THE AUTHORS

Even before they were married, Paul and Jenne Davies both had a passionate interest in wild flowers. For the past ten years and more they have travelled far and wide throughout Europe, sharing the excitement of finding and photographing rare orchid specimens as well as the better-known varieties. Now they live in Dorset, where Jenne is a housemistress and teacher at Clayesmore School and Paul works as a freelance writer, photographer and tour leader. Their photographs have been exhibited by Kodak, used for a set of postage stamps issued by the government of Cyprus, and reproduced in many publications in Europe and the USA. This, their first book, came about as a result of their extensive travels in search of wild orchids and the unrivalled collection of photographs that they accumulated, and was completed with Anthony Huxley's collaboration.

Anthony Huxley, son of the late Sir Julian Huxley, F.R.S., has for years been a leading authority on botanical and horticultural subjects. Among the best known of his thirty-five books are the *Penguin Encyclopaedia of Gardening*, *Macmillan's World Guide to House Plants*, *An Illustrated History of Gardening*, *Plant and Planet* and, most recently, *Green Inheritance: The World Wildlife Fund Book of Plants*. His classic field guide, *Flowers of the Mediterranean*, written with the late Oleg Polunin, is now available as a Hogarth Press paperback. He is a member of the Council of the Royal Horticultural Society and holds their highest award, the Victoria Medal of Honour. He is now working on a new edition of the RHS *Dictionary of Gardening*.

The Campbells
Townhill Rr Dunfermline. Fife

July 1990

WILD
ORCHIDS
of Britain and Europe

Paul & Jenne Davies
and Anthony Huxley

THE HOGARTH PRESS

LONDON

Published in 1988 by
The Hogarth Press
30 Bedford Square, London WC1 3RP

First published in Great Britain by Chatto & Windus Ltd 1983
Copyright © Paul & Jenne Davies and Anthony Huxley 1983, 1988

British Library Cataloguing in Publication Data

Davies, Paul, 1950–
Wild orchids of Britain and Europe.
1. Europe. Orchids – Field guides
I. Title   II. Davies, Jenne
III. Huxley, Anthony, 1920–
584'.15'094

ISBN 0 7012 0820 1

Printed in Great Britain by
Redwood Burn Ltd,
Trowbridge, Wiltshire

Contents

Acknowledgements

During the years of travel and throughout the production of this book many people have given willing help for which we are extremely grateful.

First of all, we are greatly indebted to the photographers who helped us to fill the gaps in our collection which time and other commitments prevented us from completing. Detailed acknowledgement to these photographers is given on page 47, just before the Plates section.

Special thanks are due to Dr Tom Norman and Dr Paul Christian, both acknowledged experts in growing orchids, who fortunately had a number of the plants we were wanting to illustrate and allowed them to be photographed. To Dr Norman we owe thanks not only for his plants but also for advice and encouragement that was much appreciated.

For the section on worthwhile areas to visit, which we have called 'In search of orchids', we could not possibly have made such good use of our limited travelling time and financial resources without the help we received from many people. With the generosity that we have found typical of orchid lovers everywhere, they have either shared with us the experiences of their own travels and knowledge, or directed us to relevant but hard-to-obtain literature. In this connection our thanks are due to the following: Sir Colville Barclay, Dr H. Baumann, David Birkinshaw, Mary Briggs, Susan Cowdy, Andreas Demetropoulis, Wilhelm Eisenreich, Ralf and Karin Hansen, Phil Holmes, David Lang, Ilse Maskow, R. D. Meikle, C. and D. Rainbow, Victor Scott, W. F. Taylor and Jeffrey Wood.

We are also appreciative of the technical skill of the Harry Smith Horticultural Photographic Collection in making 35mm colour transparencies from larger formats for colour separation purposes.

Last but not least our thanks go to John Charlton of Chatto & Windus both for his editorial skills and for the support he has given us and the confidence he has shown in the project throughout the time of our collaboration.

Foreword by Anthony Huxley

Orchids seem always to have exercised a particular fascination. The European terrestrial species, with which this book is concerned, were the first to come under the scrutiny of botanists, from the fifteenth century onwards, but long before that orchids had attracted the attention of herbalists: in fact two kinds are mentioned in the earliest surviving herbal (Dioscorides' *De Materia Medica* of the first century AD). While the doctrine of signatures held sway, orchids, with their suggestively-paired tubers, or 'stones' as they were commonly called, were thought to have significant medicinal value in terms of potential human virility not only in Europe but the Middle East. The word Orchis, after all, means testicle. (In truth, though, their tonic value is minimal.)

European orchids have a special quality about them, difficult to define, and I have often noticed many flower lovers find them more appealing than far showier plants. This clearly has nothing to do with their size, because most have relatively small blooms and humble stature, although some can reach over one metre tall. The fact that they have always been difficult to cultivate, and are for the most part only to be seen in the wild, may be an aspect of their fascination, as is the mysterious way in which they come and go.

When explorers began to visit warm countries and bring back the more showy-flowered orchids from these climates, interest in orchids generally received a fresh stimulus. During the latter part of the nineteenth century they were grown in huge numbers for their decorative and bizarre qualities, and their cultivation took on the dimensions of a cult, especially as so many tropical and sub-tropical species live epiphytically on trees or rocks and thus need growing techniques markedly different from those of most other plants. It also became clear that in world numbers the orchid family, with over 20,000 species, is barely second in size to that of the composites (daisies, dandelions, etc.) The glamour of the exotic orchids has undoubtedly enhanced the popularity of our local ones.

Charles Darwin was one of the first to probe the peculiarities of orchid pollination mechanisms, which he studied to a considerable extent from the European species. Since his book on the subject, first published in 1862, many other observers have revealed more details, with the result that orchids, as a group, are recognised as being in this respect the most highly adapted flowers of all. In remarkable contrast, the lack of elaboration in the seed, and the frequent dependence of the germinating orchid upon a fungus, have added to the mystique of these plants.

We can study and enjoy wild orchids on various levels. Most of us, perhaps, would echo the seventeenth-century German botanist Jakob Breyne, or Breynius, in our immediate response to these flowers:

If nature ever showed her playfulness in the formation of plants, this is visible in the most striking way among the orchids. . . . They take on the form of little birds, of lizards, of insects. They look like a man, like a woman, sometimes like an austere sinister fighter, sometimes like a clown who excites our laughter. They represent the image of a lazy tortoise, a melancholy toad, an agile, ever-chattering monkey. Nature has formed orchid flowers in such a way that, unless they make us laugh, they surely excite our greatest admiration.

This anthropomorphic quality, particularly evident in the European terrestrial species, combined with an astonishing variety of forms in some of them (due to the family's relatively recent development in evolutionary terms), helps to give this group of plants its special attraction for the amateur and the professional botanist alike. With roughly 200 species and sub-species in all, it is perfectly possible for the painstaking enthusiast to find and photograph the majority of this unique group within the European flora. Our wild orchids are particularly rewarding in this respect because many are rare and local, their annual appearance is by no means guaranteed, some display the extraordinary variation already referred to, and a great many hybrids are possible. One may find new localities for rarities or even new orchids: I myself have had the excitement of logging two orchids previously unrecorded for the countries concerned, and even of discovering a previously unknown, very local variety. The European orchids, in short, provide possibilities for a lifetime of travel!

Many orchid enthusiasts set out to learn everything they can about these plants, and that is really the *raison d'être* of this book. It came about as a result of a shared enthusiasm which prompted Paul and Jenne Davies to get in touch with me some years ago. My own interest in orchids was evidently apparent to them from my Royal Horticultural Society booklet, *Flowers in Greece*, and the book which I wrote with Oleg Polunin, *Flowers of the Mediterranean*. The Davieses, I soon realised, were passionate and dedicated orchid lovers. More important, they were superb photographers with an already impressive collection of orchid close-ups. They sought my advice about possible publication, feeling frustrated at the inadequate illustration in other field guides.

Although I knew of the already quite extensive literature on European orchids, and of other books in the offing, it seemed to me that there was a place for a combination of comprehensive and technically top-class photographs, and a text as informative and botanically up-to-date as possible. The Davieses proved to be indefatigable travellers and went to great lengths to make their collection of photographs and observations comprehensive, although a fair number of my own photographs have been included and some have had to be obtained elsewhere. The Davieses studied the orchid habitats on the one hand and scoured the literature on the other. Their photographic excellence culminated in the issue, in 1981, of four Cyprus stamps of native wild orchids reproduced from their transparencies.

In addition to his photographs, Paul Davies has prepared all the text drawings. These are used to point up salient identification features of closely related species and also to illustrate some species with insignificant colourless flowers.

My own part was mainly one of encouragement in the early stages, and of editorial and technical assistance during the drafting of the text and laying out the photographs. In the end our combined knowledge has, I believe, produced the most informative text of any on European orchids. It has been brought in line with *Flora Europaea*, Volume 5, in which the taxonomy of European monocotyledons has been stabilised (if only for the time being!), and recent research initiated by OPTIMA* has been taken account of.

One special attraction of the text lies in the chapter 'In search of orchids', where countries are described in terms of their orchid flora, with an account of some fascinating places to visit for its study. Here even the energy of the Davieses could not cover the whole ground in the time available, and my experience and notes from several of their friends have been put to use.

The European orchids have certain outposts – the Canaries and Azores to the west and North Africa to the south – which are included here; while the distribution of the relevant genera tails off eastwards to make the Ural mountains in the USSR a convenient boundary. However, only the more accessible countries are in fact described under 'In search of orchids'. Yugoslavia is included but most Iron Curtain countries, including the USSR itself, are not, since few western Europeans are likely to get the chance to botanise there. The inclusion of Lebanon must at the present time be called wishful thinking, but let us hope that its orchids will still be there when conflict ceases.

It must be remarked that orchids are in special need of conservation. More than many endangered plants, they are highly sensitive to human activities: even improved drainage or the use of artificial fertilizers can destroy them forever. The difficulty of seed germination and the long development of flowering maturity make orchids all the more vulnerable.

It could thus be argued that the chapter 'In search of orchids' opens the door to unscrupulous collectors. Alas, these certainly exist, both cultivators and botanists whose desire to acquire a certain species often over-rides all concern for its future. However, the exact localities of rare species are never divulged, and in our view a general idea of the orchids that may be found in particular countries can only provide encouragement and assistance to those who have limited opportunities for travelling.

Most such enthusiasts will not dream of digging up plants, and it is surely only by helping people to see orchids in the wild that co-operation can be sought from all to preserve them: knowledge begets knowledge. The casual visitor must be educated not to pick flowers indiscriminately, the enthusiast not to trample seedlings and immature plants around flowering specimens,

*Organization for the Phyto-Taxonomic Investigation of the Mediterranean Area.

and the farmer and industrialist must be persuaded not to erase unique habitats. Finally, governments can be lobbied through natural history and preservation organisations to pass laws to prevent the picking or digging up of rare plants, control their export, stop indiscriminate grazing, prevent the use of weedkillers on archaeological sites and roadsides, and to give legal protection to the most important plant sites, as indeed to any of special scientific interest.

Our hope is that this book will initiate and sustain excitement in the study of these often elusive flowers, and also be of value to botanists who need an account of the present-day taxonomic situation plus details of species distribution at a time of increasing pressure on habitats. It is, in short, addressed to all who fall under the inimitable spell of the wild orchid.

New discoveries and name changes (1988)

In the five years since *Wild Orchids of Britain and Europe* was first published, several new orchid species have been discovered and new criteria for classification have gained acceptance. The publication of this paperback edition gives us the opportunity of drawing attention to the more important changes that have taken place.

As we explained originally (p. ix above and pp. 38–9 below), the system of plant names we used was based on the scheme which had been established in the fifth volume of *Flora Europaea* not long before. We wanted to help our readers by adopting the most up-to-date and authoritative taxonomy, even though we had misgivings about the scheme ourselves and indeed had some different ideas of our own. The shortcomings of *Flora Europaea* have now become apparent: its ranking system (in which the dominant taxon is the 'species', closely related taxa are 'subspecies', and 'varieties' are excluded because of restrictions on space) simply does not work for European orchids, principally because some genera contain large numbers of closely linked taxa.

Today, the accepted practice is to identify closely related taxa as species within a 'group', e.g. the *Ophrys sphegodes* group, and to refer to individual species by the name which was formerly given to subspecies. Thus *Ophrys sphegodes* ssp. *mammosa* now becomes *Ophrys mammosa*. This applies in particular to the genus *Ophrys*, where major upheavals due to name changes have occurred in some groups. To avoid confusion, only those groups are listed with names fast gaining currency in published literature and their counterparts in this book. Many *Ophrys* which can be grouped together have been recognised as separate species for some time, and their inclusion would only serve to swell the list.

Some names have also been changed as a result of the careful and consistent application of 'rules of priority' to European species. A great deal of such work has been done in the past five years, notably in Germany by members of the AHO (see p. 190 below).

In the following lists of name changes, many new names incorporate the old subspecific and varietal names. Where this has not occurred and it seems that a new name altogether is used (even though it is one which may be found in early literature), the name used in this book is given in brackets.

Ophrys

Arachnitiformis group
O. aveyronensis, *O. morisii*, *O. sipontensis* (*O. sphegodes* ssp. *sipontensis*), *O. splendida*, *O. tyrrhena*.

Fusca group
O. atlantica (ssp. *durieui*), *O. dyris*, *O. fleischmannii*, *O. fusca*, *O. omegaifera*, *O. pallida*.

Holoserica (fuciflora) group
O. biancae, *O. biscutella* (ssp. *pollinensis*), *O. bornmuelleri*, *O. candica*, *O. crabonifera* (ssp. *exaltata*), *O. holoserica*, *O. lacaitae*, *O. levantina* (ssp. *bornmuelleri* var. *grandiflora*).

Scolopax group
O. cornuta, *O. flavomarginata*, *O. heldreichii*, *O. isaura*, *O. phrygia*, *O. scolopax*, *O. umbilicata* (includes *O. carmeli*, *O. scolopax* ssp. *attica* and *orientalis*).

Speculum group
O. ciliata (*O. speculum*), *O. regis-ferdinandii*, *O. vernixia* (ssp. *lusitanica*).

Sphegodes group
O. aesculapii, *O. araneola* (ssp. *litigosa* and *tommasinii*), *O. garganica*, *O. hebes*, *O. helenae*, *O. incubacea (ssp. atrata)*, *O. mammosa*, *O. tarentina*.
   There are still 'grey' areas as far as *O. mammosa* and *O. sphegodes* are concerned. *O. mammosa* has two very closely related taxa that might well be regarded as its subspecies: *O. transhyrcana* (ssp. *sintenisii*) and *O. amanensis*. Similarly there are taxa very closely linked to *O. sphegodes* which sometimes appear as distinct species in botanical literature: *O. cephalonica*, *O. epirotica*, *O. panormitana* (*O. spruneri* ssp. *panormitana*), *O. provincialis*, *O. sicula*.

Several new species of *Ophrys* have been described from limited areas in southern Europe and Turkey:
O. aymoninii (Breistr.) Buttler: formerly regarded as a subspecies of *O. insectifera*, this taxon differs in having a pronounced yellow border to the labellum and longer, spreading side-lobes. It is endemic to the Causse country in southern France.
O. biancae (Tod.) Macchiati: closely resembling *O. oxyrrhynchos* in appearance, it has a much-reduced speculum forming an H at the labellum base. Found in south-east Sicily.
O. isaura Renz & Taubenheim: a member of the *Scolopax* group, it has a

narrow labellum 9–11mm long with reflexed green or pinkish-green sepals. It is found in southern Anatolia.

O. lycia Renz & Taubenheim: closely related to *O. ferrum-equinum*, although it has an H-shaped speculum bordered in white. It occurs in the Lycia region of southern Turkey.

O. sphegodes ssp. *cephalonica* B. & H. Baumann and *O. sphegodes* ssp. *epirotica* (Renz) Gölz & Reinhard: local but distinctive races of *O. sphegodes*.

O. tarentina Gölz & Reinhard: also in the *Sphegodes* group, it has the same labellum surrounded by long hairs as *O. incubacea* (*O. atrata*) but lacks the distinct protruding side-lobes of that taxon and has a speculum limited to an inverted horseshoe or even a pair of small 'eyes'. It is found in southern Italy (Brindisi, Cosenza, Matera, Taranto).

Name changes:
O. cilicica is now accepted as the earliest correctly published name for *O. kurdica* and replaces it.

O. reinholdii ssp. *straussii* has been the object of investigation, and it is now realised that the name originally referred to plants from southern Turkey with a reduced speculum area and restricted markings. The plant illustrated in photograph 279 is now known as *O. reinholdii* ssp. *leucotaenia*.

Barlia

Barlia metlesiciana Teschner: restricted to the Canary Isles, this taxon differs from *B. robertiana* in having a wider, spreading labellum with intense magenta coloration.

Dactylorhiza

New species have been recognised and several 'old' ones resurrected as a result of work done in Greece and Turkey:

D. baumanniana Hölzinger & Künkele: found in north-western Greece and the Pindus.

D. euxina (Nevski) Czerep. (*D. caucasica*, *D. majalis* ssp. *caucasica*): related to *D. cordigera* and found in north-eastern Anatolia.

D. nieschalkiorum H. Baumann & Künkele (*D. maculata* ssp. *osmanica*): found in north-eastern Anatolia.

D. osmanica (Klinge) Soó (*D. cataonica*, *D. cilicica*): found in Anatolia.

D. umbrosa (Kar. & Kir.) Nevski (*D. persica*, *D. vanensis*): found in eastern Anatolia.

D. urvilleana (Steudel) H. Baumann & Künkele (*D. triphylla*): found in northern Anatolia.

Much of the investigative work done with this genus is hampered by incomplete data on distribution. Principal name changes are:
D. romana has again found favour over *D. sulphurea* ssp. *pseudosambucina*, and closely related taxa once considered subspecies of *D. sambucina* are: *D. flavescens* (*D. sambucina* ssp. *georgica*), *D. insularis* (*D. sambucina* ssp. *insularis*), *D. markusii* (*D. sulphurea* ssp. *siciliensis*).

Epipactis

E. albensis Novakova & Rydlo: found in Albania.
E. cretica Kalopissis & Robatsch: small-flowered taxon with incurved perianth segments (green tinged with red), epichile broader than long. Found in the mountains of central Crete.
E. muelleri group: Buttler treats a number of European taxa (*E. albensis*, *E. dunensis*, *E. pontica* and *E. youngiana*) together within this group of autogamous species.
E. youngiana A. J. Richards & A. F. Porter: known from sites in Northumberland, northern England.

Limodorum

L. trabutianum: formerly regarded as *L. abortivum* ssp. *abortivum*.

Nigritella

Following careful analysis of individual flower sizes and shapes, three new species closely linked in a group with *N. rubra* are now recognised:
N. archiducis-joannis Teppner & Klein: flowers half-closed, with only the lateral sepals spreading; flower colour rose-pink. Found in Austria (northeastern Alps, calcareous soil).
N. stiriaca (K. Rech.) Teppner & Klein: endemic to the Salzkammergut region of Austria; flowers bicoloured light pink/deep rose.
N. widderi Teppner & Klein: this taxon has light pink, very small flowers. Found in Austria (north-eastern Alps).

Another new species is:
N. lithopolitanica Ravnik: similar in appearance to *N. corneliana* (*N. nigra* ssp. *corneliana*), it differs in colour, there being a definite magenta tinge in the flowers near the top of the inflorescence and in detailed dimensions of the perianth segments.

Orchis

The genus *Orchis* has been treated in much the same way as *Ophrys*, with the abolition of subspecies for many taxa. Thus:
O. langei (*O. mascula* ssp. *hispanica*), *O. pinetorum* and *O. scopulorum* have become the Spanish, Turkish and Madeiran relatives respectively of *O. mascula*.

Others are:
O. albanica: in the *O. morio* group, and endemic to Albania.
O. brancifortii: formerly *O. quadripunctata* ssp. *brancifortii*.
O. conica: a relative of *O. tridentata* from the western Mediterranean region (formerly *O. acuminata*).
O. laeta: formerly *O. provincialis* ssp. *laeta*, and found in the Atlas Mountains.
O. prisca: formerly *O. spitzelii* ssp. *nitidifolia*.

Another discovery:
O. stevenii: the plant reported on p.124 as being 'lost' for many years because of confusion over the colour of the type species. It now turns out that there are purple-flowered plants in Turkey which match Reichenbach's description. The plant illustrated in this book as *O. stevenii* (photograph 165) is now known as *O. adenocheila*.

Serapias

S. nurrica: this taxon is endemic to Sardinia and Corsica; hypochile 11–13mm long and 15–18mm broad, epichile 14–18mm long, side-lobes 5.5–7.5mm broad, central lobe 7–10mm broad. The epichile is reddish-brown becoming lighter, forming a border at the edges coloured the same shade as the hood formed by the other perianth segments.

1 – Orchid biology

The orchid flower

The classification of plants into families is based almost entirely upon the characteristics of the flower, so before studying orchids in detail it is important to master the overall features which make orchids different from other plants.

The leaves do not help much. Like all monocotyledenous plants, orchids have leaves in which the veins run the whole length of the leaf and are more or less parallel, until they converge at the leaf tip; unlike the leaves of dicotyledons, in which smaller veins branch out laterally from a central vein (Fig. 1). But there are many monocotyledons, and this distinction does not narrow the field significantly. We must therefore look at the orchid flower itself if we are to find ways of identifying the plants.

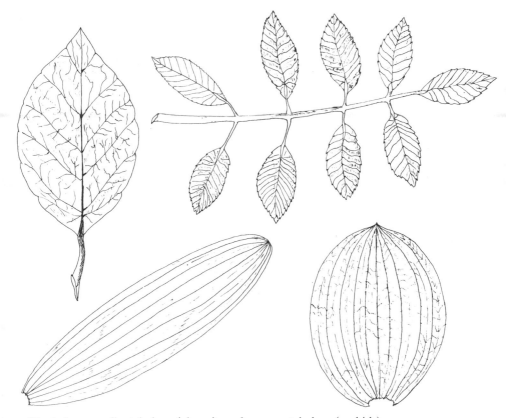

Fig. 1 Leaves: dicotyledons (above), and monocotyledons (orchids).

Few plants resemble them, although there are various louseworts (*Pedicularis*) which look like marsh orchids, and the broomrapes (*Orobanches*) are certainly more than reminiscent of orchids in both flowers and habit. However, the number of orchid species in Europe is not vast, and it is not difficult to recognise their diagnostic form.

As with many monocotyledons, we cannot readily distinguish between petals and sepals; instead we should regard them collectively as forming the perianth. Individual segments of the perianth are termed tepals. In the case of many well-known monocotyledons (such as bluebells, lilies and tulips) the perianth segments are more or less the same size; in the orchid flower they are not. Orchid flowers are zygomorphic; that is to say, there is only one way they can be cut to give two identical halves. Look at the flower from face on (Fig. 2a); it can only be cut from top to bottom to provide equal parts, whereas a tulip can be cut in many ways.

The parts of an orchid flower are present in threes; three outer perianth segments or sepals, and three inner segments which correspond to petals. The outer segments can be all alike, as in the case of the *Ophrys*, or the two side ones (laterals) may be alike and slightly different from the central one (median).

The inner segments comprise a pair of identical petals and a third, the lip or labellum, which is often so distinctive that it provides the inspiration for the common name of the plant: Man Orchid, Bee Orchid, Lizard Orchid, Fly Orchid and Monkey Orchid are examples.

The lip is usually the lowest petal in the orchid flower although there are notable exceptions – for example *Microstylis monophyllos* and *Hammarbya paludosa* have the lip uppermost. At first sight it seems that they have been twisted through 180° but the rotation is in fact 360°, for many orchid flowers are already turned through 180°. Some, like *Epipogium aphyllum*, are not twisted at all.

The part of the lip nearest its point of attachment to the rest of the flower is called the base, and in many cases this is drawn out behind the flower into a tube, called the spur, where the nectar is stored. This varies in shape: sometimes it is short and stubby like the finger of a glove, sometimes long and drawn out (as in the case of *Platanthera* or *Gymnadenia*) so that only the moths and butterflies which pollinate these species can reach the nectar with their long probosces.

Some species of orchids have lips with two parts: the hypochile near the base, while the apical part is called the epichile (Fig. 2b, c). For species of *Epipactis* and *Serapias* the shape of these parts of the labella provide important diagnostic features.

In a strict technical sense flowers have no sex since they are part of the asexual phase of a plant's life. However, flowers, or some of their parts, are commonly termed male or female, since they are responsible for the eventual male and female cells, which fuse on fertilization to produce seeds.

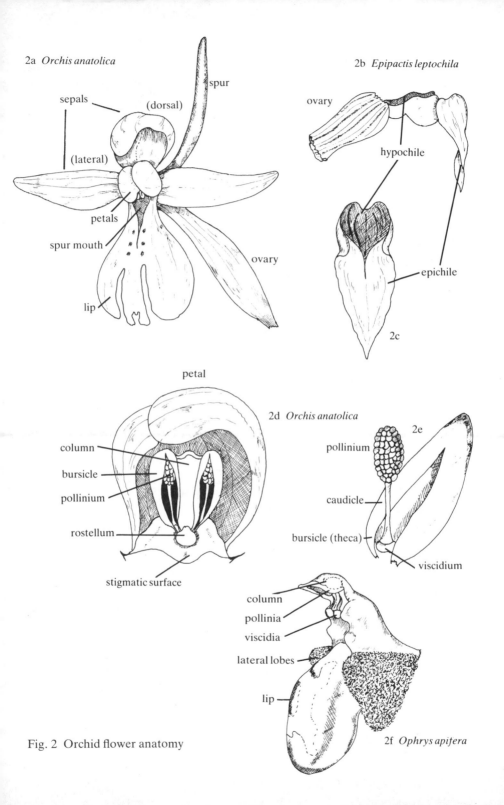

2a *Orchis anatolica*

spur
sepals
(dorsal)
(lateral)
petals
spur mouth
ovary
lip

2b *Epipactis leptochila*

ovary
hypochile
epichile

2c

petal

2d *Orchis anatolica*

2e
column
bursicle
pollinium
rostellum
stigmatic surface

pollinium
caudicle
bursicle (theca)
viscidium

column
pollinia
viscidia
lateral lobes
lip

2f *Ophrys apifera*

Fig. 2 Orchid flower anatomy

In this respect the internal parts of orchids are quite distinctive too, for, unlike other monocotyledons, the male and female parts are not completely separated. The male parts (stamens) of most flowers consist of a stalk (filament) supporting an anther which holds millions of separate pollen grains, whilst the female part (pistil) has a stigma to receive pollen, below which is the style leading to the ovary. In orchids, by contrast, male and female parts are fixed into a single structure called a column. The pollen grains are not separate but held together to form more or less solid masses called pollinia. There are thousands, even millions, of individual pollen grains in each pollinium, which is itself sticky or has a special sticky pad or viscidium. This ensures that the pollinium adheres to any insect with which it comes into contact and that it is carried off to the next flower.

Most European orchids have a single stamen placed near the top or towards the back of the column. This single stamen contains the pollinia in a pair of bag-like structures called theca or anther loculi, which are usually arranged side by side. More rarely they diverge, as in *Platanthera chlorantha*.

It is perhaps fitting that *Cypripedium calceolus*, the most exotic-looking European orchid, should provide the exception to the 'single stamen' rule. In fact it has two stamens, placed one on either side of the column, but they do not have a filament like those of other flowers. Two close relatives, *C. macranthos* and *C. guttatum*, which creep into the area covered by this book, also have two stamens. In these orchids the pollen grains are not formed into bundles as in other European orchids but neither are they free since they lie in a sticky substance (Fig. 2d, e).

One of the female parts, the ovary, is frequently rather long and thin, which makes it difficult to tell where the flower stalk ends and the ovary begins. Inside the ovary there are innumerable tiny ovules, each one a potential seed should it eventually become fertilized.

The two stigmas capable of receiving pollen are found on the column in the very centre of the flower, either below or immediately in front of the stamen. There is also a sterile third stigma in many orchids which has evolved into a curious structure called the rostellum. It serves to prevent pollen spreading from a stamen onto a stigma of the same plant, which would cause self-fertilization. The rostellum comes in a variety of shapes and sizes – from tiny ball through tooth shape to a comparatively large, complicated structure.

Finally, some orchid flowers still possess the sterile remains of stamens which have disappeared with evolution. These are called staminodes.

Pollination and sexual reproduction

Most orchids growing in Europe rely only on insects as pollinators. A few species (examples are *Ophrys apifera* and *Epipactis phyllanthes*) are usually, but not always, self-fertilized.

The sticky pollen masses or pollinia ensure that there is no wind dispersion of pollen grains, but self-fertilization is still rare because of the geometry of the orchid flower: stigma and pollinia are either positioned to make it awkward or they are separated by the rostellum, a sterile stigma.

The devices used by orchids, first to attract insects and then to ensure that pollinia are removed, are some of the most intriguing examples of engineering in the natural world.

Cypripedium calceolus has a structure which only allows suitably sized insects to follow a one-way system, brushing against the pollinia and removing them. *Gymnadenia* and *Platanthera* species produce a scent attractive to moths and butterflies, the only insects capable of reaching the nectar stored in their long spurs. While they are feeding, the pollinia stick to the base of their probosces. *Listera ovata* has an explosive mechanism which fires the pollinia onto the head of an insect visitor. The startled creature then flies off – hopefully to the next flower of *Listera ovata*, where the pollen can be placed on the stigma.

Although insects are mainly attracted to orchids for feeding on the nectar and other secretions this is not always the case. *Ophrys* are perhaps the most intriguing of all European orchids. Their insect-mimicking shape was supposed to be the attraction for the tiny wasps that act as pollinators. However, recent work has shown that the plant also secretes a chemical which is very much like the sexual attractant (pheromone) produced by the female wasp. If this were not bizarre enough the chemicals vary with the species of wasp. Thus in nature, hybrids between *Ophrys* species are not as common as one would imagine because of the faithfulness of the pollinators to particular orchid species.

The subject of pollination is one of the most fascinating in the field of botany. Darwin certainly thought so, for he turned his attention to it and produced his famous work, *The Various Contrivances by which Orchids are Fertilized*. More recently Bertil Kullenberg has done very detailed work on the genus *Ophrys*, which is published in his *Studies in Ophrys Pollination* (Uppsala, 1961) and makes fascinating reading.

For *Ophrys*, other orchids, and also for the rest of the flowering plants, *The Pollination of Flowers* by Proctor and Yeo is a mine of information.

In this book, because of the intricate links with the structure of individual flowers, the reader will find detailed descriptions of pollination mechanisms included in accounts of the various orchid genera.

Seed germination

Anyone who has planted tomato seeds soon knows when they have germin-
ated because of the appearance of the tiny seed leaves or cotyledons. And
not only tomatoes. The same is true for virtually all flowering plants and
vegetables raised from seed in the garden. But the germination of orchid
seeds is not so straightforward: their seedlings may not be recognisable as
such until two, three or even more years after the growth process has started.

To understand this we must take a closer look at the orchid seed itself. By
any standards it is tiny, and it contains very little in the way of nutriment. The
seeds from an orchid can be numbered in thousands rather than in hundreds,
and are so light that they can be blown far and wide by the wind when the
ripened capsule eventually splits. If the seed lands on favourable ground
germination can occur, but the growth rate is very slow compared with the
vigorous efforts of most seeds to throw up their first leaves and start the
photosynthetic process that ensures their food supply. The growth rate
increases after the appearance of the first leaves but progress is still slow, and
several more years pass by before flowering takes place.

Dr V. Summerhayes, in his superb book *Wild Orchids of Britain*, cites a
number of examples of the time taken from germination to flowering. These
times were measured by the observation of seedlings found in the wild at
various stages of their growth. More recent observations by successful
propagators suggest that these times are slightly pessimistic (recent work
with certain *Dactylorhiza* and *Orchis* species has shown that seed scattered
on suitable ground can reach flowering maturity in as few as three years), but
they can still serve as guides to the period of germination of wild orchids.

As examples: some of the *Dactylorhiza* and *Orchis morio* are quickest off
the mark, with four to five years from germination to flowering, whereas
most *Ophrys* and *Platanthera* species take between five and eight years. The
saprophytic *Neottia nidus-avis* takes nine to eleven years, whilst others such
as *Listera ovata*, *Spiranthes spiralis* and *Orchis ustulata* can be thirteen or
fourteen years beyond germination before they finally flower. Longest of all
is *Cypripedium calceolus*, for plants of this species can remain in a purely
vegetative state for over sixteen years before coming into bloom.

For most plants, after germination, successful growth depends on the
amount of nutriment in the soil, the drainage available, the acidity or
alkalinity (pH) of the soil. But far more important than these factors is a type
of fungus that lives in the soil and invades the orchid seed soon after
germination.

Growers have long been aware how difficult it is to get the seed from
terrestrial orchids to germinate. Attempts to germinate *Orchis* and *Dactylorhiza* seeds by sowing them in pots containing healthy, growing orchids
have met with partial success, but it is now realized that the true answer to

the problem 'lies in the soil'. There one can find the tiny fungi which invade the orchid seeds and provide them with nutriment in the early stages of their life. In many cases the association between orchid and fungus is a lifelong one.

This combination of plant and fungus is called mycorrhiza and it is not confined to orchids: beech, oak, pine and birch trees often have these fungi in their roots, as do heather and ling. Part of the fungus lives outside the root and can form an external covering. This is called ectotrophic mycorrhiza, while the part living within the root goes under the term endotrophic mycorrhiza. Cultures of the mycorrhizal fungus can be prepared from orchids and they have all been identified as members of the genus *Rhizoctonia*. Only a few species are involved and they are not plant-specific, since cultures from different orchids reveal the same mycorrhizal fungus. Care must be taken with artificial cultures of fungus for they lose their effectiveness in causing germination of the orchid seed if kept separately for too long.

The external portion of the fungus can break down the dead organic matter in the soil (humus), using enzyme action to produce simpler chemicals that can be absorbed by the fungus as food. Thus in its early stages the plant is able to survive without green leaves providing its food by photosynthesis. Those filaments (hyphae) of the fungus which actually penetrate the orchid either act as a 'channel' for simple nutrients or are themselves digested by the orchid for food – exactly which is not very clear.

In the natural world there are many examples of different species of plants and animals living together with both partners benefitting from the arrangement. The term symbiosis has been coined to describe this kind of association: it literally means 'living together'. At first sight the cohabitation of orchid seed and mycorrhizal fungus would seem to be one of those happy relationships. But this is not so. Close examination reveals a two-sided fight, with the plant staving off the attacks of the fungus. The first of the attacks, when the fungus penetrates the orchid seed, is almost certainly parasitic. The plant fights back and, if successful, restricts the fungus to parts where it can control it. In the wild, we have good reason to believe that many of these invasions result in the death of the seed.

During the early stages of the plant's life the relationship is a series of attack and counter-attack manoeuvres. The fungus makes an advance and is then partly digested by the orchid for food. Ultimately the enemies achieve a tactical balance which is sensitive enough to be affected by changes in temperature and weather. Thus, in a mature plant, the fungus can be in the ascendant in the winter months when the chemical activity of the plant is at its lowest ebb, whilst the summer months favour the plant. Then the green leaves all photosynthesise and the plant is not so reliant on the fungus.

Some European orchids have to depend completely on mycorrhiza for their food supply, whatever the time of year. These are the so-called saprophytic orchids: *Neottia nidus-avis*, *Epipogium aphyllum*, and *Limo-*

dorum abortivum. The first two have their common names (Bird's Nest Orchid, Spurred Coral Root) derived from a reference to their root structures which are distinctive in appearance and heavily infested with mycorrhizal fungi.

Corallorhiza trifida does manage to possess some chlorophyll in its stems and so is not wholly reliant on mycorrhiza.

Orchids like those of the *Ophrys* and *Orchis* tribes have tubers in their mature stages and are almost completely independent of mycorrhiza. In most cases the tubers and roots are not infected at all.

The seedling

After germination a protocorm or mycorrhizome is produced. This is rather a curious structure, something like an old-fashioned child's spinning top in appearance and very heavily infected with fungus (Fig. 3). Indeed, at this stage it depends totally on the fungus for its survival.

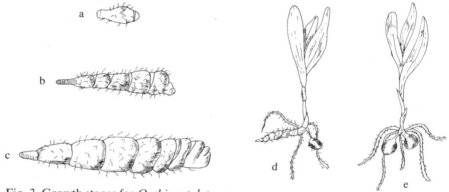

Fig. 3 Growth stages for *Orchis ustulata*
Mycorrhizome grows, adding segments annually, for about 10 years. It is later replaced by tubers. Flowering takes place 14+ years after germination.

The next stage – the subsequent growth, the first leaves and the appearance of the underground parts – varies from one orchid species to another.

With *Cypripedium calceolus* and the helleborines (both *Epipactis* and *Cephalanthera*) the mycorrhizome sends down one or more fleshy roots in the first two or three years' growth and then subsequently produces its first aerial stem, bearing leaves. Initially the roots are heavily infected with fungus but over the years this diminishes. Eventually the rhizome (underground stem) becomes free of fungus. Non-flowering stems are produced for a number of years as the plants become more and more vigorous. Finally the time arrives when the plant is able to produce flowers. *Cypripedium calceolus* and *Epipactis palustris* produce a creeping rhizome, while the

Cephalantheras and *Epipactis helleborine* have a shorter and altogether more upright rootstock.

Species of *Dactylorhiza* usually grow in damp places, as their common name of Marsh Orchids suggests. Their mycorrhizome is usually capable of producing a single foliage leaf in the second year after germination or even earlier. The first root-tuber is formed soon after and this heralds the final withering away and dying of the mycorrhizome.

Close relatives of the *Dactylorhiza* are the members of the genus *Orchis*. On the whole they are found in drier places than the Marsh Orchids and this seems to cause a slower rate of leaf growth. The first foliage leaf generally appears in the third or fourth year after germination. Exceptions are *Orchis morio*, which produces a leaf in its first year after germination and a tuber in its second, and *Orchis ustulata*, which goes to the other extreme, producing its first leaves after anything up to ten years. The mycorrhizome grows during this time by adding another segment each year without producing roots and so it remains dependent on fungal activity for its food for a long time.

Most growers of European orchids would agree that there is no set timetable for the appearance of leaves with any of the species they deal with. But certainly, if optimum conditions for growth are provided, years can be deducted from the time it takes some orchids to start flowering in the wild.

Among the European orchids *Ophrys* and *Orchis* can be propagated in the laboratory by means of a technique borrowed from growers of tropical orchids. The seed is sown in flasks under sterile conditions (fungus is completely absent) on an agar jelly enriched with necessary minerals. *Ophrys* can be brought to flowering maturity in about five years from sowing. The seed germinates about two to three weeks after sowing, and nutrients are absorbed directly through the seed coat. The first stage of growth is a prototuber which has neither roots nor leaves and is entirely dependent on nutrients in the surrounding medium. Only at a later stage when the prototuber is well developed are the leaves and roots formed and photosynthesis starts. When the plant has established normal production of carbohydrates by photosynthesis it can be transplanted to a normal potting compost.

The underground parts

The underground parts of orchids, equivalent to the root systems of more orthodox perennials, can be divided into two broad categories, namely tubers (Fig. 4) and rhizomes (Fig. 5), each adapted to the conditions in which the orchids grow.

Tubers are fleshy swollen roots capable of resisting drought, found for instance in *Serapias*, *Ophrys* and *Orchis*, all plants of grasslands which suffer

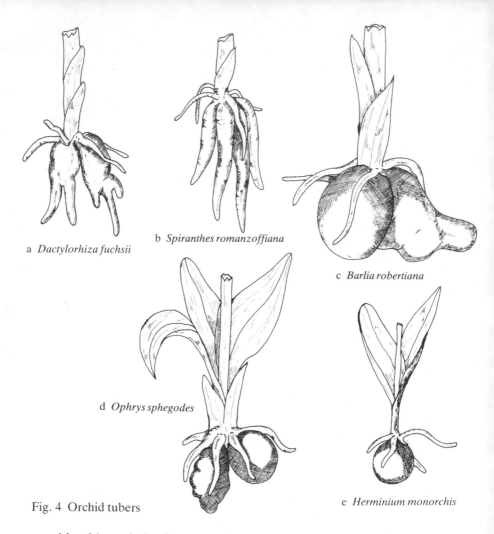

a *Dactylorhiza fuchsii*

b *Spiranthes romanzoffiana*

c *Barlia robertiana*

d *Ophrys sphegodes*

e *Herminium monorchis*

Fig. 4 Orchid tubers

considerable periods of dryness. They can be used solely for food storage, as in the case of *Ophrys* and *Orchis*, in conjunction with more orthodox, though usually fleshy, roots used for absorbing water and dissolved nutrients from the soil. In *Spiranthes aestivalis* and many of the *Dactylorhiza* the tubers have the further function of themselves absorbing water. This is achieved through narrow parts at the ends of the tubers.

The leaves and flowering stems are produced by utilising the food stored in the tuber. As the new plant produces excess carbohydrate during the growing season this is stored in a new tuber and the old, exhausted one withers away.

Just before flowering a plant will appear to have two tubers, the old one, not yet exhausted, and a new one in the process of being formed. *Spiranthes* species form two or three new tubers each year, so can appear to have as many as six at any one time.

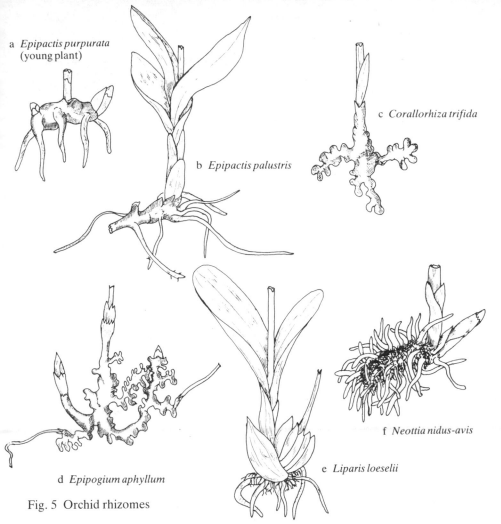

a *Epipactis purpurata*
(young plant)

b *Epipactis palustris*

c *Corallorhiza trifida*

d *Epipogium aphyllum*

e *Liparis loeselii*

f *Neottia nidus-avis*

Fig. 5 Orchid rhizomes

The resemblance of the tubers to testicles gave orchids their name – the ancient Greek ορχις means testicles. Indeed the modern Greek is not so very different, and the traveller in Greece who claims to be looking for orchids should beware!

At the stage where there are two tubers some skilled propagators have removed the new tuber carefully and grown it into a flowering plant, separate from the parent, in as little as one or two years. Meanwhile the original plant, deprived of its tuber, produces another. The result is 'two plants for the price of one'.

The production of two tubers is not restricted to man's intervention alone. Nature allows it where a particularly vigorous plant produces enough excess carbohydrate to warrant production of an extra tuber. In the Mediterranean region it is certainly not uncommon to find what look like 'clumps' of *Serapias* or *Ophrys* (e.g. *O. scolopax* ssp. *orientalis*) but which are in fact a group of separate plants produced by the tubers becoming separate on the death of the parent. This process is repeated over the following years, when conditions allow it, and the clump forms.

With orchids such as the *Ophrys*, *Orchis*, *Serapias* and *Platanthera* which have short tuberous roots, the new tuber is formed from one of a number of buds in the axils of the rudimentary leaves at the base of the stem. Normally only one of these buds develops but others can be encouraged, either by the need for greater carbohydrate storage capacity or by removal of the new tuber as mentioned above – the best time being when the flowers of the parent plant are fading.

The case of *Herminium monorchis* is worth mentioning because it produces its new tubers at the ends of stolons, which allows the offspring to spread out from the parent.

Rhizomes are underground stems which occur in all shapes and sizes in the case of European terrestrial orchids. They present a variety of ways in which the plants can propagate vegetatively. Some rhizomes take the form of a short vertical rootstock, as in some of the helleborines – *Cephalanthera damasonium*, *Epipactis helleborine* and *E. purpurea*.

C. damasonium has a rather deep-seated, erect rootstock with a large number of thick deep roots that enable it to survive on dry chalky slopes. The rootstock usually produces one bud each year which becomes an aerial stem. Under suitable conditions more can be produced, but those large clumps of stems one sees in young beech woods on occasions are not produced in this way. They arise from buds produced by the roots and not the stem. These root buds often develop into plants at some distance from the parents. Some rhizomatous orchids only produce root buds occasionally, as in *Neottia*, while in other orchids they are always produced, for instance in *Cephalanthera rubra*, *Listera cordata* and *L. ovata*.

Epipactis helleborine again is a plant which tends to produce a single bud each year (occasionally more). It has a number of thick, deep penetrating roots with a degree of fungal infection depending on the soil in which the orchid grows. Plants found in the soil of a beechwood rich in humus will be affected to a much greater extent than plants found on coastal sand-dune systems. Out of necessity in such a harsh environment, the latter plants have an exceptionally long root system.

Epipactis purpurea may have had, in the past, an existence somewhere between a true saprophyte and less fungally infected orchids. Perhaps the purple tinge to its colouring encouraged this idea. It does in fact seem that the colouring enables the plant to make more efficient use of what light is available, for the roots are not fungally infected.

Certain orchids have creeping underground rhizomes which grow forward each successive year of the plant's life. The rear parts of the rhizome decay gradually after they have served their purpose. This type of growth is found with *Listera ovata* and *Epipactis palustris*. In the case of the latter the rhizome frequently branches, and eventually, on the death of the part of the rhizome where branching occurred, two separate plants exist.

Rather similar to the rhizome is the stolon or runner, a thin branch from the main stem ending in a new shoot, and finally becoming detached from the parent after eventually establishing itself as a plant. In *Epipogium aphyllum* these stems are entirely underground like the rest of the vegetative parts (in some cases even the flowers are underground, not surfacing above a mass of beech litter). In *Goodyera repens*, which usually flourishes in soft moss cushions, the stolons thread their way above the actual soil into which the roots penetrate. In *Goodyera* these stems become detached early in the development of the new plant, while in *Epipogium* they produce lateral buds which swell up and become new rhizomes before final detachment from the parent plant. The new individuals of both species grow rapidly because they have a high degree of fungal infection.

Finally, one must mention that a very few European orchids do not rely on underground tubers or rhizomes. These are *Hammarbya paludosa*, *Liparis loeselii* and *Microstylis monophyllos*, all of which store food in a swelling at the base of the stem called a pseudobulb, which is often found in tropical orchids, especially epiphytes. In addition *Hammarbya* develops small buds called bulbils at the tips of its leaves. These bulbils fall off, quickly become infected by the mycorrhizal fungi associated with the parent, and develop into separate individuals with their own roots in the bogs in which the plant makes its home. Such bulbils are found in other plants, including many with a markedly northern distribution, since they afford the plant a means of propagation in cold seasons when flowers and seeds may not be formed at all.

Flowering span

Orchids are basically perennials, which means that growth, flowering and fruiting take place over many years. When finally they do flower, what can be expected? Will they keep on flowering and for how long, or will they die?

If conditions are good most orchids can flower in successive seasons over a period of years. One can often find the dried-up fruiting stems of the previous year next to a new bloom.

The number of years of flower production for each orchid varies according to conditions. At one end of the scale there are records of rhizomes of *Listera ovata* with the remains of up to twenty-four old flowering stems (and the first would not have been produced until the plant was about twelve or thirteen years old). At the other end of the scale *Ophrys apifera* is sometimes not truly perennial but monocarpic, flowering once and then dying. However, this occurs mainly in Britain, where the optimum conditions for growth of

Ophrys (a predominantly Mediterranean genus) do not exist, so that the plant often exhausts itself in producing a single flowering stem and then fruiting.

In more congenial natural climates than Britain can offer and in cultivation it certainly flowers for several years, and can thus be termed a true, if short-lived, perennial.

In cultivation most of the European orchids can be kept flowering for five years or more. Some years orchids take a 'rest' from flowering if the light levels and weather conditions of the previous year were not in favour of food production. The plant could then possibly flower the following year, although this is by no means guaranteed.

The majority of European orchids 'go underground' in winter, the leaves dying on the surface, and the stored carbohydrate in the rhizome, tuber or pseudobulb being used for growth the following spring (or late winter).

In Britain *Spiranthes spiralis* and *Ophrys apifera* develop a rosette of leaves in autumn, and these remain green throughout the winter, manufacturing food by photosynthesis. Both orchids behave in this respect like other orchids in the Mediterranean region, where the leaves are sent up after the autumn rains begin and persist throughout the winter. In the field one can easily find their rosettes, and it is tantalising to wonder exactly which species of orchid is present, for at this stage the leaf rosettes of many orchids are so similar that identification is extremely difficult.

Mediterranean orchids receive very different treatment in summer from orchids living in Britain or Germany (Fig. 6). All the *Ophrys*, *Orchis* and *Serapias* species which thrive around the Mediterranean actually need the baking they get during the summer months. The new tuber, formed in the late winter or early spring, exists in moist (often cledgy) soil during the time the parent plant is alive. After flowering and fruiting has occurred, the weather starts to get very warm and the soil is literally baked hard by the sun. The tuber escapes dehydration because a hard earth shell is formed around it as the ground dries out.

The onset of the next winter rains causes this shell to soften, and growth starts again when moisture reaches the plant. Without this period of summer dormancy orchid tubers are almost always doomed to fail in cultivation. Many Mediterranean *Ophrys* and *Orchis* grow in places where the moisture retention in winter is sufficient to promote a good growth of moss.

Some of our European orchids can go into a state of dormancy if, for example, they live in woodlands where the light level drops as the trees grow and provide a denser leaf cover each successive year. It seems that if light levels are not high enough the plant reverts to dependence on mycorrhiza for its food supplies.

A good example of this type of behaviour is found with *Cephalanthera rubra*. Most of its roots are long and comparatively slender and they grow out horizontally – especially in the humus-rich upper layers of the soil. They

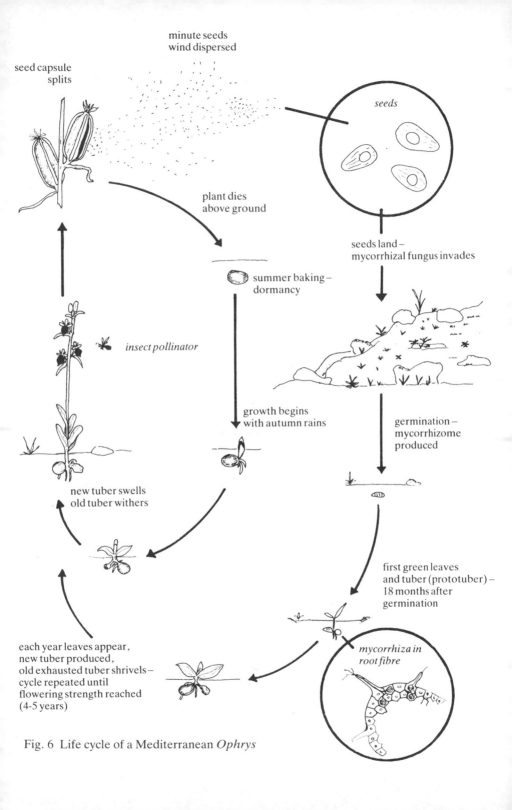

minute seeds
wind dispersed

seed capsule
splits

seeds

plant dies
above ground

seeds land –
mycorrhizal fungus invades

summer baking –
dormancy

insect pollinator

growth begins
with autumn rains

germination –
mycorrhizome
produced

new tuber swells
old tuber withers

first green leaves
and tuber (prototuber) –
18 months after
germination

each year leaves appear,
new tuber produced,
old exhausted tuber shrivels –
cycle repeated until
flowering strength reached
(4-5 years)

*mycorrhiza in
root fibre*

Fig. 6 Life cycle of a Mediterranean *Ophrys*

are normally heavily infected with fungus, and food from this is usually stored in the root and not in the rootstock. As long as the light level is high enough the leaves produce food, which is used for the next year's aerial leaves and flower spike. If the leaf cover above the plant becomes too dense then the leaves cannot produce enough food and the onus is again on the fungus. Flowering does not take place and the plant can persist in this vegetative state for some time (as it is forced to do in one of its British sites). *Goodyera repens* is another woodland orchid which can revert to a purely vegetative state, depending on mycorrhizal activity for its food.

Even *Cypripedium calceolus*, which is very little infected by fungus in its adult state, can revert to its childhood dependence in adverse conditions. Reinfection takes place from the surrounding soil.

All the plants mentioned above can, during a period of fungal dependence, exist entirely underground. In this case no leaves appear above the surface except for the occasional almost transparent leaf or prophyll. *Epipogium aphyllum* is thought to spend much of its life in this way, surfacing after very long intervals of time (sometimes ten or twenty years). It is wholly dependent on mycorrhiza for its nutrition as it contains no chlorophyll.

Ophrys are virtually independent of mycorrhiza in their adult stages, but some growers have noticed that, very rarely, a plant will send up no more than a prophyll (an embryonic leaf), yet when the tuber is lifted it is found to have increased substantially in size. This can only be explained by fungal activity.

2 – Orchid ecology

A close study of the wild orchids of Europe and the Mediterranean region reveals a complex and subtle interplay of factors – historical, geographical and ecological – which determine where orchids are to be found.

First, there is the climate, with rainfall, mean annual temperatures and seasonal extremes of temperature all playing leading roles. Then there is the climate of previous eras. Was the land, for example, a victim of the ice sheets that covered most of Europe during the various glacial epochs?

Geological history is important, too, because land masses have separated considerably during the period associated with orchid evolution. It is often thought that orchids first appeared on Planet Earth somewhere in the region of what is now Malaya during the Cretaceous period, which was the time when dinosaurs became extinct and birds and mammals flourished.

Finally, orchids cannot be considered in isolation from other types of plants in the surrounding vegetation. Grasslands, marshes, woods – all provide different environmental conditions and consequently support distinct orchid populations.

In what follows we make an arbitrary division between highlands and lowlands; that is, land below 600m is regarded as lowland, and land above this as highland or montane. Within each of these broad categories there are grasslands, woodlands, rocky areas and wetlands, each with its own orchids which change in type as one moves from northern Europe, through the western and central European countries to the Mediterranean lands.

Obviously there are orchids which can grow in more than one type of habitat, and this poses a problem for anyone attempting a closely defined division of orchids according to the habitat they prefer. The range of types of countryside included here should, however, give the reader some idea of the species of orchids that may be found in a particular place.

One of the most important factors determining orchid distribution is the nature of the soil. Whether a soil is basic (e.g. limestones and chalks) or acidic (e.g. peat) plays an important part in dictating which plants will grow there. For example, a gardener who wants to plant rhododendrons on a lime-rich soil has either to make a peat bed or resort to expensive chemical preparations.

The presence of calcium in a soil can prevent the uptake of other essential elements such as magnesium and iron, making it impossible for some plants to survive.

The flora of chalk and limestone areas is markedly different from that of acid heaths and bogs, and we can divide plants roughly into two groups – calcicoles, plants which thrive on basic soils, and calcifuges or calciphobes, the plants which inhabit acidic ground where calcium cannot affect their mineral uptake.

Many of the richest orchid populations occur on basic soils. One has only to visit Greece or Italy to see orchids in evidence wherever the red soil (*terra rossa*), derived from the weathering of limestone, is found. In Britain the chalk soils of Kent and Buckinghamshire support by far the most impressive collection of British orchids. In Holland, too, the limestone karst of south Limburg carries an impressive display of orchids. France and Germany have much larger areas of calcareous soils, and where these are not farmed orchids flourish.

Listera ovata is one orchid which flourishes on basic or acidic soils, while *Orchis mascula* and *O. morio* are frequent on neutral soils composed, for the most part, of clay.

Many marsh species do not need soils that are themselves lime-rich so long as the drainage water flowing into or through the marsh contains enough lime to neutralise the natural acidity of the marsh soils.

A few orchids are restricted to acidic soils; only in exceptional cases do they occur elsewhere. The most common is *Dactylorhiza maculata* ssp. *ericetorum* and, far less frequently met with, *Hammarbya paludosa* and *Listera cordata*.

Other factors affecting the distribution of orchids are, first of all, the surrounding vegetation: different habitats of grassland, woodland and marsh provide conditions and vegetation types which suit quite distinct groups of orchids.

Secondly, controlled grazing (i.e. grazing by sheep or other animals at certain times of the year) is essential to preserve the character of some types of grassland. Downlands, for example, would gradually be taken over by trees and shrubs as part of a natural process, called succession, if grazing animals did not devour the young shoots of these plants. Unfortunately, if these lands are grazed when orchids are in leaf, or in flower before seeds are produced, the numbers of orchids growing there can rapidly dwindle to zero.

Throughout Europe vast areas of calcareous grassland, which once held rich orchid populations, have been used to satisfy man's insatiable demands for meat and dairy produce.

Around the Mediterranean the ubiquitous goat is by far the most important contributor to dwindling populations. Goat-grazed land is easily recognisable because of the absence of plants. Spurges, spiny brooms and asphodels thrive, but gone are the anemones, orchids and bulbous plants that once dotted the ground.

Aspect is the third important factor, especially in the hotter countries around the Mediterranean. Here the south-facing slopes receive the full effect of the sun's rays, and conditions can prove too harsh for orchids. The north-facing slopes are noticeably different in appearance; far less arid and more favourable for orchid survival.

Finally there is drainage to consider. Some orchid species will occur at the bottom of a slope, some prefer plateaux at the top, while others are quite content with both. It all depends on their water requirements, how long water is retained after the rain, and for how much of the year.

It may help if we set out in tabular form the environmental headings which we have adopted in the rest of this chapter.

Lowlands

GRASSLANDS
Moderately Dry Grasslands
Mediterranean Dry Grasslands
Heath and Moorland

STONY AREAS
Limestone Pavement

WOODLANDS
Pinewoods – West, Central and Northern Europe
Mediterranean Pinewoods
Beechwoods (on chalk or limestone)
Immature Beech and Other Broad-leaf Woods.
Maquis and Garigue.

WETLANDS
Sphagnum Bogs
Fens
Marshes
Dune Slacks

Highlands

GRASSLANDS
Montane Meadows (Central Europe)
Mediterranean Montane Meadows
Alpine and Sub-alpine Meadows

WOODLANDS
Beechwoods
Coniferous Woodland
Mediterranean Mountain Woods

WETLANDS
Mid-European Wet Meadows (including the Alps)
Mediterranean Wet Meadows and Mountain Seepages.

Lowlands

Grasslands

Moderately Dry Grasslands. These generally have short grass on well aerated calcareous soils: such areas are found on low hillsides or in sparse meadows. Examples are 'downland' in Buckinghamshire, Kent and Sussex in the British Isles, and much of the Massif Central and Auvergne in France.

The surroundings are often very attractive, with low trees and bushes of juniper, hazel, blackthorn, hawthorn and various whitebeams. On these chalky soils one can recognise two distinct types of grassland. The first, where the grasses reach a height of 30cm or so, is formed by the grasses *Bromus erectus, Brachypodium pinnatum, Arrhenatherum elatius* and others; the second is an altogether shorter turf, up to 15cm, composed mainly of *Festuca ovina, F. rubra, Cynosurus cristatus* etc. The flowering plants found in these grasslands – *Polygala vulgaris, P. comosa, Pulsatilla vulgaris* (unfortunately rare in Britain), *Anthyllis vulneraria, Onobrychis viciaefolia* and *Gentiana germanica* – afford a good way of recognising the habitat.

Examples of the orchids to be found are: 'Long grass' – *Anacamptis pyramidalis, Aceras anthropophorum, Gymnadenia conopsea, Orchis militaris*; and 'Short grass' – *Ophrys apifera, O. sphegodes, O. fuciflora, Herminium monorchis, Coeloglossum viride, Orchis ustulata* and *Spiranthes spiralis*.

Another group of orchids is found in either long or short grassland. Members of this group are: *Orchis mascula, Listera ovata, Platanthera chlorantha*. Other orchids sometimes found in these places are *Orchis purpurea, O. simia, Himantoglossum hircinum* and *Ophrys insectifera*. In the British Isles *Ophrys fuciflora, Orchis simia, O. militaris* and *Himantoglossum hircinum* are all very rare, while *Ophrys sphegodes*, although more frequently met with, has a restricted distribution (Dorset, Sussex and Kent).

Unfortunately these grasslands make ideal farm land, and urban expansion claims its share as well. As a result this type of habitat is disappearing at an alarming rate.

Mediterranean Dry Grasslands. In and around the Mediterranean lands one finds stony meadows where *Asphodelus microcarpus* is a familiar sight in spring. Again there are olive groves, where the undergrowth has not been unduly influenced by cultivation, and the so-called secondary grasslands, formed over the years after scrub clearance had removed the original vegetation. Together with roadsides, disused vineyards, areas around ruined habitations and sometimes archaeological sites, we have a collection of places where the orchid flora can be hard to rival.

Ophrys in particular seem to thrive on land where there has been some agricultural disturbance in the past, provided that modern chemical fertilizers (which are ruinous to most of our orchids) have not been used.

These places tend to be moderately grassy in spring, drying out with the onset of summer, and are usually on fairly flat ground (the hillsides are often scrub-covered).

The abundance of species is unusually great because a number of orchids find their optimum conditions for growth on this sort of terrain. The content of the flora varies around the Mediterranean but the following species are often to be found: *Ophrys sphegodes* (various subspecies depending on geographical location), *Ophrys lutea* and its ssp. *murbeckii* (sometimes called var. *minor*), *O. fuciflora* (again in a number of possible forms), *O. fusca, O. fusca* ssp. *iricolor, O. bombyliflora, O. tenthredinifera, Orchis tridentata, O. italica, O. papilionacea, O. coriophora* ssp. *fragrans, O. simia, Barlia robertiana, Serapias lingua, S. vomeracea* and *Aceras anthropophorum*.

Heath and Moorland. These two types of habitat, which frequently grade one into the other, support plant communities on non-calcareous soils covered with a variable depth of raw humus or peat. In drier places where the thickness of the peat is not too great we have heathlands, whereas those damper places which allow a much more extensive peat formation become moorlands. The vegetation on heathland is dominated by members of the *Ericaceae* (heaths and heathers), and by coarse grasses and sedges (e.g. cotton grass, deer grass, purple moor grass) in the case of moorland.

Very few orchids occur in heather, although as always with orchids there is an exception (in this case *Listera cordata*) on some of the northern and Scottish heaths in the British Isles. When the heather is mixed with heaths (*Erica cinerea* and *E. tetralix*) and bilberry (*Vaccinium myrtillus*), *Dactylorhiza maculata* is frequent, whilst *Platanthera bifolia* is a much less common find.

Other types of moorland with cotton grass and deer grass or, at higher altitude, crowberry, bilberry and cowberry are devoid of orchids except for the ever-present *D. maculata*.

In Scandinavia the lists of heath and moorland species is supplemented by *Platanthera obtusata* ssp. *oligantha* and *P. hyperborea*. The first mentioned is a very rare orchid, growing in birch and conifer woods and on calcareous heaths. It is restricted to Finland, Norway, northern Russia and Arctic Sweden, where it grows only in the Abisko National Park, on the slopes of Mt Nuolja and in the marshes of Torne. *P. hyperborea* is an orchid of heaths and moorlands, restricted to Iceland but by no means rare there.

A very distinctive type of heathland exists in Scandinavia, on mountains with lime-rich rocks. It is called Dryas-heath because it is covered with a very low 'scrub' of the attractive *Dryas octopetala*. It also supports a rich flora which can include *Epipactis atrorubens*.

Lowland stony areas

Limestone Pavement. Although grass grows in the fissures and cracks, limestone pavement is not strictly grassland. In appearance it resembles a vast area of crazy paving. Fissures are formed by the erosion of softer material and can be several metres deep. Within these clefts the microclimate allows moist humus to form, and many calcicoles grow there.

Limestone pavement occurs in many places in the Massif Central in France, on the Gargano peninsula in Italy, in Yorkshire, Cumberland and Westmorland in Britain, in Durness and Inchnadamph in Scotland, and in the Burren region of western Ireland.

The orchid flora depends very much on the geographical location and often has the same species as one finds on well-established sand dunes. In northern England one finds *Ophrys apifera, Orchis mascula, Epipactis helleborine*, *E. atrorubens* and *Spiranthes spiralis*. In the Burren region in Ireland, one of the most famous regions of limestone pavement, there are relicts of a Mediterranean flora which escaped the ravages of the ice sheets that covered much of Britain a long time ago. Apart from the above mentioned orchids the speciality here is *Neotinea maculata* in its only British site. In France the Massif Central has vast areas of pavement degrading into boulder-strewn meadows (the flora of these is covered in the section 'Moderately Dry Grasslands'). Here *Orchis purpurea* and *O. militaris* can be added to the orchid list as frequent finds.

Wherever limestone occurs in the Mediterranean one finds fissures, often filled with the rich red *terra rossa*, where orchids flourish. The species found will be the same as those mentioned for 'Maquis and Garigue' or 'Mediterranean Dry Grasslands'. In fact the latter is something of a misnomer since few places in the Mediterranean hold what western Europeans regard as grasslands. The grass cover is altogether more sparse and the areas are usually very rocky and stone-strewn.

In northern England vast areas of limestone pavement have been destroyed, and their unique wild flowers are thus gone forever. The irony, in this case, is that the stone has been taken for garden rockeries.

Lowland woodlands

Pinewoods – West, Central and Northern Europe. These are usually found in dry places on calcareous soils – a similar background to that of the 'Moderately Dry Grasslands'. The pinewoods occur in parts of the Jura and Auvergne in France as well as in many other places in Europe. The usual orchid flora includes: *Cephalanthera damasonium*, *Gymnadenia conopsea*, *Platanthera chlorantha*, *Epipactis helleborine*, *Ophrys insectifera* and *Neottia nidus-avis*. More rarely the following orchids stray into this type of woodland: *Goodyera repens*, *Cephalanthera rubra*, *Epipactis atrorubens*.

In Britain the only coniferous woodlands with any claim to being natural are those formed by the Scots pine (*Pinus sylvestris*) in the Highlands of Scotland. Most of the pinewoods are found in valleys up to 600m or more above sea level and thus, in terms of our arbitrary division, are not definitely montane woods. Yet because of their northern latitude their flora is very much like that of a sub-alpine wood. *Listera cordata* grows in clearings or under a light leaf canopy, *Goodyera repens* threads its way through moss cushions, and *Corallorhiza trifida* favours fairly dense shade.

Pinewoods which have arisen in the last hundred years as a result of direct colonisation of healthy areas by means of windblown seed have an interesting orchid flora. Both *Epipactis dunensis* and *E. phyllanthes* occur in such woods in Anglesey and Southport in Great Britain. The soil is calcareous as it is formed from sand containing crushed shells of long-dead molluscs.

In Sweden and Finland the special prize of some damp, mossy pinewoods is the exquisite *Calypso bulbosa*.

Mediterranean Pinewoods. In many places around the Mediterranean, near the coast, plantations of the Aleppo pine (*Pinus halepensis*) and, less frequently, the Stone pine (*Pinus pinea*) are a common sight. They are good places to find orchids, especially after the trees have been thinned out. For anyone who has fought his way through the densely packed trees of a British pinewood this kind of Mediterranean woodland comes as a very pleasant surprise. One can actually walk between the trees, there is a light undergrowth of cistus species, and herbs (e.g. *Rosmarinus officinalis*) are everywhere. The pinewoods of calcareous soils invariably consist of *Pinus halepensis* although the tree is not confined to these soils.

Frequent finds among the orchid flora are: *Ophrys sphegodes* (in various guises, depending on where the wood is situated in the region), *Ophrys fusca* (the species and ssp. *omegaifera* in eastern Mediterranean lands) *O. tenthredinifera*, *O. bombyliflora*, *O. fuciflora* (again a range of subspecies is possible, depending on geographical location), *O. lutea*, *O. speculum*, *Orchis morio* ssp. *picta*, *O. coriophora* ssp. *fragrans*, *O. italica*, *Serapias vomeracea*, *Neotinea maculata* and *Limodorum abortivum*.

In France the Aleppo pine used to form extensive woodlands around the Riviera, while the woods of stone pine were particularly good near Hyères and in the Argens valley near St Raphael, although urban development has now taken its toll of both regions. The two pines are frequent on the Italian coast, and in Cyprus there are plantations of Aleppo pine in a number of places along the southern coast from Larnaca to Paphos. A species closely related to the Aleppo pine, called *Pinus brutia*, forms very extensive woods in Cyprus, away from the coast, and these are mentioned in connection with 'Mediterranean Mountain Woods' (c.f. p. 34).

Similar collections of orchids can be found in woods of *Cupressus sempervirens* which, in Greece in particular, occurs wild as the horizontal spreading form var. *horizontalis*.

The soil on which all these trees grow is often sandy but calcareous.

Beechwoods (on chalk and limestone). In Britain the finest beechwoods are to be found in Buckinghamshire, Surrey and Kent, where they often exist as 'hangers' on the sides of chalk hills. In France beechwoods are found over very large areas, and in Germany, too, large parts of the broad-leaved forests are beech.

Mature beechwoods are characterized by an absence of thick ground cover, although *Mercurialis perennis*, *Paris quadrifolia*, *Galium odoratum*, *Lathyrus vernalis* and, outside the British Isles, *Hepatica nobilis* and *Daphne mezerum* all thrive in the shaded conditions, as do certain orchids.

In Britain the beechwood is unrivalled for the diversity of its orchid flora.

This is due to two factors. First, they occur in the southern half of Britain where the climate is more suitable for orchids; and secondly, they occur on calcareous soils. The greater number of orchids in a beechwood grow on the shallow chalk soils found on slopes. On the flatter summit plateaux, where much of the lime has been washed away, or on the sands and gravels overlying the chalk, the orchid flora is far less abundant.

Characteristic orchids of the beechwoods are: *Cephalanthera damaso-nium*, *Epipactis helleborine* and *Neottia nidus-avis*. Where the leaf cover overhead is not so dense one can find *Platanthera chlorantha*, *Listera ovata*, *Orchis mascula*, *Cephalanthera rubra* and the occasional *Orchis purpurea*. Less frequently met with is *Epipactis leptochila*, and beechwoods at higher levels (e.g. the Jura) are the home of *Epipactis atrorubens*.

In those parts of beechwoods where the shade is heaviest one can look for (but seldom find) *Epipogium aphyllum*. This grows in one or two sites in Buckinghamshire in Britain, but is reputedly more frequent in the Jura and occurs in some good colonies in Germany's Black Forest. It is one of the great rarities amongst European wild orchids.

Immature Beech and Other Broad-leaf Woods (on chalk or limestone). At the edges of beechwoods there are often extensive thickets of young beech trees where orchids can be found – especially if these trees are now growing on what was once calcareous grasslands.

One of the first orchids to colonise these areas (and young beech planta-tions made by man) is *Cephalanthera damasonium*. In these places it is at its best, often existing in clumps of large numbers of flowers. *Epipactis helle-borine* is another colonist but it takes a few more years to establish itself than does its cousin *C. damasonium*.

One can often find 'relict' populations of orchids (more frequent in grassland haunts) that persist until the leaf cover becomes too dense. These are: *Anacamptis pyramidalis*, *Gymnadenia conopsea* and *Ophrys apifera* (after the heat of the summer of 1976 in Britain a colony of *O. apifera* appeared under the shade of beech trees where grassland had been some twenty years previously, but this was not repeated the following year, in 1978).

The edges of beechwoods are often good places to look for *Platanthera chlorantha*, *Ophrys insectifera* and *Orchis militaris*. This latter orchid is frequently found in such places in France and Germany and, many years ago, it was to be found in Britain throughout the Chilterns. Sadly this is no longer the case.

As one travels to more northerly and western areas in Britain and Europe beechwoods on calcareous soils are often replaced by woods of ash. The orchid flora is similar to those of the beechwoods, but most of the species favouring southern Europe are absent. *Orchis mascula*, *Dactylorhiza fuch-sii*, *Listera ovata*, *Platanthera chlorantha*, *Ophrys insectifera* and *Epipactis helleborine* are all possible finds. Other less frequent species are: *Ophrys apifera, Anacamptis pyramidalis, Platanthera bifolia* and *Cephalanthera longifolia*.

Oakwoods outside the Mediterranean region are usually composed of *Quercus robur* (pedunculate oak) or *Quercus petraea* (sessile oak) or, very occasionally, both. Pedunculate oakwoods occur usually on soils with more bases present, although these soils may be heavy or light in different places, whereas sessile oakwoods are more characteristic of well-drained soils poor in bases. This makes a great difference to the orchid flora. In parts of Europe there are woods filled with shrubs of hazel, ash and other woody plants. Every fifteen years or so these shrubs are cut back and allowed to sprout again – an ancient practice known as coppicing. The shrubs can cast a very heavy shade, but when cut back they allow *Orchis mascula* to flourish in large numbers a few years later. Such sites are becoming rarer as forests are cut down or the practice of coppicing is neglected. The only other orchids to appear in these woods with any regularity are the two Helleborines, *Epipactis helleborine* and *E. purpurata*.

Woods of sessile oak are not the best places to look for orchids. They have what could perhaps be described as 'very impoverished orchid flora'.

Maquis and Garigue. Two characteristic types of vegetation in the Mediterranean region are maquis and garigue. Strictly speaking maquis is 'bush' wood, from one to three metres in height and composed mostly of evergreen shrubs. Typically one can find: *Quercus ilex* and *Q. coccifera, Arbutus unedo, Olea europaea, Erica arborea, Rosmarinus officinalis, Pistacia lentiscus* etc. The growth is so thick that undergrowth is usually absent. Orchids and various bulbs occur where there are spaces, and we have grouped garigue with maquis because, although it is an altogether sparser type of vegetation, it houses the same orchids.

One very striking feature of garigue is the number of scented low-growing shrubs. Indeed local names for garigue are given according to the character of the 'scent' predominating. For example, in Spain the thyme and other Labiates form the 'tomillares', in Greece the garigue has a different but no less fragrant composition and is called 'phrygana', whilst in Palestine it is 'batha'. Over two hundred different species of plants are estimated to make up 'phrygana', and many of our culinary herbs (hyssop, sage, savory, garlic and rue) have their progenitors there.

In springtime it is the variety of bulbous plants and annuals flowering in the garigue that produces the floral explosion so characteristic of the Mediterranean. The sudden burst of flowering in March and April (or earlier in Cyprus and Israel) is soon followed by a dry and parched landscape where the dusty fruitheads are the only reminders of the glory.

Between maquis and garigue there are many gradations which only the pedant would trouble to enumerate. What really concerns us is that such lands reaching up to about 600m above sea level provide a home for a dazzling array of orchids. The list includes all those mentioned above in connection with 'Mediterranean Dry Grasslands', but we can add to them *Ophrys speculum* and a host of other orchids, altogether more restricted in distribution. These include (in Greece and Italy) the various forms of *Ophrys scolopax*, numerous distinctive varieties of *Ophrys sphegodes* and *O. fuciflora*, the beautiful *Ophrys cretica* (in Crete), and its close relative across the water in Cyprus *Ophrys kotschyi*. Both *Ophrys argolica* and *O. ferrum-equinum* are found in phrygana in parts of Greece and also, to some extent, in grassier places.

Lowland wetlands

Wetlands are some of the most vulnerable habitats in Europe. They are an attractive prospect for the farmer because the ground, when drained, is very fertile. They are decreasing at an alarming rate despite attempts by conservation bodies to make people aware of the irreparable damage that has already been done to vast areas of bog, marsh and fen.

Throughout the region covered by this book there are a number of distinct types of wetland.

The Sphagnum Bog. A bog is a distinctly 'acid' wetland found on non-calcareous soils in regions where the rainfall is usually high, although they may occur locally in a 'dry' area where the drainage is poor. Bogs are usually associated with moorlands and heaths of acid soils. Ireland, with its damp climate, possesses bogs covering large areas of land, even on slopes and low hills.

Bogs are found in most countries of Europe except the Mediterranean lands, where the low rainfall and predominantly calcareous soils operate against them.

In very acid conditions the peat is formed almost entirely by sphagnum mosses, and the characteristic orchid of such bogs is the tiny Bog Orchid, *Hammarbya paludosa*. It grows on the surface of moss cushions in the company of *Drosera* and *Pinguicula* species. Other orchids found in bog conditions are *Listera cordata* and a form of *Dactylorhiza incarnata* (suggested as ssp. *sphagnicola*) which has been identified from specimens growing in sphagnum bogs in Germany. In slightly drier places one may find *Dactylorhiza maculata* and *Platanthera bifolia*.

Fens. These are wetlands formed on a peat base where the drainage water is either neutral or basic in nature. Fen vegetation consists of tall sedges, grasses, rushes and various flowering plants such as *Filipendula ulmaria*, *Iris pseudacorus* and *Caltha palustris*. The plant list varies from one fen to another or even between parts of a fen, depending on the water level.

In Britain there are still extensive fens in East Anglia, although drainage for agriculture and excessive use of the waterways by holidaymakers has had (and is still having) a deleterious effect. Holland also has extensive fens, although many have been reclaimed for farm land.

The most frequently encountered orchids are, appropriately enough, the 'marsh' orchids or *Dactylorhiza* group. The most widespread is *Dactylorhiza incarnata*, which can occur in a number of forms (ssp. *coccinea* and *ochroleuca*, as well as the type). *Dactylorhiza traunsteineri* is another rather scarce fen inhabitant, though a number of texts cite it as a 'bog' resident. This is almost certainly due to the great similarity that exists between species of *Dactylorhiza*. Confusion is rife in the genus, and many records for *D. traunsteineri* are probably for narrow-leaved forms of the ubiquitous *D. maculata* or for hybrids of *D. majalis* with other marsh orchids.

Epipactis palustris is a plant characteristic of reedy swamps and so is often found in fens. A very much rarer plant is the inconspicuous *Liparis loeselii*, which is found in a number of places in Europe but is very thinly distributed. Both *E. palustris* and *L. loeselii* also occur in the dune slacks of the South Wales coastal regions (c.f. p. 29).

In Ireland *Spiranthes romanzoffiana* occurs in fen areas around Lough Neagh but is not particular in its requirements and can be found in marshes or bogs with neutral or slightly acid ground water.

The presence of peat in fens and bogs means that the distinction between the two environments is often blurred, and sometimes a mixed vegetation results. Thus in parts of Ireland *S. romanzoffiana* can be found in company with *D. majalis* ssp. *occidentalis*.

Marshes. These differ from fens and bogs in the complete absence or poor development of peat. They occur on any soils where drainage is poor but are especially well developed on clays and marls. Marshes are also found along valleys of streams or rivers in lowland or upland regions.

The amount of lime in the water varies greatly and so, as a result, do the associated flora. Plants to be found in marshes, from the simple 'hollow in the ground' sort to the extensive ones covering many hectares, include: *Juncus inflexus*, *Juncus effusus*, *Juncus conglomeratus*, *Ranunculus flammula*, *Cardamine pratense*, *Lychnis flos-cuculi*, *Mentha aquatica*, *Iris pseudacorus*, *Epilobium hirsutum*, *Caltha palustris* and *Equisetum* species.

Again marsh orchids are the most frequently found. *Dactylorhiza majalis* is quite common in the southern half of England and Wales in the form *D. majalis* ssp. *praetermissa*. This is rare in northern France, Belgium, Holland and Germany where other forms of *D. majalis* are much more common. In north-western Europe, including northern parts of England and Wales, *D. majalis* ssp. *purpurella* takes over from *D. majalis* ssp. *praetermissa* as the orchid found in great purple 'drifts' where it finds favourable conditions.

Other orchids found in marshes are *Epipactis palustris* and a very robust form of *Gymnadenia conopsea* called var. *densiflora*. In highly calcareous marshes in Mayo and Galway in Ireland there is a marsh orchid whose status alternates between that of a species and a subspecies, depending on the whim of current botanical opinion. This is *D. incarnata* ssp. *cruenta*, also known from the European mainland, especially in the Alps.

Dune Slacks. Sand-dune systems are one of the most underrated of all habitats in which one can find orchids. Although it is not widely recognised, the overall flora and fauna of a dune system can indeed be not only unique but rich in species that elsewhere are scarce.

In a floristically impoverished country like Britain a dune system is one of the few places where one can gain an impression of the sheer abundance of flowers that makes alpine or Mediterranean localities so memorable.

Most dune systems consist of high ridges alternating with low valleys or 'slacks'. The most recently formed dunes are near the sea, whilst the older ones farther inland are consolidated to varying degrees, often bearing a dense grassy turf. The flora of the ridges and slacks are in most cases distinct, the former consisting of various types of grassland, whereas the latter are often very marshy.

Both ridges and slacks are calcareous in nature, and for this reason they both support rich orchid populations. On the sides of the ridges, not too far from the dampness of the slacks, *Ophrys apifera* and *Epipactis helleborine* are possible finds, whilst on the older, well-consolidated dunes *Spiranthes spiralis*, *Coeloglossum viride*, *Orchis morio* and *Anacamptis pyramidalis* can occur. The dune systems in South Wales hold enormous populations of *Epipactis helleborine* in a bewildering variety of colour forms; the plants are often much more robust than those from beechwoods, particularly where the turf is thick on the older dunes. Other helleborines can be found on dunes: *E. phyllanthes* is rather rare but does flower in South Wales and Lancashire, whereas *E. dunensis* is restricted to Lancashire, Anglesey, and a few similar sites in western France, Holland and Belgium. *Himantoglossum hircinum*, too, occurs on sand dunes, sometimes in abundance, on the Dutch and French coastal dune systems and in small colonies in similar habitats in Britain (Kent and, at one time, Somerset). Calcareous dunes in western Ireland have occasionally afforded sites for *Neotinea maculata*, and in many of the Hebridean islands they are the special habitat for *Orchis fuchsii* ssp. *hebridensis*.

But despite this comparative richness the ridges cannot compete for floral colour with the wet dune slacks. Much of the slack area can be under water in a wet winter, only to dry out in the summer leaving a thick cushion of *Salix repens*, various bryophytes, *Anagallis tenella*, *Hydrocotyle vulgaris* and, on the South Wales coast, great drifts of *Pyrola rotundifolia*.

Dactylorhiza praetermissa occurs in very large numbers in dune slacks in

South Wales, and *D. purpurella* in more northerly parts, both favouring damper places than *D. incarnata* ssp. *coccinea* (a form of Early Marsh orchid found in dune slacks, often in fairly dry conditions). A special member of the orchid flora of the dune slacks in South Wales is *Liparis loeselii* in a broad-leaved form (var. *ovata*). It is very local in its distribution within the dune slacks but in some years can be found in large numbers in its chosen spots. After a hot summer, when the slacks dry, it can all but disappear for a few years until seedlings, unaffected by the drought, reach maturity.

Highlands

Grasslands

Montane Meadows (Central Europe). There are large areas of calcareous grassland in Europe which exist somewhere between 600m and 1600m above sea level. Botanically they owe an allegiance both to the 'Moderately Dry Grasslands' already described (c.f. p. 19) and to the grasslands of the alpine and sub-alpine zones covered later in this section.

The mountain regions of France and Germany, together with parts of the alpine areas of Switzerland, Austria and northern Italy, are the places to find these grasslands and the considerable number of orchid species they carry.

At the right season of the year (mid-June through to July) as many as nine or ten different orchids can be found at any one time: *Gymnadenia conopsea, Listera ovata, Orchis mascula, O. morio, O. ustulata, Coeloglossum viride, Platanthera bifolia* and the occasional *Orchis militaris* have all been mentioned before as members of the orchid flora of calcareous grasslands at lower altitudes. Now we can include the possibility of finding *Pseudorchis albida* and *Dactylorhiza sambucina*, both orchids of high mountain areas.

Not infrequently *Platanthera chlorantha* can be found where woodlands and grasslands meet, and *Epipactis atrorubens* where there are stone-strewn hillsides.

In parts of the Southern Alps, where the climate tends to be less harsh than in the Central and Northern Alps, there are a few strays from the warm lands of the Mediterranean regions to be found on the lower dry, grassy slopes. *Anacamptis pyramidalis, Orchis purpurea, O. tridentata,* an occasional *Himantoglossum hircinum* and several *Ophrys,* including *Ophrys insectifera* and *Ophrys fuciflora* can all be found here, although in very limited areas.

In parts of Austria's Southern Tyrol there is a form of *Ophrys bertolonii* which has a number of differences from the familiar plant of the French and Italian Rivieras. The discrepancies have been sufficient to warrant the suggestion that it was in fact a distinct species and should be regarded as

Ophrys benacensis. Now it is included with *Ophrys bertoloniiformis* (p. 167).

Serapias vomeracea, a plant with a marked preference for Mediterranean climes, reaches the most northerly limits of its distribution in a few valleys in southern Austria and Switzerland.

Mediterranean Montane Meadows. Mountain meadows in the Mediterranean area bear more than a passing resemblance to those in the central parts of Europe. Apart from the presence of many plants characteristic of the Mediterranean, they tend to occur at altitudes of between 600m and 1200m and have the same fresh and open appearance as their counterparts further to the north.

In places where calcareous rocks predominate, the meadows are often stone-strewn and carry a rich bulb collection in the spring. Autumn sees a repetition of the floral display, but with a more restricted list of late-flowering crocuses, colchicums and sternbergias.

The number of orchid species does not rival the abundance one is used to at lower altitudes in the Mediterranean, but nevertheless there are some attractive plants to be found: *Orchis morio, O. mascula, O. tridentata, O. purpurea* and *O. quadripunctata* are widespread over much of the area, *Orchis pallens* occurs less frequently, and *Dactylorhiza sambucina*, a familiar orchid in alpine surroundings, descends to these levels in places.

Orchis anatolica is another orchid which shows a definite preference for montane habitats in the eastern Mediterranean: Crete, Rhodes, Turkey, Lebanon and Cyprus. In the last mentioned island it occurs in great abundance in places in the central Troodos massif, sometimes with small numbers of another orchid, *Dactylorhiza sulphurea* ssp. *pseudosambucina* (formerly *D. romana*), which in Cyprus is only found in its yellow form (a pink form does exist in some countries).

Mountains of moderate height are a distinctive feature of most countries bordering on the Mediterranean, so there is little difficulty in finding mountain meadows – even if they contain relatively little grass. In Italy there is the backbone formed by the Apennines; most of mainland Greece and her islands are mountainous; much of Yugoslavia close to the Adriatic coast, Cyprus with the Kyrenia mountains and the Troodos massif; Spain; Provence and the southern slopes of the Maritime Alps in France; and parts of Turkey – this is by no means a complete list but an indication of the choice available.

Alpine and Sub-alpine Meadows. In late May, June and July the display of flowers in the Alps is something that not even the most ardent devotee of the urban environment could fail to notice. The Alps are justifiably famous for the parade of flowers, which begins with the crocuses pushing their way up through the melting snow, to be followed by soldanellas, anemones and narcissi taking their turn as spring progresses. One considerable bonus for flower-lovers in the Alps is that plants which are past their best lower down can always be searched for higher up where spring is only just beginning.

Unfortunately man has long realized that the Alps provide grazing land second to none, together with a plentiful supply of hay to last livestock through the harsh winter months. Thus in many places overgrazing and the use of fertilizers have killed off the natural flora. Skiing and hiking can prove ruinous to the plant population, especially when large numbers of tourists are involved.

Happily, however, there are still beautiful meadows where man has not intervened, where there are flowers as well as grass and where excessive mowing, fertilizing and grazing have not yet taken their toll. Also, in some countries (in particular Austria, Switzerland and, more recently, France) people are beginning to realize that the floral beauty of the high mountains is a natural asset which many people journey to see, and a more protectionist policy with regard to the mountain flora is emerging.

Below the uppermost tree-line lies the sub-alpine zone which marks the limit of any cultivation and provides a rich floral display. Towards the upper reaches of this zone the trees (generally birch, pine or juniper) become dwarf and stunted.

When conditions become too rigorous to support tree growth we enter the true alpine zone. Here the floral display is less obvious than that in the lower zone but the highly specialized nature of the plants able to survive in these regions leads to beautiful dwarf species, often in clumps which colour the ground.

In the sub-alpine zone orchids are an attractive component of the flora, occurring with such plants as *Hedysarum hedysaroides*, *Helianthemum oelandicum* ssp. *alpestre*, *Astragalus alpinus*, *Pedicularis verticillata* and *Oxytropis campestris*.

Gymnadenia conopsea occurs with the closely related *Gymnadenia odoratissima* which, as its name suggests, has a very strong fragrance. Both species rely on day- and night-flying Lepidoptera for pollination, and Danesch records that butterflies and day-flying moths seem attracted to the dark-coloured forms of both species, whereas the light-coloured plants are favoured by night-flying moths.

Nigritella nigra (with a host of local names to its credit) must be the best known of all the alpine orchids. Its scent and colour combine to give it the English name by which it is known, the Black Vanilla Orchid. When it occurs in large numbers with both *Gymnadenia* species hybrids are frequently found. Such hybrids are quite readily distinguished from their parents by a combination of shape and colour, although it is as well to remember that there is a wide range of colour forms of *N. nigra* besides the deep red-black. The 'Marsh' orchids are represented by the rather variable *Dactylorhiza maculata* and by the two colour forms of *D. sambucina*, purple and yellow, which often occur together.

Other orchids which are found in the sub-alpine zone include *Coeloglossum viride*, *Orchis ustulata*, *Platanthera bifolia* and *Traunsteinera globosa*. This latter (unlike its companions) is not found lower down: it is very much an inhabitant of alpine and sub-alpine places – wherever there is damp earth to its liking in grasslands or at the edges of woods.

Often well-hidden in the grass, camouflaged successfully by its green colour, is the tiny *Herminium monorchis* whose strong, honey-like scent attracts the tiny flies on which it relies for pollination. *Cypripedium calceolus*, one of the loveliest of all European orchids, is sometimes found in parts of the Alps on open, stone-strewn slopes, although more often in woodlands.

Above the tree-line and into the alpine zone proper the plants of *Dryas octopetala*, *Salix reticulata* and *Salix retusa* reign supreme, covering the stony ground in places with a thick mat of stems and leaves. *Gentiana clusii*, *Saxifraga aizoides* and *Androsace chamaejasme* are among a host of plants that thrive in the environment the Alps provide. A tiny orchid, *Chamorchis alpina*, is perfectly at home here too. It occurs sparsely throughout the Alps, but perhaps its reputation for rarity is a direct consequence of the difficulty of seeing it, for its grass-like leaves, dwarf stature and insignificant flowers make it hard to spot. *C. alpina* does not venture below 1600m, and its only orchid companions are likely to be *Coeloglossum viride*, *Pseudorchis albida* and *Nigritella nigra*.

In more northerly latitudes the sub-alpine and alpine zones occur at a much lower level. For example, in parts of Norway, Finland and Arctic Sweden true alpine plants occur well below 1000m and indeed are found at sea level. *Chamorchis alpina* is quite frequently found at low levels in northern Scandinavia.

Mountain woodlands

Woodlands contribute as much as flower-filled meadows and snow-capped mountains to the overall beauty of the Alps. At lower levels there are extensive mature beechwoods where the underlying rock is basic in reaction, and these give way to similarly well established coniferous woods which clothe the mountain sides up to the topmost reaches of the sub-alpine zone. Mixed deciduous woodland is met with in some places, although this tends to be at lower levels, around 600m, so the orchid flora are those mentioned in the earlier section dealing with low level woodlands. One tree that can form woods up to about 1500m is the White Oak, *Quercus pubescens*. The habitat these woods afford and the orchid flora they carry are described in more detail below.

Beechwoods. The orchid flora in a beechwood on calcareous soil has already been dealt with in detail (c.f. p. 23), but a few additions are possible when we consider some of the beechwoods of the Alps. Although parts of the beech forests of the Jura are below 600m and can be embraced by the earlier section on 'Beechwoods', much exists at higher altitudes. The limestone Alps of the North Tyrol and many parts of Switzerland and the Dolomites of northern Italy all have superb beechwoods where orchids are certainly to be found.

Various helleborines are a feature of the orchid flora in a mountain beechwood; those in the *Cephalanthera* group include *C. damasonium*, *C. longifolia*, and the incomparable *C. rubra* whose rosy blooms are by no means rare in some places. *Epipactis helleborine* and *E. leptochila* are two helleborines to be seen in beechwoods in general but there are two close relatives which are found in mountain beechwoods although both are rare – a close relative of *E. helleborine*, called *E. muelleri*, and a rather curious small-flowered plant with tiny leaves, *E. microphylla*. Finally, the darker recesses of these woods hide plants of *E. purpurata* and, almost by way of contrast, *E. atrorubens* which favours the stony slopes at the edges of woods where the sun's rays are not completely absent.

The lighter parts of the woodland are usually the home, too, of *Cypripedium calceolus* whose almost exotic blooms have made it a target for flower pickers and gardeners. It is now protected by law in Switzerland and Austria and by a 'Do not pick the flowers' approach in France.

The yellow *Orchis pallens* is an uncommon plant of grassy places at the edges of beechwoods up to about 1800m, and is far less likely to be met with in these places than *Platanthera chlorantha*, another orchid enjoying the same preferences for this habitat.

The beech litter of the dark woodland recesses provides an ideal environment for two saprophytic orchids, *Corallorhiza trifida* and the very much rarer *Epipogium aphyllum*. The former occurs in both beech and pine woods up to 2700m, whilst the latter shows a marked preference for lower altitudes, being found up to 1900m, although its choice of woodland is the same. The third saprophyte, *Neottia nidus-avis*, is common, often appearing in colonies in the general gloom of the wood. Where there are mossy cushions and the decay of plant matter has made for slightly acidic conditions the tiny creeping stems of *Goodyera repens* can be found threading their way through the cushions.

Coniferous Woodland. Coniferous woods can be made up of several species of tree, the stateliest to our mind being *Larix decidua*. Perhaps this choice has been influenced by the orchids we have found in such places, for other conifers are no less magnificent: *Pinus nigra*, *Pinus sylvestris*, *Picea abies* and *Abies alba*.

The pine and fir woods are evergreen and tend to be dark, so that few orchids are capable of surviving there unless the trees are fairly far apart. *Listera cordata* is one of those orchids occurring on damp mossy banks in the woods; *Corallorhiza trifida* is another, and *Epipogium aphyllum* is as likely to be found here as it is anywhere. Again mossy places at the edges of the woods provide shelter for *Goodyera repens*.

A mixed larch and pine wood is very different in character from the pure pinewood. It tends to be far lighter because the crowns of a larch are not nearly so dense as those of pines, and consequently the flora are richer. Mosses grow far better, and there are the attractive wintergreens *Pyrola rotundifolia, Moneses uniflora* and *Orthilia secunda*, growing with *Vaccinium myrtillus* and *Erica carnea*. In the early spring *Daphne mezereum* is not uncommon, and autumn sees the flowering of *Gentiana asclepiadea*.

Bees, wasps, butterflies and beetles are some of the insects that thrive in these woods and act as pollinators for the flowering plants, among which we can number an impressive collection of orchids.

Ophrys insectifera with its inconspicuous blooms is the only *Ophrys* that regularly ventures to these altitudes; *Platanthera bifolia* flowers in open places, and *Goodyera repens* occurs in colonies or sometimes just as individuals.

Damp shady places afford a habitat for another orchid that can be difficult to spot – *Corallorhiza trifida*. *Listera ovata* is frequently encountered and is about as common in these woods as *Neottia nidus-avis*, a plant favouring the darker recesses rather than places where the sun penetrates the overhead branches.

Both *Dactylorhiza fuchsii* and forms of *D. maculata* are found, although they are so similar in places that one often wonders about their true identity.

Helleborines are again in evidence. First, there is *Cephalanthera rubra* and its relation *C. longifolia*, often flowering close together. Then we have *Epipactis helleborine*, the most widespread of all, flowering in light or shade – in contrast to *E. atrorubens* which shows a marked preference for thin overhead cover and stony, calcareous slopes.

Wherever these woods occur in the Austrian Tyrol there is a possibility of finding *Cypripedium calceolus* at its photogenic best, with light filtering gently through the larches. This plant likes mountain woods up to an altitude of 1800m and calcareous soils with a light humus.

Mediterranean Mountain Woods. Most Mediterranean mountains viewed from the air give an appearance of being sparsely wooded. When woodlands do occur they are usually leafy places where the cool air provides a blessed relief from the heat of the summer sun.

Both broad-leaved and coniferous woodlands can be found, and on Mt Olympus in Greece (Thessalian Olympus to distinguish it from numerous other mountains of the same name on the islands) both occur in true alpine fashion at different altitudes.

Some superb mountain beechwoods are to be found on the unique Gargano peninsula in south-east Italy. Here, on a limestone substratum, orchids thrive both at lower levels in the open and on the high parts in the beechwoods of the Foresta del Umbra. The purple and yellow colour forms of *Dactylorhiza sulphurea* ssp. *pseudosambucina* are particularly attractive here, and a vast range of *Orchis* and *Ophrys* occur at the woodland edges where the trees give way to a landscape strewn with limestone boulders.

Quercus pubescens* is quite capable of forming deciduous woodlands but such woods are seldom if ever extensive. Mountain pinewoods are, in fact, usually formed from *Pinus brutia* or *Pinus halepensis*. More infrequently cedar (*Cedrus libani*) or fir (*Abies cephalonica*) can be the main tree. Examples are the famous cedars of Lebanon and the once extensive forests of *Cedrus libani* ssp. *brevifolia* in Cyprus. Again in Cyprus the mountains of the Troodos massif are particularly well wooded. At low levels there is a mixed woodland, mainly of *Pinus brutia* but with some other interesting and attractive trees; an endemic oak with leaves more like a holly (*Quercus alnifolia*) and the flaking red bark of *Arbutus andrachne*. During May in places on the southern slopes of the massif one can find huge, deep rose blooms of *Paeonia mascula* in this mixed woodland, growing with the white form of *Neotinea intacta* and a rather curious orchid – a green form of *Platanthera chlorantha* which has at times been awarded specific status as *Platanthera holmboei*. In this respect it has at least as much claim to specific status as some of the *Ophrys*.

An endemic helleborine, *Epipactis troodii*, occurs here too, but a month or so later, and in the interim period there are large numbers of *Limodorum abortivum*.

Towards the heights of Troodos the pinewoods take on a completely different appearance, with *Pinus nigra* ssp. *pallasiana* the dominant tree. In this zone the orchid flora is particularly impressive from mid-June to early July. There are helleborines at their most confusing: *Epipactis troodii* and *E. microphylla* (some opinion has been voiced that these are very closely related and that the variable *E. persica* found in countries further east is another part of the tangle), *E. condensata* (a much rarer plant), spikes of *Limodorum abortivum*, *Platanthera chlorantha* (both green and white forms looking distinctly different), and finally *Cephalanthera rubra*, not widespread but in good colonies in one or two places.

In pinewoods on the south-west coastal mountains of Turkey one has the possibility of finding the intriguing *Comperia comperiana*, a plant which also occurs in broad-leaved mountain woodland on the Greek island of Lesbos.

In Lebanon *Comperia comperiana* turns up again with *Himantoglossum affine*, two plants which are found in the mountain woods of northern Syria with the rare and impressive pink *Cephalanthera kurdica*.

Mountain wetlands

Mid-European Wet Meadows (including the Alps). In mountainous parts of France, Germany, Austria, Switzerland and northern Italy one can frequently encounter wet meadows beside streams, or in other places where spring water runs down the hillside turning it into a wetland ('seepage'). The soil reaction can range from lightly acidic to neutral or distinctly basic, and moss is absent or present only in small amounts – which makes a considerably different environment from a peat bog.

Flowering plants to be seen in such places include *Parnassia palustris*, *Pinguicula vulgaris* and *Tofieldia calyculata* when the wetland is in Alpine regions, and *Cirsium oleraceus*, *C. palustre*, *Caltha palustris* with *Equisetum palustre* at lower altitudes.

The orchid list is not very large but it is possible to find in one hillside seepage as many as four of the Marsh Orchids, together with a whole array of confusing hybrids. *Epipactis palustris*, *Listera ovata*, various forms of *Dactylorhiza majalis*, *Gymnadenia conopsea* (and its var. *densiflora*), *D. incarnata*, *D. maculata*, *Platanthera bifolia*, *Orchis morio*, *Orchis laxiflora* ssp. *palustris* and the occasional *Orchis militaris* are the species most likely to be seen up to about 1000m, although *O. laxiflora* ssp. *palustris* and *E. palustris* will only very rarely occur at such an altitude. The rather confusing *Dactylorhiza traunsteineri* occurs in a number of places but often hybridises readily with any other Marsh Orchids present.

In higher regions, up to about 1500m, *D. maculata*, *D. incarnata* (and the ssp. *cruenta*), *G. conopsea* and the occasional *O. militaris* persist. The most frequent orchid in these wet places is *D. majalis* which occurs with its 'alpine' form, *D. majalis* ssp. *alpestris*. Towards the south of Europe there are other orchids which make an appearance in wet meadows. Examples are *Spiranthes aestivalis* and *Dactylorhiza elata*.

As one moves east towards the 'Iron Curtain' countries, slightly different species of Marsh Orchid begin to appear: *Dactylorhiza saccifera* in wet mountain pastures in Greece and the Balkans, and the attractive *Dactylorhiza cordigera* in similar places in southern Yugoslavia, Bulgaria, Greece and western Russia and *D. cilicica* in eastern Turkey.

In Russia itself there is the attraction of *Spiranthes sinensis*, found in wet meadows in the Volga Kama region and so unfortunately inaccessible to most of us.

Mediterranean Wet Meadows and Mountain Seepages. Wetlands in the Mediterranean area are very different from those in Central Europe. For example, there is only one orchid likely to occur in large colonies and that is *Orchis laxiflora*. *Serapias lingua* occurs in damp places in the south of France, Italy and Greece, *Serapias neglecta* in similar places in Corsica and northern Italy. Another of the 'Tongue Orchids', *S. neglecta* ssp. *ionica*, often grows in large numbers in the Ionian Islands of Greece – as its name suggests.

In Cyprus, high up in the Troodos massif, there are a few streams that run all the year round, with limited areas of wetland near them. In such places *Epipactis veratrifolia* grows, often in large numbers, with the tiny *Pinguicula crystallina* for a companion. Lower down, where grass grows under trees and beside a trickle of water that passes as a stream, *Dactylorhiza iberica* flowers. Both orchids have to be searched for at altitudes above 1300m, and also occur in wet mountain areas of Syria, Lebanon and Turkey.

3 – Classification

Numerous schemes for orchid classification have been proposed and rejected in the years since Linnaeus first attempted to impose his ideas of order on the animal and plant world.

In this book we have decided to use the scheme set out in *Flora Europaea*, Volume 5, which is certainly simpler than some of its past or present-day rivals.

There was a tendency in past works to split the family *Orchidaceae* into subfamilies and then further into tribes and subtribes. In the *Flora Europaea* only two distinct subfamilies are considered:

Cypripedioideae – plants with two fertile stamens, pollen not united in pollinia and three fertile stigmas;

Orchidoideae – plants with one fertile stamen, pollen united in pollinia and two fertile stigmas (often confluent).

Plants within each subfamily can be subdivided into *genera* and then into *species*. This is not the end of the matter for further splitting can sometimes result in *subspecies* and *varieties*, as explained later.

The classification of orchids poses considerable problems for amateur and professional botanists alike: scarcely a year passes without some subspecies being raised to specific rank or demoted to varietal status. Again, throughout orchid literature numerous synonyms are in use for the same species of orchid. In recent years, almost in desperation, botanists have agreed to use the earliest name proposed for a plant in its correct genus. This demands a great deal of accurate historical research and is generally a move to be welcomed – although when the process turns a simple name such as *Dactylorhiza romana* into the unwieldy *Dactylorhiza sulphurea* ssp. *pseudosambucina* one can see there are shortcomings.

In order to appreciate the problems with orchids we must first look at the factors which determine whether an orchid is granted specific, subspecific or varietal status. It is worth first mentioning that in orchid classification one man's subspecies is another's variety, and that any list of orchid species and varieties, however well researched, inevitably changes with the tide of current botanical opinion.

Species. If similar plants can interbreed and produce fertile offspring under natural conditions then they are considered as belonging to the same species. Related species are classified under the heading of a genus.

Subspecies. These form populations differing from the type plant and other races of the same species not only in form (morphological differences) bur usually in their geographical or ecological distribution.

Populations of different subspecies are usually well isolated from one another, meeting only on the boundaries between their respective territories. These populations are capable of interbreeding freely if they are brought together.

Varieties. In any race of an orchid species individuals with differing characteristics can arise by genetic mutation. The characteristics are usually unimportant (e.g. overall colour) and the plants occur with normal forms of the race. Without a geographical distribution different from the race they cannot be termed subspecies and are classed as varieties.

It would be extremely convenient if all the orchids in this book could be fitted neatly into the three categories defined above but this is not possible.

What does one call forms of a species which are quite distinct in appearance, breed true and yet overlap partially in their geographical and ecological distribution? Where they occur freely they interbreed and form a spectrum of plants intermediate between the parents – something often called a cline with animal forms.

Overlapping raises such plants above subspecific status yet because they interbreed freely they cannot be 'true' species.

In the Mediterranean area there are numerous *Ophrys* forms that present this dilemma to the taxonomist. As an example we can take *Ophrys sphegodes* since it has numerous distinct races, each with a clearly defined area of distribution. *Flora Europaea* lists these as subspecies, for example ssp. *atrata*, ssp. *garganica* and ssp. *mammosa*.

Many botanists think that these races are closely related species – a 'species complex' in fact – and one should then name them as species. Thus in literature from the OPTIMA project one finds *Ophrys atrata, O. garganica* and *O. mammosa*.

Professor Hans Sundermann proposed a further category for plants which do not satisfy accepted criteria for specific and subspecific status. He called these *prespecies*, and it has always seemed an attractive alternative, since one does not have to challenge long-accepted ideas of what a species or subspecies is. This approach has not found favour with many botanists, so we have followed *Flora Europaea* and used the idea of numerous subspecies. Ultimately it is just a question of attaching a label, and even with sophisticated methods of chromosome analysis, biochemical analysis and studies of pollen ultra-structure, it will be a long time before groups of botanists come to a final agreement on how to name an orchid.

Hybrids. These are plants which arise from cross-breeding between different species and show some characteristics of each parent. They are often, but not always, infertile.

Hybrids are not nearly as common as one would expect from the large populations of different orchids that are found growing together. This can be accounted for by the high degree of fidelity shown by insect pollinators to one particular orchid species.

The only exception occurs with the genus *Dactylorhiza* whose members interbreed with ease and cause great confusion to the field botanist.

A very wide range of orchid hybrids is known, and they can be of two types: *interspecific* (between different species in the same genus) and *intergeneric* (between members of different genera).

Hybridisation is an important factor in evolution. Interspecific hybridisation can lead to a new fertile species in one step but this is unlikely. Much interbreeding and back-crossing with parents must take place, and a 'gene pool' is built up from which new lines can emerge. Natural selection then dictates whether or not these lines succeed.

In most plant families two distinct species should not be able to hybridise, but in the case of orchids interspecific hybrids do occur. This happens when two species are not sufficiently distinct to prevent it, or because distinction which once existed is now breaking down. The former is called primary intergradation and the latter secondary intergradation.

The highly variable *Ophrys arachnitiformis* is an example of a species which is thought to have arisen from hybrid origins. The parents are thought to be *O. fuciflora* and *O. sphegodes*, and there is still much doubt whether one can consider a single species *O. arachnitiformis* or split the races into another species complex.

Finding the putative parents of any hybrid demands some detective work. If one is lucky, there are only a few species growing together and any hybrids are identifiable as the intermediates between them. In practice this seldom happens, so there are three useful criteria that can be borne in mind. Proposed by Cockayne in 1923 they are:

i. The plant should be intermediate in form between the parents;

ii. There should be a population of both parents somewhere in the vicinity of the hybrid;

iii. If a fertile hybrid results (often the case with *Dactylorhiza*) then, when two first generation hybrids (F1) cross to give the F2 and future generations, there is some segregation into forms that are closer to one parent than to another.

The final composition of a hybrid swarm will often depend on the surrounding habitat; e.g., in crosses between *D. majalis* ssp. *praetermissa* and *D. traunsteineri* offspring closer to the former will predominate in dry areas, since this parent is more tolerant of such conditions and can pass on this character. Indeed in cases where a fen is slowly drying out one can see forms close to *D. traunsteineri* gradually decrease year by year. In the end, one of the parents can disappear altogether and then it is very difficult to decide on the origins of the hybrid swarm.

Sometimes hybridisation results in a particularly successful combination, and the offspring is far more robust than either parent. In such cases the offspring have inherited 'hybrid vigour'. It is just as likely that inherited characters prove totally inadequate for the survival of the plant and the result is fatal.

Orchid names

The scientific or Latin names of plants have two main parts. The first identifies the genus to which the plant belongs, begins with a capital letter and is known as the *generic* name. This is followed by a different name for each plant in the genus, which is written with a lower case letter and termed the *specific* name. The name *Anacamptis pyramidalis* signifies that the plant belongs to the genus *Anacamptis* and has the specific name *pyramidalis*. Specific names can refer to a variety of things such as shape, colour, size, habitat or even discoverer.

If a plant is a subspecies or variety then these also have names with the order of arrangement genus-species-subspecies-variety, e.g. *Ophrys fuciflora* ssp. *oxyrrhynchos* var.*lacaitae*.

Here we use the following abbreviations: sp. = species (spp. plural); ssp. = subspecies (sspp. plural); var. = variety (vars. plural). In some books one can find subsp. replacing ssp.

It is becoming increasingly common to see a plant name followed by what are termed *Authorities* or *Citations*. For example, take *Anacamptis pyramidalis* (L.) L. C. M. Richard. The initial in brackets signifies that the plant was first described by Linnaeus, the father of biological classification. In his work the plant was described as *Orchis pyramidalis*. L. C. M. Richard was the botanist who first placed it in the genus *Anacamptis* and used the now accepted name. If the original name is the accepted name then a single name follows the plant and the bracket is omitted, e.g. *Serapias cordigera* L.

In the text these citations are omitted for the sake of clarity but if needed they can be found in each of the species descriptions. Even an unwieldy name such as *Ophrys fuciflora* ssp. *oxyrrhynchos* var. *lacaitae* could be correctly expanded to *Ophrys fuciflora* (F. W. Schmidt) Moench ssp. *oxyrrhynchos* (Tod) Soó var. *lacaitae* (Lojacono) Camus. Whereas the first name is an awkward title the second needs no comment from us.

There are some additional points to note when naming hybrids, and the way one writes the name depends on whether the hybrid is interspecific or intergeneric. As an example consider hybrids formed by *Orchis militaris*. An interspecific hybrid with *O. simia* is known and has been called *Orchis* x *beyrichii* Kern. One of the intergeneric hybrids possible occurs with *Aceras anthropophorum* and it is named x *Orchiaceras spurium* (Reichenb. fil.) Camus. In the former case the plant is still an *Orchis* but the x between generic and specific names shows its hybrid origins. In the latter it is quite apparent that the new generic name is a combination of the parents but now to show it is a hybrid the x precedes the generic name.

Most European orchids have undergone at least one change of name in botanical literature. Some, like *Aceras anthropophorum*, have been known under a dozen or more Latin names depending on the way botanists viewed its affinities to different genera. To avoid confusion we have decided only to include the more important synonyms used in works written this century. Earlier names are listed in monographs by Nelson, Camus and Godfery (see Bibliography)

All synonyms included are listed in the Index with their equivalent names as used in Chapter 4, 'Species Descriptions'.

Common names have been included wherever we are aware of a name in popular published works, but the practice of making up names of rarities by translating the Latin name into English, French, German or Italian seems pointless. It is surprising how quickly scientific names become familiar, and they have the advantage of being the same in all languages.

Key to the orchid genera

Most people using this book in the field will find that orchids can be identified from the photographs and use of the species descriptions. However, sooner or later one is bound to come upon an orchid which seems to defy classification. A key can be of considerable use for fitting an orchid to a genus but is by no means foolproof and has to be used with care.

A small hand lens is essential for distinguishing those features that will aid identification, and we have tried to ensure wherever possible that the features specified preclude digging up the orchid – a practice to be deplored, for the welfare of the plant is more important than naming it.

When the genus is located, further keys can be used to determine the plant's identity at specific and subspecific level.

In this book further keys are provided only for more difficult genera such as *Dactylorhiza*, *Orchis*, *Serapias*, *Ophrys* and *Epipactis*. They are not true botanical keys, for they make use of location as well as plant characteristics – in fact anything to make identification as easy as possible.

To use the key. Start at **1**, where a choice of characters is offered. Decide which of the alternatives is applicable, then proceed to the choice indicated by the number at the right. Carry on until the name of a genus appears on the right, and then move to the species descriptions and photographs for a more detailed study.

1	Orchids without green leaves	*2*
	Orchids with green leaves or green bract-like scales on a green stem	*5*
2	Spur long, slender	*3*
	Spur very short or absent	*4*
3	Lip entire, directed downwards	*Limodorum*
	Lip 3-lobed, directed upwards	*Epipogium*
4	Stem with numerous scales, lip twice as long as other perianth segments (flowers pale brown)	*Neottia*
	Stem with 2–4 sheathing scales (flowers greenish or yellowish)	*Corallorhiza*
5	Flowers without a spur	*6*
	Flowers having a spur	*20*
6	Lip large, inflated, slipper-shaped	*7*
	Lip not inflated or slipper-shaped	*8*
7	Plant with one foliage leaf, one pseudobulb and one anther	*Calypso*
	Plant with 2–4 leaves, creeping rhizomes and two anthers	*Cypripedium*
8	Lip with distinctively coloured and shaped central area (speculum), glabrous or hairy resembling an insect body	*Ophrys*
	Lip without speculum, flowers not insect-like	*9*
9	Lip directed upwards	*10*
	Lip directed downwards	*12*
10	Plant very small with lip shorter than sepals, petals about half the length of sepals	*Hammarbya*
	Plant small with lip, sepals and petals of roughly equal length	*11*
11	Sepals short, not more than 3mm, single foliage leaf borne above pseudobulb	*Microstylis*
	Sepals at least 5mm; plant with 2 pseudobulbs growing alongside one another, joined by a small stolon, 2 foliage leaves sheathing stem	*Liparis*
12	Lip divided by a constriction into 2 parts: hypochile or concave basal part, epichile or downward, forward pointing distal part	*13*
	Lip not divided as above	*15*
13	Hypochile with lateral lobes erect, epichile downward pointing, tongue-shaped	*Serapias*
	Hypochile without marked side lobes, lip not distinctly pendant	*14*
14	Flowers erect or sub-erect, stalks absent or very short, spike more or less one-sided	*Cephalanthera*
	Flowers held horizontal or pendant, distinctly stalked column short	*Epipactis*

15 Flowers white, arranged in 1–3 spiral rows or
    in a one-sided spike   *16*
    Flowers yellowish, greenish or purplish not
    arranged spirally or in a one-sided spike   *17*

16 Leaves with parallel veins (not net-veined),
    lip and sepals equal in length   *Spiranthes*
    Leaves conspicuously net-veined; lip shorter than
    sepals   *Goodyera*

17 Leaves slender and linear, about equalling the stem,
    lip entire or slightly lobed, plant small   *Chamorchis*
    Leaves distinctly shorter than stem, oblong to
    linear-lanceolate, lip deeply lobed   *18*

18 Leaves numerous, lip with long lateral and median
    lobes – shaped like a man   *Aceras*
    Stem with two ovate bract-like leaves, lip not
    man-shaped   *19*

19 Lip very definitely 3-lobed   *Herminium*
    Lip deeply 2-lobed, stem with 2 broadly
    oval leaves   *Listera*

20 Flowers with a spur   *21*

21 Lip divided by a constriction into 2 parts:
    hypochile or concave basal part, epichile or
    downward or forward pointing distal part   *Cephalanthera*
    Lip not divided in this way   *22*

22 Spur not more than 2mm   *Nigritella*
    Spur at least 5mm   *23*

23 Lip with median lobe much exceeding the laterals
    and spirally twisted, sepals and petals forming a
    helmet (galea), bracts equal to or shorter than
    the flowers   *Himantoglossum*
    Median lobe of lip not twisted spirally, sepals
    spreading   *24*

24 Plant extremely robust, lateral sepals spreading not
    forming helmet, bracts longer than flowers   *Barlia*
    Plants not outstandingly robust   *25*

25 Lip strap-like   *26*
    Lip not strap-like   *28*

26 Lip entire, flowers greenish-white   *Platanthera*
    Lip lobed   *27*

27 Lip 3-lobed, flowers green, endemic to Canary
    Islands   *Habenaria*
    Lip strap-like 3-lobed at apex, lateral lobes
    parallel, longer than median lobe   *Coeloglossum*

28 Lip with lobes extended to long spiral thread-like
    processes   *Comperia*
    Lip not extended into processes   *29*

29 Inflorescence definitely globe-shaped, tips of
         perianth segments spatulate, flowers pink   *Traunsteinera*
         Inflorescence not globe-shaped, tips of perianth
         segments not spatulate   *30*

30 2 heart-shaped leaves on stem, flowers
         greenish-yellow   *Gennaria*
         Without 2 heart-shaped leaves on stem   *31*

31 Lip more or less converged with other perianth
         segments, flowers white, small (2–3mm)   *Pseudorchis*
         Lip and perianth segments not converging   *32*

32 Dorsal and lateral sepals fused almost to apex, flowers
         predominantly greenish, stem with single basal leaf
         and 2 leaves sheathing stem above   *Steveniella*
         Dorsal and lateral sepals not fused to apex   *33*

33 Lateral sepals and petals fused at base, sepals
         short less than 4mm   *Neotinea*
         Lateral sepals and petals not fused   *34*

34 Flowers in one-sided spike, bursicle absent, flowers
         pinkish   *Neottianthe*
         Flowers not arranged in one-sided spike   *35*

35 Some perianth segments converging to form a hood;
         lip 3-lobed; spur very long and slender, at
         least 11mm   *36*
         Perianth segments either converging or spreading;
         lip variable, entire, 3-lobed or tridentate at
         apex; spur usually not slender; at least 5mm   *37*

36 Lip deeply 3-lobed with two longitudinal basal ridges   *Anacamptis*
         Lip shallowly 3-lobed without ridges at base   *Gymnadenia*

37 Floral bracts membranous; tubers entire   *Orchis*
         Lower floral bracts leaf-like; tubers divided
         like fingers at extremities (palmately lobed)   *Dactylorhiza*

The plates

The 328 photographs reproduced in the 64 plates that follow represent virtually all the orchid species described in the next chapter. The few species that have eluded photography are illustrated by drawings in the text.

In many cases both the whole plant and a close-up of its flowers are placed alongside each other. In some cases, however, notably *Ophrys*, where growth habit is similar throughout the group, we have chosen close-ups of the florets to illustrate the extraordinary variation within the species.

There are some cases where an individual species varies considerably, often according to locality, without separate names being given to the different forms. Here we have sometimes placed a number of variations together: examples are *Orchis papilionacea* (numbers 129–135) and *Serapias cordigera* (213–216).

References to the numbered illustrations are given by bold numerals after the descriptions in Chapter 4. It is unfortunately impracticable to provide a direct reference from plates to text; but the description of the plant illustrated can be found easily enough by reference to the Index.

The order of the colour illustrations follows that of the species descriptions, but not always exactly. This is partly due to the arrangement of the text (thus varieties are described within the species description but are illustrated after the species as such), and partly to problems of picture lay-out, the aim always being to group species and subspecies together in a visually logical way. *Nigritella nigra* is thus shown in three adjacent pictures where the numbering is not consecutive (72, 75, 76), while the respective habitat and close-up views of *Orchis pallens*, *O. provincialis* and *O. provincialis* ssp. *pauciflora* (183–188) have each been placed one above the other for ease of reference, the numbering again being disturbed.

A number of orchid photographers have filled difficult gaps, and the authors are extremely grateful for the help so generously provided. They are as follows: Ivor Barton, 122; D. Birkinshaw, 30; R. Hansen, 38, 44, 48, 51, 52, 68, 75, 76, 183, 186, 196, 247, 314; C. Henderson, 39, 289; Dr G. Hermjakob, 3, 4, 28, 61, 71, 102, 203, 233; Dr V. Hoffman, 16; W. Neeth, 62; M. Norman, 29, 121, 175, 178, 279, 310; G. & S. Phillips, 50, 92, 118, 181, 249, 302, 303; Dr J. Renz, 24, 120, 165, 204, 285, 286; P. Scholes, 195; H. Sigg, 37.

ERRATUM

Photograph number *132*, *Orchis papilionacea*,
has been reproduced upside down

Cypripedium calceolus

2 C. calceolus

C. guttatum

4 C. macranthos

5 Epipactis palustris

6 E. palustris

7 E.p.var. ochroleuca

8 E. veratrifolia

Epipactis helleborine

10 E. helleborine

1 E. helleborine

12 E. helleborine

13 Epipactis leptochila

14 E. leptochila

15 E. muelleri

16 E. dunensis

7 Epipactis purpurata

18 E. purpurata

9 E. condensata

20 E. phyllanthes

21 Epipactis atrorubens

22 E. microphylla

23 E. troodii

24 E. persica

25 Cephalanthera damasonium

26 C. damasonium

27 C. longifolia

28 C. cucullata

29 Cephalanthera epipactoides

30 C. kurdica

31 C. rubra

32 C. rubra

33 Limodorum abortivum

34 L. abortivum

35 L. abortivum

36 L.a. var. rubrum

37 Epipogium aphyllum

38 E. aphyllum

39 Neottia nidus-avis

40 N. nidus-avis

41 Listera ovata

42 L. ovata

43 L. cordata

44 L. cordata

45 Spiranthes spiralis

46 S. spiralis

47 S. aestivalis

48 S. aestivalis

49 Spiranthes sinensis

50 S. romanzoffiana

51 Goodyera repens

52 G. repens

53 Herminium monorchis

54 H. monorchis

55 Platanthera bifolia

56 P. bifolia

57 Platanthera chlorantha

58 P. chlorantha

59 P.c. ssp.holmboei

60 P. algeriensis

61 Neottianthe cucullata

62 Chamorchis alpina

63 Gymnadenia conopsea

64 G. conopsea

5 Gymnadenia conopsea var. densiflora

66 G.c. var. densiflora

7 G. odoratissima

68 G. odoratissima

69 Pseudorchis albida

70 P. albida

71 P. frivaldii

72 Nigritella nigra

73 Coeloglossum viride

74 C. viride

75 Nigritella nigra

76 N.n. ssp. rubra

77 Dactylorhiza iberica

78 D. sambucina

79 D. sambucina

80 D. sambucina

81 Dactylorhiza sambucina ssp. insularis

82 D.s. ssp. insularis var. bartonii

83 D.sulphurea ssp. pseudosambucina

84 D.sulphurea ssp. pseudosambucina

85 D.sulphurea ssp. pseudosambucina

86 D.sulphurea ssp. pseudosambucina

87 D. incarnata

88 D. incarnata

39 Dactylorhiza incarnata ssp. coccinea

90 D.i. ssp. pulchella

91 D.i. ssp. cruenta

92 D.i. ssp. ochroleuca

93 Dactylorhiza majalis

94 D. majalis

95 D.m. ssp. alpestris

96 D.m. ssp. alpestris

97 D.m. ssp. purpurella

98 D.m. ssp. purpurella

99 D.m. ssp. praetermissa

100 D.m. ssp. praetermissa

101 D. baltica

102 Dactylorhiza cordigera

103 D. traunsteineri

104 D. traunsteineri

105 D. elata ssp. sesquipedalis

106 D. elata ssp. sesquipedalis

107 D. elata ssp. sesquipedalis

108 D. foliosa

109 D. foliosa

110 D. cilicica

111 D. maculata ssp. ericetorum

112 D.m. ssp. ericetorum

113 D.m. ssp. lancibracteata

114 Dactylorhiza fuchsii

115 D. fuchsii

116 D. fuchsii

117 D.f. ssp. hebridensis

118 D.f. ssp. okellyi

119 D. saccifera

120 Steveniella satyrioides

121 S. satyrioides

122 Comperia comperiana

123 Traunsteinera globosa

124 T. globosa

125 Comperia comperiana

126 Neotinea maculata

127 N. maculata

128 N. maculata

129 Orchis papilionacea

130 O.p. var. grandiflora

131 O. papilionacea

132 O. papilionacea

133 O. papilionacea

134 O. papilionacea

135 O. papilionacea

136 O. boryi

137 O. boryi

8 Orchis morio   **139** O. m. ssp. picta   **140** O.m. ssp. picta

1 O.m. ssp. champagneuxii   **142** O.m. ssp. libani   **143** O.m. ssp. libani

4 O. longicornu   **145** O. longicornu   **146** O. longicornu

147 Orchis coriophora

148 O.c. ssp. fragrans

149 O. sancta

150 O. sancta

51 Orchis ustulata

152 O. ustulata

53 O. tridentata

154 O. tridentata

155 Orchis tridentata ssp. commutata

156 O.t. ssp. commutata

157 O. lactea

158 O. lactea

159 Orchis italica

160 O. italica

161 O. militaris

162 O. militaris

163 Orchis simia

164 O. simia

165 O. steveni

166 O. galilea

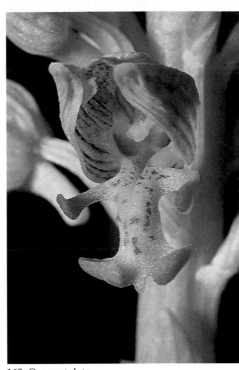

167 Orchis punctulata

168 O. punctulata

169 O.p. ssp. sepulchralis

170 O.p. ssp. sepulchralis

171 Orchis purpurea

172 O. purpurea

173 O. saccata

174 O. saccata

75 Orchis patens

176 O. canariensis

77 O. spitzelii

178 O. spitzelii

179 Orchis mascula

180 O. mascula

181 O. mascula ssp. signifera

182 O. mascula ssp. olbiensis

83 Orchis pallens   184 O. provincialis   185 O.p. ssp. pauciflora

186 O. pallens   187 O. provincialis   188 O.p. ssp. pauciflora

189 Orchis quadripunctata

190 O. quadripunctata

191 O. anatolica

192 O.a. var. troodii

193 Orchis laxiflora

194 O. laxiflora

195 O. laxiflora ssp. palustris

196 O. laxiflora ssp. palustris

197 Aceras anthropophorum

198 A. anthropophorum

199 A. anthropophorum

200 A. anthropophorum

201 Himantoglossum hircinum

202 H.h. ssp. caprinum

203 H.h. ssp. calcaratum

204 H. affine

205 Barlia robertianum

206 B. robertianum

207 B. robertianum

208 B. robertianum

209 Anacamptis pyramidalis

210 A. pyramidalis

211 A.p. var. brachystachys

212 A.p. var. brachystachys

213 Serapias cordigera

214 S. cordigera

215 S. cordigera

216 S. cordigera

17 Serapias neglecta   218 S. neglecta   219 S. vomeracea

20 S. vomeracea   221 S.v. ssp. laxiflora   222 S.v. ssp. orientalis

23 S.v. ssp. orientalis   224 S.v. ssp. orientalis   225 S.v.o. var. cordigeroides

226 Serapias lingua

227 S. lingua

228 S. parviflora

229 S. olbia

230 Ophrys insectifera

231 O. speculum

232 O.s. ssp. lusitanica

233 O.s. var. regis-ferdinandi

234 Ophrys lutea

235 O. lutea

236 O.l. ssp. melena

237 O.l. ssp. murbeckii

238 Ophrys fusca   239 O. fusca   240 O. fusca

241 O.f. ssp. fleischmannii   242 O.f. ssp. omegaifera   243 O.f. ssp. dyris

244 O.f. ssp. iricolor   245 O.f. ssp. durieui   246 O. pallida

247 Ophrys sphegodes

248 O. sphegodes

249 O.s. var. planimaculata

250 O.s. ssp. litigiosa

251 O.s. ssp. provincialis

252 O.s. ssp. atrata

253 O.s. ssp. mammosa

254 O.s. ssp. mammosa

255 O.s. ssp. sintenisii

256 Ophrys s. ssp. aesculapii   **257** O.s. ssp. helenae   **258** O.s. ssp. garganica

259 O.s. ssp. garganica   **260** O.s. ssp. sipontensis   **261** O.s. ssp. sicula

262 O. spruneri   **263** O. spruneri   **264** O.s. ssp. panormitana

265 Ophrys ferrum-equinum

266 O. ferrum-equinum

267 O.f. ssp. gottfriediana

268 O. bertolonii

269 O. bertolonii

270 O. bertoloniiformis

271 O. catalaunica

272 O. lunulata

273 O. lunulata

74 Ophrys argolica   **275** O. argolica   **276** O.a. ssp. elegans

277 O. reinholdii   **278** O. reinholdii   **279** O.r. ssp. straussii

280 O. cretica   **281** O. cretica   **282** O. cretica

283 Ophrys kotschyi

284 O. kotschyi

285 O. kurdica

286 O. schulzei

287 Ophrys scolopax   **288** O.s. ssp. apiformis   **289** O.s. ssp. cornuta

290 O.s. ssp. heldreichii   **291** O.s. ssp. heldreichii   **292** O.s. ssp. orientalis

293 O. carmeli   **294** O. carmeli   **295** O. carmeli

296 Ophrys fuciflora

297 O. fuciflora

298 O.f. ssp. apulica

299 O.f. ssp. maxima

00 Ophrys fuciflora ssp. candica

301 O.f. ssp. oxyrrhynchos

302 O.f. ssp. oxyrrhynchos

303 O.f.o. var. lacaitae

304 Ophrys fuciflora ssp. bornmuelleri   **305** O.f.b. var. grandiflora   **306** O.f.b. var. grandiflor

307 O.f. ssp. exaltata   **308** O.f. ssp. exaltata   **309** O. morisii

310 O. arachnitiformis   **311** O. arachnitiformis   **312** O. arachnitiformis

3 Ophrys apifera

314 O. apifera ssp. jurana

15 O. apifera var. chlorantha

316 O. apifera var. bicolor

317 Ophrys tenthredinifera

318 O. tenthredinifera

319 O. tenthredinifera

320 O. bombyliflora

321 Corallorhiza trifida

322 C. trifida

323 Calypso bulbosa

324 Microstylis monophyllos

325 Liparis loeselii

326 L. loeselii

327 Hammarbya paludosa

328 H. paludosa

4 – Species descriptions

Cypripedium

Of all European orchids the members of this genus have the most exotic appearance. The large flowers have a characteristically inflated lip which, with its slipper- or clog-like form, has led to the popular name of Lady's Slipper.

Some taxonomists have suggested that the various genera of Slipper Orchids should be considered as a group apart from the *Orchidaceae*, because of certain detailed structural differences. For example, most orchids have a single stamen whereas Slipper Orchids have 2. Again, the bundles of pollen grains or pollinia are a familiar feature of most orchids, but in the Slipper Orchids pollen grains are separate though held together by a sticky paste.

In some ways one can consider Slipper Orchids as intermediate between Lilies and the rest of the *Orchidaceae*, but the tendency now is to treat them as a sub-family encompassing 5 separate genera: *Cypripedium, Paphiopedilum, Phragmipedium, Selenipedium* and *Criosanthes*.

The first of the genera is the only one that concerns us in this book as 3 species are found in the area dealt with. Unfortunately Europe is one of the regions in the northern hemisphere least rich in this sub-family of orchids which includes some 50 known species.

All plants in the genus have creeping rhizomes, with no tubers, and leaves which are broad and prominently veined. The flowers are distinctive, with widely spread perianth segments and the inflated lip. The median sepal is broad and the laterals partly fused, pointing downwards behind the lip. The petals are thong or strap-like, often with a spiral twist. The third petal forms the labellum and is swollen into the shape of a clog or slipper to protect the reproductive organs. These latter comprise a short column and 3 stamens: unusually for European orchids, two of these are fertile and the third has evolved into a petal-like structure called the staminode.

The shape of the lip allows for a very interesting pollination mechanism. A visiting insect slips down into the lip, where veins guide it past a series of hairs towards a narrow exit. Along this route it brushes against the stamens and some of the pollen sticks to it. All this proves rather exhausting for an insect, and if it shortly comes into contact with another flower it has no strength to resist falling into the lip. This time some pollen is transferred onto the stigma, thus causing cross-pollination.

The path followed by an insect is an ingenious one-way system with retreat via the obvious large opening rendered impossible by the slippery sides of the lip. Hairs inside the lip provide the only footholds as the insect makes its way towards a set of transparent 'window panes' at the lip base. Cross-pollination is assured in almost all cases because only one flower per stem is open at any give time.

Small pollen-collecting bees of the genus *Andrena* are the usual pollinators of European flowers but other smaller insects can be attracted to the lip where, proving too small to brush the stigma, they are also too small to contact the stamens and rub off any of the precious pollen. Wastage is thus eliminated.

The obvious beauty of *C. calceolus*, the best-known European species, has led to its being picked to the point of extinction in many places. In Switzerland and Austria, where good colonies still flourish, it enjoys the protection of the law and the people of the countries bring this fact home to walkers and others through an effective publicity campaign. In Italy it was once common in the Dolomites but now one must search well away from the beaten track. Friends tell horror stories of mountain hotels with their vases filled with specially picked blooms.

In Britain it hangs on in a site known to far too many. In the same area of Yorkshire it used to thrive in the woodlands, but its sale in bunches in market places, and efforts to transfer plants to gardens, brought about its demise.

The exotic appearance of its blooms has inevitably led to several legends, and one of these concerns the goddess Venus.

In days of old when gods and goddesses walked the earth, Venus was strolling through a forest when a sudden thunderstorm surprised her. She ran for shelter and in so doing lost one of her golden slippers. The next day a young shepherdess, leading her flocks through the woods to pastures beyond, saw the exquisite little shoe and ran to pick it up. However, just as she reached for it the treasure vanished and left there a flower in the shape of a slipper.

Hybrids
Only one European hybrid has been recorded: *C. calceolus* x *C. macranthos* = *C.* x *barbeyi* Camus & Berg.

Cypripedium calceolus L.
LADY'S SLIPPER; SABOT DE VÉNUS
(F); FRAUENSCHUH; FORFALLONE
(I).

The plant stands 20–50cm tall, with 3–4 broadly elliptic leaves arranged alternately up the stem. The leaves are furrowed and prominently veined, with a basal part that sheaths the stem, and a tip that ends in a sharp point.

Underground there is a horizontal rhizome which entangles itself with the roots of neighbouring vegetation. The flowering stem starts from this as a horizontal runner which later grows upwards.

The flowers are large and usually solitary but robust plants can bear 2, 3 or even 4 blooms on the same stem. The flower bract is large and leaf-like.

All the perianth segments are coloured the same shade of deep maroon red which ages to a dark purple-brown. The median sepal is large and can be erect or curve forward in freshly opened blooms. The laterals are fused for most of their length, and have the appearance of a single downward-pointing tepal with a slightly forked tip. Two of the petals are strap-like and twisted along their 3–5cm length. The third petal forms the lip. In colour this is bright yellow and it contrasts strongly with the other perianth segments. It is clog-shaped, with a hairy basal region and the edges folded over to leave a small opening. The third stamen is sterile and has evolved into a white petal-shaped staminode which is sometimes spotted with red. The flowers are delicately scented and the ovary is hairy.

Varieties: Var. *flavum* Rion is an all-yellow form which has been recorded on occasions from continental Europe.

Flowers: May to July depending on altitude.

Habitat: shady deciduous and mixed woodland or less frequently stone-strewn slopes, always on calcareous soils up to an altitude of 1700m. In some sites it occurs out in the open growing in high-altitude valleys often accompanied by *Dryas octopetala*.

Distribution: England (extremely rare); Germany; Scandinavia (as far north as latitude 70°); France; Austria (frequent in some parts of the Tyrol up to 1700m); Switzerland (some populations with hundreds of plants); Italy (especially the Dolomites); Yugoslavia (Julian Alps); northern Turkey (Pontus); Poland; Hungary; Bulgaria; Rumania; Czechoslovakia; Russia (Caucasus and Siberia). It is now believed to be extinct in northern Greece. **1, 2**

Cypripedium guttatum Swartz
This is a species from central Russia eastwards to Japan. It is a rather slender plant reaching a height between 15 and 30cm. The stems are slightly hairy and bear two leaves, both oval in shape, with a length of 7–12cm.

The solitary flower is smaller than that of *C. calceolus*, and the flower bract is large and leaf-like. The dorsal sepal is a broad oval in shape. It is also markedly concave, white on the outside and spotted purple on the inside. The lateral sepals are greenish-white in colour and are united almost to their apex. The

petals are spreading and spotted with purple for most of their length. The third petal forms the lip and is strongly inflated, with a broad orifice and incurved edges.

Fig. 7

The lip colouring is the same as that of the other petals, with the purple spotting producing a very attractive effect. In plants from the far eastern end of the range the ground colour takes on a decidedly yellowish tint.

Varieties: Var. *redowski* Reichenb. fil. is a form without spotted flowers. The overall colour of the blooms is greenish-white

Flowers: May to June.

Habitat: birch woods, coniferous and mixed woodland, often between shrubs, shady glades (accompanied in some places by *C. macranthos*).

Distribution: central Russia, through Siberia, to Manchuria in northern China and finally to Korea and Japan. **3**

Cypripedium macranthos Swartz
This orchid, which barely enters our European definition, resembles *C. calceolus* in form but is very different in colour. The plant usually reaches a height of 20–45cm and has 3–4 broadly ovate leaves arranged alternately up the stem. In common with a number of plants in the same genus, it has leaves

which are broadly furrowed and prominently veined.

The flowering stem rises from a short thick rhizome and usually carries a single bloom, although like *C. calceolus* robust plants may carry more. The flower bracts are large and leaf-like.

The colour of the perianth segments varies from a pale rose to reddish purple, and there is no difference between the lip and the other segments. The perianth segments are only just longer than the lip, with a broad dorsal sepal that is folded forwards and laterals that are united and point downwards. The lip is large (4–6cm), inflated, and possesses a rather narrow orifice. The staminode is whitish with violet speckling.

Varieties: Var. *speciosum* Rolfe. Flowers with a light pink ground colour, and with magenta veining that gives them a striped appearance, are sometimes separated from the nominate race as var. *speciosum*.

Var. *ventricosum* Swartz: in this form the petals and sepals are longer than the lip and the dorsal sepal is rather narrow. The flower colour tends to be paler than in the usual form.

Habitat: birch woods and forest glades; more rarely pine forests. It sometimes occurs with *C. guttatum*.

Distribution: central Russia from Moscow eastwards, Urals, Siberia and further east to northern China and Korea. Within its range it is not a rare orchid, sometimes occurring in large colonies in suitable territory.   4

Epipactis

The genus *Epipactis* comprises about thirty species. Distribution is widespread, with species found throughout Europe, southwards to Ethiopia and eastwards through temperate Asia to Japan. Only one species is native to north America.

Similarity in growth and general appearance makes *Epipactis* closely related to *Cephalanthera* and, in common with the latter genus, the lip is clearly divided into two parts, hypochile and epichile. Both these genera were at one time called *Helleborine*.

The principal differences between the genera are: *Epipactis* have distinctly stalked flowers and an ovary that is not twisted, while *Cephalanthera* have no noticeable stalk and a spirally twisted ovary; *Epipactis* is more highly developed for pollination than *Cephalanthera*, with some of the species possessing the sterile third stigma (rostellum) which separates the pollinia from the fertile stigmatic surface.

A number of species in the genus rely on self-pollination and in these the rostellum has not developed or withers away soon after the flowers open. This rostellum is quite a primitive organ consisting, as it does, of a thin-skinned bag containing a liquid glue which sets hard on contact with the atmosphere.

In those species which are insect-pollinated the pollinia fall from the anther on to the rostellum where they stay until an insect visitor comes along and breaks the rostellum, releasing the glue that will stick them to the insect. The pollinia adhere to the antennae or head of the insect (often a wasp) and are carried along to the next flower, where they come into contact with the sticky stigma. In colonies of *Epipactis purpurata*, in late September, one can see wasps that are so laden with pollinia stuck all over their head region that they can barely get into the air.

There are few problems in recognising members of this genus for they all possess distinctive characteristics: they have rhizomes, not tubers; the flowers have stalks and an ovary without a twist in it; the perianth segments are either spreading or incurved, and the lip is in two parts. Near the base of the lip lies a cup-shaped hypochile which ranges from a shallow depression in some species to a deep cup in others. The apex of the lip forms an epichile which can be a heart-shaped or triangular lobe which points downwards. The column is short.

It is when one tries to identify particular species that problems arise. In this genus, as much as any other, plants have been granted specific status on the grounds of quite fine criteria. Much meticulous analysis has been done by Dr D. P. Young, but there are still grey areas and there is little doubt in our minds that the number of distinct species recognised will change more than once in the coming years.

E. helleborine is the most common member of the genus and can show considerable variation in flower shape, size and colour. Furthermore it can occur in the same locality as far rarer species, which presents problems in identification for many orchid enthusiasts. There is nothing for it but to examine the flowers carefully with a hand lens, make a note of important features, and then set to work with key and species descriptions.

Key

To avoid confusion, only those species one would expect to meet in Europe and north Africa are included in the key. There are several other species which are not encountered outside the eastern end of the region described in this book. These are *E. veratrifolia*, *E. condensata*, *E. troodii*, *E. persica*, and *E. pontica*. Of these *E. veratrifolia* is related to *E. palustris* but is such a distinctive plant that confusion with any other species is unlikely. *E. condensata* has a similar appearance to *E. purpurata* and the same clump-forming tendency. *E. pontica* is restricted to parts of Turkey on the Black Sea coast. Difficulties might arise with *E. troodii*, which occurs with the closely related *E. microphylla* in Cyprus. Similarities between these two species and *E. persica* are discussed in detail in the species descriptions.

1	Hypochile with its lateral lobes erect, connected to the epichile via a narrow hinged joint	*E. palustris*
	Hypochile without lateral lobes, and the connection to the epichile formed from one or more folds	*2*

2   Flowering stem, flower stalks and ovary densely covered
    with fine hairs   *3*
    Flowering stem, flower stalk and ovary more or less
    hairless or with a slightly roughened appearance   *4*

3   Leaves from 4–10cm long forming 2 rows up the stem,
    flowers coloured deep wine-red   *E. atrorubens*
    Leaves from 1–3cm long arranged spirally, flowers
    greenish with a reddish tinge   *E. microphylla*

4   Leaves arranged in 2 rows up the stem, rostellum
    absent in mature plants, flowers often not
    opening fully   *5*
    Leaves arranged spirally, rostellum prominent and
    persistent even in mature plants, flowers opening
    fully   *6*

5   Flowers spreading or slightly pendent, hypochile
    purplish or pinkish inside   *E. leptochila*
                                                                       group (including
                                                                       E. muelleri and
                                                                       E. dunensis)

    Flowers distinctly pendent, hypochile greenish-
    white inside   *E. phyllanthes*

6   Leaves greyish or purplish, epichile at least as
    long as wide   *E. purpurata*
    Leaves green, epichile not longer than wide   *E. helleborine*

Hybrids
Mainly interspecific hybrids have entered the record books but there are only two
examples of intergeneric hybrids with the genus *Cephalanthera*:
E. atrorubens x *E. palustris* = E. x pupplingensis Bell
E. atrorubens x *E. microphylla* = E. x *graberi* Camus
E. atrorubens x *E. helleborine* = E. x *schmalhausenii* Richt.
E. helleborine x *E. microphylla* = E. x *barlae* Camus
The parentage of the hybrids with *Cephalanthera* is not certain but the following has
been proposed:
E. helleborine (?) x *C. damasonium* = x *Cephalopactis hybrida* (Holuby ex Soó)
    Dom.
E. atrorubens (?) x *C. damasonium* = x *Cephalopactis speciosa* (Wettstein) A. & Gr.

***Epipactis palustris* (L.) Crantz**
MARSH HELLEBORINE; EPIPACTIS
DES MARAIS (F); ECHTE
SUMPFWURZ, SUMPFSTENDELWURZ
(G); MUGHETTI PENDOLINI (I).
    Plants of this species can range in
height from 15–50cm, but 15–25cm is
more usual for those in open habitats
such as sand-dune slacks. There are 4–8
oblong-lanceolate leaves which decrease
markedly in size higher up the stem, and
the base is surrounded by violet sheaths.
The stem grows up from a creeping rootstock, which enables the plant to spread
quite quickly over suitable ground.
There are cases of well over one hundred
flowering stems being attributable to the
same root system.
    There are from 4–20 flowers carried in
a lax, one-sided spike, with flower bracts

that are longer than the ovary low down on the inflorescence but become shorter as they go up the spike.

The flowers are rather striking in appearance, with sepals that are greenish-grey tinged with purple on their exterior surfaces and reddish inside. The petals are shorter in length than the sepals and coloured off-white with reddish-brown tinges. All the perianth segments are spreading so that the flowers open fully.

The lip is a complicated structure in this species: the hypochile is slightly concave, with triangular red-striped side lobes and an orange-yellow plate-like structure in its upper portion which produces nectar; the epichile is joined to it by a narrow hinge-like part, has a wavy margin, is coloured white and has yellow ridges at its base.

The hinged joint between the lip sections is an important part of the pollination mechanism. Bees are the usual insect visitors that effect pollination by landing on the lower portion of the lip, which springs up as the insect leaves, forcing it to fly slightly upwards so that its head brushes against the rostellum. The fragile membrane covering the rostellum is easily removed by an insect moving upwards then backwards, the glue is released and, as the insect flies out, the pollinia are neatly removed. When alighting at the next flower the position of the epichile is arranged so that the pollinia stuck to the insect are in exactly the right place to strike the stigma while it feeds on the nectar.

Varieties: Var. *ochroleuca* Barla is a form of the plant which lacks the red colouring and striping of the normal race. It is an uncommon form which occurs most frequently in sand-dune slacks. The name var. *albiflora* Luscher refers to the same plant.   7

Flowers: late June through to September.

Habitat: found in large colonies in marshes, fens, deserted gravel pits and slacks in well established dune systems, always in alkaline conditions. Occurs up to 1600m in the Alps.

Distribution: although it has been hard hit by the disappearance of its habitat as land is drained and 'reclaimed', this species is still locally common and occurs over a very wide region: northern Spain; France; UK; southern Scandinavia; Germany; Benelux countries; Switzerland; Austria; Italy; Yugoslavia; northern Greece; Turkey (Pontus); Poland; Czechoslovakia; Hungary; Bulgaria; Rumania; Russia (Crimea and Caucasus), to Iran and further east into Japan.   **5, 6**

Epipactis veratrifolia Boiss
SCARCE MARSH HELLEBORINE;
GERMERBLÄTTRIGE STENDELWURZ
(G).

This species can produce plants with exceptionally long stems (20–150cm) which rise from a short rhizome, are densely leafy and carry anything from 8–20 broadly lanceolate to slender leaves. The lower leaves sheath the stem, and the upper ones grade into flower bracts.

The flower spike is lax and carries 10–30 flowers which are horizontal when they first open but then tend to droop slightly with age. The flower bracts are very long low down on the stem (about 15cm) so that the flowers have the appearance of emerging from leaf axils. Higher up the stem the bracts become progressively shorter, finally reaching a minimum of around 1cm.

The flowers are quite large and showy, having a diameter of 15–35mm, with spreading perianth segments. The petals and sepals have a similar broadly ovate shape, and their ground colour is green, through greenish-yellow, to buff, overlayed with areas of rich reddish- or purplish-brown. The colour scheme alone is sufficient to distinguish this impressive orchid from all other members of the genus described in the text, but it is worth mentioning that the flowers do bear some similarity to a North American species, *E. gigantea* (also found in the Himalayas).

The lip is slightly shorter than the sepals and the hypochile is curved upwards, with rounded basal lobes and a dark purple interior. The epichile is triangular and coloured buff, with a horizontal reddish stripe. Both segments of the lip are connected by a narrow part that forms a sort of hinge, as in the case of *E. palustris*, its closest relative amongst the European *Epipactis*. The rostellum is present in this species and there is no spur.

Flowers: late May (Cyprus) through to August.

Habitat: stream banks and on damp ground in sheltered gorges, hillside seepages and wet mountain meadows, always in mountain areas – from 500m to 2000m altitude.

Distribution: restricted to the far eastern part of the region covered in this book, where it is decidedly rare and local; Cyprus in the Troodos massif, on volcanic soils; Turkey (Anatolia); Syria; Lebanon; Israel; Iran; Iraq.

Although *E. veratrifolia* is a rather rare and local orchid, it can occur in large numbers in some sites where it is found in clumps of anything up to 40 flowering stems.   **8**

Epipactis helleborine (L.) Crantz
BROAD-LEAVED HELLEBORINE;
EPIPACTIS À LARGES FEUILLES (F);
BREITBLÄTTRIGE SUMPFWURZ (G);
ELLEBORINE CRESTATA (I).

This is by far the best known and most variable in appearance of all the genus *Epipactis*. Flowering stems can range from 35–100cm in height and carry anything from 4–10 leaves, in a spiral, on the stem. In shape the leaves are a broad oval, often with a purple tinge, and the lower leaves are reduced to sheaths.

The spike is dense and many-flowered, with the blooms carried horizontally, or drooping slightly, in a one-sided inflorescence. Near the base of this spike the flower bracts tend to be longer then the flowers but, in common with most other species of *Epipactis*, they decrease in length relative to the flowers the higher they are on the spike.

The flowers are variable, both in size and colour, to the extent that unusual forms of this species are responsible for numerous erroneous records of other members of the family.

Sepals and petals are large and end in a blunt point. Possible colours can range from the usual green, through pinkish-violet, to deep red, with the greatest range of colour forms often being found in its duneland habitat.

The hypochile is cup-shaped, with its inner surface a dull purple-brown and the outer surface green. The epichile is ovate, with its apex much recurved. It has two protuberances near its base and varies in colour from greenish-white, through pink, to a purple shade. The lip has a length of 9–11mm but in width it can vary from the common broad structure to a narrow pinched one in some populations.

There is an effective rostellum, and it persists even until the flowers start to wither when fertilisation does not take place.

Varieties: Var. *albiflora* Graber, as suggested by its name, is a form with white flowers.

Large-flowered forms from the mountains of southern Spain and Morocco are considered by some botanists to warrant specific status in their own right as *E. tremolsii* Pau. These plants differ mainly in having large well-opened flowers in which the inner surface of the hypochile is coloured green.

Flowers: from June through to August, depending on altitude and habitat.

Habitat: it can be found on both calcareous and slightly acidic soils in a wide range of surroundings. It is equally at home in beechwoods with a dense overhead leaf cover as it is on open, well-established sand dunes. In fact, in the latter habitat the plants are often robust and show a considerable range of flower colours. It also occurs in coniferous and mixed woodland, thickets and scrub up to an altitude of 1800m.

Distribution: widespread throughout most of the region covered by this book, it is one of the commonest woodland orchids, and it occurs with equal frequency on established dunes: north Africa; Spain; Balearic Isles; France; Ireland; England; Wales; Scandinavia (as far as latitude 71°); Germany; Benelux countries; Austria; Switzerland; Italy; Corsica; Sardinia; Sicily; Yugoslavia; Greece; Rhodes; Cyprus (has not been found for many years); Turkey; Lebanon; Poland; Czechoslovakia; Hungary; Bulgaria; Rumania; Russia; Crimea; Caucasus and further east into central Asia.   **9, 10, 11, 12**

Epipactis leptochila (Godfery) Godfery
NARROW-LIPPED HELLEBORINE; SCHMALLÍPPIGE STENDELWURZ (4).

Plants of this species range from 30 –60cm in height and carry from 5–10 oval to lanceolate leaves. There are two well defined rows of leaves on the stem and they vary in colour from yellowish-green to dark green.

The flower spike is lax, with 7–20 blooms which are horizontal at first, then droop within a few days of opening. Low down on the stem the bracts are longer than the flowers but higher up they become shorter.

Petals and sepals spread in most flowers and are pale green in colour. They are narrow and invariably have pointed ends. In any colony of this species one will find individuals where the flowers do not open fully.

The lip varies in length from around 4–9mm, with a hypochile that is capable of producing nectar and has a reddish-brown inner surface. The epichile is the noteworthy feature in this species because it is long and pointed. Where it is separated from the epichile, there is a narrow constriction and also two smooth or slightly roughened basal protuberances.

There is no rostellum, and the anthers are carried on a short stalk called a clinandrium.

In its beechwood environment it often grows accompanied by the variable *E. helleborine* and, when the forms of this latter plant have no red colouring and are etiolated due to gloomy conditions, confusion can result. Matters are further complicated if the plants of *E. hellebor-*

ine have flowers in which the epichile is not recurved. The following points should serve to separate these species in all but the more perverse cases that one encounters: the leaves of *E. leptochila* are arranged in two rows up the stem, those of *E. helleborine* form a spiral; the pointed epichile of *E. leptochila* is about 1.5 times as long as that in *E. helleborine* even in plants where it has not curved under; and *E. leptochila* has no rostellum being, for the most part, self-fertilised.

Varieties: Var. *cleistogama* (C. Thomas) D. P. Young has a greenish epichile and flowers that barely open.

Flowers: July through to early August.

Habitat: in beech or conifer woods, usually growing on well-drained slopes, always on calcareous soils. It is a rare inhabitant of dune systems, growing under willow scrub, and it is known to have colonised gravels contaminated by zinc waste in the north of England.

Distribution: France (Jura), England, Denmark, Germany, Switzerland, Austria and, possibly, northern Greece.
                                        13, 14

Epipactis muelleri Godfery
MUELLER'S HELLEBORINE; MÜLLERS STENDELWURZ (G).

This is a species which has often been confused with the similar *E. helleborine*. It ranges from 25–70cm in height, with 7–10 broadly lanceolate, pointed leaves arranged in two rows up the stem.

From 4–20 flowers are carried in a lax one-sided spike, and although the lower flower bracts are longer than the flowers the upper ones are not.

Sepals and petals curve inwards to form a bell-shaped structure which is pale green inside and out, lacking the reddish tinge so often present in *E. helleborine*.

The lip is 7–9mm long and the hypochile, which does not contain nectar, is cup-shaped with a reddish inner surface. The epichile is heart-shaped, broader than long with a slightly recurved apex and is coloured pale pink or greenish. At its base there are 2 (rarely

3) smooth basal protuberances.

The rostellum is usually absent and, unlike *E. leptochila*, the anther is not held on a short stalk but is attached almost directly above the stigma.

Records for this species have sometimes been unreliable because of ts close resemblance to the variable *E. helleborine* but the following features serve to separate them: *E. muelleri* has no rostellum as a rule (there are records claimed for this species where a rostellum is present but ineffective; it has a lip where the apex is only slightly recurved; the inflorescence is invariably lax – *E. helleborine* is often dense-flowered; *E. muelleri* has light green flower segments without a reddish tinge, and the inner surface of its hypochile is reddish rather than the dull brown associated with *E. helleborine*.

Flowers: July through to August.

Habitat: open woodlands (in light shade), forest edges, mixed grass and scrub, always on calcareous soils.

Distribution: this is a local and uncommon species found in south-east France; west Germany; Belgium; Holland; Luxembourg; Switzerland (Vaud Alps).

Plants from north-east England have proved to be virtually identical with this species, and investigation into *E. muelleri* as a British species is proceeding.

15

Epipactis dunensis (T. & T. A. Stephenson) Godfery
DUNE HELLEBORINE;
DÜNENSTENDELWURZ (G).

This species is closely linked to *E. muelleri*. It varies from 20–40cm in height, with those of smaller stature growing on open dunes and the taller ones living under planted pines. There are 7–10 broadly lanceolate leaves arranged in two rows on a hairy stem.

The spike is lax, with 7–20 blooms that droop slightly or are held practically horizontal.

The sepals and petals are slightly incurved so that the flowers do not open fully and there are two colour forms: those in open situations usually have pink-tinged perianth segments, whilst those growing in shade are often a pale yellowish-green.

The epichile is triangular, with the apex only slightly recurved in many flowers. Usually it is greenish-white in colour but can at times carry a pink tint. The hypochile is often mottled with red on its internal surface but can be dark green in some flowers.

Some plants have a rostellum but it withers away soon after they open and, to all intents and purposes, the flowers are self-fertilised.

Records of this plant from continental Europe have often proved on detailed analysis to be for *E. muelleri*, from which it differs only in that it has an epichile that is as long as it is wide (in *E. muelleri* it is broader than long) and the anther is attached by a very short stalk.

Flowers: June to July, but because of its sand-dune habitat it is susceptible to drought conditions, and in a dry year plants shrivel quickly. In a normal British summer the plants are at their best in or near the second week in July.

Habitat: on stabilised open dunes or under planted pines.

Distribution: north Wales, north England (Lancashire). In continental Europe its distribution is improperly known because of the confusion with *E. muelleri*, already mentioned above. This species is claimed to grow in north-west France, Belgium, Holland and Germany.

16

Epipactis pontica Taubenheim
PONTIC HELLEBORINE; PONTISCHE
STENDELWURZ (G).

This slender species is not likely to be encountered unless one is looking for orchids near the Black Sea coast. The plants are small: from 15–30cm tall, with 3–5 narrow lanceolate leaves arranged in two rows on the stem.

The flower spike is lax, with up to 15 pendulous blooms and bracts that are longer than the flowers.

The sepals and petals are green and are incurved so that the flowers do not open fully.

Fig. 8

The epichile has a rounded tip and is white with a noticeably green patch near the base where it is joined to the hypochile. The hypochile itself is cup-shaped, and its internal surface is reddish-green.

Flowers: a rather late-flowering species, blooming from August to September.

Habitat: always on limestone, in beech-woods from 500–1500m.

Distribution: restricted to north-eastern Turkey (central and eastern Pontus near the Black Sea coast).

Epipactis purpurata Smith
VIOLET HELLEBORINE; EPIPACTIS
POURPRE (F); VIOLETTE
STENDELWURZ (G).

The flowering stems of this species are usually found in clumps, where they can range from 20–90cm in height, and carry 6–10 leaves arranged in a spiral. The overall length of the leaves is barely greater than the distance between them on the stem, they are oval, greyish-green with a pronounced purple tinge.

The flowers are arranged in a compact spike (15–30cm long) and tend to hang downwards slightly. The stems have a covering of fine greyish hairs, and the flower bracts are noticeably longer than the flowers.

The sepals and petals spread widely, so that the flowers open fully, and their outside surfaces are green, with a whitish appearance to the inner surfaces.

The hypochile is cup-shaped, with its outside green and its inside mottled with violet. The epichile is triangular and pointed, with its apex slightly recurved and two or three bosses or protuber-ances near its attachment to the hypochile. Although its ground colour is white, it develops a pinkish tint around and on the basal protuberances.

There is an effective rostellum in *E. purpurata* which is pollinated mainly by wasps.

Beneath the soil there is a vertical rootstock with a mass of roots which, in mature plants, can number in excess of 40 and penetrate up to 1m into the ground.

Varieties: Var. *chlorotica* Erdner is a plant with pinkish lilac stems and leaves completely lacking in chlorophyll.

Flowers: a late flowering species coming into bloom in August or even September.

Habitat: in woodland (usually beech) on chalk or limestone. A particularly favoured site occurs on or near the tops of chalk hills, where the chalk is over-layed with clay and flints.

Distribution: mainly in north, west and central Europe; Portugal; southern England; Germany; France (central and eastern); Benelux countries; Austria; Switzerland; northern Italy; Yugoslavia; Poland; Czechoslovakia; Hungary; Bulgaria; Rumania and Russia. **17, 18**

Epipactis condensata (Boiss.) D. P. Young
EASTERN VIOLET HELLEBORINE;
DICHTBLÜTIGE STENDELWURZ (G).

This robust species varies in height from 30–70cm and, like the closely related *E. purpurata*, has a tendency to grow in clumps.

From 6–10 leaves are carried in a spiral up the stem and in shape they are boadly oval, tapering to a sharp point. In colour they are greyish-green, and sometimes there is a reddish tinge, particularly to the lower surfaces.

The spike is fairly dense, with numerous blooms and bracts that exceed them in length. The flowers are held horizontally or droop slightly, and have a fully opened appearance because of the spreading perianth segments.

The sepals are broad, pointed and slightly concave, with a delicate green colouring that turns to yellow at their free ends. The yellow colouring is even visible in unopened flower buds. The petals, too, are broad and pointed, but they differ from the sepals in colour, being green flushed with delicate pink. The cup-shaped hypochile is greenish, with its inside surface dark brown or purple black. The epichile is heart-shaped and greenish-white near the apex. Towards its base the colour turns to pinkish red where one finds the two prominent basal humps arranged in a 'V'.

There is a rostellum but it tends to be effective only in young flowers. Freshly opened flowers can be found, with the pollinia already removed by insects, but, if this does not happen quickly, the rostellum withers and the flowers are then autogamous.

E. condensata is an easily recognisable species which, although resembling *E. purpurata*, has a completely different distribution. It differs from *E. purpurata* in having shorter, broader, yellowish-green leaves and a fine covering of brownish-yellow hairs. Its flowers, too, are smaller and differently coloured.

Flowers: mid-June to early August.

Habitat: in coniferous mountain forests often on stony, sunny slopes where the overhead cover is light.

Distribution: Cyprus (rare and found only in the *Pinus nigra* ssp. *pallasiana* zone, high in the Troodos massif); Turkey (Anatolia); Lebanon; Syria; Caucasus (Georgia).   **19**

Epipactis phyllanthes G. E. Smith
PENDULOUS-FLOWERED HELLEBORINE; GRÜNE STENDELWURZ (G).

This rather slender species can range from 20–45cm in height, the smaller specimens occurring in dry beechwoods and the taller ones in willow holts or under pines on sand dunes. There are 3–6 broadly oval leaves which are rather thin and are carried in two rows up a glabrous stem.

The lax flower spike bears 12–30 blooms which are pendulous even in the early stages, and the flower bracts are longer than the flowers low down on the spike, becoming shorter high on the stem.

The sepals and petals are pale green, occasionally with a violet tinge, and are very incurved, sometimes so much so that the flowers scarcely open. This species is invariably self-pollinated, and some of the forms mentioned below are cleistogamic; that is, the flowers fertilise themselves without first opening.

The hypochile forming the basal portion of the lip is a shallow hollow and in some plants is further reduced to a barely discernible depression. The inside surface of the hypochile is white or greenish in colour. The epichile is sometimes not clearly separable from the hypochile and is variable in shape, ranging from ovate-lanceolate, through heart-shaped, to a narrow pointed triangle. The single factor linking all these shapes is that the length of the epichile is in most cases greater than its width.

The wide range of lip shapes and flower sizes has been regarded by some authorities as justification for separating *E. phyllanthes* into a number of distinct species. One problem that arises is the number of intermediate forms found, so that it is not practicable to recognise these forms above varietal level. Plants once regarded as species but now included with *E. phyllanthes* with distinct rank are:

Epipactis cambrensis C. Thomas: a robust form, with stems up to 40cm and light green leaves, found rarely on sand dunes at Kenfig in South Wales (UK). The flowers are partly opened and records of its occurrence are confused because it grows with the extremely variable dune forms of *E. helleborine*.

Epipactis confusa D. P. Young. This plant has a better claim to specific status than the other three forms because it is restricted to Sweden, Denmark and northern Germany – though recently similar plants have been found in two populations in the UK (south Northumberland). It has narrower leaves than other forms of *E. phyllanthes*, flowers which open wider, and a lip with a pink tinge. The column has a spike-like projection which forms a false rostellum immediately below the pollinia. Most authorities are of the opinion that it does not merit a higher status than a variety.

Epipactis pendula C. Thomas. This form ranges from 20–40cm, depending on its habitat. In pine plantations on sand dunes it is tall and robust but in shady beechwoods it becomes a small, rather slender plant. The flowers open more fully than in other forms and, as the specific name suggests, they hang downwards. The leaves of this form tend to have a wavy edge, and at the base of the stem there are several funnel shaped sheaths. In colour the leaves are a rich green – those of *E. dunensis* with which it grows in some sites are a yellowish-green. It was first recorded from pine plantations in Britain in the county of Lancashire and was then 'discovered' in other countries, mainly in the south of England.

Epipactis vectensis T. & T. A. Stephenson. Once called the 'Isle of Wight Helleborine', this form has flowers which scarcely open and a shallow depression which serves as the hypochile. It is a small plant, ranging from 15–25cm tall, and it occurs infrequently in beech woodland in the southern counties of England.

In all the forms mentioned there is no rostellum, so that the flowers are autogamous.

Flowers: June to September, plants in exposed locations being earlier to flower than those in dense woodland.

Habitat: edges of coastal dune slacks, conifer plantations on well established dunes, beechwoods, always on calcareous soils.

Distribution: essentially a western European species, with a wide distribution in that area, but always local and uncommon: England; Wales; Ireland; Denmark; southern Sweden; northern Germany and western France.   **20**

Epipactis atrorubens (Hoffm.) Besser.
DARK RED HELLEBORINE; EPIPACTIS ROUGE (F); BRAUNROTE STENDELWURZ; STRANDVANILLE (G).

In most forms of this plant the dark red colouring of the floral parts makes it hard to confuse with any other species.

Plants can range from 20–70cm in height, with 5–10 oval leaves well separated into two rows. There is often a reddish tinge to the leaves, and towards the top of the stem they tend to change shape and become more elongated. The upper stem and ovaries are quite densely covered with fine tufts of hair.

The sepals are roughly triangular and the petals elliptical, all ending in a sharp point and coloured a similar shade of wine-red, brick-red or purple. Some plants have flowers which are mainly dark green but in which there is inevitably a reddish tinge.

The lip is 5.5–6.5mm in length and is coloured in the same or slightly brighter shade of the colour of the other perianth segments. The width of the epichile exceeds its length and it has a recurved tip. Near its base there are two crinkled bosses which have joined together to produce what looks like a flap on the main portion of the epichile.

The flowers have an effective rostellum and are fragrant, with a pronounced vanilla scent. The ovary has a velvety texture and is coloured green with a violet tinge.

Varieties: Var. *albiflora* Camus has a white labellum and cream or greenish-white perianth segments.

Flowers: May to August, depending on altitude.

Habitat: always in limestone areas; as in cracks in limestone pavement or on cliffs where its long penetrating roots serve it admirably, stony slopes often under light tree cover, woodland margins and, more rarely, dry pastures or established sand dunes. It is a plant of mountain regions up to 2200m, while in northern latitudes it occurs down to sea level (e.g. on Dryas heath in parts of Scandinavia).

Distribution: Spain; France; Ireland;

northern England; northern Wales; Scandinavia; Germany, Benelux countries; Switzerland; Austria; northern Italy; Yugoslavia; northern Greece; Poland; Czechoslovakia; Hungary; Rumania; central Russia; Crimea; Caucasus; possibly Turkey and Lebanon.

21

Epipactis parviflora (A. & C. Nieschalk) E. Klein
Although long considered as a subspecies of E. atrorubens, this is so distinct that it is now listed as a separate species.

The stems are relatively short, from 15–50cm high, and the leaves are not as elongated as those of E. atrorubens.

The flowers are small, with sepals and petals about 5mm in length, and are coloured pale brown or greenish.
Flowers: June to July.
Habitat: mountain woods on calcareous soils.
Distribution: south-east Spain.

Epipactis microphylla (Ehrh.) Swartz
SMALL-LEAVED HELLEBORINE;
EPIPACTIS À PETITES FEUILLES (F);
KLEINBLÄTTRIGE STENDELWURZ (G).

This is the slenderest species in the genus, with a height of 15–40cm and a delicate appearance, due to its very small leaves. The stems are solitary or in small groups and can be straight or slightly flexuous. From 2–6 leaves are carried in a spiral, with the lowest ovate or elliptical and the others becoming progressively narrower and bract-like. On some plants the leaves are suffused with purple.

The spike is lax, with few blooms (exceptional plants have up to 30) and bracts that equal or exceed the flowers low down the stem, diminishing in size higher up.

The sepals and petals are slightly incurved to form a bell shape with a whitish-green inside surface, and green, tinged with purple-red, outside. The sepals are slightly concave, 6–8mm long and 3–4mm wide, with a hairy external surface. Petals are 6–7mm long, 3–4mm

wide, with a more or less triangular-ovate shape.

The lip is about 6mm long and consists of a hypochile that forms no more than a shallow cup and is abruptly pinched at its front end. The epichile can be whitish-green to pale pink, is heart-shaped and 3–4mm long. Its special feature is the crinkled apron formed by the humps at its base giving an appearance quite distinct from any other Epipactis species.

The rostellum is persistent, and the ovary is comparatively long and cigar-shaped.

The flowers have a strong spicy vanilla scent which is more apparent towards the evening.
Varieties: Var. *firmior* Schur., a little-known form from Transylvania, first described in 1866. It is supposed to differ from the nominate race in having larger oval leaves. According to Hautzinger (1976) this form also occurs in Austria, south-east Europe and the larger Mediterranean islands, such as Sicily and Cyprus (although the only forms we have found in the latter island agree very well with the nominate plants).
Flowers: from May (at low altitudes in the south) through to August.
Habitat: in beech or pine woods, often on limestone. In Cyprus it grows only under hazel.
Distribution: east Spain; Balearics; Germany; Benelux; Switzerland; Austria; Corsica; Sardinia; Sicily; Yugoslavia; Greece; Cyprus (rare); Turkey; Czechoslovakia; Hungary; Bulgaria; Rumania; Russia (Crimea and Caucasus). Although widespread, this species tends to be local and uncommon.

22

Epipactis troodii Lindberg
CYPRUS HELLEBORINE;
ZYPERNSTENDELWURZ (G).

The erect, slender stems of this species range from 14–45cm in height and can occur singly or in groups. The stem is straight and leafy, with 3–4 sheaths near the base which are brownish-green flushed with purple. There are 3–5 leaves and these are dark green, stained with purple-violet particularly on their lower surfaces. They are ovate in shape, shorter in length than the internodes and arranged spirally up the stem.

The flower bracts are narrowly elliptical, stained purple-violet, with the lower ones as long as, or exceeding the flowers. The spike is lax with few pendulous flowers though exceptional cases of 20 or more blooms are on record.

The sepals are slightly concave in shape, being 10–12mm long, 4–5mm wide and coloured yellowish to dull olive green. The petals are ovate to ovate-elliptical, with a pointed end. They are whitish-green in colour, though the margins often become suffused with purple, and are 8–10mm long and 5–7mm wide.

The lip has a total length of 6–8mm, with a cup-shaped hypochile which is olive green edged with purple, or even completely reddish-purple on its inner surface. The epichile is more or less triangular, with a pointed apex and slightly crinkled margins in some cases. Near the base of the epichile lie two humps or calli which are reddish-purple with a slightly ridged surface.

The rostellum is effective only in recently opened flowers, and the ovary is rather short and slender.

At one time it was thought that this species was endemic to Cyprus but it is so similar to forms of the highly variable *E. persica* that it is probably no more than one of its subspecies. Some of the Cypriot plants have a heart-shaped rather than triangular labellum and look remarkably like forms of *E. persica* shown to us.

E. troodii has also been treated as conspecific with *E. microphylla* and is claimed to resemble its little known form var. *firmior*. There are few opportunities in Cyprus to view *E. troodii* and *E. microphylla* together but where they grow in hazel woods it is quite apparent there are similarities in stature; but the leaves of *E. troodii* are broader and oval in shape all the way up the stem, the flowers are larger and open wider. The most obvious diagnostic difference is the shape of the lip as can be seen in the photographs.

Certainly the question of the *troodii–microphylla–persica* relationship needs a lot more field work before a solution is reached.

Flowers: mid-June, through to mid-July.
Habitat: mainly under pines in the *Pinus nigra* ssp. *pallasiana* zone on basic soils derived from igneous rocks.
Distribution: Cyprus in the higher reaches of the Troodos massif from 1200m to 1800m.   **23**

Epipactis persica Hauskn. ap. Soó
PERSIAN HELLEBORINE; PERSISCHE STENDELWURZ (G).

Plants of this species can range from 10–15cm in height, with 3–4 broadly lanceolate leaves arranged in two rows up the stem. Near the base of the stem there are a number of purplish-brown sheaths. Like many other species of *Epipactis* the lower flower bracts are longer than the flowers themselves, becoming shorter higher up on the stem.

From 5–12 flowers are carried in a lax spike and, although they are horizontal when freshly opened, they droop slightly as they age.

The sepals and petals are broad, spreading and coloured pale green to whitish. The hypochile is cup-shaped and the epichile is greenish-white and triangular.

There is a rostellum, but it tends to be ineffective in preventing self-fertilization.
Flowers: June to July.
Habitat: mountain woodlands, broadleaf, coniferous or mixed; from 800–2500m.
Distribution: Turkey; Iran; Afghanistan.   **24**

Ssp. **troodii** is an unofficial title for *E. troodii*, used in some works. There is a very close link between *E. persica* and *E. troodii*, so this name should not be ruled out for future use.

Epipactis greuteri H. Baumann & Kuenkele
Plants of this recently discovered species are known only from a very limited area

of Greece.

Flowering stems reach 20–60 cm in height and carry 5–25 blooms which barely open.

The perianth segments are greenish on their outer surfaces, becoming reddish towards their tips. The total lip length is 7–9mm, which includes a cup-shaped hypochile with its inner surface greenish-yellow to reddish, and a triangular epichile with its tip curved backwards. There is a rostellum but it is only effective in freshly opened flowers.

Flowers: late June to early August.

Habitat: coniferous and beech woods on calcareous soils, from 1200–1500m.

Distribution: north-central Greece (Trikala area).

Cephalanthera

The name *Cephalanthera* is derived from two Greek words, *kephale* (head) and *anthera* (stamen), which refer to the shape of the single stamen possessed by these orchids.

The members of the genus are restricted to the temperate parts of Europe, Asia and north Africa, although of the five species falling within the scope of this book only three are found on the European mainland. They are regarded as one of the most primitive groups of monandrous (single stamen) orchids, retaining certain ancestral features (such as their means of vegetative propagation) yet having evolved some of the more familiar orchid characteristics. For example, they have one of the least sophisticated pollination mechanisms, with little specialised development of structures in the flower – a factor which makes them unique amongst European orchids. There is no specially adapted stigma or rostellum. Instead, the single stigma is sticky, and any insect visitor picks up this natural glue from the stigma when it penetrates the tubular cavity between the lip and the column, and the constriction presses its thorax against the stigmatic surface. The pollinia protrude so that the insect brushes against them as it leaves and they stick to the tacky thorax. In the next flower parts of the pollinia are pulled off on contact with the sticky stigma and cross-pollination takes place.

Self-pollination is not usual though it can occur in some members of the genus (it has even been recorded whilst the plant is still in the bud stage).

The roots of *Cephalanthera* species are fibrous and form no tubers. In fact there is a close similarity in appearance with the stems and underground parts of *Cypripedium*. The vegetative growth has been mentioned earlier (cf. p. 12) and it involves root buds which develop into aerial stems. This is very effective in deep shade where flower and seed production is at a minimum, and it also occurs with members of the *Liliaceae* and various tropical monocotyledons.

All the perianth segments have very nearly the same length and converge, so that the flowers do not open wide. Flowers of *Cephalanthera* species, like those of the closely related *Epipactis*, have a lip divided into two parts by a constriction. This produces a basal part, called the hypochile, and an apical part called the epichile. The epichile is recurved at its apex and carries longitudinal ridges near its attachment to the hypochile. The spur is absent in some species, very small in others and the flowers produce no nectar. The flowers are very nearly or completely stalkless, which distinguishes them from the clearly stalked *Epipactis*. Instead the flowers are held erect on stalk-like ovaries which are spirally twisted.

The name 'Helleborine' has been used to embrace both *Cephalanthera* and *Epipactis* species.

Hybrids

A series of both interspecific and intergeneric hybrids is known, although in the case of the latter the only genus involved is *Epipactis*:
C. damasonium x *C. longifolia* = *C.* x *schulzei* Camus & Berg.
C. damasonium x *C. rubra* = *C.* x *mayeri* (Zimm.) Camus
C. longifolia x *C. rubra* = *C.* x *otto-hechtii* Keller

C. damasonium x *Epipactis helleborine* (?) = x *Cephalopactis hybrida* (Holuby ex Soó) Dom.
C. damasonium x *Epipactis atrorubens* (?) = x *Cephalopactis speciosa* (Wettstein) A. & Gr.

Cephalanthera damasonium (Miller) Druce
WHITE HELLEBORINE;
CÉPHALANTHÈRE BLANCHE (F);
WEISSES WALDVÖGELEIN (G);
ELLEBORINE GIALLOGNOLA (I).

C. damasonium grows to a height of 15–60cm and has a leafy stem with numerous leaves that are oval or broad oblong-ovate in shape and become more lanceolate higher up the stem. The basal leaves are reduced to sheaths.

The flowers number from 3–16 (3–8 being most common) and are arranged in a lax spike, with broad flower bracts that are longer than the ovary. The comparatively large flowers have perianth segments that converge to such an extent that the flowers seem to open very little. Sometimes one can find blooms that have opened wide enough for their inner parts to be visible. The overall flower colour is a creamy off-white. The lip is shorter than the sepals, and the epichile carries 3–5 orange ridges at its base whilst the hypochile has an orange-yellow basal mark.

Self-pollination is possible and can occur in the bud stage: if conditions prove too dry the flowers are readily aborted.

The rootstock is vertical and carries a number of rather thick roots anything between 25 and 50cm in length. These roots penetrate deeply into the soil and enable the plant to survive on steep, well drained, chalky slopes.

C. damasonium is one of the first woodland orchids to colonise beech plantations on chalk hills, and the plants seem to flourish under the young trees before the overhead leaf cover becomes too dense. In such places clumps of stems produced from a single plant by root-budding are not uncommon, and the authors have seen as many as 16 stems in a single clump.

Varieties: Var. *chlorotica* Tahourdin has leaves which are lacking in chlorophyll.
Flowers: May to July (usually at its best towards the end of May)
Habitat: fairly shady woodland, especially young beech (25 years or thereabouts) on calcareous soils up to an altitude of 1300m.
Distribution: eastern Spain; Balearic Islands; France; southern Sweden (Götland); Denmark; Germany; Belgium;

Austria; Switzerland; Italy; Corsica; Sardinia; Sicily; Yugoslavia; Greece; Cyprus (very rare); Turkey; Syria; Israel; Poland (rare), Hungary; Bulgaria; Rumania; Czechoslovakia; southern Russia; Crimea and the Caucasus. In the UK it is a common plant of beechwoods on the south eastern chalk hills of England. It becomes progressively rarer further north and west and is absent from Wales, Ireland and Scotland.
25, 26

Ssp. *kotschyana* Renz & Taubenheim. Plants from eastern Turkey have recently been considered to be a separate subspecies of *C. damasonium*. They have lanceolate leaves 6–10cm in length which are often folded and bent outwards. The flowering spike is dense and many-flowered.

Flowers are large and white-to-ivory in shade. They open more widely than plants of the nominate race and have an epichile which is broadly heart-shaped.
Habitat: oak scrub.
Distribution: east Turkey.

Cephalanthera caucasica Kränzl.
This species, sometimes treated as a subspecies of *C. damasonium*, is robust with a height of up to 60cm. The stem is densely leafy with 7–9 dark green, broad leaves up to 16cm in length.

The inflorescence is dense and congested with large white flowers that open fairly wide.

The lip is broad with 3 (sometimes 4) ridges at the base of the epichile, and the ovaries are slender.

J. Renz, in *Flora Iranica*, mentions a tendency for the shoots of non-flowering plants to turn downwards after a while, forming spirals; something that was earlier recorded by Reichenbach in his observations of *C. longifolia*.
Flowers: end of April to early June.
Habitat: humid mountain woodlands.
Distribution: endemic to the forest area of Talysh and Gilan around the Caspian sea.

Cephalanthera longifolia (L.) Fritsch
SWORD-LEAVED HELLEBORINE; CÉPHALANTHÈRE À LONGUES FEUILLES (F); LANGBLÄTTRIGES WALDVÖGELEIN (G); ELLEBORINE BIANCA (I).

The plant is characterised by its large, fresh green leaves, arranged in an erect fan shape. The leaves are reduced to sheaths near the base of the stout glabrous stem, but are long and lanceolate higher up. The common name of Sword-leaved Helleborine is an apt one.

The flowers are carried in a moderately dense spike, and the height of the plant varies from 15–60cm. The usual number of flowers is about 10 but exceptional plants can have up to 20. The broad flower bracts are shorter than the ovary.

The perianth segments are all of equal length and converge so that the flowers do not open fully (although they open wider than those of *C. damasonium*). In colour they are pure white, in contrast to the cream colour of *C. damasonium*, and the lip is heart-shaped and covered with small fine hairs. At the base of the hypochile there is a small orange-yellow patch whilst the base of the epichile carries 5–7 orange ridges.

The rootstock is erect, and there are two sorts of roots produced; short thick ones that are fungus-free, and numerous fine ones that are infected with mycorrhizal fungus.

Only cross-pollination is known in *C. longifolia*, with small bees acting as the usual agents. The anther is equipped with an elastic hinge which allows it to spring back to its original position after the insect has left.
Flowers: May to July.
Habitat: it is tolerant of both dry and damp conditions in beech, oak or ash plantations on calcareous soils, also in undergrowth, such as bushes and brambles, in mountain regions.
Distribution: north Africa; Britain (local); northern Spain; France; southern Scandinavia; Germany; Belgium and Luxembourg; Austria and Switzerland; Italy; Corsica; Sardinia; Sicily; Greece;

Yugoslavia; Turkey; Lebanon; Poland; Czechoslovakia; Hungary; Bulgaria; Rumania; Crimea; Caucasus and eastwards into Iran. Dubious records exist for Crete, Cyprus and Rhodes. **27**

Cephalanthera cucullata Boiss & Heldr.
HOODED HELLEBORINE; KRETISCHES WALDVÖGELEIN (G).

One of the least impressive members of the genus, this rather dingy-coloured plant grows some 15–30cm high and has few leaves, all sheathing the stem. The leaves are 2.5–6cm long and are oblong lanceolate in shape.

The inflorescence is relatively lax, with 7–20 blooms, and the flowers exceed the bracts in length, except in the case of those lower down on the stem.

The perianth segments spread slightly to provide a partially opened flower and are most often a pale creamy white in colour. Occasionally the flowers are a more attractive rose pink. The lip is divided, as with all members of the genus, and the hypochile has lateral lobes whilst the epichile is heart-shaped, with 3–6 ridges near its base. There is a conical spur but it is very short (1–2mm).
Flowers: March to early June, depending on altitude.
Habitat: mountain thickets, scrub and forests.
Distribution: this species is endemic to Crete and even there it has a restricted distribution, being confined to the region around Mt Ida. **28**

Cephalanthera epipactoides Fischer & C. A. Meyer
EASTERN HOODED HELLEBORINE; GESPORNTES WALDVÖGELEIN (G).

A more robust plant than the related *C. cucullata*, it usually grows from 30–90cm in height. The lower leaves sheath the stem as in *C. cucullata* but the upper leaves are broadly lanceolate and end in a sharp point. They spread out from the stem at an acute angle.

The inflorescence is fairly dense with some 10–30 blooms on a stem. The flower bracts are as long or just longer than the ovary.

The flowers are opened to about the same degree as those of *C. longifolia* and are pure white. The epichile of the lip is triangular, with 7–9 ridges at its base, whilst the hypochile has lateral lobes with a truncate appearance. The spur is 3–4mm long and this, with the form of the leaves, serves to distinguish it from *C. cucullata*.
Flowers: late March to early June.
Habitat: open coniferous woods and hillside scrub.
Distribution: the northern Aegean Isles; Turkey (western Anatolia). **29**

Cephalanthera kurdica Bornm. & Kranzl.
KURDISCHES WALDVÖGELEIN (G).

This strikingly attractive species grows from 10–70cm tall with a deep seated rhizome below ground. The erect stem is slightly flexuous with sheaths in the lower portion and ovate-elliptical leaves up to 5cm long clasping the stem. Higher up on the stem the leaves grade into bracts.

The inflorescence occupies as much as 40cm in some plants and can be dense- to few-flowered.

The flowers are bright rose pink with oblong-lanceolate, slightly spreading sepals up to 2.5cm in length. The petals are narrowly oblong and shorter than the sepals. The lip is divided into a pale rose hypochile and a whitish epichile. The spur is conical with a length of about 4mm.

This species is sometimes regarded as no more than a subspecies of *C. epipactoides* but there are subtle differences in lip structure as well as flower colour and a completely different distribution.

Sundermann cites *C. kurdica* as a possible subspecies of *C. cucullata*.
Flowers: May to June, although end of March to April is possible in lower regions.
Habitat: woodlands both mixed and pine up to 2100m.
Distribution: eastern Turkey; northern Syria; Iraq and Iran. **30**

Cephalanthera floribunda Woronow
This little-known plant is closely related

to *C. epipactoides*, *C. cucullata* and *C. kurdica*. It has the fairly lax-flowered spike of *C. kurdica*, but the flowers are yellowish-white and both the lip and ovary are hairy.
Habitat: similar to *C. kurdica*.
Distribution: restricted to eastern Pontus in Turkey and the Caucasus.

Cephalanthera rubra (L.) L. C. M. Richard
RED HELLEBORINE; CÉPHALANTHÈRE ROUGE (F); ROTES WALDVÖGELEIN (G); ELLEBORINE ROSEA (I).

A slender-stemmed plant, some 20 −60cm high, with 5−8 short lanceolate to linear-lanceolate leaves.

The flower spike is usually lax, carrying 3−15 blooms on a slightly zigzagged stem. The flower bracts are very long in the case of the lower flowers, and although they get shorter for flowers higher up the stem they are always longer than the glandular ovary.

The perianth segments are wide and pointed, and the spreading sepals ensure that the flowers open wider than any other members of the same genus. The overall colour is a bright pink, occasionally with a lilac tinge, making it one of the finest coloured of all European orchids. The lip is white with a pointed epichile that carries a pink-tinted margin and, near the constriction that separates it from the hypochile, it has 7−9 narrow yellow ridges arranged longitudinally. The spur is barely indicated or absent altogether, and the plant possesses no nectar.

The rootstock is fairly deep-seated with quite slender horizontal roots that have the rootbuds as small outgrowths. These buds eventually extend upwards and penetrate the surface of the soil, where they can form several narrow leaves − but no flowers unless the light level is high enough.

Cephalanthera rubra is notorious for its tendency to disappear then mysteriously reappear in a known locality. This is entirely due to its ability to exist in a purely vegetative state for a lengthy period whilst it depends on mycorrhizal activity for its food. In very overgrown conditions leaves can all but disappear, with the roots carrying out a completely saprophytic existence underground, living with the help of the fungus on decayed organic matter in the surrounding soil. Should local conditions change, the plant can develop fully if the ambient light level is high enough.
Varieties: Var. *albiflora* Harz is a form with white flowers.
Flowers: May to early August (June and early July in Britain, early June in lower regions in France and Germany, to July in mountain woodlands).   **31, 32**
Habitat: usually on calcareous soils (in Cyprus it is found on the igneous soils of the Troodos massif, growing with calciphobes such as bracken). Open woodlands − usually of beech or pine, clearings or thickets in scrubby places, roadside verges in lightly wooded country. From sea level up to 1800m.
Distribution: North Africa; Britain (very local); Spain, France (in some places the most frequent of the European *Cephalanthera*); Scandinavia; Germany: Belgium; Austria and Switzerland (found in many areas in mountain woods); Italy; Corsica (?); Sardinia; Sicily; Yugoslavia (especially the Julian Alps); Greece (central and northern mountain areas); Cyprus (limited to one or two places on the Troodos massif); Turkey; Poland; Czechoslovakia; Hungary; Bulgaria; Rumania; Russia; Crimea and the Caucasus.

Limodorum

The single species in this genus is a large, often robust plant, with a violet colouring that makes it easy to identify.

The name is derived from some confusion with *Haemodorum*, an ancient name give to a parasite with red flowers.

The characteristics of this genus are: a short rhizome bearing thick, almost tuber-like roots; no green leaves – the stem is sheathed with purple-brown scales; flowers with free perianth segments, carried in an erect spike; a long column; a long, slender up-curved spur; a single viscidium, without bursicles so that the pollinia are exposed.

Limodorum abortivum is generally regarded as a saprophyte but there have been suggestions that at least part of its existence might be parasitic. One invariably finds it growing where there are living pines close by, but exactly what degree of parasitism there might be is not known, for the physiology of the plant is not perfectly understood. Proving parasitism is always fraught with difficulties, since there has to be some very careful dissection of root systems, in situ.

Limodorum abortivum (L.) Swartz
VIOLET LIMODORE; LIMODORE À
FEUILLES AVORTÉES (F); DINGEL
(G); FIAMMONE (I).

At its best *Limodorum abortivum* can be a magnificent orchid, with robust spikes up to 80cm tall and large spreading flowers. In suitable locations it is not unusual to find groups of three or more flowering stems together. When the rainfall in early spring and winter proves inadequate the plants suffer and then the stems can be little more than 20cm tall, with flowers that barely open. In this case they have a distinctly dingy appearance, because there are no green leaves; instead the stem is sheathed with brownish-purple scales along the greater part of its length.

The flower spike is lax, with 4–25 flowers spaced over 15–33cm. The perianth segments are long (around 2cm), with the sepals rather broad and the petals much thinner and a little shorter. In colour the segments are usually reddish violet or violet but in large colonies one can occasionally find plants with white flowers.

The lip is large and triangular, with a wavy margin and a bright colour scheme of violet and yellow. The spur is slender, about the same length as the ovary. The column is long and prominent, with the pollinia easily visible since there are no bursicles to protect them.

Varieties: Var. *rubrum* Ruckbrodt, a name sometimes used for a form from southern Turkey and Cyprus, has rosy pink flowers but resembles the nominate race in all other aspects.   **36**

Flowers: mid-April to July, depending on latitude and altitude.

Habitat: usually on calcareous soils, from sea level to 1750m, in bushy grassland, shady banks in pine or mixed woodland but invariably near growing pines.

Distribution: mainly in the Mediterranean countries, with limited incursions into some territories to the north of this region. North Africa; Spain; Balearics; France; Germany (limited to Kaiserstuhl and the Trier area); Benelux countries; Switzerland and Austria (to 1200m); Italy; Corsica; Sardinia; Sicily; Yugoslavia; Greece; Crete; Rhodes; Cyprus (to 1750m); Turkey; Lebanon; southern Czechoslovakia; Hungary;

Bulgaria; Rumania; Crimea and the Caucasus.   33, 34, 35

Plants from west-central Portugal (north of Lisbon) and north Africa have been singled out for subspecific status, *L. abortivum* ssp. *trabutianum* (Batt.)

Rouy. They differ from the nominate race in their possession of a very short spur and a linear rather than triangular lip.

They occur intermingled with the typical form and probably only deserve varietal status.

Epipogium

There are two species in this genus but only one, *E. aphyllum*, occurs in the area covered by this book. The other, *E. roseum*, is widely distributed throughout the tropics of the old world. These species have lost the ability to produce chlorophyll, and their mode of existence is completely saprophytic.

E. aphyllum is a rare orchid in spite of its wide distribution and this, coupled with irregular flowering and an effective camouflage against a background of dead leaves, makes it a very difficult plant to find.

The name *Epipogium* derives from *epi* (on) and *pogon* (a beard or lip), and the spelling *Epipogon* was once used for the genus.

The genus characteristics are: coral-like rhizomes heavily infected with mycorrhizal fungus and covered with fine hairs not roots; a stem with sheathing scales and no green leaves above; flowers with free perianth segments held downwards; a three-lobed lip directed upwards; a slender upward-pointing spur; a short column with a small rostellum and two distinct viscidia without bursicles.

Epipogium aphyllum usually propagates by means of underground stolons which can spread out over a large area. Buds at their tips then grow into plants which eventually become separate on the death of the parent. The plant is capable of spending a long time underground without flowering; up to ten years can elapse between successive flowering stems – a part of the rhizome dies after a stem is produced and takes years to reform.

In most cases flowering only takes place after a wet spring, which enables the rhizome to store up water. This aids the development of an aerial stem, but if later conditions prove too dry then the plant will abort it while the rhizome keeps on growing.

The flowers are scented, and the inner walls of the spur secrete nectar. Bumble bees are the most successful insect pollinators as their size is just right for the operation of the pollination mechanism. After the bee lands on the exposed part of the lip it climbs inside the flower and makes its way towards the spur. Once at the mouth of the spur it can reach the nectar inside, but on backing out it breaks the delicate rostellum when it comes into contact with it. As it leaves, the anther cap is pushed away and the pollinia revealed. These then stick to the head parts of the insect, which hopefully visits another flower of the same species. Seed is seldom produced, unless the plants are growing in large colonies.

Epipogium aphyllum Swartz
SPURRED CORAL-ROOT OR GHOST
ORCHID; EPIPOGON SANS FEUILLES
(F); OHNBLATT (G).

Plants of this species seldom exceed 20cm in height and can be no more than 5cm tall.

There are no leaves: only 2–5 brownish scales sheath the pinkish-coloured stem. Beneath the ground there is a whitish rhizome, with many short-lobed branches and one or two narrow stolons. The underground parts resemble certain kinds of coral, hence the common name of Spurred Coral-root.

From 1–5 flowers are carried in a lax arrangement, they are large for the size of the plant, pendent, and their ovaries are attached to the stem by slender stalks (pedicels). The bracts are small.

The perianth segments curve downwards, with the sepals narrow and yellowish, whilst the petals are slightly shorter and yellowish with short violet lines.

The lip is three-lobed, with short rounded lateral lobes and a triangular middle lobe which points upwards. In colour the lip is white or pinkish, with reddish-violet spots and papillae. Its edges are distinctly crinkled.

Cases are on record where flowers have opened under the humus in which the plant flourishes. *E. aphyllum* is not unique in this respect, because the same thing can happen with another saprophyte, *Neottia nidus-avis*, and there is even an orchid, *Rhizanthella gardneri*, discovered accidentally in western Australia in 1928, which has a completely subterranean existence.

Varieties: Var. *lacteum* Keller has milky white flowers without any yellow colouring.

Flowers: May to September (in Britain) but usually in July and August elsewhere.

Habitat: in decaying vegetable matter in pine, beech or oak woods.

Distribution: widespread but always local and rare: France; England (known only from two beechwood sites in southern England); Scandinavia (up to 66°, occurs fairly frequently in Jämtland in Sweden); Germany (some superb colonies in the Black Forest); Belgium; Switzerland and Austria (up to 1900m); northern Italy; Yugoslavia; northern Greece (recently rediscovered); Poland; Czechoslovakia; Hungary; Bulgaria; Rumania; Russia; Crimea; the Caucasus and eastward through Iran to Japan.

37, 38 (Black Forest, Germany)

Neottia

All members of this genus are saprophytes, gaining their food from a close association with mycorrhizal fungi in their roots and rhizomes. Only one species, *Neottia nidus-avis*, occurs in Europe but a number of species grow in the Himalayas, western China and Japan. Of these *Neottia listeroides* has the most westerly distribution, but it reaches no further west than western Pakistan.

The name *Neottia* means nest, and it refers realistically to the tangled mass formed by the roots. The specific name *nidus-avis* (bird's nest) serves to drive the point home.

Although *N. nidus-avis* has no green leaves there are a few stunted scales sheathing the stem and it has not completely lost the ability to produce chlorophyll. Experiments have been carried out where the light levels are artificially increased, compared with the shady conditions of normal growth, and small amounts of chlorophyll are manufactured in the stem. Even in low light conditions it seems that minute quantities of chlorophyll do exist in the plant but it is used for food production in conjunction with the mycorrhizal fungi.

The members of this genus have the following characteristics; they are saprophytes, with short creeping rhizomes, covered with thick fleshy roots, forming a nest-like mass; an absence of green leaves; stem covered with brownish scales; numerous flowers in a spike-like raceme; perianth segments more less equal in length or the inner slightly shorter, converging slightly to form a helmet; 2-lobed labellum; no spur; a long slender column, with a wide flat rostellum but no viscidia or bursicles.

N. nidus-avis propagates vegetatively by forming new shoots from the root tips after flowering, when a part of the root system and rhizome dies. If several flowering stems occur, growing closely together, they generally grow from a number of distinct but entangled plants. These can arise by division, vegetative propagation or even from seed. Plants are seldom strong enough to produce two flowering stems from the same rhizome.

The flowers do not have a spur but they can produce nectar from the slightly concave part near the base of the lip. Small flies are seen visiting the flowers, but the plants are mainly self-pollinated.

Like *E. aphyllum*, there are cases where flower buds develop under a covering of moss or even completely underground, where a stone or other obstacle prevents the vertical growth of the stem. These plants can even flower underground and, more surprisingly, set seed which then germinates in the seed pod.

Neottia nidus-avis (L.) L. C. M. Richard
BIRD'S-NEST ORCHID; NÉOTTIE NID D'OISEAU (F); NESTWURZ (G); NIDO D'UCCELLO (I).

The stems and flowers of this species are coloured a uniform honey-brown. The plants can be 20–45cm in height, with 3–5 bract-like brown scales sheathing the stem in the place of green leaves.

The flowers are held in a fairly dense raceme, occupying some 5–21cm of the stem length, and the bracts are shorter than the ovary.

The perianth segments are 4–6mm long, ovate or elliptical in shape, and curve inwards to form a hood.

The lip is 8–12mm long and deeply divided into two lobes at its apex (this is especially noticeable in the case of the lower flowers). The undivided part of the lip is slightly convex, and its surface is capable of secreting nectar.

There is no spur, and the column is elongated with a rather long beak, over which the anther projects.

Varieties: Var. *nivea* Magnus ap Schulze is a form with pure white flowers.

Flowers: May to July (in some years flowers are still found in mountain woods during August).

Distribution: widespread throughout Europe, where it is a frequent inhabitant of beech and pine woods on calcareous soils: north Africa (rare); Spain; France (common in the Jura); Ireland; Wales (rare); Scotland (not north of Inverness); England (frequent in beechwoods on southern chalk hills); Scandinavia (up to 62°); Germany; Benelux countries; Switzerland and Austria (up to 1700m); Italy; Corsica; Sardinia; Sicily; Yugoslavia: Greece; Turkey; Poland; Czechoslovakia; Hungary; Bulgaria; Rumania; Russia; the Caucasus and eastwards, to middle and north Asia.   **39, 40**

Listera

This genus is restricted to the cold and temperate parts of Asia, north America, and Europe. M. Lister, an English scientist, was the source of the generic name, and out of around ten species only two occur in Europe. One of these, *Listera ovata*, is a well known orchid, easily recognised by its green flowers and two large oval leaves arranged opposite one another on the stem.

The genus characteristics are: short rhizomes and slender roots which are free of mycorrhizal fungi in the mature plants; a lax inflorescence forming a spike-like raceme; 2 leaves arranged more or less opposite one another and borne just below the middle of the stem; perianth segments approximately equal in length and held patent or slightly convergent; lip 2–3 times the length of the other segments, deeply bifid from its apex, rarely carrying two small basal lobes; no spur, but nectar secreted in the central furrow of the lip; column short and erect, rostellum wide and flat; no viscidia or bursicle.

Listera ovata has a very effective pollination mechanism that can be triggered by a wide variety of insects such as beetles, flies and various small Hymenopterans.

The lip has a long shiny ridge and this has a nectar channel in it. An insect visitor climbs up this until it reaches the rostellum. Even if touched gently an internal 'explosion' takes place in the rostellum and a droplet of liquid is forced out where it hits the head of the insect and the pollinia together. In two to three seconds this liquid sets hard, cementing the pollinia firmly to the insect's head and, startled by the action, it flies off.

At the next flower the insect again follows the nectar trail and, if it has been open for sometime, the rostellum is bent up, exposing the stigma. This is the first thing the insect touches, and fragments of the pollinia stuck to its head region cling to the stigma and ensure pollination.

Listera cordata has a similar mechanism operated by small insects, such as ichneumon flies, which distribute the pollen as they crawl over the flowers. Again, fragments of the pollinia can fall onto the stigma an cause self-fertilization. This is obviously an effective and speedy process, for seed pods can be found at the same time as flowers on some plants.

Both European species can increase vegetatively. *Listera ovata* is slow growing but can produce root buds which give rise to rhizomes which send up their own aerial stems and become separate plants on the death of the root. This enables the plant to increase during the early years of its growth when it can draw on food in the rhizome. *Listera cordata* is capable of producing root buds on a larger scale than *L. ovata*. These are formed from the underground stem and root system. Food is stored in the roots and underground stems after its production by the mycorrhizal fungi on which this species is heavily dependant. Buds grow from the swollen parts of the underground stem and eventually send up aerial shoots which become separate plants and flower as soon as three years after their formation.

Both species were at one time included in the genus *Neottia*.

Listera ovata (**L.**) **R. Br.**
TWAYBLADE; GRANDE LISTÈRE (F); GROSSES ZWEIBLATT (G); ORCHIDE-DI-PRIMAVERA (I).

Plants are found with a height ranging from 30–60cm and a pair of broad oval leaves without stalks, arranged on opposite sides of the stem, somewhere under half way up it. Occasional plants are found with a third, smaller, pointed leaf above or below this pair.

The inflorescence is lax, with numerous flowers and short bracts. The flowers are green, sometimes with a reddish-brown tinge; petals and sepals incurve to form a loose hood.

The lip is strap-like and points downwards, with a deep division into two lobes, starting at the apex. A ridge runs longitudinally on the lip and is capable of producing nectar. There is no spur.

Flowers: May to August depending on altitude. On sand dunes near the coast May is usual, whilst in mountain woodlands it can still be flowering well into August.

Habitat: this is one of the few orchids that can grow happily on acidic or calcareous soils in a wide range of surroundings; deciduous and mixed woodlands; scrub and grassland (especially on chalk downs and old established sand dunes where the soil is damp) – either in shade or exposed conditions up to 1900m above sea level.

Distribution: widespread throughout Europe, it is one of the few orchids that can be described as common; Spain; France; British Isles; Scandinavia (up to 70°) Germany; Benelux countries; Switzerland; Austria; Italy; Sicily; Corsica; Sardinia; Yugoslavia; Greece;

Crete; Turkey; Poland; Czechoslovakia; Hungary; Rumania; Russia; Crimea; Caucasus, eastwards into central Asia.

41, 42

Listera cordata (**L.**) **R. Br.**
LESSER TWAYBLADE; LISTÈRE EN COEUR (F); KLEINES ZWEIBLATT (G).

This species is usually inconspicuous because of its small stature (5–20cm) and the way it grows concealed in the surrounding vegetation.

There are 2 heart-shaped leaves arranged more or less opposite each other half way up the stem and 1–2 brownish membraneous sheaths at the stem base.

The inflorescence is lax, with few flowers (4–12) and tiny bracts. Sepals and petals are small (2–2.5mm) and tend to spread much more than those in *L. ovata*; hardly, if at all, converging to form a hood.

The lip is strap-like and three-lobed: the laterals are very small, and the middle lobe is deeply forked to form a two pointed lobules.

The flowers are reddish-green to a deep purplish-brown and there is no spur.

Flowers: late May to early September.

Habitat: coniferous woodlands; moorland amongst heather; peat bogs from sea level in the north of the region up to 2000m in the Alps, always on acidic soils.

Distribution: widespread but local throughout Europe; Spain (Pyrenees); France; Iceland; British Isles (Ireland, north Wales, Scotland and north England – with occasional records form the south); Scandinavia (71°); Austria; Switzerland; Germany; Italy (Alps and the Apennines); Yugoslavia; northern Greece; Turkey (Pontus); Poland; Czechoslovakia; Bulgaria; Rumania; Russia; Caucasus and circumpolar to north Asia; north America and Greenland. **43, 44**

Spiranthes

There are approximately thirty species in this genus, with a large number of them native to north and central America. Only four species occur in the area covered, and of these *S. spiralis* is the most frequently encountered, as it has by far the widest distribution. Another, *S. aestivalis*, has a fairly wide distribution but is disappearing from many of its haunts at an alarming rate as the wetlands it inhabits are drained for farming. *S. romanzoffiana* is something of an enigma, for it is found only in Western Ireland, parts of Scotland and Devon, with its nearest neighbours in north America. *S. sinensis* is widespread in the Middle East, Far East and Australasia, but reaches its westernmost limit in the Volga Kama region of the USSR.

A fifth species, *S. cernua*, has become established as an introduction on sand dunes in Holland but is really a north American species.

The name *Spiranthes* refers directly to the spirally twisted flower spike. The arrangement of the flowers looks like plaited hair and was no doubt the inspiration behind the common name of 'Lady's Tresses'.

The characteristics of the genus are: 2–6 fleshy roots that are more or less tuberous; the axis of the spike is twisted, so that the flowers are arranged in one or more spiral rows; sepals united to form a tube-like hood; a lip about as long as the other segments; fragrant flowers with no spur; a horizontal column and a rostellum which is deeply bifid, with a single viscidium between the lobes; the anther is largely hidden behind the rostellum.

The closely related genus *Goodyera* has similar flowers and stems but also possesses well-developed creeping rhizomes and stolons. The spiral arrangement of the flowers is far less obvious, and the flowers are held in a more or less one-sided spike.

Insects are attracted to the flowers for the nectar, which is secreted by two small glands near the base of the lip. When the flowers first open the rostellum lies very close to the lip and leaves a narrow aperture which only allows access to the relatively long probosces of humble and other bees. An insect visitor lands on the spreading front portion of the lip and inserts its proboscis to seek out the nectar, touching the sticky viscidium at the same time. The pollinia are then glued onto the proboscis as it is withdrawn. At the next flower the pollinia fragment as the insect insert its proboscis and the pieces come into contact with the sticky stigma, allowing fertilization to take place. This tends to work better with older flowers because the rostellum withers with age and creates a bigger opening. As the insect crawls up the spike it gets covered with pollen from younger flowers.

Hybrids

Because of the late flowering of *S. spiralis* hybrids are unlikely. In late August and September, when it is in bloom, most orchid species have withered. A single interspecific hybrid is known:
S. spiralis x *S. aestivalis* = *S.* x *zahlbruckneri* Fleischm.

Spiranthes spiralis (L.) Chevall.
AUTUMN LADY'S-TRESSES;
SPIRANTHÉ D'AUTOMNE (F);
HERBSTDREHWURZ (G).

This species is usually small in stature, especially where it grows in short, open turf. It ranges from 5–20cm in height, but larger plants can occur under pine trees such as those in Cyprus, where the authors have found most of the plants between 25 and 35cm tall.

The flowering stem has small, bract-like sheaths along its lower part, and it grows alongside the leaf rosette of the following year's plant. Its own rosette has long withered by the time flowers appear and its remains can be found near the base of the stem. The new rosette is produced in the autumn, lasts through the winter and dies away in late spring. The slender flower spike develops from the centre of this rosette, with 6–25 flowers in one tight spiral row. The flower bracts are about 6–7mm long, making them just exceed the ovary.

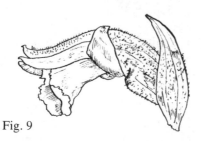

Fig. 9

The sepals and petals are 6–7mm in length, oblong in shape and coloured white – often with a greenish tinge near their bases. The dorsal sepal and the petals form a 'tube' with the lip, while the lateral sepals spread horizontally. The lip is 6–7mm long with curved white margins which appear crinkled near the apex. Away from the edges and towards the base the lip becomes green in colour.

The flowers have a sweet scent during the daytime, whereas those of *S. aestivalis* are reputed to be more strongly scented at night.

Groups of plants are often found growing together and the individuals arise from lateral buds on a single stem, producing separate root tubers. Each tuber becomes a distinct plant when the connecting stem dies away. This process, repeated over several years, can produce a large group of plants.

Flowers: August to September (October in hot Mediterranean countries). It is irregular in flowering, with some populations not producing spikes for many years then suddenly, one year, copious flowering stems appear.

Habitat: mainly a lowland species, often flourishing in turf on coastal cliff tops or well established sand dunes. It also occurs in short grass on chalk and limestone hills, up to 1000m. In the Mediterranean it flourishes in coastal pine plantations.

Distribution: widespread throughout Europe and the Mediterranean region; north Africa; Spain; Balearic Islands; France; British Isles (absent from northern England and Scotland); Denmark; Germany; Benelux countries; Austria and Switzerland (up to 1000m); Italy; Corsica; Sardinia; Sicily; Yugoslavia; Greece; Crete; Rhodes; Cyprus; Turkey; Lebanon; Poland; Czechoslovakia; Hungary; Rumania; Bulgaria; Caucasus.   **45, 46**

Spiranthes aestivalis (Poiret) L. C. M. Richard
SUMMER LADY'S-TRESSES;
SPIRANTHÉ D'ÉTÉ (F);
SOMMER-DREHWURZ (G).

This slender species stands between 12 and 30cm tall, with 4–6 linear-lanceolate leaves at the stem base. These point more or less upwards and, higher up the stem, they degenerate into one or two bract-like scales.

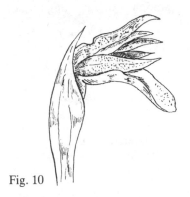

Fig. 10

The flower spike is rather lax, carrying from 6–20 flowers in a spiral row over a length of 3–10cm. The bracts are slightly longer than the ovary, with a length of 6–9mm.

The petals, sepals and lip all converge to form a tube, unlike *S. spiralis* where the lateral sepals spread outwards.

The lip is slightly longer than the other segments, with a deflected apex and margins which curve upwards. The flowers are white or yellowish-white and are possibly moth-pollinated, since some workers report their scent is noticeably stronger towards the evening.

Just like *S. spiralis* this species can multiply vegetatively by forming lateral buds.

Flowers: June to August.

Habitat: damp grassland and mountain pastures on slightly acidic soils up to 1200m above sea level.

Distribution: now rather rare, and decreasing rapidly as its former haunts are subjected to drainage or other land improvement schemes. Unlikely to survive until the end of the twentieth century in most places, and the best hope for its preservation is in sites in southern Europe. It occurs in north Africa; Spain; Balearics; France; southern Germany; Benelux countries; Switzerland; Austria; Italy (only in the north); Corsica; Sardinia; Yugoslavia; Greece; Turkey and Hungary.

In England, as in other places in northern Europe, it appears to be extinct. It once grew in the New Forest in Hampshire, and many have searched for it since, in the hope that it remains, waiting rediscovery.   **47, 48**

Spiranthes sinensis (Pers.) Ames
PINK LADY'S-TRESSES; CHINESISCHE DREHWURZ (G).

This species closely resembles *S. aestivalis* but has bright rose-pink flowers. It grows from 15–30cm tall, with 4–5 basal leaves which are linear-lanceolate in shape and held erect. The upper leaves are bract-like.

The inflorescence is rather dense, with a large number of flowers and bracts longer than the ovary.

The perianth segments form a tube-like flower and are around 5mm in length. The lateral sepals spread only slightly, if at all, and the lip has a wavy margin. The flowers are usually pink or rose-purple and only very rarely whitish.

Flowers: May to September in general, though the Russian plants usually flower in July and August.

Habitat: wet meadows near lakes and rivers and in peat bogs.

Distribution: this species is found, throughout tropical Asia (China, New Guinea, Japan) and Australia (Australia, Tasmania, New Zealand) and is widely cultivated as a hot-house plant. In Europe it reaches no further west than the Volga Kama region of Russia.   **49**

Spiranthes romanzoffiana Cham.
IRISH LADY'S-TRESSES; AMERIKANISCHE DREHWURZ (G).

European plants of this species tend to be small, with a height of 12–15cm, whereas in north America they can grow to 50cm.

There are 5–8 linear-lanceolate leaves, with those above the basal rosette becoming shorter but not reducing to the scales one finds in *S. spiralis*.

The flowers number 12–35 and are arranged in 3 spiral rows on a rather dense spike, with bracts that exceed the ovary in length.

The perianth segments are longer than

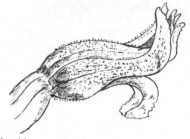

Fig. 11

those of *S. aestivalis* and *S. spiralis* (around 12mm), converging to form a tube-like structure, with the lip sharply deflexed near its apex. The flowers are white, with a green or cream tinge. *Varieties*: Some workers separate plants into two types: *Spiranthes gemmipara* Lindley being used for the Irish form with whiter flowers and flatter leaves than *S. romanzoffiana* var. *stricta* Wilm., the northern form. Most normal populations of *S. romanzoffiana* will be found

to contain plants answering to both descriptions, together with intermediates, so the value of such a splitting is questionable.
Flowers: late July and August.
Habitat: acid bogs and peaty marshes
Distribution: this species has one of the most interesting ranges since in Europe it is restricted to the western parts of the British Isles, with the nearest sites across the Atlantic in north America.

It grows in western Ireland with two other north American plants, *Sisyrinchium bermudianum* and *Eriocaulon aquaticum*, and so it has been suggested that they are all relics of a flora that existed prior to the last ice age 10,000 years ago: Ireland (west Cork, south Kerry, Lough Neagh); western Scotland (Argyll and Inverness); Scottish islands (Coll and Colonsay in the Hebrides); England (recently found on Dartmoor in Devon); elsewhere in parts of Asia and in north America.   **50**

Goodyera

The orchids in this genus bear a close superficial resemblance to *Spiranthes*. The genus is named after John Goodyer, a seventeenth-century Englishman, and comprises about one hundred species distributed throughout the forests and woodlands of the world. In our area there are only two species: one, *G. repens*, is widespread and the other, *G. macrophylla*, is confined to the island of Madeira.

Goodyera species differ from *Spiranthes* in the following characteristics: creeping rhizomes rather than tubers, which give rise to shoots bearing leaf clusters and flowering stems; leaves with a conspicuous 'net' of veins; stolons which spread over ground; the spiral arrangement of the flowers is less marked or absent altogether; lip shorter than the sepals; hypochile of the lip strongly concave; epichile triangular and flat.

As one would expect from the similarity of the flowers, pollination in *Goodyera* and *Spiranthes* is effected by a similar mechanism. The flower tube is only wide enough initially to allow the removal of pollinia on the insect's proboscis. Later it widens, as the lip moves downwards, allowing pollinia from other flowers to be introduced and contact the sticky stigma. Nectar is secreted in the cup-shaped hypochile (the flowers have no spur) and this attracts insects such as humble bees.

One can often find ripe seed pods in the woods where *G. repens* grows, and it seems that pollination is effective even if there are few insects to be seen on the wing in these pinewood haunts.

The plants can increase vegetatively by the stolons, which sprout from buds at the tip of the rhizome sometime in the autumn. These stolons thread their way through mossy cushions and, if they are lifted, one can see them interwoven with the rhizomes and fungus threads. Plants are formed from buds at the ends of the stolons and, in most cases, they remain heavily dependent on their fungus partners for a regular food supply.

Goodyera repens (L.) R. Br.
CREEPING LADY'S-TRESSES;
GOODYÈRE RAMPANTE (F);
MOOSWURZ (G); SATIRIO
SERPEGGIANTE (I).

This small species grows from 10–25cm tall, with few short roots, a long creeping rhizome and branching stolons which run overground.

Most of the leaves are held in a rosette at the base of the stem and are ovate, with their dark green surface covered in a network of lighter nerves. The upper leaves are reduced to sheaths.

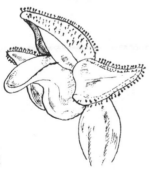

Fig. 12

The inflorescence is slender, often with a slight twist, and carries the small flowers in a lax, one-sided arrangement, from 3–7cm long.

The sepals and petals are similar in length and about 3–4mm long. The median sepal and the petals form a tight hood, whilst the laterals spread outwards. The edges of the sepals are covered with white glandular hairs.

The lip is separated into two parts: a strongly concave hypochile at the base, and a triangular, downward-pointing epichile forming the apex. Inside the flower the reproductive parts are orange-yellow in colour, in contrast to the pure white of the perianth segments.

The flowers are fragrant and lack a spur but nevertheless they can produce nectar from the inner surface of the hypochile.

Flowers: July and August.

Habitat: grows in coniferous or mixed woodland, often where the light level is fairly low and there are cushions of moss on the ground. Here its rhizomes and stolons thread their way through the cushion and humus beneath.

Distribution: widely distributed in northern, central and western Europe, from sea level (in northerly latitudes) to 2000m (Alpine regions): France; Britain (Scotland and northern England, with one colony in pinewoods in Norfolk); Scandinavia (70°); Germany; Benelux countries; Austria; Switzerland; Italy (Alps); Yugoslavia; northern Greece; northern Turkey; Poland; Czechoslovakia; Hungary; Bulgaria; Rumania; Russia; Crimea and the Caucasus.

51, 52

Goodyera macrophylla Lowe
MADEIRAN LADY'S-TRESSES; GROSS-
BLÄTTRIGES NETZBLATT (G).

Plants of this species are much more robust than *G. repens*. They grow from 20–50cm in height, with 5–7 broadly lanceolate leaves spread out over the lower part of the stem rather than forming a basal rosette. The upper leaves are reduced to sheaths.

The spike is rather dense, with numerous flowers arranged more or less along one side and bracts that are as long as the ovary.

The sepals and petals are white, curving inwards to form a hood. The lip is shorter than the sepals and there is no spur.
Flowers: April to September.

Habitat: damp woodlands in mountain areas.
Distribution: restricted to the island of Madeira (endemic).

Habenaria

Habenaria tridactylites is the only member of this genus found in the area covered here, and it is endemic to the Canary Isles.

The lip is the distinctive feature of this orchid, and the specific name 'tridactylites' refers to its 3 finger-like lobes.

Characteristics of the genus are as follows: a pair of ovoid, tapering tubers; 2 large, ovate basal leaves; spreading lateral sepals; a hood formed from the dorsal sepal and petals; lip divided into 3 strap-like lobes.

Habenaria tridactylites Lindley
THREE-LOBED HABENARIA;
KANARENSTENDEL (G).

Plants of this species range from 10–40cm in height and have 2 large ovate basal leaves, above which grows a leafless flowering stem.

The spike is lax, with 10–30 flowers and bracts which are shorter than the ovary.

The pale green flowers have spreading lateral sepals and a hood formed from the incurved petals and dorsal sepal.

The lip is deeply 3-lobed, and all the lobes are long and narrow, but the middle lobe is slightly shorter than the laterals. The spur is longer than the ovary.

Flowers: a very early flowering species, coming into bloom as early as November and only lasting until January.
Habitat: forest cliffs and cliff ledges in

Fig. 13

mountainous areas, from 200–1400m.
Distribution: restricted to the Canary Isles, where it is a locally frequent endemic; Tenerife (forests 800–1400m); Hierro; Las Palmas and Gomera.

Gennaria

The single species in this genus has a distribution restricted to the lands of the western Mediterranean and to the Canary Isles.

Like *Herminium monorchis* there is only a single tuber in evidence at the time of flowering, but the distinctive feature is the pair of leaves to which the name 'diphylla' refers.

The genus characteristics are: an oblong tuber; a stem bearing 2 alternate leaves in its upper half; flowers in a dense spike; free perianth segments; a 3-lobed labellum; short spur; short rostellum; viscidia small without bursicles.

Gennaria diphylla (Link) Parl.

GRÜNSTENDEL; GENNARIE (G).

Fig. 14

The 2 leaves placed at different heights on opposite sides of the stem are the noticeable feature of this orchid. They are both heart-shaped and about the same length, but the lower is much broader than the upper. The plant grows from 15–30cm in height and, with its small green flowers, is not a particularly imposing orchid. The flower bracts are short, and the flowering stem is leafless.

Numerous flowers are carried in a loose spike of up to 10cm length. Each of these blooms has perianth segments which converge to form a tapering hood or in some plants diverge slightly.

The lip has 3 pointed lobes, with the median lobe longer than the laterals. The overall flower colour is light yellowish-green, and there is a small rounded spur.

Flowers: an early flowering species which usually blooms in February and March. In the Canary Isles it starts to flower in January, while in the Mediterranean it can last until early May.

Habitat: shady places in evergreen woods and scrubby thickets, up to 1000m.

Distribution: over much of its distribution the species is local and uncommon: Canary Isles (fairly frequent); Madeira; north Africa; Portugal: southern Spain; Corsica; Sardinia.

Herminium

The common name of the single species is 'Musk Orchid' but it is a misnomer because the sweet-smelling flowers have a scent rather like honey.

Small insects, such as flies and beetles, are readily attracted to the flowers, being forced to enter them sideways because of the construction of the floral parts. In doing this they contact the relatively large saddle-shaped viscidia which stick onto their body or legs, together with the pollinia.

Self-fertilization can take place, too, because the stigma is rather extended and pollinium fragments can easily fall onto it.

Herminium monorchis has sometimes been described as 'migratory' because new tubers are produced on the ends of stolons, making the next year's plant appear in a different place. At the time of flowering, only one tuber is in evidence beneath the plant, and this is the source of the name *monorchis*. Other tubers are forming, however, but they are possibly no more than slight swellings at the ends of the slender stolons. From a single parent plant as many as 5 new tubers can be formed.

Besides the 'single' tuber and the stolons the genus has the following characteristics: a pair of basal leaves; perianth segments which are erect and spreading or slightly convergent; a lip which is conspicuously 3-lobed and slightly longer than the other perianth segments; no spur; distinct viscidia and a rudimentary bursicle.

Herminium monorchis (L.) R. Br.
MUSK ORCHID; ORCHIS MUSC (F);
EINKNOLLE (G).
It is easy to overlook this species because the combination of green colouring and small stature makes it difficult to see in grassland.

Plants grow from 7–25cm tall and carry 2–3 lanceolate or oblong leaves low on the stem and bract-like leaves higher up the stem. At the time flowers appear there is only a single tuber in evidence, but others are formed, later, on the ends of slender stolons.

The spike is usually lax, with numerous small green flowers in a more or less one-sided spike, and bracts that are shorter than the ovary.

The ovate-lanceolate sepals are 2.5–3mm long while the oblong-lanceolate petals are slightly longer at 3.5mm, with shallow lobing near the base. Both sets of perianth segments converge slightly to form a rather loose, tapering hood.

The lip is 3-lobed, with the lateral lobes projecting forwards almost at right angles to the rest of the lip. The middle lobe is the longest, having an overall length of 3.5–4mm.

There is no spur, and the flowers have a distinct sweet smell of honey.

Flowers: June to August, depending on altitude.

Habitat: ideal growth conditions are found in moist grasslands and grassy banks on chalk and limestone. In mountainous areas plants can be found in damp meadows up to 2000m above sea level.

Distribution: widespread and occurring in large numbers in some areas, but it is fast decreasing and is now decidedly uncommon: Spain; France; UK (England); Scandinavia; Germany; Benelux countries; Austria and Switzerland; Italy (Alps and Appennines); Yugoslavia; Turkey; Poland; Czechoslovakia; Hungary; Bulgaria; Rumania; Russia; Caucasus and then east to central Asia and Japan.   **53, 54**

Platanthera

Only two of about 80 species in this genus occur with any frequency in the area covered in the text. The largest numbers of species are found in Asia and America, with a mere half-dozen in Europe and the lands bordering the Mediterranean.

Platanthera chlorantha and *P. bifolia* are the best-known of the European species, and both have highly scented flowers which are pollinated by the larger night-flying moths. Nectar is stored in a long spur and is only accessible to insects with long probosces. The scent produced by the flowers is particularly noticeable in the evening and this attracts the moths: they are helped, too, by the white colouring which makes the flower spikes conspicuous, even in low light levels. In their efforts to reach the nectar the moths dislodge the pollinia, and these, stuck to the insect's head region, are carried away to the next flower. The members of the genus are characterised by: possession of two tubers, ovoid or cigar-shaped, usually tapering at the end; few leaves, with the two largest oval in shape near the stem base – the upper ones are not well-developed and are more like bracts sheathing the stem; white or green flowers in a moderately dense spike; lateral sepals which spread but point slightly downwards; the dorsal sepal and petals incurve to form a helmet; the lip is long and strap-like; the spur is more or less cylindrical; there is a single, flat stigma and an inconspicuous rostellum.

Hybrids
Interspecific
P. bifolia x *P. chlorantha* = *Platanthera* x *hybrida* Bruegg

Intergeneric
P. bifolia x *Anacamptis pyramidalis* = x *Anacamptiplatanthera payotii* Fournier
P. bifolia x *Dactylorhiza sambucina* = x *Rhizanthera fournieri* (Royer) Soó
P. bifolia x *Gymnadenia conopsea* = *Gymnaplatanthera chodati* (Lendn) Lamb
P. chlorantha x *Coeloglossum viride* = x *Coeloplatanthera brueggeri* Ciff. & Giac.
P. chlorantha x *Gymnadenia odoratissima* = x *Gymnaplatanthera borelii* Lamb
P. chlorantha x *Orchis pallens* = x *Orchiplatanthera andreasii* Kümpel.

Platanthera chlorantha (Custer) Reichenb.
GREATER BUTTERFLY ORCHID; ORCHIS VERDÂTRE (F); GRÜNLICH WALDHYAZINTHE (G).

Often forming robust spikes where it grows at woodland edges, this species ranges from 25–50cm in height, with two large oval leaves near the base of the stem. The leaves are, in fact, sub-opposite; that is, they are situated on opposite sides of the stem, with one just below the other. Higher up on the stem the leaves become more like bracts in sheath form. The spikes varies from lax to fairly dense-flowered, and the flower bracts are about as long as the ovary.

The outer sepals are white, often with a green tinge, and spread widely. The petals and median sepal are similarly coloured and form a hood. The anther lobes are easily seen and taper so that their bases are further apart than their tips. This is a useful distinguishing feature from the similar *P. bifolia*, where the anther lobes are closer together and parallel. Again, one can distinguish *P. chlorantha* from *P. bifolia* in the following ways: it has larger flowers, usually more green than those of *P. bifolia*; its spur is 18–27mm long, compared with 25–30mm for *P. bifolia*; and the end of the spur is often slightly swollen at the apex, whereas *P. bifolia* has a spur with the sides more or less parallel. The flowers are fragrant.

Flowers: May to August, usually a few weeks earlier than *P. bifolia*.
Habitat: usually on calcareous soils at woodland edges, thickets or in dry grassland and scrub, up to 2000m in Alpine regions. On the whole it has more of a preference for calcareous soils and shady places than *P. bifolia*.
Distribution: widely distributed throughout Europe, this plant is locally frequent on suitable soils: north Africa; Spain; Balearics (?); France; Ireland; UK; Scandinavia (up to lat. 63°); Ger-

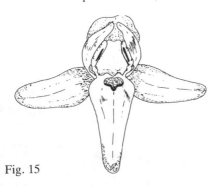

Fig. 15

many; Benelux; Switzerland and Austria; Italy; Corsica; Sardinia; Yugoslavia; northern Greece; Cyprus (rather rare, compared with ssp. *holmboei*); Turkey; Poland; Czechoslovakia; Hungary; Bulgaria; Rumania; Russia; Crimea; Caucasus. **57, 58**

Ssp. *holmboei* Lindb. fil.

Plants of this form are usually shorter and less robust than the nominate race, with a height from 15–30cm. The stems have a square cross-section and are slightly flexuous. Flower bracts are about as long as the ovary.

The flowers themselves are small and completely green, with anther cells that converge towards their free ends. The lateral sepals are narrow, with a slight twist towards their tips, while the dorsal sepal forms a helmet with the petals. The lip is narrow, downward pointing (sometimes slightly deflexed) with a whitish area around the mouth of the spur. In all plants examined by the authors the spur is long (up to 3cm), parallel, and lacks the slightly swollen tip found in plants of the nominate *P. chlorantha*.

Some workers have granted the plants specific status but it seems to us to be a montane form of *P. chlorantha*. In Cyprus it grows in quite large colonies on the Troödos massif, well above the winter snow line, while plants of the nominate race occur in lower valleys in the same area. All forms of *P. chlorantha* growing in Cyprus have green flowers, and it seems to us that differences in the montane forms are just those that allow it to survive winter snows and summer baking. We feel the distinct distribution of this plant merits subspecific status but no more. Plants from the north African mountains, often called *P. algeriensis*, are very similar to ssp. *holmboei* and perhaps they should be considered together as a single subspecies.

Flowers: the two basal leaves appear in late April-early May, with flowers at the end of the latter month. In years when snow persists on the mountains flowers can still be found in early July.

Habitat: open pine forests on soils formed from igneous rocks, from 1300 to 1800m.

Distribution: best known from the upper parts of the Troodos massif in Cyprus wherever there are woods of *Pinus nigra* ssp. *pallasiana*. Formerly thought to be endemic, it has also been recorded from Turkey and is supposed to grow in northern Syria. **59**

Platanthera algeriensis Batt. & Trabut
ALGERIAN BUTTERFLY ORCHID;
ALGERISCHE WALDHYAZINTHE (G).

This robust species ranges from 40–80cm in height. It is closely related to *P. chlorantha* but has much larger basal leaves and smaller flowers. The anther lobes are much closer together at their free ends than at their bases, giving them the appearance of converging more sharply than is the case with *P. chlorantha*.

It bears such a close resemblance to *P. chlorantha* ssp. *holmboei* that to us it seems they should be grouped together.

Flowers: July to August.

Habitat: mountain woodland, 1400–1600m.

Distribution: Algeria and Morocco. **60**

Platanthera bifolia (L.) L. C. M. Richard
LESSER BUTTERFLY ORCHID; ORCHIS
À DEUX FEUILLES (F);
ZWEIBLÄTTRIGE WALDHYAZINTHE
(G).

This plant is similar in stature and overall appearance to the closely related *P. chlorantha*. It has two foliage leaves

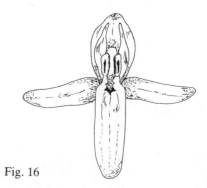

Fig. 16

near the stem base, with bract-like leaves sheathing the stem higher up. The flower spike tends to be denser than in *P. chlorantha*, forming a closer packed 'cylinder' of flowers. The flower bracts have approximately the same length as the ovary.

The lateral sepals spread widely, and a hood is formed from the median sepal and the petals. In colour the flowers are white, usually with less of a greenish tinge than that commonly found in *P. chlorantha*. The flowers are generally smaller than those of *P. chlorantha*, too, with lateral sepals 8–10mm long and the lip 8–12mm long. The spur is long, slender and almost horizontal, with less variation in length than in *P. chlorantha* (25–30mm). The anther cells are parallel and close together. The flowers are fragrant.

Flowers: late May to early August, depending on altitude.

Habitat: It is usually found in more open places than *P. chlorantha*, either on acid or calcareous soils, in open woodland, heath, moorland and on edges of thickets.

Distribution: North Africa; Spain; Balearics; France; Ireland; UK; Scandinavia; Germany; Belgium; Austria & Switzerland; Italy; Corsica; Sardinia; Sicily; Yugoslavia; Greece; N. Turkey; Poland; Czechoslovakia; Hungary; Bulgaria; Rumania; Russia; Caucasus.

55, 56

Platanthera hyperborea (L.) Lindley
NORTHERN BUTTERFLY ORCHID; ISLÄNDISCHE WALDHYAZINTHE (G).

Plants of this species grow from 6–35cm tall, with 4–7 leaves distributed evenly on the stem. The lowest leaf is short, broad and resembles a 'trumpet' from which the rest of the plant emerges.

Fig. 17

The remaining leaves are broadly lanceolate, becoming smaller and narrower higher up the stem, where they are finally indistinguishable from the flower bracts. The flower spike is lax, with yellowish-green flowers and bracts that are longer than the ovary. The perianth segments are 3–4mm long, with the lateral sepals spreading and a hood formed from the petals and the dorsal sepal. The lip is 3–7mm long, broadly lanceolate in shape, and held anywhere between the horzontal and vertical position. The spur is shorter than the ovary, being some 3.5–4.5mm in length, and curves downwards and forwards. The flowers are fragrant.

Flowers: throughout June and July.

Habitat: grows in a variety of surrounds in open country: dryas heath, moorland, moist tundra.

Distribution: Within the area covered in the text it occurs only in Iceland, where it is widely distributed in the northern part of the island. It also occurs in Greenland, eastern Asia and north America.

Platanthera obtusata (Pursh) Lindley
ONE-LEAVED BUTTERFLY ORCHID; WENIGBLÜTIGE WILDHYAZINTHE (G).

The subspecies *oligantha* Turcz. is the only form of the plant occurring in Europe. It is an inconspicuous orchid, which can range from 6–20cm in height, but is often no more than 10cm tall. There is a single, broadly elliptical foliage leaf near the base of the stem, and another narrow, upright leaf just below the flowers. From 3–6 blooms are carried in a lax spike, and the bracts are about as long as the ovary. The perianth segments are 2–3mm long, with a lip that is 3–3.5mm in length and is shaped like a narrow tongue. The flower colour is whitish-yellow, with some green markings, and the lip is held horizontally or is deflexed. The spur varies from about ½ to equal the ovary length, and the flowers are unscented. W. T. Stoutamire (1968, *Misc. Bot.*) suggested that mosquitoes were responsible for pollinating the flowers.

Flowers: July to August.
Habitat: birch and conifer forest or calcareous heaths, accompanied by *Pinguicula alpina* and various dwarf *Salix* species. Its diminutive stature and sporadic flowering make it very easily overlooked.
Distribution: The nominate *P. obtusata* occurs widely in north America and some parts of northern Asia, but the ssp. *oligantha* is very rare, with a restricted

Fig. 18

distribution. The latter occurs in northern Sweden (Abisko National Park, Mt. Nuolja and Torne marshes); northern Norway. Forms intermediate between the two races occur in Alaska.

Platanthera micrantha (Hochst.) Schlechter.
AZORES BUTTERFLY ORCHID;
AZOREN-WALDHYAZINTHE (G).

This rather slender species grows 20 –50cm high, with two large, broadly

Fig. 19

elliptical leaves near the base of the stem. The remaining leaves are much smaller and sheath the stem until they eventually merge with the bracts. The flower spike is quite dense, with numerous flowers held in an inflorescence 8–13cm in length. The flowers are pale green, with small perianth segments (2 –4mm in length) and a lip which is oblong, 2–4mm in length and held almost horizontal. The spur is variable in length, ranging from ⅓–⅘ the length of the ovary. This makes it 2–3.5mm in most plants, but occasional specimens are found with a 5–8mm spur. The latter forms are attributed to *P. azorica* (see below).

Platanthera azorica Schlechter
The validity of this plant as a species in its own right is rather dubious. It differs from *P. micrantha* in its longer, broader leaves, longer perianth segments and lip, and in a much longer spur (7–8mm), which is almost as long as the ovary.

The characteristics mentioned above are by no means constant and, since the plants have no clear ecological or geographical separation, there is little justification for allotting it more than varietal status.
Flowers: June to July.
Habitat: mountain grassland in sphagnum moss, amongst *Erica* bushes, on acid soil.
Distribution: endemic to the Azores.

Neottianthe

There is a single species in this genus, and the name *Neottianthe* suggests that its flowers resemble *Neottia*. Whereas this is perhaps true with some members of the genus *Neottia* there is no possibility of confusing *Neottianthe cucullata* with the European *Neottia nidus-avis*. To start with, the colours are completely different: *N. nidus avis* is a brownish saprophyte, whilst *N. cucullata* has pink flowers and green leaves.

The genus *Neottianthe* has the following characteristics: two globular tubers; two elliptical leaves low on the stem, with one or two small lanceolate leaves above; a lax inflorescence; lanceolate sepals, united with the petals to form a hood; a slender conical spur which is strongly curved and about 5mm in length; a deeply 3-lobed lip which is densely papillose; viscidia close together above the stigma and no bursicles.

Neottianthe cucullata (L.) Schlechter
PINK FROG ORCHID; GYMNADENIA À CAPUCHON (F); KAPUZENORCHIS (G).

This rather slender species grows from 10–30cm tall and has a pair of elliptical basal leaves, with one or two small bract-like leaves higher up the stem.

Fig. 20

From 6–20 flowers are carried in a lax spike which is more or less one-sided,

with bracts equalling the ovary in length. The lilac-pink sepals and petals are united to form a pointed hood or cowl. White-flowered forms are known but they are rare.

The lip is 7–9mm long and points forwards slightly from the vertical. It is deeply 3-lobed, with the median lobe longer than the laterals and a light, whitish area with pink or reddish-purple spots near the base.

The spur is slender, with a slight swelling at its apex, a length of about 5mm, and it points downwards and forwards.
Flowers: July and August.
Habitat: in damp mossy places in coniferous and mixed forests, occasionally in mountain meadows.
Distribution: a local and uncommon orchid within the area covered in this book, where it is restricted to eastern Europe, which represents the western limits of the range: north-east Germany; northern Poland; Russia, east to Siberia, China and Japan. **61**

Chamorchis

The name *Chamorchis* is derived from *kamai* (on the ground) and is certainly an apt description of this plant, because it has a small stature and is extremely difficult to see. In some books the name *Chamaeorchis* is used instead of the contracted *Chamorchis*.

Although unscented, the flowers are visited by a variety of small alpine insects which serve as pollinators.

After fertilization, the closed withered flowers persist for some time at the ends of the seed pods.

The genus characteristics are: two ellipsoidal tubers; all leaves basal and grass-like; perianth segments converging to form a hood, with the sepals equal in length but longer than the petals; a lip which is entire or shallowly 3-lobed and slightly longer than the other perianth segments; no spur; an inconspicuous rostellum, with distinct viscidia and a simple bursicle.

Hybrids

A single hybrid with *Gymnadenia* has been recorded:
C. *alpina* x G. *odoratissima* (?) = x *Chamodenia heteroglossa* (Reichenb. fil.) Peitz

Chamorchis alpina (L.) L. C. M.
Richard
ORCHIS DES ALPES (F);
ZWERGORCHIS (G); TESTICOLO
GRAMIGNOLE (I).

This tiny orchid is probably easier to overlook than any other European species, a factor which contributes to its reputation as a rather rare orchid.

Plants grow from 6–12cm tall, with 4–8 narrow, grass-like leaves rising from the base of the stem.

There are 3–10 flowers held in a short, rather lax spike with slender bracts that exceed the flowers in length.

The perianth segments curve inwards to form a hood, with the sepals broadly oblong in shape, with a length of around 3.5mm. The petals are narrower and just slightly shorter. In colour sepals and petals are greenish-yellow, tinged with purplish-brown.

The lip varies in shape from entire to 3-lobed, although in the latter case the side lobes are tiny. It has a length of approximately 4mm and is yellowish-green in colour.

Flowers: July to August.

Habitat: damp mountain pastures on limestone where its grass-like leaves and diminutive stature conceal it in colonies of *Dryas octopetala*. It occurs from 1500 –2700m above sea level in the Alps and at much lower altitudes in Scandinavia.

Distribution: Scandinavia (especially in Lapland where it occurs at low altitudes in exposed heathland); Germany (only in the Alps); Switzerland; Austria; northen Italy (Alps); Yugoslavia (High Tatras); Rumania; Russia.

An unusual (1976) record exists for the New Forest in Hampshire and is the only sighting in the UK.   **62**

Fig. 21

Gymnadenia

Only two species of *Gymnadenia* occur in Europe, though at one time *Pseudorchis albida* and *P. frivaldii* were also included in the genus.

Superficially there is a resemblance to *Orchis* and, like them, *Gymnadenia* are orchids of the northern hemisphere. Close examination reveals a number of differences between the genera: in *Gymnadenia* the lip is 3-lobed and the spur is long and slender; the viscidia at the base of the pollinia have no bursicle to cover them. This latter fact is referred to directly by the name *Gymnadenia* which is derived from *gymnos* (exposed) and *aden* (gland).

The general characteristics shared by the genus members are: tubers palmately lobed for about half their length; a leafy stem; flowers in a spike; lateral sepals spreading or curved downwards; dorsal sepal and petals converging to form a helmet; lip downward pointing and shallowly 3-lobed; spur long and slender; column short and erect with a long rostellum; viscidia two in number, long and linear, without bursicles.

The plants are fragrant and attractive to moths and butterflies which have long probosces and can reach the nectar stored in the spur. Insect visitors come into contact with the narrow exposed viscidia and these stick to the insect's proboscis. On the way out of the flower the insect removes the pollinia, which start off in an upright position but swivel to point forwards so that they strike the stigma of the next flower visited.

In the Alps, where the two European species can be found growing together, there is evidence to suggest that the light-coloured *G. odoratissima* is more easily visible to nocturnal moths which are the main pollinators, whereas *G. conopsea* is pollinated by both butterflies and moths. Bees have a harder task to reach the nectar, but they do visit the flowers and are often caught by the crab spiders that lurk in them. These insects also visit short-spurred orchid species, and hybrids can sometimes be formed as a result.

Hybrids
G. conopsea x *G. odoratissima* = *G.* x *intermedia* Peterm.

Intergeneric hybrids
G. conopsea x *Anacamptis pyramidalis* = x *Gymnanacamptis anacamptis* (Wilms) A. & Gr.
G. conopsea x *Coeloglossum viride* = x *Gymnaglossum jacksonii* Druce
G. conopsea x *Dactylorhiza incarnata* = x *Dactylodenia vollmannii* Schulze
G. conopsea x *Dactylorhiza maculata* = x *Dactylodenia legrandiana* Camus
G. conopsea x *Dactylorhiza majalis* = x *Dactylodenia lebrunii* Camus
G. conopsea x *Dactylorhiza sambucina* = x *Dactylodenia zollikoferi* Stoj.
G. conopsea x *Orchis laxiflora* = x *Orchigymnadenia burdigalensis* Keller & Jean
G. conopsea x *Orchis morio* = x *Orchigymnadenia reserata* Pau Sofio
G. conopsea x *Platanthera bifolia* = x *Gymnaplatanthera chodati* Lendn
G. conopsea x *Pseudorchis albida* = x *Pseudadenia schweinfurtii* Hegelmann
G. conopsea x *Traunsteinera globosa* = x *Gymnotraunsteinera vallesiaca* Spiess
G. odoratissima x *Anacamptis pyramidalis* = x *Gymnanacamptis odoratissima* Wildhaber
G. odoratissima x *Chamorchis alpina* = x *Chamodenia heteroglossa* Reichenb.
G. odoratissima x *Dactylorhiza maculata* = x *Dactylodenia regeliana* Godfery
G. odoratissima x *Platanthera chlorantha* = x *Gymnaplatanthera borelii* Lamb
G. odoratissima x *Pseudorchis albida* = x *Psuedadenia strampfii* Asch.

Gymnadenia conopsea (L.) R. Br.
FRAGRANT ORCHID; ORCHIS MOUSTIQUE (F); MÜCKEN HANDELWURZ (G); ORCHIDE GAROFANATA (I).

This is one of the best known orchid species in Europe. It varies in height from 15–45cm and has 2–3 brownish basal sheaths with 4–8 unspotted, linear-lanceolate leaves above them. The up-per leaves are small and bract-like, and all the leaves are keeled.

There are numerous flowers (nearly 200 in particularly robust plants) arranged in a dense spike which can be pyramidal at first but then lengthens into a cylinder from 6–16cm in length. The flower bracts are at least as long as the ovaries.

The lateral sepals spread out horizon-

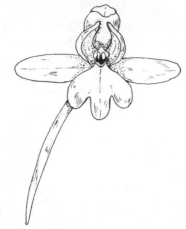

Fig. 22

tally, whilst the dorsal sepals and petals are incurved to form a hood. The lip has three lobes, all of which have approximately the same length and are downward pointing with rounded tips. The flowers are usually pink or reddish-lilac in colour, but white or even purple spikes can be found.

The spur is long and slender, being up to twice the length of the ovary, and it projects downwards.

There is a strong fragrance, usually with a hint of carnations, but there is a lot of evidence to suggest that populations of various forms exist with quite different scents. The problem with substantiating this lies in the fact that scent is subjective and almost impossible to quantify.

Varieties: Var. *borealis* P. F. Hunt
This name is proposed for a form of the plant with clove-scented flowers which are dark pink in colour. The lobes of the lip are less distinctly divided than in flowers of the nominate race and the lip is smaller. It occurs mainly in north England and in Scotland, although plants agreeing with this description are found in southern England where they flower later than the usual form. Unlike the nominate race, it sometimes grows on acidic soils.

Var. *densiflora* (Wahlenb.) Lindley
These are plants with particularly robust

growth found in wet areas throughout the entire range of the species. They have a marked clove scent, with flowers packed into a dense spike. The plants can be as much as 80cm tall.   **65, 66**

Var. *insulicola* H.-Harr.
This form is found in the Outer Hebrides. The plants are small, with dull reddish-purple flowers and a rather unpleasant scent which has been described as 'rubber-like'.

Var. *leucantha* Schur
This is a form with white flowers.

Flowers: May to August depending on altitude and latitude.

Habitat: it occurs in a variety of surroundings, from grassland on calcareous soils to high mountain pastures, moorland and open woods up to 2500m.

Distribution: Spain; France; Britain; Scandinavia; Germany; Benelux countries; Switzerland; Austria; Italy; Sicily; Yugoslavia; Greece; Turkey (Pontus); Poland; Czechoslovakia; Hungary; Bulgaria; Rumania; Russia; Crimea and the Caucasus, then east to Iran and into Siberia, north China and Japan.   **63, 64**

In a paper in *Feddes Repert* (1967) J. Bisse suggested there were three distinct subspecies growing in Germany. Leaf dimensions and placing, density of flowering spike, size, scent and spur width were the features dealt with in the analysis and used as criteria for the separation. In volume V of *Flora Europaea* it suggests that further work is needed to find out whether these characteristics are valid over the range of the species.

Gymnadenia odoratissima (L.) L. C. M. Richard
SHORT-SPURRED FRAGRANT ORCHID; GYMNADENIA ODORANT (F); WOHLREICHENDE HANDWURZ (G).

This species is superficially similar to *G. conopsea* but is generally a smaller plant. It grows from 15–30cm tall, with 4–6 linear-lanceolate leaves which possess a keel but no spots.

The inflorescence is dense and many-flowered but appears more lax than *G.*

conopsea because of the shorter spurs on the flowers. The bracts are as long as the ovaries.

Fig. 23

Overall flower shape is similar to *G. conopsea* but the dimensions are smaller: *G. odoratissima* has perianth segments which are 2.5–3mm in length, whilst those in *G. conopsea* are 4–5mm long. The lateral lobes of the lip are much smaller than the middle lobe, and the spur is 4–5mm long, whereas in *G. conopsea* it is 11–18mm.

The flowers are paler in colour than those of *G. conopsea*, with a range from pale pink to white. The specific name *odoratissima* infers that the scent is particularly strong. This is certainly true, for one can sometimes locate the plant by smell alone, though its scent is reputed to be stronger than that of *G. conopsea* only during the daytime.

Varities: Var. *alba* Zimmerman is a form with white flowers.

Flowers: from the end of May to August (on high ground).

Habitat: it is restricted to mountainous regions where it occurs in fairly dry grasslands, marshes, mountain pastures, open conifer woods usually on calcareous soils but also in bogs and places where water stands in spring or winter.

Distribution: widespread over the mountainous regions of Europe, often growing with *G. conopsea*; northern Spain; France; southern Sweden; Germany; Switzerland; Austria; northern Italy; Yugoslavia; Turkey (?); south-west Poland; Czechoslovakia; Rumania; Russia (here it occurs in pine forests but is rapidly decreasing). There is one record of this plant from the UK on oolitic limestone near Durham. This dates from the last century and the plant has not been seen since. **67, 68**

Pseudorchis

The two European members of this genus have had a chequered taxonomic history, having been incorporated at various times with *Habenaria*, *Gymnadenia* and even *Orchis*. The name means 'false orchis', and in older literature one often finds the name *Leucorchis* E. H. F. Meyer for the same genus.

The plants are closely related to *Gymnadenia* and share many of the same features. They differ in having a shorter spur, sand perianth segments that more or less converge to form a helmet.

Pollination is similar to that in *Gymnadenia* and *Coeloglossum*, with moths, butterflies and other insects attracted by the scent of the flowers.

In older flowers self-pollination occurs when pollinia fall on to the stigma.

Hybrids
P. albida x *Dactylorhiza maculata* = x *Pseudorhiza bruniana* Bruegg.
P. albida x *Dactylorhiza sambucina* = x *Pseudorhiza albucina* Ciff. & Giac.
P. albida x *Gymnadenia conopsea* = x *Pseudadenia schweinfurtii* Hegel.
P. albida x *Gymnadenia odoratissima* = x *Pseudadenia strampfii* Asch.
P. albida x *Herminium monorchis* = x *Pseudinium aschersonianum* Bruegg.

P. albida x *Nigritella nigra* = x *Pseudadenia micrantha* Kern
P. frivaldii x *Nigritella nigra* = x *Pseudadenia borisii* Stoj. & Steff.

Pseudorchis albida (L.) A. & D. Löve
SMALL-WHITE ORCHID; ORCHIS
BLANC (F); WEISSZÜNGEL (G).

This rather slender species grows from 12–35cm tall, with 3–5 broadly lanceolate leaves and 2–3 membraneous scales which sheath the stem base. There are two tubers, each of which is divided almost as far as its base and has pointed ends which act as roots.

The spike is dense, with numerous flowers occupying a length of 3–7cm, and bracts that exceed the ovary in length.

Fig. 24

The flowers are small, rarely more than 2–3mm in diameter, with a uniform dingy greenish or yellowish-white colour. The sepals and petals are incurved to form a hood, although in some plants the lateral sepals spread slightly.

The lip is 3-lobed, with the lateral lobes shorter and narrower than the central lobe.

The spur is ⅓ to ½ as long as the ovary, with its apex thickened slightly, and a downward curve.

Flowers: May to August.
Habitat: pastures, grassy heaths and mountains up to 2500m.
Distribution: a rather local orchid with a fairly wide distribution in Europe: northern Spain; France; Iceland; British Isles (Ireland, north Wales, Scotland and northern England, with a few records from the south); Scandinavia; Germany; Benelux countries (except Holland); Austria; Italy; Switzerland; Corsica; Yugoslavia; Greece (?); Poland; Hungary; Bulgaria; Czechoslovakia; Rumania and Russia. **69, 70**

Ssp. *straminea* (Fernald) A. & D. Löve.
This form is restricted to northern latitudes and has leaves that are more or less patent, with an oblong ovate shape. The flower spike is often shorter and less dense than in the nominate race. The flower bracts exceed the ovary in length and in some cases have crinkled margins. The lateral sepals have a diameter exceeding 3mm (in the nominate race it is less).

Distribution: mountains of northeastern Europe and southern Norway.

Pseudorchis frivaldii (Hampe ex Griseb.) P. F. Hunt
FRIVALD'S FROG ORCHID; BALKAN
WEIßZÜNGEL (G).

In this species the two tubers are divided for just half their length. The stem is 14–30cm tall and carries 3–4 leaves which are narrower than those of *P. albida*. The upper leaves are narrow, pointed and bract-like.

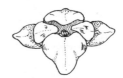

Fig. 25

The flower spike is shorter than in *P. albida* and the flowers are slightly larger (around 5mm in diameter). The bracts are about as long as the ovary and have a single vein.

The lip is barely 3-lobed, and the overall colour is usually pure white but can be a pale pink.

The spur is small and slender, being only 1.5mm long.

Flowers: June to August.
Habitat: damp pastures and mountain seepages between 1500 and 2500m.
Distribution: this rather local orchid is restricted to the mountainous parts of the Balkans: Rumania; Bulgaria; Albania and southern Yugoslavia. **71**

Nigritella

The single orchid in this genus is one of the best known and best loved flowers in the Alps. It is certainly not a large orchid, but its dark, almost black-red flowers and strong vanilla scent make it easily noticed.

There are probably more local names for this orchid than for any other, from the Scandinavian 'brown woman' to the German 'Brunelle', 'Kohlröschen' or Italian 'Christi fragantissima'. The Latin names both come from *niger*, black.

The numerous butterflies in the Alpine pastures where these orchids flourish are the usual pollinators.

The characteristics of this genus are: 2 oval tubers divided into fingers at their ends; numerous narrow leaves at the base of the stem; a dense inflorescence; spreading sepals with a triangular lance-like shape; a small blunt spur; a small rostellum and an ovary which is not twisted.

Hybrids
A number of intergeneric hybrids are known with orchids that grow in the same alpine meadows as *N. nigra*:
N. nigra x *Dactylorhiza maculata* = x *Nigorchis tourensis* Godfery or x *Dactylodenia tourensis* Godfery
N. nigra x *Gymnadenia conopsea* = x *Gymnigritella suaveolens* Wettstein
N. nigra x *Gymnadenia odoratissima* = x *Gymnigritella heufleri* Wettstein
N. nigra x *Pseudorchis albida* = x *Pseudadenia micrantha* Kern
N. nigra x *Pseudorchis frivaldii* = x *Pseudadenia borisii* Stoj. et Steff.

Nigritella nigra (L.) Reichenb.
VANILLA ORCHID; NIGRITELLE NOIRE (F); SCHWARZES KOHLRÖSCHEN (G); CHRISTI FRAGANTISSIMA (I).

This species reaches 8–25cm and has numerous slender, channelled leaves, mainly growing from the base of the stem. The stem is ridged, so that it has a triangular or polygonal section.

The spike is dense-flowered with a conical shape when flowers first open, becoming ovoid as it elongates.

The lance-shaped sepals spread wide-ly, while the lip points upwards since the ovary in this species is not twisted. The lip is entire or indistinctly 3-lobed. The flowers are usually blackish-crimson but can exist in a variety of colour forms as the list below shows.

The spur is short and blunt; the flowers are strongly scented with vanilla, and the rostellum is small.

Varieties: A number of colour forms are known and most at one time or another have been classed as varieties:
Var. *alba* Harz has pure white flowers;
Var. *flava* Jaccard, a form with pale creamy yellow flowers;
Var. *fulva* Keller, a plant with reddish-yellow flowers;
Var. *pallida* Keller has white flowers, with the points of the perianth segments tinged reddish (it seems to be the form now called ssp. *corneliana*);
Var. *rosea* (Visiani) Wettstein has pink flowers;

Fig. 26

Var. *sulphurea* Keller has sulphur yellow flowers;

Var. *ustulata* Keller, the flowers are whitish, with brown tips to the perianth segments.

Flowers: June to August.

Habitat: high mountain pastures, where it often occurs in large numbers provided the ground is not heavily grazed, woodland edges from 1000–2800m. Although primarily an alpine orchid it occurs at low altitudes in Scandinavia.

Distribution: Scandinavia (where it has recently been the subject of a strong conservation campaign); France (Massif Central, Jura Alps); Italy (Alps, Apennines); Austria; Switzerland; Germany (Alps); Carpathians and Balkan mountains.   **72, 75**

Ssp. **rubra** (Wettstein) Beauverd
ROTES KOHLRÖSCHEN (G).

Many consider this to be a species in its own right – *N. miniata* (Crantz) Janchen. It differs from the nominate race in having fewer basal leaves, a more or less cylindrical spike and red flowers.

Fig. 27

The petals carry 2 veins whereas there are often 3 in the nominate race.

Flowers: from late May onwards, usually slightly earlier than the nominate plants.

Distribution: an uncommon and local form, found in the central and eastern Alps (especially the Dolomites); Rumanian mountains.   **76**

Ssp. **corneliana** Beauverd. This form has numerous basal leaves (12–18), a conical spike and white flowers tinged with pink or reddish. The petals possess a single vein.

Flowers: same time as the nominate race.

Distribution: south-west Alps.

Coeloglossum

The single European member of this genus has a very wide distribution in central and northern Europe.

The characteristics of genus members are: 2 ovoid tubers with palmate lobes; flowers in a lax spike; lateral sepals erect and spreading; the median sepal and petals connivent to form a helmet; lip with 3 teeth at the apex; spur very short; column short; rostellum 3-angled, with 2 lateral lobes; viscidia oblong and a rudimentary bursicle.

Small insects visit the flowers and come into contact with the sticky viscidia at the mouth of the spur. These fasten the pollinia onto the head region of the insect, where with their forward-pointing direction they are positioned to contact the stigma of the next flower.

Hybrids

C. viride x *Dactylorhiza incarnata* = x *Dactyloglossum guilhotii* Camus et Bergon

C. viride x *Dactylorhiza maculata* = x *Dactyloglossum dominianum* Camus et Bergon

C. viride x *Dactylorhiza majalis* = x *Dactyloglossum drucei* Camus

C. viride x *Dactylorhiza sambucina* = x *Dactyloglossum erdingeri* Kerner

C. viride x *Gymnadenia conopsea* = x *Gymnaglossum jacksonii* Druce
C. viride x *Platanthera chlorantha* = x *Coeloplatanthera brueggeri* Ciff. et Giac.

Coeloglossum viride (L.) Hartman
FROG ORCHID; ORCHIS GRENOUILLE (F); HOHLZUNGE (G); TESTICOLO DI VOLPE (I).

This well-known species can be difficult to find when the plants are small, because their colour scheme blends well with their grassland surroundings.

Plants range from 10–35cm in height, with 2–6 leaves that are broadly lanceolate, low on the stem but become narrower higher up.

5–25 flowers are held in a rather lax cylindrical spike, with ovaries twisted to various degrees so that the flowers appear irregularly arranged.

Fig. 28

The sepals and petals converge to form a well rounded hood and are green or yellowish-green, edged in reddish and suffused with a purplish shade.

The lip is 6–8mm long, with a strap-like shape and 3 lobes at its apex. The middle lobe is reduced to a small tooth and is shorter than the lateral lobes. The lip is usually yellow or yellowish-brown in colour.

Forms of this orchid from northern Europe are usually darker in colour than those in the southern part, and on high mountains the plants are often stunted, but have their stems and flowers tinged heavily with purple or brown.

Flowers: May to August.

Habitat: plants show a strong preference for calcareous soils but are not completely confined to them, growing in: grasslands; grassy banks; scrub and woodland margins. In southern Europe it is confined to mountains but in north, west and central Europe it occurs from sea level up to 2500m in the Alps.

Distribution: widespread and fairly frequent in places: Spain; France; Iceland; British Isles; Scandinavia; Germany; Benelux countries; Austria; Switzerland; Italy; Yugoslavia; Greece; Turkey; Poland; Czechoslovakia; Hungary; Bulgaria; Rumania; Crimea and the Caucasus.   **73, 74**

Dactylorhiza

Without doubt plants in this genus cause more problems of identification than any other European orchids. Not only are there close similarities between plants regarded as distinct species but there is also a lot of hybridisation. Indeed the hybrids are often more vigorous than their parents and show a high degree of fertility.

Botanists specialising in this genus can never agree on a suitable system of classification. It is often just a matter of personal opinion that one plant is accorded specific or subspecific status, and the criteria which support the decision seem to be changed with alarming frequency.

In recent years a lot of the research on this genus has been concentrated on understanding the chromosome structure. This is helping to put the classification on a rigorous experimental basis. Most schemes have had to rely on field work, and when hybrids are as frequent as the parents in a genus which is clearly still actively evolving it comes as no surprise that confusion reigns.

A classification scheme is offered in *Flora Europaea V*, and although it does not appeal to all botanists it seems to us to provide a logical basis for categorising these plants in a way helpful to the field worker.

Orchis and *Dactylorhiza* are obviously closely related because their appearance is so similar, and until comparatively recently they were both regarded as belonging to the same genus. The main difference between them is found in the shape of the tubers: *Orchis* tubers are globose and entire but those of *Dactylorhiza* are palmately lobed. The name *Dactylorhiza* means 'hand-rooted' and refers to the way the tubers are divided into fingers. This genus was originally referred to as *Dactylorchis*.

Whether a tuber is divided or entire, its main function is to store the food manufactured in the leaves. *Dactylorhiza* species are usually found where the ground is damp or marshy, and their tubers have a second purpose of absorbing water through the narrow parts of their ends.

Dactylorhiza plants are amongst the quickest of terrestrial orchids to develop mature flowering plants from seeds. They produce a first leaf in the second year, and their first true tuber in the third or fourth year.

In mature plants new tubers are produced in association with a lateral bud at the base of the current season's stem. Sometimes more than one bud develops and two or more new tubers are produced in the year. The following year two or more serial stems may be produced; these form their own tubers and, with the death of the parent plants, become completely separated. In the wild this process, carried on over a few years, allows clumps to form.

The pollination mechanism of *Dactylorhiza* is similar to that of *Orchis*, as one would expect, given the similarity of the flower structure. It is obviously an effective mechanism, judging by the number of fruiting stems found in a population of these orchids. Bees seem to be the main pollinating agents.

The general characteristics of the genus are: 2 (sometimes 3) tubers, each palmately divided into 2–5 lobes with an elongated apex; the perianth segments are free and equal in size (or with the inner smaller than the outer); a spur; a 3-lobed rostellum with a short central lobe and viscidia in one simple bursicle; lower bracts which are leaf-like – in *Orchis* they are thin and membraneous.

Hybrids

It was mentioned earlier that interspecific hybrids are often formed and that their fertility is high. In some populations the hybrids are more frequent and more vigorous than the parents. Some instances are known of more or less stabilised hybrid segregates, and it has been suggested that new 'species' have arisen from such groups. Forms of *D. incarnata*, *D. majalis* and *D. maculata* often grow together with confusing results because of the crossing and back-crossing that takes place. It is virtually impossible to distinguish the hybrids from the range of forms shown by the parents; one is just aware of a large number of plants each with slight differences from the next.

The following interspecific hybrids have been recorded:

D. iberica x *D. sulphurea* ssp. *pseudosambucina* Klinge
D. iberica x *D. cilicica* Klinge
D. iberica x *D. maculata* ssp. *lancibracteata* (?) Klinge
D. sambucina x *D. majalis* = *D.* x *ruppertii* (Schulze) Borsos et Soó
D. sambucina x *D. maculata* = *D.* x *altobracensis* (Coste) Soó
D. incarnata x *D. majalis* = *D.* x *aschersoniana* (Hauskn.) Borsos et Soó
D. incarnata x *D. maculata* = *D.* x *ambigua* (Kern)
D. majalis x *D. maculata* = *D.* x *braunii*

Numerous intergeneric hybrids have been recorded with: *Aceras*; *Anacamptis*; *Coeloglossum*; *Gymnadenia*; *Nigritella*; *Platanthera* and *Pseudorchis*. These are listed in the descriptions of each of the other genera. Because of their similarities a large number of the European species divide conveniently into two groups: *D. incarnata* group; *D. maculata* group. The remaining species *D. iberica*, *D. sambucina* and *D. sulphurea* are quite readily distinguished and do not present too many problems of identification.

In addition there are three species with a much more restricted distribution; *D. foliosa* occurs in Madeira, and *D. cataonica* and *D. cilicica* are Turkish species. To try and avoid unnecessary confusion these three are not included in the key given below but can be referred to directly in the species descriptions.

Key

1	All 5 perianth segments forming a hood; stem with stolons	*D. iberica*
	Lateral sepals not forming part of the hood; stolons absent	2
2	Tubers shallowly divided into 2–4 fingers	3
	Tubers deeply divided into 2–5 fingers	4
3	Stem with 4–5 leaves spaced along it in the lower part, spur shorter than 15mm	*D. sambucina*
	Stem with up to 10 leaves in a lax basal rosette	*D. sulphurea*
4	Lateral sepals sub-erect; stem usually hollow	*D. incarnata* group
	Lateral sepals spreading; stem usually solid	*D. maculata* group

Dactylorhiza iberica (Bieb.) Soó

This slender species is quite distinct in appearance from others in the genus. The stems grow from 25–50cm tall and carry 3–5 linear-lanceolate, unspotted leaves on their lower portion. There are stolons at the base of the stem which allow the plants to increase their numbers easily by forming new plants from buds. The highest leaves more or less sheath the stem, and the bracts are narrow but usually exceed the ovary in length.

The inflorescence is lax, with 6–10 flowers, and is unusual in having the hoods to the flowers formed from the lateral sepals as well as the dorsal sepal and petals. All the perianth segments are pink, and the sepals are 8–10mm long with 3 veins, whilst the petals are up to 8mm in length with a single vein.

The lip spreads towards its apex and is usually 3-lobed, with the middle lobe more slender than the laterals. It is pink like the other perianth segments, with the addition of purple or magenta spots which often merge together near the edge of the lip to give it a coloured margin.

The spur is narrow, cylindrical and curved. It is about half the length of the ovary with a whitish region near its base.

Flowers: May to August, depending on altitude.

Habitat: marshes, mountain seepages and shady stream banks, usually above 800m.

Distribution: an uncommon and local orchid in the area covered: northern Greece; Cyprus (rare); Turkey; Lebanon; Caucasus; Crimea, eastwards into Iran (where it occurs in large numbers in some mountain marshes, spreading readily by means of its stolons).   **77**

Dactylorhiza sambucina (L.) Soó
ELDER-FLOWER ORCHID;
HOLUNDER-KNABENKRAUT (G).

The tubers in this plant are often only slightly lobed. The stem grows from 10 –30cm in height, with 4–5 broadly lanceolate, unspotted leaves spaced out along its lower half.

The inflorescence is dense and many-flowered, with bracts that are longer than the ovary.

The dorsal sepal and the petals are incurved to form a hood, whilst the lateral sepals are only slightly incurved. The lip is shallowly 3-lobed, with all the lobes short.

Two distinct flower forms are found, sometimes growing together: one, with yellow flowers, has a fine brown speckling on the lip, which is less obvious in the uncommon magenta form. Bicoloured varieties are certainly rare but can be most attractive orchids.

The spur is up to 15mm long, about as long as the ovary, and is curved slightly to point downwards.

The flowers are hardly scented, so that the common name of 'Elder-flower Orchid' is a misnomer. The rather similar *Orchis pallens*, which exists in the same mountain habitats, is the plant with a strong elder (*Sambucus*) smell.

Flowers: late March to early July, depending on altitude.

Habitat: mountain meadows, scrub and open woods, often forming large colonies. It usually grows in mountainous regions from 500–2000m above sea level. In parts of Scandinavia it grows on low ground, often near the coast.

Distribution: northern Spain; France; Scandinavia (especially islands near Stockholm); Germany (very rare); Switzerland and Austria; Italy; Sicily (in high parts of the Madonie and Nebrodie); Yugoslavia; Greece; Turkey (?); Poland; Czechoslovakia; Hungary; Bulgaria; Rumania and Russia.   **78, 79, 80**

Ssp. *insularis* (Sommier) Soó. In this form the inflorescence is lax and the spur is shorter (8–10mm). The lip has 2–4 red-orange spots at its base.

It is restricted to parts of southern Spain, Corsica, Elba, Sardinia and possibly Sicily.   **81**

A striking form with a red inverted V at the base of the lip is sometimes distinguished as var. *bartonii* Huxley and Hunt. It was first linked to *D. romana* (now = *D. sulphurea* ssp. *pseudosambucina*) and later to *D. insularis* as it then was. The shape and attitude of the spur, and the arrangement of the leaves, seem to us to insist on this rare plant, found only in the Montes Universales in Spain, being a variety of *D. sambucina* ssp. *insularis*, not of *D. sulphurea*.   **82**

Dactylorhiza sulphurea (Link) Franco
The name *sulphurea* was resurrected with the publication of *Flora Europaea*, volume V. It had long been regarded as just another synonym for the well-known *D. romana* but in that work was used to describe a race of orchids retricted to western Spain and northern Portugal. When the rules of botanical nomenclature were applied strictly the

name *D. romana* was suppressed completely, and plants answering that description were called *D. sulphurea* ssp. *pseudosambucina*.

If common sense prevails, it seems to us that *D. romana* should be retained on two counts: first, these plants have by far the widest distribution; and secondly, the name is well-established.

D. sulphurea has flowering stems 15–35cm tall, with a basal rosette of up to 10 narrowly oblong unspotted leaves. It thus differs from *D. sambucina* which has its leaves spaced out along the lower stem.

The inflorescence is moderately dense with upwards of 7 flowers and bracts that exceed the ovary in length.

The lateral sepals are held more or less erect and tend to become broader near their bases. The dorsal sepal and petals incurve to form a hood, and the flower colour is yellow.

The lip is 3-lobed, with the middle lobe longer than the laterals; it has an oblong or rectangular shape.

The spur is cylindrical and shorter than the ovary, upturned to near-vertical.

Flowers: April to June.

Habitat: bushy or stony slopes in lower mountain pastures or maquis up to 1800m.

Distribution: north Portugal; western Spain.

Ssp. **pseudosambucina** (Ten.) Franco = *D. romana* (Seb. & Maur.) Soó. this form grows from 20–40cm tall and has 8–12 lanceolate unspotted leaves.

The inflorescence is lax, and the bracts are longer than the ovary. The flowers are similar to those of the nominate plants but have the central lobe of the lip shorter than the lateral lobes and a lip which is almost square in shape.

The spur is cylindrical and definitely longer than the ovary, with its end curved upwards. Just like *D. sambucina* it has two colour forms – yellow and magenta. Again the yellow form is more frequent than the other and, in some places, it is the only form found.

Flowers: March to June.

Habitat: stony slopes, maquis mountain woods: pine (Cyprus) or beech (Gargano peninsula, Italy).

Distribution: north Africa (?); Spain (?); Italy (frequent in mountain woodland on the Gargano peninsula); Sicily; Yugoslavia; Greece; Crete; Rhodes (?); Cyprus (only the yellow form occurs on the volcanic soils of the Troodos massif); Turkey; Bulgaria; Crimea. **83, 84, 85, 86**

Ssp. **siciliensis** (Klinge) Franco = *D. romana* ssp. *siciliensis*. This race closely resembles ssp. *pseudosambucina* but the spur is conical and generally shorter than the ovary. The flowers are yellow.

Distribution: southern Italy (Calabria); Sicily; Sardinia; south-west Spain; Morocco (?).

A race closely related to ssp. *siciliensis* grows in the Caucasus and Transcaucasia. Nelson lists it as *D. romana* ssp. *georgica* (Klinge) but remarks that it probably does not deserve subspecific status. Sundermann lists it as *D. sambucina* ssp. *georgica* (Klinge) and includes a white-flowered race as var. *candida* Rouy.

It is a race with small flowers and a broader rosette than the similar ssp. *siciliensis*. The spur points upwards, and although the yellow form is the usual one there are reports of a red-flowered form in eastern Turkey and Transcaucasia.

The distinct geographical distribution together with the slight differences in flower structure probably merit subspecific status.

The *Dactylorhiza incarnata* group

The species belonging to this group usually have hollow stems and lower bracts which equal or exceed the flowers in length and are lanceolate in shape. The lateral sepals are sub-erect, i.e. they are held more or less upwards, and the median sepal converges with the petals to form a helmet.

Key

1   Lower leaves, with a length no more than 4 times their width, are more or less elliptical in shape and widest at or below their middle **2**
Lower leaves, with a length more than 4 times their width, usually lanceolate in shape, gradually tapering from the base to the apex **4**

2   Stem not more than 20cm, sepals and lip only 6–7mm long *D. pseudocordigera*
Stem usually 20–60cm, sepals 6–12mm, lip 5–12mm **3**

3   Leaves 4–8 with the upper ones often reaching the base of the inflorescence *D. majalis*
Leaves 2–5, the upper ones seldom reaching the base of the inflorescence *D. cordigera*

4   Lip 5–7.5mm often with a deflexed margin, sepals 5–6mm *D. incarnata*
Lip 5.5–10mm, sepals 7–13mm **5**

5   Sepals 7–8mm (exceptionally 10mm) **6**
Sepals 8–13mm **7**

6   Flowers magenta-purple, lip with slightly deflexed margin, central lobe of lip noticeably longer than the laterals *D. traunsteineri*
Flowers pink, lip flat, with a triangular middle lobe, restricted to eastern Europe *D. russowii*

7   Stem not more than 30cm, leaves usually with dark spots *D. cordigera*
Stem 30–110cm leaves without dark spots *D. elata*

Dactylorhiza incarnata (L.) Soó
EARLY MARSH ORCHID; FLEISCHFAR-
BENES KNABENKRAUT (G).

Several distinct races of this species exist, and some of them are often considered to be worthy of specific status in their own right.

The nominate race has deeply divided tubers, forming 3–5 fingers which become more or less elongated at the apex.

The stem can be as tall as 70cm in particularly robust plants, with 4–5 leaves spaced along the stem. Leaf shape ranges from slender to broadly-lanceolate, without spots on the surfaces and with the apex of each often curved over to form a hood.

The inflorescence is packed densely, with numerous flowers arranged in a cylindrical shape and bracts that exceed the ovary in length.

The lateral sepals spread but are also slightly recurved. The lip tends to be small and is either entire or shallowly 3-lobed, with a small central 'tooth'. An important feature of all forms of this plant is the folded back edges of the lip. In large populations, where variously coloured forms of *D. majalis* and *D. incarnata* occur together, this can be a helpful distinguishing feature, though their hybrids can also possess it.

The spur points downwards, is not curved and is shorter than the ovary.

Flower colour varies from white through shades of pink to reddish purple.

Flowers: April to July.

Varieties: Var. *alba* is the name given to the pure white albino form, which is quite distinct from the yellowish ssp. *ochroleuca*.

Habitat: fens, bogs (where the drainage water is slightly alkaline or neutral), dune slacks (often in large numbers), damp grassland.

Distribution: widespread over much of Europe but decreasing due to land drainage. Rare in the Mediterranean area: northern Spain; France; Britian; Scandinavia; Germany; Benelux countries; Austria and Switzerland; northern Italy; Yugoslavia; Greece (?); northern Turkey; Poland; Czechoslovakia; Hungary; Bulgaria; Rumania; Russia; Crimea (?) and Caucasus (?).   **87, 88**

D. incarnata readily hybridises with other closely related species, and one often finds plants, or even whole populations, whose parentage is difficult to ascertain.

A number of distinct colour forms have been given varietal or subspecific status according to the views of the botanist dealing with them. Here they are listed as subspecies, but their status is by no means certain.

Ssp. *coccinea* (Pugsley) Soó. This race thrives best in dune slacks, where it seldom exceeds 30cm in height, although taller plants have been recorded from time to time.

The leaves are erect, hooded at the ends and usually unspotted. The striking feature of these plants is the deep crimson colour of the flowers. Another name *D. incarnata* var. *atrirubra* Godfery also refers to this race.

Habitat: dune slacks in neutral or alkaline conditions.

Distribution: UK and Ireland, with unconfirmed records from Holland.   **89**

Ssp. *pulchella* (Druce) Soó. Flowers of this form are purple, often with the addition of red streaks. The stems are up to 70cm in height with erect unspotted leaves.

Habitat: hillside bogs or boggy woodlands where the soil reaction is slightly acidic.

Distribution: UK and Ireland.   **90**

Ssp. *cruenta* (O. F. Mueller) P. D. Sell. This race is sometimes treated as a distinct species, *D. cruenta* O. F. Mueller, since it is the only form of *D. incarnata* which invariably has spotted leaves. Spotting does happen in some of the other forms but it is the exception rather than the rule.

The stems are 12–30cm tall with leaves that are not quite erect, have dark spots on both surfaces, and lack the hooded tip of some of the other forms.

The flowers are purplish-red or crimson, often with red streaks and the edges of the lip are not folded as much as in the nominate race.

Varieties: Var. *albiflora* Lec. & Lamotte is a form with pure white flowers.

Habitat: marshy place and hillside seepages often on high ground.

Distribution: France (Alps); north-west Ireland; Scandinavia; Denmark; north Germany (?); Switzerland (up to 1800m in the Alps); Austria (rare in the south Tyrol).   **91**

Ssp. *sphagnicola* (Höppner) Soó. This is a race of uncertain status, restricted to sphagnum bogs in Germany.

The tubers are deeply divided and the leaves are rather narrow and unspotted. The flowers are usually rose-pink but the occasional white flowered form has been noticed. The lip is often almost entire but can also occur with three distinct lobes and is spotted or streaked with red.

The spur is nearly as long as the ovary.

Habitat: sphagnum bogs.

Distribution: north Germany.

A number of races occur sporadically throughout all or part of the range of the nominate race. Possibly they are no more than varieties but in this genus, as with *Ophrys*, a cut-and-dried separation into subspecies and varieties using accepted definitions is just not possible. These plants are:

Ssp. haematodes (Reichenb. fil.) Soó. This form is very similar to the nominate race but has leaves spotted with brownish-purple.
Distribution: occurs sporadically in north and central Europe.

Ssp. ochroleuca (Boll) P. F. Hunt & Summerhayes. This form, also referred to as var. *straminea*, has yellowish-white flowers and is quite different from the albino form var. *albiflora*. The plants are rather tall and robust, with leaves that are broader nearer their bases than in other forms of the species. They are capable of forming quite large colonies on their own and tend to flower after the normal pink forms.
Habitat: fens.
Distribution: a very local and uncommon race, occuring here and there throughout the range of the species. In the UK it is restricted to fens in East Anglia where drainage of its sites has made it rare. **92**

Ssp. gemmana (Pugsley) Soó. Sometimes, particularly robust plants with a height in excess of 50cm and 6 or more leaves are given subspecific status as ssp. *gemmana*.
Distribution: west Ireland; east England (Norfolk).

Ssp. serotina (Hausskn.) Soó & D. Moresby Moore. The name above refers to small forms with 3–4 narrowly lanceolate leaves and few flowers. They are thought to be synonymous with a number of localised races such as: var. *borealis* Neuman; var. *dunensis* Druce; and var. *cambrica* Pugsley.
Distribution: west, north and north central Europe.

Dactylorhiza pseudocordigera (Neuman) Soó
This species seldom grows more than 20cm tall and is often no bigger than 10cm. 3–4 leaves are carried on the stem; the lower ones are elliptical and spreading, whilst the upper ones are more or less erect, and all are densely spotted with dark purple-brown.

The inflorescence carries comparatively few flowers in a fairly lax raceme. The petals, sepals and lip are all about 6–7mm in length and coloured purplish-red with some darker markings.

The spur is only about half as long as the ovary and has a conical shape.

This species is sometimes classed as a form of *D. traunsteineri* and is then referred to as ssp. *blyttii* (see p. 105).
Flowers: July and August.
Habitat: marshes and damp calcareous grassland.
Distribution: Norway and north Sweden.

Dactylorhiza majalis (Reichenb.) P. F. Hunt & Summerhayes
BROAD-LEAVED MARSH ORCHID; BREITBLÄTTRIGES KNABENKRAUT (G).

This is another member of the genus in which some of the races are so distinct that many botanists consider them as species in their own right.

Plants of the nominate race have a pair of tubers, divided at their ends into 2–5 elongated fingers. They often have robust stems which grow from 20–75cm in height and have a hollow interior. From 4–8 broadly lanceolate leaves are carried spaced out along the stem. They are broadly lanceolate in shape, with the upper ones reaching or exceeding the base of the inflorescence and the lower ones held more or less erect. The widest part of each leaf is near its centre, and the upper surface is spotted with purplish-brown.

The inflorescence is dense, with numerous flowers carried in a raceme which varies from ovoid to cylindrical in its overall shape. The bracts are noticeably longer than the ovary, often exceeding the flowers themselves.

The sepals range from 6–12mm in length, are spreading or slightly reflexed and have an ovate–oblong lanceolate shape.

The lip is rather variable in size and shape but is invariably wider than long with three shallow lobes. The lateral lobes are much broader than the middle lobe, which is often no more than a triangular tooth. Plants sometimes occur with entire lipped flowers. A wide range of flower colours is possible, from deep magenta to purplish-lilac, with darker spots and streaks on the lip, which also has a whitish area near its base.

The spur is about half as long as the ovary and points downwards. Sometimes the lip can be so broad that the flowers resemble those of *D. cordigera*, an orchid of the Balkan mountains. Records of *D. cordigera* from the Swiss, French and Austrian alps are almost certainly wide-lipped forms of the highly variable *D. majalis*.

Flowers: May to July.

Habitat: swamps and marshy places on low ground or in hillside seepages up to 2000m in the Alps.

Distribution: this is the most widespread and often the most common of the *Dactylorhiza* on the European mainland. The nominate race is not found with any certainty in Britain; northern Spain; France; Scandinavia (up to 63°); Germany; Benelux countries; Switzerland; Austria; northern Italy; Yugoslavia; Poland; Czechoslovakia; Hungary; Russia.
93, 94

Ssp. *alpestris* (Pugsley) Senghas. This race is easily recognised by its large elliptical lower leaves, which are widest towards the apex and carry large irregular dark spots. The flower stems range between 15–30cm in height.

Flower colour varies from lilac to deep magenta, and the lip is more or less entire (rarely 3-lobed), without markings on its middle portion.

Flowers: July and August.

Distribution: the Alps and the Pyrenees, where it grows in marshy places and high mountain seepages.
95, 96

Ssp. *purpurella* (T. & T. A. Stephenson) D. Moresby Moore & Soó

NORTHERN MARSH ORCHID; PURPURNBLÜTIGES KNABENKRAUT (G).

Plants are usually 20–30cm tall but exceptionally grow to 40cm.

There are 5–8 lanceolate leaves, with their widest part below the middle and in many cases a collection of small purple spots near the apex.

The flowers are bright or deep reddish-purple in colour, with regular dark markings of lines and spots on a lip which is almost entire and shaped like a broad diamond.

Flowers: late June to early August.

Distribution: north-west Europe and northern Britain (where it replaces ssp. *praetermissa*): Norway (west coast); Sweden (north Götland); Faroes; Ireland; northern England; north Wales and Scotland.
97, 98

Ssp. *praetermissa* (Druce) D. Moresby Moore & Soó

SOUTHERN MARSH ORCHID; ÜBERSEHENES KNABENKRAUT (G).

This form ranges from 20–70 in height, with 5–7 lanceolate leaves which lack the spotting of the nominate race and have their widest part below the centre of the leaf.

The flowers vary in colour from pale pinkish-red to rose-purple. The lip is 10–14mm long, with 3 shallow lobes and a cluster of small spots near its centre. The lip is not folded at its edges, and this is usually enough to separate it from *D. incarnata*, with which it often grows.

Varieties: a form with heavily ring-spotted leaves has been called *D. pardalina* Pugsley. Nelson lists it as a sub-species of *D. majalis*. It tends to occur with ssp. *praetermissa* and probably deserves to be no more than a variety, although its status is certainly not properly resolved. It is restricted to southern England and Holland.

Flowers: slightly later than *D. incarnata* from mid-June to July.

Distribution: restricted to north-western Europe, it is abundant in some parts of southern Britain and the sand-dunes of south Wales but rather local and uncommon on the European mainland: northern France; Britain; northern Denmark; Belgium; Holland.   **99, 100**

Ssp. *occidentalis* (Pugsley) P. D. Sell. This is consistently one of the smallest races, with plants from 10–25cm tall. The leaves are broadly lanceolate, with large irregular spots, and their widest part near the centre.

The lip varies from distinctly 3-lobed to almost entire and has a length of 9–10mm.

The flowers are violet-purple, with darker markings in the form of broken loops or lines on the lip.

Flowers: May to early June, though occasional individuals appear in flower in late April in some years.

Habitat: boggy pastures and wet dune-slacks.

Distribution: British Isles, mainly in Ireland where it occurs in wet places in the west and also in the limestone district of the Burren. It has also been recorded in parts of Scotland and from Anglesey in north Wales.

The Welsh and Scottish forms have been separated by some workers on the basis of small structural differences. *D. majalis* ssp. *cambrensis* (Roberts) Nelson is the form from Anglesey in north Wales, while the plants from the Hebrides and parts of north Scotland are called *D. majalis* ssp. *scotica* Nelson.

Dactylorhiza baltica (Klinge) Orlova
This species is very closely related to *D. majalis* ssp. *purpurella* but has narrower leaves, a distinctly 3-lobed lip and slightly longer spur.

Its status is still uncertain and it is possibly no more than another subspecies of *D. majalis*.

Distribution: north and eastern Europe.   **101**

Dactylorhiza cordigera (Fries) Soó
HEART-SHAPED ORCHID;
BALKANKNABENKRAUT (G).

In some schemes this is classed as yet another subspecies of *D. majalis*, to which it bears a close resemblance.

The tubers are divided into 2–4 elongated fingers, and the stem ranges from 15–30cm in height. There are 2–5 lanceolate-oblong leaves, spaced along the stem but seldom reaching the bottom of the inflorescence (in *D. majalis* they frequently exceed it). The leaves are spotted with dark purple on both surfaces and are not held erect.

The inflorescence can be lax or moderately dense, with the flowers held in an ovoid-oblong raceme and bracts that are noticeably longer than the ovary.

The lateral sepals are 8–12mm long and held erect, whilst the dorsal sepal and petals converge to form the helmet.

The lip is the remarkable feature of this orchid because it is often very broad (as wide as 16mm) and heart-shaped, which accounts for the specific name *cordigera*.

The flowers are coloured deep rose to magenta, with darker line markings on the lip. The spur, which is half the length of the ovary, hangs downwards.

Flowers: July and August.

Habitat: marshy places in mountainous areas, from 1000–2400m above sea level.

Distribution: mainly confined to the Balkan mountains: southern Yugoslavia; Bulgaria; Rumania; northern Greece (also the northern Peloponnese on Mt. Chelmos); western Russia.

Wide-lipped forms of *D. majalis* from the alpine regions of Europe have been confused with *D. cordigera* and given rise to erroneous records already mentioned (p. 103).   **102**

Ssp. *bosniaca* (G. Beck) Soó. This race has long-stemmed plants and a dense inflorescence. The lip is more or less square but becomes wedge-shaped near its base; occasionally it is 3-lobed. The spur is 6–8mm long, which makes it less than half the length of the ovary.

Distribution: Albania; Yugoslavia; Bulgaria.

Ssp. *siculorum* (Soó) Soó. These plants are similar to ssp. *bosniaca* but have lanceolate petals and a more or less circular lip which ranges from entire to deeply 3-lobed. The spur is 8–11mm long and up to ¾ the length of the ovary. *Distribution*: Rumania and western Russia.

Dactylorhiza traunsteineri (Sauter) Soó
IRISH MARSH ORCHID; TRAUNSTEIN-ERS KNABENKRAUT (G).

This usually slender species ranges from 15–45cm in height, with a slightly flexuous stem carrying 4–7 lanceolate leaves, which can be spotted or plain and are held more or less erect.

The inflorescence is rather lax, with few to many flowers and bracts longer than the ovaries; often with a purplish-brown tint.

The sepals are 7–8mm long, spreading or slightly reflexed, with an oblong-lanceolate shape. The lip of this species can be shallowly 3-lobed or even entire, often with a deflexed margin, but the main feature is a distinctly elongated apex.

The flowers are coloured light magenta or purple, with dark reddish-purple markings on the lip.
Flowers: late June to August.
Habitat: marshes and fens on calcareous ground.

There seems to be some confusion about the preferences of this orchid. Most authors cite it as growing in lime-rich conditions but others mention it in sphagnum bogs where the water is distinctly acidic.

One reason for this dichotomy could lie in the close similarity of some forms of *D. traunsteineri* to *D. incarnata* ssp. *cruenta* and narrow-leaved variants of *D. majalis* which grow in bogs. Again, *D. traunsteineri* hybridises readily with other members of the genus and the offspring can form stable populations on their own. As growth conditions change – for example a fen dries out or build-up of rotting plant material makes the environment acidic – the hybrids able to tolerate the changes survive whilst the parents progressively die out.

Distribution: north and central Europe but the true extent is not certain because of confusion with other similar orchids. It is definitely known from Britain and most of Scandinavia but probably occurs widespread throughout north and central Europe.   **103, 104**

Ssp. *lapponica* (Laest. ex Hartman) Soó
LAPLAND MARSH ORCHID; LAPPLAND KNABENKRAUT (G).

This small race grows from 10–20cm tall and has been considered as a species in its own right or, again, as a form of *D. incarnata* ssp. *cruenta*. It has 2–4 leaves, with the upper one bract-like and erect whilst the lower ones are patent.

The inflorescence is lax with few flowers. The sepals spread, and the lip is indistinctly 3-lobed, with a length of 5.5 –7mm and lateral lobes longer than the middle lobe.

The flowers are mauve to reddish in colour, with darker markings on the lip. The spur is conical, with a length about ⅔ that of the ovary.
Flowers: July to August.
Habitat: sphagnum bogs.
Distribution: north Scandinavia; northern Russia.

Ssp. *curvifolia* (Nyl.) Soó. These orchids have 2–4 spreading leaves, which are strongly curved, with a keel on their upper surfaces.

The lip is almost entire or shallowly 3-lobed, with a length of 7–9mm, and the middle lobe only just longer than the laterals.

The flowers are pale magenta with darker markings on the lip.
Distribution: Sweden; Finland; northern Russia.

Ssp. *blyttii* Blytt. This is treated as *D. pseudocordigera* in line with *Flora Europaea*, Volume 5 (see p. 102).

There are close and confusing links between *D. pseudocordigera*, *D. incarnata* ssp. *cruenta* and *D. traunsteineri*. No grouping at present in use seems to us to deal with them satisfactorily, and it will be some time before their interrelationship is properly understood.

Dactylorhiza russowii (Klinge) Holub
This is another orchid having close links with *D. traunsteineri*, and its status has not finally been decided to the satisfaction of some workers.

In overall appearance it is similar to *D. traunsteineri*, with an erect stem and 4–5 leaves. It differs in having a dense inflorescence, with pink flowers and a flat lip (in most plants of *D. traunsteineri* the edges are slightly deflexed). The central lobe of the lip is triangular and pointed. The spur is only just shorter than the ovary.
Distribution: from east Germany into central Russia.

Dactylorhiza elata (Poiret) Soó
ROBUST MARSH ORCHID; HOHES
KNABENKRAUT (G).
Often a very robust species, this plant has stems from 30–110cm in height, carrying from 8–14 broadly lanceolate leaves. These are unspotted and held nearly erect, with the upper ones becoming bract-like.

The raceme is dense, with numerous flowers arranged in a cylindrical spike and bracts that exceed the ovary in length.

The lateral sepals spread but are slightly reflexed, with a length of 10–13mm. The lip ranges from almost entire to 3-lobed, with the lateral lobes frequently deflexed, so that it has a folded appearance.

Flower colour ranges from pink to purplish-red, occasionally white, and although some forms can resemble robust plants of *D. incarnata* they are distinguishable by their much broader lips. This is a useful diagnostic feature when one encounters the occasional slender spike of *D. elata* (e.g. **106**).

The spur is cylindrical or slightly conical and is about as long as the ovary.
Flowers: April to the end of June.
Habitat: wet meadows, hillside seepages, roadside ditches, bogs.

Distribution: southern and central Spain; south-west France; Corsica; Sicily and north Africa.

Two races of this orchid are now widely recognised: the first *D. elata* ssp. *elata* (Poiret) Soó is confined to north Africa and has smaller flowers than the European form *D. elata* ssp. *sesquipedalis* (Willd.). Soó which is illustrated. It also has a lip with a length that just exceeds its width.   **105, 106, 107**

A third race *D. elata* ssp. *brennensis* Nelson is restricted to a small area around Brenne in France and is separated from ssp. *sesquipedalis* on the basis of a short inflorescence (6–8cm) and 15–20 smallish flowers.

Plants from the Cilician Taurus in Turkey are often considered as another subspecies, *D. elata* ssp. *anatolica* Nelson.

Dactylorhiza foliosa (Verm.) Soó
MADEIRAN ORCHID;
MADEIRAKNABENKRAUT (G).
This fairly robust species is not likely to be confused with any other since it is endemic to the island of Madeira and is the only member of the genus found there.

The flowering stems reach 40–60cm and carry 4–5 unspotted lanceolate leaves.

The inflorescence is fairly dense, with numerous blooms and bracts that exceed the ovary in length.

The lateral sepals are slightly incurved, so that they point forwards, and have a twist, so that their back surfaces are turned to face upwards.

The lip is broad and 3-lobed, with the lateral lobes rounded and edges that are sometimes slightly upturned. The middle lobe is pointed and much narrower than the lateral lobes.

The flowers are usually pink but can be found in a range of shades from pink to light reddish-purple, with darker spots arranged regularly near the centre of the lip.

The spur is slender and about ½ the length of the ovary.
Flowers: May to June.

Habitat: marshy pastures in mountain areas.
Distribution: endemic to Madeira.
108, 109

Dactylorhiza cilicica (Klinge) Soó
ANATOLIAN MARSH ORCHID;
ZILIZISCHES KNABENKRAUT (G).

With its distribution restricted to eastern Turkey and Anatolia this is a species not likely to be encountered unless one is specifically searching for it.

It grows from 30–75cm tall, with 6–7 lanceolate to broadly lanceolate leaves which are not spotted and normally held erect.

The inflorescence is dense and carries numerous flowers, with bracts that exceed them in length and are tinged purple-brown.

The lateral sepals spread and the lip is entire, with an extended apex.

The flowers are pink to purple in colour, with darker markings, and the thick spur points downwards and is shorter than the ovary.
Flowers: May to July.
Habitat: wet pastures and seepages in the Montane zone.
Distribution: Turkey; mountains of central Anatolia; eastern Taurus.   **110**

Dactylorhiza kalopissii E. Nelson
This recently described species from Greece resembles *D. cilicica* in a number of characteristics but has quite different flowers.

It is slender in appearance, with narrow leaves which are usually plain but can also be lightly spotted in purplish-brown.

The inflorescence is short and dense-flowered, with bracts that exceed the ovaries in length and can sometimes be longer than the flowers.

The lateral sepals spread but point upwards slightly and the median sepal makes a helmet with the petals.

The lip is the feature which separates this species from *D. cilicica* since it is distinctly 3-lobed – *D. cilicica* has an entire lip. All the lobes are rounded at their ends but the central lobe is the largest in width and length. The flowers are magenta, and the lip has a lighter area towards its base where there is a pattern of dark red spots and lines.
Flowers: mid-June to mid-July.
Habitat: flat ground in wet meadows and along stream banks in mountain areas from 1350–1600m.
Distribution: northern Greece in the Pindus mountains (north and west of the Katara pass).

Dactylorhiza cataonica (Fleischm.) Holub
CAUCASIAN MARSH ORCHID;
KAUKASISCHES KNABENKRAUT (G).

This species is restricted to eastern Turkey and Armenia where it grows from 10–30cm tall, with a few spotted leaves that are held horizontal to erect.

The inflorescence is lax and carries few flowers, with bracts that exceed the ovary in length.

The lateral sepals are spread widely, and the lip is broad and entire.

The flowers are dark red to magenta in colour, with darker markings near the central part of the lip.

The spur is rather thick with a length ⅔ that of the ovary.

There is a close superficial resemblance to *D. cordigera* but the two species have a quite different range of distribution and there is no overlapping.
Flowers: June to July.
Habitat: wet mountain pastures and hillside seepages upto 2500m above sea level.
Distribution: eastern Turkey (Pontus) and Armenia.

The *Dactylorhiza maculata* group

There are a number of closely related species that can be linked in a group, as in the case of *Dactylorhiza incarnata*, and they share the following features: tubers that are divided deeply into three or four fingers, more or less elongated at their tips; a stem up to 60cm high which is erect or slightly flexous and usually has a solid cross section; erect spreading leaves with the upper set bract-like; a conical raceme which extends to an oval or oblong shape as the flowers open; lanceolate bracts; flowers which show a range of colours from yellowish-white through pinkish-lilac to reddish or purple; oblong-ovate sepals with spreading laterals and a lip which is flat and 3-lobed; a spur which varies in length according to species from shorter than to longer than the ovary.

Dactylorhiza maculata (L.) Soó
HEATH SPOTTED ORCHID;
GEFLECKTES KNABENKRAUT (G).
This species occurs as a number of quite distinct geographical races. The nominate forms have solid stems, from 15–60cm tall, carrying 5–12 lanceolate leaves which are usually spotted.

The inflorescence is dense, with few to many flowers, and bracts that only rarely exceed them in length.

Sepals range from 7–11mm and either spread horizontally or curve inwards slightly. The lip is broad and 3-lobed, with the middle lobe much narrower than the laterals and shorter than them in length – exceptions occur where it is longer.

The flowers are variable in colour, with a range embracing white, pale pink, mauve or even reddish; always with darker markings on the lip.

This species can cause confusion in the field because of the wide variation in lip size, shape and colour. It also hybridises readily with other species of *Dactylorhiza* to form stable populations which add further to the problems of positive identification.

Flowers: late April to August, depending on latitude and altitude.

Habitat: heaths, moorland bogs and lightly wooded areas, invariably on damp acidic soils.

Distribution: a fairly common orchid over much of Europe, except in the south-eastern countries. Unconfirmed in north Africa.

For the person trying to come to grips with this species in the field there has been an unfortunate tendency on the parts of taxonomists to separate *D. maculata* into numerous races. This is done on the basis of slight differences in morphology, which can often be explained by the natural variability of the species. It is clear that *D. maculata* is one of those orchids which has not yet 'settled down' and is still probably evolving. Some of the races below hardly deserve the subspecific status they seem to enjoy in botanical literature, and any close similarities between races are pointed out.

Ssp. *ericetorum* (E. F. Linton) P. F. Hunt & Summerhayes
HEATH SPOTTED ORCHID.
This is the British and Irish race which is not always regarded as separate from the highly variable nominate plants. It is treated as a distinct subspecies by some on account of the following: short stems – up to 30cm tall; narrower leaves which can sometimes be unspotted; pale flowers which range from light pink through lilac to reddish; a spur which is only ½ the length of the ovary, compared with ⅔ in the nominate race.

Distribution: Britain; Ireland; Sweden; Holland (common on heaths and peat moorland).   **111, 112**

Ssp. *elodes* (Griseb.) Soó. This race is so similar to ssp. *ericetorum* that many include them together as a single subspecies. Those that separate them use as criteria: the smaller number of leaves growing from the stem (4–6 compared with 5–12 in ssp. *ericetorum*); and a slightly longer spur in ssp. *elodes*.
Distribution: over much of the region of the nominate race.

Ssp. *schurii* (Klinge) Soó. This is similiar to ssp. *elodes* but has 5–12 sparsely spotted leaves growing from the stem, and a lip with a median lobe that equals or exceeds the other lobes.
Distribution: Carpathians.

Ssp. *transilvanica* (Schur) Soó. This distinctive race has stems up to 60cm tall, with 6–10 unspotted leaves spaced along the stem. The flowers are yellowish-white, with the middle lobe of each either equal to or much longer than the laterals.
Distribution: Yugoslavia and the eastern Carpathians.

Ssp. *islandica* (A. & D. Löve) Soó. Plants of this race have small hollow stems from 10–20cm in height. There are 5–7 unspotted leaves growing along the stem, with the lower ones broadly-lanceolate, ovate or even elliptical in shape.
The flowers are pink, pale lilac or reddish, and the middle lobe of the lip equals the laterals in length. The spur is shorter than the ovary.
Distribution: Iceland.

Ssp. *lancibracteata* (C. Koch) Soó. This race from Turkey is readily recognised by the long bracts which extend far beyond the flowers and are green with purple spots. The flowers are pale mauve-lilac spotted with a darker shade of purple. The name ssp. *osmanica* (Klinge) Nelson also refers to this race.
Distribution: Pontus, eastern Turkey and the Caucasus. **113**

Ssp. *rhoumensis* (H.-Harr.) Soó. Plants from Rhum and adjacent islands of the Scottish coast seem to have markings which are consistently much stronger than in ssp. *ericetorum*, and this has led to the suggestion that they constitute a separate subspecies.

Dactylorhiza fuchsii (Druce) Soó
COMMON SPOTTED ORCHID;
FUCHS'SCHES KNABENKRAUT (G).

In overall appearance this species resembles *D. maculata* closely and is listed as one of its subspecies by both E. Nelson and H. Sundermann.
The outstanding difference between them is the preference that *D. fuchsii* shows for fairly dry calcareous soils, compared with the wet acidic haunts of *D. maculata*. The other distinguishing feature is the long pointed central lobe of the lip in *D. fuchsii*.
Plants of the nominate race vary in height from 20–60cm and have solid stems. The leaves are broad and heavily spotted, running from 7–12 in number. They are spaced out along the stem and are held erect or spreading.
The inflorescence is dense and many-flowered, with bracts that are usually shorter than the flowers.
The lateral sepals spread and have a length of 6–9mm. The lip is variable in size and deeply 3-lobed, with all lobes of approximately equal width, but the middle lobe is at least as long as the laterals and frequently longer. In *D. maculata* the side lobes are noticeably broader than the centre lobe.
The flowers are pale pink, mauve or white, with dots or lines of deep red or purplish. Lip shape and flower colour are so variable that some botanists have been encouraged to identify numerous races.
Flowers: June to August.
Habitat: grassland, open scrub, woodland margins, usually on calcareous soils.
Distribution: over much of western and mid-Europe where it is a fairly common species. It is absent from much of the south, occurring also in: Iceland (?);

Norway; Sweden; Finland (?); Italy (north and north-west); Spain; Russia.
114, 115, 116

Ssp. *psychrophila* (Schlechter) Holub. This small race has stems up to 25cm tall and only 1–2 leaves. The flowers are pink or reddish-purple and rarely white. *Distribution*: central Europe to Scandinavia.

Ssp. *soóana* (Borsos) Borsos. This form has 7–12 leaves on stems up to 60cm tall. The flowers are white, except for stripes and spots of purple on the labellum. *Distribution*: Hungary.

Ssp. *hebridensis* (Wilmott) Soó. This is a dwarf form, seldom more than 10cm tall, with 5–6 narrow leaves which are finely spotted or unmarked.

The flower spike is short, dense and almost spherical in shape, with blooms that have a ground colour of deep rosy purple.

Distribution: Hebrides; Tiree; Jura and Islay. In these Scottish islands it often occurs in great numbers in the 'machair'.
117

Ssp. *okellyi* (Druce) Soó. This has slender leaves which are normally unspotted. The spike has a square top, with strongly scented flowers which are small, white and have faint markings. The lip is divided into three almost equal lobes.
Distribution: north-west Ireland and parts of north-west Scotland.   **118**

Dactylorhiza saccifera (Brongn.) Soó
A rather slender species with a height of 30–50cm, this plant has 4–5 broadly lanceolate or elliptic leaves, without spots.

The inflorescence is fairly lax, with few to many flowers. The bracts are about twice the length of the flowers and protrude way beyond them.

The sepals are up to 10mm long, with the laterals spreading. The lip is deeply divided into three pointed lobes of approximately the same length and width, with the laterals toothed at the apex.

The flowers are pink, with dark red spotting on the lip.

The spur is thick, with a length equal to the ovary.

Flowers: May to July.
Habitat: open woodland and wet pastures in the subalpine zone up to 2500m.
Distribution: north Africa (?); Spain; Portugal; Balearics; southern France; Italy; Corsica; Sardinia; Sicily; Yugoslavia; northern Greece; Albania; Bulgaria; Rumania.   **119**

Dactylorhiza gervasiana (Tod.)
H. Baumann & Kuenkele
This name has been recently applied to plants from the Italian mainland that are often regarded as forms of *D. saccifera*.

Overall flower shape is very similar to *D. saccifera*, with a deeply 3-lobed lip, the lateral lobes of which have 'toothed' edges. *D. gervasiana* differs mainly in that the flower colour is uniform pink as opposed to the veined appearance of *D. saccifera*.

In large populations of *D. saccifera* one finds some plants with uniformly coloured flowers, just as one does in populations of the better known *D. fuchsii*.

If as a result of more research it is accepted generally that the Italian forms are distinct, then the name *D. saccifera* will only be used for plants from the Balkan peninsula and some Greek islands.

Flowers: mid-May to late June or early July.
Habitat: woodlands (pine and chestnut) from 400–1500m.
Distribution: Italy (western mainland), Sicily, Sardinia, Corsica.

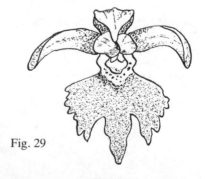

Fig. 29

Steveniella

The single orchid in this genus is a very rare plant and it is named after the botanist C. von Steven, whose life spanned part of the eighteenth and nineteenth centuries.

The genus characteristics are: 2 tubers which are round or oblong; a single lanceolate leaf above the base, with 2 sheathing leaves higher up the stem; sepals fused almost to their ends; small petals about as long as the anther; a 3-lobed lip with rounded lobes; divided spur; 3-lobed rostellum, with an erect middle lobe and viscidia contained in a 2-lobed bursicle.

Steveniella satyrioides (Steven) Schlechter

HOODED ORCHID; KAPPENORCHIS (G).

Plants of this species vary from 15 –35cm in height and have three leaves, two of which are sheaths, with the third near the base. The leaves vary from oblong ovate to lanceolate in shape and are usually tinged reddish or purple. The flower bracts are shorter than the ovary and are lanceolate to ovate in shape, whilst the spike is cylindrical and carries 7–20 flowers, fairly densely bunched. The sepals are fused into a hood, whilst the petals are free but very short (i.e. 4mm, compared with 6–8mm for the sepals). In colour the perianth segments are green or yellowish-green, usually tinged with purple or reddish-brown. The lip is 3-lobed, with all the lobes rounded at the end and the laterals shorter than the middle lobe. The lip is coloured green, with a purple or reddish area where the lip is constricted towards its base. The twin spurs are short (2– 2.5 mm), conical, and point downwards.

Flowers: April to May.

Habitat: open woodlands, mountain pastures.

Distribution: This orchid is certainly local and rare. It has a very restricted range of distribution, and few sites are known, although in some of the sites there are good colonies to be found. It is known from Turkey (the Pontus region and one or two other recently discovered localities); Crimea; Caucasus; Iran. **120, 121**

Comperia

Like *Steveniella* the single plant in the genus is named after an early botanist; in this case Komper is the person so honoured.

The genus characteristics are: 2 ovoid tubers; perianth segments fused into a hood – only the tips are free; a convex lip with 3 lobes, the ends of which are prolonged into four filiform processes; a spur which is shorter than the ovary and viscidia in a simple bursicle.

Comperia comperiana (Steven) Ascherson & Graebner

KOMPER'S ORCHID; BARTORCHIS (G).

This orchid cannot possibly be confused with any other species in this book. Plants can grow from 25–55cm, with 3–4 oblong or oblong-ovate basal leaves and 2–3 sheaths higher up the stem. The spike is usually cylindrical, but the arrangement of the flowers can vary from lax to dense. The sepals are fused for most of their length into a hood –

only their tips are free and slightly reflexed, resembling 3 teeth. The lip is 3-lobed, with the middle lobe split into two and all the divisions are drawn out into fine thread-like processes up to 2.8cm long. The total lip length from the tip of one of the processes to the base can be as much as 4cm. This lip gives the plant a bizarre appearance, especially when some of the flowers are only just opening, for the processes are tangled into tight spirals which unwind as the flowers open. The petals, too, are drawn into fine processes but they cannot be seen until one looks inside the hood formed by the sepals. Like *Barlia robertiana* this species seems to have two distinct colour forms: the first has a greenish helmet, suffused with purple, and the lip whitish with green processes; the second has a darker appearance, with a brownish-purple helmet and the basal area of the lip pale pink, streaked and tinged with a deeper red. In this form the processes are the same colour as the hood.

Flowers: April to July (August) depending on altitude. In Rhodes, Lesbos and western Turkey it starts to flower in mid to late April; in the mountains of Lebanon it is at its best in late May.

Habitat: essentially a plant of mountain conifer woods on limestone soils, up to 2000m.

Distribution: This plant is decidedly local and rare, having a mainly eastern distribution: Greece (Lesbos & Rhodes – very limited numbers in small colonies in pinewoods on both islands; only recently discovered in Rhodes, but known in Lesbos since the last century); Turkey (particularly in the west); Iran; Lebanon (several known colonies, one where it flourishes in abundance and is one of the sights of the orchid world).   **122, 125**

Traunsteinera

The single species in this genus is named *T. globosa* and is one of a small group of orchids characteristic of high mountain meadows in the subalpine zone. The generic name comes from J. Traunsteiner, a Tyrolean chemist, and the characteristics of the genus are: 2 ovoid tubers without divided ends; perianth segments, varying from ovate to ovate-lanceolate and often tapering then broadening at the tip to form a spathulate apex; downward pointing labellum with 3 lobes; a short spur; 3-lobed rostellum, with the middle lobe erect; viscidia in a rather rudimentary 2-lobed bursicle.

This species was at one time included in the genus *Orchis* but its leaves arise about halfway up the stem, leaving the base with a few sheaths. *Orchis* plants always have some of their leaves in a basal rosette. Another difference between the genera is the way the viscidia are carried; in *Orchis* they are held in a single bursicle whilst in *Traunsteinera* there are 2 bursicles.

Hybrids
Traunsteinera globosa x *Gymnadenia conopsea* = x *Gymnotraunsteinera vallesiaca* Spiess

Traunsteinera globosa (L.) Reichenb.
GLOBE ORCHID; ORCHIS GLOBULEUX (F); KUGELORCHIS (G).
    The rather slender stems of this orchid grow from 15–65cm in height, and the plant is not likely to be confused with any other species of orchid.
    There are 2–3 oblong leaves near the

base of the stem which partly sheath it, while spaced out along the upper part of the stem are a series of bract-like leaves. The flowers are carried in a dense globose or pyramidal inflorescence which elongates as the flowers open. From a distance, the flower head looks quite like an *Allium*. The bracts have 1–3 veins and can equal or exceed the ovary in length.

The sepals are about 5–6mm long and the petals are slightly shorter. Both sets of segments spread outwards and narrow sharply towards the apex, then spread to form a small spatula shape.

The lip points downwards and is deeply 3-lobed, with an oblong median lobe and ovate-lateral lobes. The central lobe is sometimes toothed at its apex. The flowers are pinkish-lilac in colour, and the lip and petals are spotted in purple.

The spur ranges from ⅓ to ½ the length of the ovary, is cylindrical with a slight taper and points downwards. *Varieties*: Var. *albiflora* Schur has white flowers.

Flowers: May through to August, depending on altitude.

Habitat: mountain meadows and light woodland, often where the surrounding vegetation is quite tall, on neutral or limestone soils from 1000–3000m but usualy above 1500m.

Distribution: Spain; France; Germany; Switzerland; Austria; Italy; Yugoslavia; Turkey; Poland; Czechoslovakia; Bulgaria; Rumania; Russia; Caucasus.

123, 124

Ssp. *sphaerica* (M. Bieb.) Soó. Sometimes this form is treated as a species in its own right. It differs from the nominate race in the colour of its flowers which are white with purple speckling. The shape of the central lobe of the lip is different too; it is attenuated and has a spathulate tip.

Neotinea

V. Tineo, a Sicilian botanist who lived in Palermo in the nineteenth century, gave his name to this genus. In early works the genus appears as Tinea. The genus is characterised by: two ellipsoidal tubers; 2–4 basal leaves and a more or less one-sided flower spike; a 3-lobed lip which has about the same length as the other perianth segments; sepals and petals converging to form a helmet; a very short spur; stigmas which are close together at the base but diverge to form a V shape; distinct viscidia in a 2-lobed bursicle.

The flowers contain nectar, which probably attracts small insect visitors to plants growing in the Mediterranean region, but in Ireland self-fertilization normally takes place. The small pollen masses (massulae) which make up the pollinia are not very tightly bound, so that they readily break up and are generally found scattered around the interior of the flower almost as soon as it opens.

Neotinea maculata (Desf.) Stearn
DENSE-FLOWERED ORCHID; ORCHIS INTACT (F); KEUSCHORCHIS (G); SATIRIONE MACCHIATO (I).

Often a plant of small stature and insignificant appearance, this species ranges from 10–30cm in height, with 3–6 leaves. The lower leaves are broad-oblong and spreading, whilst the upper leaves are rather narrow and erect, forming loose sheaths to the stem. There are two distinct colour forms of the flowers and the leaves vary accordingly. Plants with white flowers have plain, rather dark green leaves, whilst those with pink flowers have purplish-brown spots in longitudinal lines. The flower bracts are very short, and the small flowers are densely packed into a cylindrical spike 2–6cm in length (though up to 10cm is possible). The sepals and petals form a hood, and the lip is flat and 3-lobed, with the laterals linear and the central lobe longer but divided into 2 (rarely 3) lobes at its apex. The flower resembles a tiny man with an oversized helmet. Of the two colour forms the pink-flowered species is often more robust than the white, and both forms occur together. The spur is very short and difficult to find, and the flowers have a light vanilla scent.

Flowers: mid-March to May (depending on altitude).

Habitat: Garigue, stony grassland, woods, on limestone or even slightly acid soils.

Distribution: mainly Mediterranean; Canary Isles; Madeira; N. Africa; Balearics; south-west & southern France; mid & southern Italy; Corsica; Sardinia; Sicily; Yugoslavia; Greece; Crete; Rhodes; Cyprus; Turkey; Lebanon; Ireland (southern); England (Isle of Man).

Its presence in Ireland, in the Burren region of western Ireland, is a reminder of days gone by when the plant had an altogether wider distribution and only managed to survive where the climate was warm, even during the glacial epochs. In its two western sites it is significant that the coast is warmed by the Gulf stream.

In Cyprus it occurs in two distinct kinds of habitat: on low ground near the sea, on bare chalky soils, where both colour forms occur together, while high in the mountain forests of the southern part of the Troodos massif only the white form seems to occur.   **126, 127, 128**

Orchis

Of all the terrestrial orchids in Europe the members of the genus *Orchis* are probably the best-known; even for those with only a passing interest in wild flowers the words 'wild orchids' conjure up images of purple spikes of *Orchis* species in fields and woodlands. Indeed, many people are surprised to realize that there are other genera of wild orchid in Europe.

In addition to being the most well-known, the genus *Orchis* is one of the largest orchid genera in Europe. All these plants are orchids of the temperate regions of the northern hemisphere, extending throughout Europe to Morocco and Algeria in north Africa, then across Asia to the Japanese islands in the extreme east and the Himalaya mountains in the south.

Members of the genus show great differences in appearance between species but have the following factors in common:

There are two rounded or ovoid tubers. At one time the genus *Dactylorhiza*, with divided tubers, was included with *Orchis*.

The leaves are variable in shape and are spotted or not, depending on the species.

The perianth segments are free, but converge to form a hood in a wide range of species, or again the lateral sepals can be spreading and the hood formed by the dorsal sepal and the petals.

The lips are variable in shape and colour, ranging from entire to 3-lobed, and there is a spur.

The flower bracts are thin and membranous – another aspect in which *Orchis* differs from *Dactylorhiza*, since the members of the latter genus have leaf-like bracts.
The rostellum is 3-lobed and the viscidia are carried in a 2-lobed bursicle.

Within the genus there are a number of distinct groups, distinguished by the arrangement of their petals and sepals:

Orchids with the lateral sepals spreading and not combining with the petals to form a hood: *O. anatolica*; *O. boryi*; *O. canariensis*; *O. laxiflora*; *O. mascula*; *O. pallens*; *O. patens*; *O. provincialis*; *O. quadripunctata*; *O. saccata*; *O. spitzelii*.

Orchids where sepals and petals combine to form a hood:

A. Lip entire and narrowing towards the base: *O. papilionacea*.

B. Lip 3-lobed, with the middle lobe divided at the apex producing the appearance of 'arms and legs'; spur very short: *O. galilaea*; *O. italica*; *O. lactea*; *O. militaris*; *O. punctulata*; *O. purpurea*; *O. simia*; *O. steveni*; *O. tridentata*; *O. ustulata*.

C. Lip 3-lobed, broader than long, with the middle lobe about the same length as the laterals: *O. longicornu*; *O. morio*.

D. Lip 3-lobed but longer than broad, with middle lobe longer than the laterals: *O. coriophora*; *O. sancta*.

Orchis flowers are highly developed for pollination by insects. The pollen grains are clumped in small masses which are then held by elastic threads in club-shaped pollinia. These threads run together to form the slender stalk or caudicle, at the base of which is the sticky disc or viscidium.

The sterile third stigma, the rostellum, forms a protective pouch or bursicle which covers the viscidia. The other two stigmas are sticky and lie on the upper face of the spur entrance. An insect visitor landing on the flower inserts its proboscis into the spur in search of nectar, and in doing so touches the rostellum, which splits and exposes the sticky viscidia. One or both of these can touch the insect, which then flies off with them firmly fixed to its proboscis, since the 'glue' provided by the flower sets hard extremely quickly and is very strong.

Initially the pollinia lie almost parallel to the proboscis, but after 20–30 seconds, as the viscidium dries out, the pollinia are pulled forward through a right angle. Darwin includes drawings of a pencil point substituted for the insect proboscis, an experiment which is easily reproducible.

Insect visitors are not rewarded in any way for their role in pollination since the spur contains no free nectar. Darwin thought that the proboscis could pierce the cell wall of the spur and that the insect would feed on the cell sap. Careful investigation has shown that this is not so and that the spur is just a dummy nectary, with the insect deluded long enough to ensure removal of the pollen.

Various insects – social and solitary bees, hoverflies and droneflies – are known to visit the flowers, and a wide range of interspecific and intergeneric hybrids has been recorded.

Hybrids
Orchis species hybridise fairly frequently with one another if there are large populations of different types growing together. In other cases hybrids are quite rare but a wide range has been recorded over the years.

Many intergeneric hybrids are known particularly with *Serapias* and *Dactylorhiza*.

Interspecific Hybrids
O. anatolica x *O. provincialis* ssp. *pauciflora* = *O.* x *thriftiensis* Renz
O. coriophora x *O. morio* = *O.* x *olida* Breb.
O. coriophora x *O. purpurea* = *O.* x *celtiberica* Pau
O. coriophora ssp *fragrans* x *O. sancta* = *O.* x *kallitheae* Klein
O. coriophora x *O. tridentata* = *O.* x *tremezzinae* Keller
O. coriophora x *O. ustulata* = *O.* x *franzonii* Schulze
O. longicornu x *O. papilionacea* = *O.* x *bornemannii* Ascherson
O. mascula x *O. laxiflora* ssp. *palustris* = *O.* x *dolocheilos* Maus
O. mascula x *O. pallens* = *O.* x *loreziana* Bruegg.
O. mascula x *O. provincialis* ssp. *pauciflora* = *O.* x *colemannii* Cortesi
O. mascula x *O. provincialis* = *O.* x *penzigiana* Camus
O. militaris x *O laxiflora* ssp. *palustris* = *O.* x *bouneriana* Camus
O. militaris x *O. morio* ssp. *picta* = *O.* x *ladurneri* Murr
O. militaris x *O. simia* = *O.* x *beyrichii* Kern.
O. morio x *O. laxiflora* = *O.* x *alata* Fleury
O. morio x *O. longicornu* = *O.* x *cortesii* Camus
O. morio x *O. mascula* = *O.* x *vilmsii* Camus
O. morio x *O. papilionacea* = *O.* x *gennarii* Reichenb. fil.
O. morio ssp. *picta* x *O. quadripunctata* = *O.* x *adriatica* Soó
O. morio ssp. *picta* x *O. saccata* = *O.* x *semisaccata* Camus
O. pallens x *O. provincialis* = *O.* x *plessidiaca* Renz
O. papilionacea x *O. boryi* = *O.* x *lasithica* Renz
O. papilionacea x *O. laxiflora* = *O.* x *caccabaria* Verguin
O. papilionacea x *O. mascula* = *O.* x *peltieri* Keller
O. papilionacea x *O. provincialis* = *O.* x *neo-gennarii* Camus
O. patens x *O. mascula* = *O.* x *ligustica* Ruppert
O. patens x *O. provincialis* = *O.* x *subpatens* Camus = *O.* x *fallax* de Notaris
O. punctulata x *O. purpurea* = *O.* x *wulffiana* Soó
O. purpurea x *O. mascula* = *O.* x *wilmsii* Richter
O. purpurea x *O. militaris* = *O.* x *hybrida* Boennigh.
O. purpurea x *O. morio* = *O.* x *perretii* Richter
O. purpurea x *O. simia* = *O. angusticruris* Franch. ap. Humicki
O. quadripunctata x *O. provincialis* = *O.* x *bueelii* Wildhaber
O. quadripunctata x *O. provincialis* ssp. *pauciflora* = *O.* x *pseudoanatolica* Fleischm.
O. spitzelii x *O. mascula* = *O.* x *petterssonii* Keller ex Pettersson
O. tridentata x *O. italica* = *O.* x *diversifolia* Gaudagno
O. tridentata x *O. mascula* = *O.* x *untchjii* Schulze ap. A. & Gr.
O. tridentata x *O. militaris* = *O.* x *canuti* Richter

O. tridentata x *O. morio* = *O.* x *huteri* Schulze
O. tridentata x *O. purpurea* = *O.* x *fuchsii* Schulze
O. ustulata x *O. morio* = *O.* x *christii* Keller
O. ustulata x *O. simia* = *O.* x *doellii* Zimmermann
O. ustulata x *O. tridentata* = *O.* x *dietrichiana* Bogenh.

A number of unnamed hybrids appear in orchid literature. Some of these are:
O. papilionacea x *O. saccata* leg. Paterny
O. patens x *O. anatolica* Mouterde
O. patens x *O. spitzelii* Teschner
O. simia x *O. italica* leg. Baumann & Halx
O. tridentata x *O. galilaea* Mouterde
O. ustulata x *O. militaris* Fuller

Intergeneric Hybrids
Listed below are those hybrids formed between *Orchis* and *Dactylorhiza*. Hybrids are also known between *Orchis* and *Aceras*, *Anacamptis*, *Gymnadenia*, *Platanthera* and *Serapias*. These are listed in each of these genus descriptions.

O. coriophora x *D. incarnata* = x *Orchidactyla drudei* Schulze
O. coriophora x *D. majalis* = x *Orchidactyla schulzei* Hausskn.
O. coriophora ssp. *fragrans* x *D. sambucina* = x *Orchidactyla carpetana* Willk.
O. laxiflora ssp. *palustris* x *D. incarnata* = x *Orchidactyla uechtriziana* Hausskn.
O. laxiflora ssp. *palustris* x *D. majalis* = x *Orchidactyla rouyana* Camus
O. mascula ssp. *signifera* x *D. sambucina* = x *Orchidactyla speciosissima* Wettst. et Sennh.
O. mascula ssp. *signifera* x *D. maculata* = x *Orchidactyla pentecostalis* Wettst. et Sennh
O. militaris x *D. incarnata* = x *Orchidactyla jeanpertii* Camus et Luiz.
O. morio x *D. maculata* = x *Orchidactyla bouderi* Camus
O. morio x *D. incarnata* = x *Orchidactyla arbostii* Camus
O. morio x *D. sambucina* = x *Orchidactyla luciae* Royer
O. pallens x *D. sambucina* x *Orchidactyla chenervardii* Schulze
O. provincialis x *D. maculata* = x *Orchidactyla* (unnamed) Harbeck
O. purpurea x *D. majalis* = x *Orchidactyla guestphalica* Richter

Orchis papilionacea L.
BUTTERFLY ORCHIS; ORCHIS
PAPILLON (F); SCHMETTERLINGS-
KNABENKRAUT (G); CIPRESSINI (I).

Perhaps one of the most attractive members of the genus, this orchid can occur as small, delicate plants, 15–20cm in height, or as robust, thick-stemmed specimens up to 40cm tall.

There are 6–9 lanceolate leaves, with the lower ones in a basal rosette and the upper ones sheathing the angular stem. The flower spike is lax, with few (3–8) flowers. In rare cases the inflorescence can be dense and cylindrical. The flower bracts are longer than the ovary and have a reddish tinge. The sepals and petals are only slightly uncurved and so form a loose hood. The hood is deep red or purplish, with veining in a deeper shade, and the lip is entire, with a slightly toothed edge, and shows a large variation in shape and size. In colour it is usually pale pink, although it can be the same shade as the hood and its edges are curved forwards.

Varieties: var. *grandiflora* Boiss. has a much larger, flatter, lip which has a pale pink ground colour and deep magenta 'veining', broken into spots or streaks.

The lateral sepals are spreading, and the petals and median sepal form what remains of the hood. The hood is more magenta than red in colour and is heavily veined. (This form is found in southern Greece; Crete; southern Spain; North Africa – Algeria and Morocco; Sicily). Forms from Yugoslavia with a narrow, plain magenta lip are called var. *rubra* Lindl. or even *O. rubra* Jacq.

Flowers: March to May (depending on altitude).

Habitat: dry areas in garigue, olive groves, open pinewoods and roadsides, in calcareous or slightly acid soils.

Distribution: throughout the Mediterranean region; N. Africa; southern Spain; Balearics; southern France; Italy; Corsica; Sardinia; Sicily; Yugoslavia; Greece; Corfu; Crete (flowers early and large flowers of var. *grandiflora* suffer damage from the storms in early March); Rhodes; Turkey; Lebanon; Bulgaria; Rumania; Caucasus. One old record exists for Cyprus but its presence there now is doubtful.

Forms vary from country to country. The photographs were taken as follows: **129, 130**, Spain; **131**, Sardinia; **132**, Italy; **133, 134**, Greece; **135**, Corfu.

Ssp. **bruhnsiana** (Gruner) Soó. This is a Trancaucasian subspecies which has a small lip (7mm wide and 8–10mm long). The sepals are short, with 3 veins. Soó identifies *Orchis caspia* Trautv. from Talysh and northern Iran as identical with ssp. *bruhnsiana*.

Varieties: Var. *candida* Soó has white sepals and petals, with green veins.

Orchis boryi Reichenb. fil.
BORY'S ORCHID; KRETISCHES KNABENKRAUT (G).

A rather slender orchid, ranging from 20–45cm in height, with most plants closer to the lower limit. The basal rosette consists of 3–5 slender lanceolate leaves, with sheaths crowding the stem above. The flower bracts are lanceolate, about ½ the length of the ovary, and the spike is short and fairly dense, carrying 2–8 small flowers. The upper flowers

open before the lower ones – one of the factors that separates *O. boryi* from the closely related *O. quadripunctata*. The sepals are about 7mm in length and slightly incurved, forming a helmet with the petals. The lip is 3-lobed (but often not markedly so) and the median lobe is slightly larger than the laterals, with a tiny indentation at its apex. The helmet, ovary and buds are a deep, reddish-purple, which contrasts strongly with the much lighter pink lip (*O. quadripunctata* has uniformly coloured flowers). Lip markings are restricted to 2–6 red spots, borne on the pale whitish area near the base of the lip.

Flowers: throughout April.

Habitat: in open maquis, sparse hillside grassland and thickets, always on limestone.

Distribution: local and uncommon, confined to Greece (Peloponnese – some good populations in the south of the region) and Crete (fairly frequent in some mountain areas).   **136, 137**

Orchis israelitica Baumann & Dafni
This orchid, recently discovered in Israel, closely resembles a pale form of *Orchis boryi*.

Plants are delicate in appearance, being no more than 20–25cm tall with unspotted leaves and pinkish white flowers which unlike most species bloom from the top of the spike downwards.

Fig. 30

The sepals converge to form a loose helmet and the lip is 3-lobed with conspicuous red dots, and the central lobe is wider then the side lobes. The spur is thin and held more or less horizontal

with a length equal to the ovary.
Flowers: February to March.
Habitat: hillside scrub.
Distribution: Israel.

Orchis morio L.
GREEN-WINGED ORCHID; ORCHIS
BOUFFON (F); KLEINES
KNABENKRAUT (G); ZONZELLE (I).
The plant can range from 5cm tall in
exposed dry grassland to 50cm tall in
shady damp places. There are 5–9
broadly lanceolate leaves, with the lower
ones forming a basal rosette and the
upper ones appearing as sheaths, crowding the stem. The flower bracts are lanceolate, with several veins, sometimes
tinged reddish, and they vary in length
from less than to more than the length of
the ovary. The flowers form a loose spike
which is oblong or pyramidal in shape
(rarely cylindrical) and the lower flowers
open first. The sepals and petals converge to form a hood, and the lip is
3-lobed, rather broad, and usually
folded almost in two. The median lobe
has a small indentation at its apex. Flower colour is very variable, varying from
white, through greenish, to reddish-pink
or purplish-violet. The lateral sepals are
usually suffused with green and prominently veined, and the lip has a central
region with dark spotting. The spur is
about ½ the length of the ovary, cylindrical in shape, and with a stubbed tip. It
is horizontal or slightly upward pointing.
Flowers: March to June (depending on
altitude).
Habitat: old-established dunes, pasture-
land, open woodland, roadsides, maquis, usually on calcareous soils but
sometimes occurring where the soils are
slightly acid.
Distribution: Widespread throughout the
area covered by the book, except in the
extreme north (where it is absent) and
the Mediterranean, north Africa and the
Middle East, where it is replaced by its
subspecies.
   This orchid once occurred in pasture-
land in enormous numbers, indeed it
was one of the sights of late spring, often
growing with cowslips. In the UK and

Germany its numbers have decreased
dramatically, owing to intensive farming
methods and urban expansion.   **138**

Ssp. *picta* (Loisel) Arcangeli. Very similar to the nominate race, but the sepals
are shorter (6–8mm compared with 8–
10mm), the lip is not as folded and the
flowers are paler and smaller. The spur
tapers towards the apex and is as long as
the ovary. This subspecies replaces the
nominate race in much of the Mediterranean region.   **139, 140**

Ssp. *champagneuxii* (Barn.) Camus.
This has sepals 6–8mm in length and a
longer slender spur which widens towards its apex. The lip is only spotted
lightly, if at all, and the plant tends to
form clumps.
Distribution: Morocco;   Balearics;
Spain; southern France.   **141**

Ssp. *libani* Renz is similar to ssp. *picta*. It
has a dense rosette of rather narrow
leaves and is usually 10–25cm tall. The
flowers have pink to pale reddish hoods,
suffused with green, and a lip which is
white and unspotted.
Habitat: light pine woods and garigue.
Distribution: it occurs in the extreme
south-east in Lebanon, in south-east
Turkey, Israel and in Cyprus (common).
An albino form with pure white flowers
occurs regularly.   **142, 143**

Orchis longicornu Poiret
LONG-SPURRED ORCHID; ORCHIS À
LONGUE CORNE (F); LANGSPORNIGES
KNABENKRAUT (G); GALETTI DI
LUNGO CORNU (I).
   The plant grows 10–35cm tall, with
6–8 oblong-lanceolate leaves, the lower
ones in a basal rosette and the upper
ones in a series of sheaths which crowd
the stem. The flower bracts are lanceolate, green or tinged red, carry several veins and are about the same length as
the ovary. The flower spike is fairly lax
and oblong. In particularly strong plants
there are enough flowers to form a cylindrical spike. Sepals and petals converge
to form a helmet; the sepals are about

6mm in length and oblong, the petals are similar but smaller. In colour, petals and sepals range from white, through pink, to purplish-red,and are veined in a darker shade. The lip is 3-lobed, with the lateral lobes longer than the median lobe. The edges are so recurved that the lip appears folded in two. The lateral lobes are usually a deep purplish-violet (in Sardinia, where the orchid is at its best, they can be pink, or even red), and the median area is white with purple spots. The spur is as long as the ovary (about 16mm) and upturned, with a thickened tip.

Varieties: Var. *albiflora* Camus has white flowers.

Flowers: February to April.

Habitat: dry grasslands, open pine woods, roadside banks and, less frequently, in maquis.

Distribution: mainly a western Mediterranean species; north Africa; Spain; Portugal; Balearics (very local in Majorca but, where it does occur, there are large numbers in some years); southern France (only in Var; recorded in Thompson's *Flowering Plants of the Riviera* – probably now extinct); Italy; Corsica; Sardinia (this seems to be the ideal place for the plants – a wide range of colour forms has been recorded); Sicily (frequent).   **144, 145, 146**

Orchis coriophora L.

BUG ORCHID; ORCHIS PUNAISE (F); WANZEN-KNABENKRAUT (G); CIMICIATTOLA (I).

The plant reaches 15–40cm in height and has 4–7 rather narrow, channelled leaves low on the stem, with sheaths higher up. The flower bracts are as large as the ovary and have a single vein; the spike is dense-flowered and oblong or cylindrical in shape.

The sepals are about 5–10mm long, whilst the petals are slightly longer and converge to form a hood which ends in a sharp point. It is dark violet-brown in colour. The lip is 3-lobed and gently incurved, with the side lobes slightly toothed and their lower edges and the median lobe only a little longer than the

Fig. 31

side lobes. The colouring of the lip is a dark purple-red, with greenish streaks and a light area with dark spots near the base. Light-flowered forms occur, with a white or greenish-white ground colour and red markings. The spur is about ½ the length of the ovary, conical, and downward pointing. The whole plant has a sickly, foetid scent which resembles that of 'squashed bed bugs' – something which few modern botanists have had the misfortune to substantiate.

Flowers: late April to June.

Habitat: damp grasslands, usually on slightly acid soils (in parts of Spain where acid soils give way to limestone regions one finds the nominate race surviving in the former soils, with the ssp. *fragrans* on the latter).

Distribution: mainly through central Europe, where it is becoming increasingly rare as its damp habitat is used for farmland and urban expansion; France; southern Germany (now very rare); Austria & Switzerland (lower mountain regions); Spain (local); Yugoslavia; Poland; Czechoslovakia; Hungary; Russia; Crimea; doubtful records for Benelux, Caucasus.   **147**

Ssp. *fragrans* (Pollini) Sudre. A much more common plant than the nominate race, from which it differs in the following respects: the central lobe is noticeably longer than the side lobes, the spur is about as long as the ovary, and the flowers are paler in colour, with whitish bracts. Two quite distinct colour forms exist, one with flowers which are mainly maroon and white, the other with flowers which have a greenish tinge. Both forms are spotted with red and are sweetly scented.

Fig. 32

Varieties: Var. *albiflora* Macchiati has white flowers with sparse red spotting.
Flowers: April to early June (one of the later Mediterranean orchids, flowering in the eastern Mediterranean at the same time as the closely related *O. sancta*).
Habitat: damp grassland on hillsides, cledgy *terra rossa*, drier places in garigue (though these places will have been well soaked in early spring), usually on calcareous soils.
Distribution: it replaces the nominate race in much of the Mediterranean region; N. Africa; Spain; Balearics; southern France; Italy; Corsica; Sardinia; Sicily; Yugoslavia; Greece; Crete; Rhodes; Cyprus; Turkey; Lebanon; Crimea; Caucasus. **148**

Ssp. **matrinii** (Timb.-Lagr.) Nyman. Very similar to ssp. *fragrans* but with a much longer spur and shorter labellum. The plants are usually robust in appearance, with thick stems, whilst ssp. *fragrans* is a rather slender plant. The flowers are not sweet-scented, having the same unpleasant odour as the nominate race.

Distribution: western and central Spain; Portugal; southern Italy (Apulia).

Orchis sancta L.
HOLY ORCHID; HEILIGES KNABENKRAUT (G).
This plant is closely related to *O. coriophora*. It has 5–7 leaves, in a rosette, around the base of the stem, with sheaths higher up. It grows 15–45cm tall. The flower bracts are larger than the ovary, with 3–5 veins, and the inflorescence is more lax than with *O. coriophora*. The sepals and petals are 9–12mm long, pale lilac-red in colour, and converge to form a hood with a long upturned point. From the side the hood closely resembles in shape the headgear worn by medieval monks; hence the name. The lip is 3-lobed, with the side lobes so strongly toothed that there appear to be more than 3 lobes. The lip colouring is a uniform pale pink to reddish-purple, without the spotting of *O. coriophora*. The spur is curved downwards, strongly narrowed towards the apex and about equal in length to the ovary. This species is one of the first to push up its leaf rosette after the onset of the winter rains. The leaves remain green after other orchids have flowered and died, before the spike is pushed up.
Flowers: April – usually after other Mediterranean orchids, on low ground, when the grass is already drying off.
Habitat: dry grassland on calcareous soils, garigue, often near the coast.
Distribution: eastern Mediterranean: Aegean isles (Chios, Lesbos, Samos); Rhodes; Cyprus; western and southern Turkey; Syria; Lebanon; Israel. **149, 150**

Orchis ustulata L.
BURNT ORCHID; ORCHIS BRÛLÉ (F); BRAND KNABENKRAUT (G); SIPHO MACHIETTATO (I).
One of the smallest of the *Orchis*, the plant stands between 10 and 25cm tall, with 2–3 oblong, basal leaves and 1–3 sheathing leaves higher up the stem. The flower bracts are usually shorter than the ovary, but can be as long, and the inflorescence is dense, with numerous

small flowers in a cylindrical spike. Unopened flower buds are dark purple and give the spike its 'burnt tip'. Sepals and petals converge to form a rounded hood, which is coloured brownish-purple on the outside. The lip is only 4–8mm in length and is 3-lobed, with spreading laterals and the median widening near the apex where it becomes indented. There is no apical protuberance, and the spur is about ¼–½ the length of the ovary, cylindrical in shape, and points downwards. The lip is white with sparse red spotting, and the flowers have a delicate scent. *O. ustulata* is unusual amongst *Orchis* species for the time the mycorrhizome exists before the first green leaves appear (10 years or more). *Varieties*: Var. *albiflora* Thielens has a pale hood and the lip is not spotted.
Flowers: April to early August (depending on altitude).
Habitat: grasslands on downs, mountains and subalpine meadows (up to 2100m), usually on calcareous soils but also on sand or gravel.
Distribution: widespread over much of the region covered by this book (absent from the extreme north and south); northern Spain; France; UK; southern Scandinavia; Germany; Benelux; Austria; Switzerland; Italy; Yugoslavia; Greece; Poland; Czechoslovakia; Hungary; Bulgaria; Rumania; Russia; Caucasus.   **151, 152**

Orchis tridentata Scop.
TOOTHED ORCHID; ORCHIS DENTELÉ (F); DREIZÄHNIGES KNABENKRAUT (G).

The plant stands between 15 and 45cm tall, with 3–4 oblong leaves at or near the base and the rest sheathing the stem higher up. The flower bracts are less than ½ the length of the ovary and the inflorescence is rather dense, starting as conical but becoming ovoid in shape as the upper flowers open. The sepals taper into long points, whilst the petals are oblong. Both sets of perianth segments converge to form a hood. The lip is 3-lobed, with the lateral lobes spreading outwards and the median lobe more or less triangular, with the apex of the triangle starting just below the lateral lobes (in the closely related *O. lactea* the sides of the median lobe are parallel just below the laterals, but then spread outwards). The median lobe is shallowly divided into 2 'lobules' with serrated edges, and a small 'tooth' is sited between them. The flowers are variable in colour and range from white, through pink, to a pale reddish-violet. The hood is prominently veined in a darker shade than the ground colour, and the lip is speckled or blotched with pink or reddish-purple. The spur is as long as the ovary and the flowers are scented.
Flowers: April to June.
Habitat: grassy hillsides, woodland, maquis and garigue.   **153, 154**

Distribution: Spain; France; Germany; Austria and Switzerland (only up to 1500m); Italy; Sicily; Corsica; Sardinia; Yugoslavia; Greece; Crete; Turkey; Lebanon; Poland; Czechoslovakia; Hungary; Bulgaria; Rumania; Crimea; Caucasus. There is one highly dubious record from northern Cyprus.

Ssp. **commutata** (Tod.) Nyman. This tends to be an altogether more slender plant than the type, with a lax flower spike carrying far fewer but larger flowers (lip 8–10mm long, as opposed to 6–9mm in the nominate race). The sepals and petals are larger, producing a more attenuated and less convergent hood. The lip is wider, with the lateral lobes almost horizontal. Flowers found by the authors in Sicily had a noticeably stronger scent than flowers of the nominate race.

Although the plant has characteristics which set it apart from the nominate race, it has a similar geographical distribution and perhaps deserves no more than the varietal status it has been given by some writers.   **155, 156**

Orchis lactea Poiret
Sometimes classed as a subspecies of *O. tridentata*, this plant reaches up to

20cm in height. It is generally more robust in appearance than *O. tridentata*, with a thicker stem and broader, oblong, lanceolate leaves. The flower bracts are short, and the inflorescence is a dense cylinder or ovoid with a whiskered appearance because of the long fine points to the sepals forming the hood. The sepals and petals are white or pale pink, prominently veined (in green or purplish-red) and suffused with green towards their bases. The lip is 3-lobed, with a white or cream ground colour and fine red or purplish spots. In some plants these spots are close enough at the lip edge to merge into a continuous border. The lateral lobes are spreading, and the central lobe has parallel edges for part of its length, flaring towards the apex where it is usually only slightly indented (sometimes it is entire). It differs from the closely related *O. tridentata* in its small stature and robust appearance, cylindrical whiskery spike, and lip where part of the central lobe has parallel edges.

Varieties: Var. *albiflora* Post has white unspotted flowers.

Var. apiculata – this is a name sometimes given to Majorcan plants.

Flowers: February (N. Africa) to April.

Habitat: dry grassy hillsides and garigue.

Distribution: widespread but local throughout the Mediterranean region; N. Africa; Spain; Balearics; southern Italy; France (?); Corsica; Sardinia; Sicily (frequent in mountain pastures on limestone); Yugoslavia (?); Corfu (very rare, but a good form); Greece; Crete; Rhodes; Lebanon; Turkey (?). **157, 158**

Orchis italica Poiret

WAVY-LEAVED MONKEY ORCHID; ORCHIS ONDULÉ (F); ITALIENISCHES KNABENKRAUT (G); UOMO NUDO (I).

This orchid varies from 20–40cm in height, with 5–8 leaves in a basal rosette and sheaths higher up the stem. In shape the leaves are broadly lanceolate and an important characteristic for identification is their wavy edge (sometimes they are blotched in dark purple-brown. The bracts are short (about ¼–⅓ the length

of the ovary) and the inflorescence is farily dense, conical at first but becoming ovoid as the upper flowers open. The sepals and petals are about the same length (10mm) and converge to form a pointed hood which is pale pink/lilac in colour, with purple or, occasionally, deep red veins. The lip is 3-lobed, with the laterals slender and pointed, the median lobe deeply divided, with pointed divisions and an apical protuberance. The ground colour is pink, often with purplish spots. The spur is only ½ the length of the ovary and is cylindrical and downward pointing.

Confusion can sometimes arise between dark-coloured forms of *O. italica* and *O. simia* but *O. italica* has leaves with a wavy edge and the flowers open from bottom to top. Also the lobes of the lip taper to a point (in *O. simia* they are linear).

Varieties: Var. *albiflora* Nicotra ex Paol. – with white flowers, not unusual in large colonies of the usual form.

Var. *purpurea* Vöth has dark red flowers.

Flowers: March to April.

Habitat: on calcareous soils in grassy areas, garigue and open woodlands (pine).

Distribution: frequent around the Mediterranean; N. Africa; Spain; Balearics; mid- & southern Italy; Sicily; Yugoslavia; Greece; Crete; Rhodes; Cyprus; Turkey; Lebanon. **159, 160**

Orchis simia Lam.

MONKEY ORCHID; ORCHIS SINGE (F); AFFEN-KNABENKRAUT (G).

The plant stands 20–45cm tall, with 3–5 broadly lanceolate leaves near the base and others sheathing the stem higher up. The flower bracts vary from ⅕–½ the length of the ovary, and the inflorescence is short and fairly dense, forming an ovoid or cylindrical shape. The flowering sequence is from top to bottom. The sepals and petals are approximately the same length (about 10cm) and converge to form a peaked helmet, which ranges in colour from pale greyish-pink, through pink, to red, and often streaked in a reddish shade. Inside, the helmet is spotted or veined in red. The lip is 3-lobed, with the median lobe deeply divided and a small apical appendage. The laterals and the divisions of the median are all slender and coloured deep magenta or red at their extremities, while the base of the lip and the undivided part of the median lobe is whitish with fine reddish hairs forming 'spots'. The spur is cylindrical and about ½ as long as the ovary. It points downwards. The flower spike looks very much like a collection of tiny, dancing monkeys, with slender arms, legs and tails.

Varieties: Var. *alba* Zimm. with white flowers.

Flowers: end of March (in the south) to early June (in the north).

Habitat: Usually on calcareous soils in open grasslands, hillsides, scrub, garigue, open woodlands (pine).   **163, 164**

Distribution: N. Africa; Spain; France; UK (very rare in south-east England, but good colonies have been encouraged by hand pollination in Kent); Germany (only in Kaiserstuhl and Saarland area); Benelux; Switzerland (only in southwest); Italy; Yugoslavia; Greece (abundant in some sites); Crete; Rhodes; Turkey; Cyprus (mostly in north; very infrequent in south and centre of island); Lebanon; Hungary (in the south); Bulgaria; Crimea; Caucasus.

Orchis steveni Reichenb. fil.
This orchid had been little studied until recently, when descriptions appeared together with a range of superb photographs, in *Flora Iranica* (J. Renz – in the volume dealing with the *Orchidaceae*).

Nevsky considered it as a stabilised hybrid of *O. simia* and *O. militaris* or possibly just a geographical variant of *O. militaris*. Unfortunately these conclusions were based on illustrations in Reichenbach's work of 1851 and he had made his drawings from a dried herbarium specimen collected by Steven. Later work was affected because the colour of the plants in the illustration did not correspond with any of the colour forms found by Renz and others.

It is obviously closely related to the group of orchids including *O. purpurea*, *O. punctulata*, *O. militaris* and *O. simia* but has the following characteristics that seem to make it worthy of specific status:

The plants are robust and up to 60cm tall. The stem is leafy with 4–7 erect spreading shining bright green leaves. They are unspotted and have a length of up to 20cm.   **165**

The inflorescence is dense, with numerous flowers arranged in a cylindrical shape which can in especially robust specimens be 25cm long. The bracts are minute, being no more than 3–4mm long.

The flowers are rather large with sepals up to 12mm long coloured greenish with a brownish-purple flushing on the outside and dotted inside with the same shade of purple along the nerves. The lip is deeply lobed, with a ground colour of greenish-cream and the ends of the lobes flushed with green, rose, yellow or even pure white. Its centre carries thick dark purple hairs, and the side lobes are linear with a length of 5–7mm and a width of 1mm. Like *Orchis militaris*, the median lobe is split to form two lobules ('legs'). These are 3–5mm long and 2.5–4mm broad, with a small tooth between.

The spur thickens towards the apex and is about half as long as the ovary.

Flowers: end of April to May.

habitat: often in forests of oak, grassy places in woodlands up to 1500m.

Distribution: a rare plant confined to Turkey (north-east Anatolia); Caucasus, Crimea; Transcaucasia and northern Iran.

A plant found in Turcomania on the Russian side of the Kophet Dag mountain has been called *O. adenocheila* E. Czernjakovska. Little is known of it but it seems to be identical to *O. steveni*.

Orchis galilea (Bornm. & Schulze) Schlechter
GALILEAN ORCHID; GALILÄISCHES KNABENKRAUT (G).

An altogether more slender plant than the closely related *O. punctulata*, this orchid varies from 15–35cm in height and has 5–8 lanceolate leaves. The flower bracts are very short – about ¹⁄₆ the length of the ovary. The inflorescence forms a fairly lax cylinder, with flowers blooming from top to bottom. The sepals and petals converge to form a hood and are greenish-yellow, either with red veining or without. The lip is 3-lobed, with the median lobe deeply divided, again giving an 'arms and legs' appearance but with a much smaller (almost imperceptible) apical protuberance than with *O. punctulata*. The ground colour is invariably greenish-yellow, and there are reddish spots near the base of the lip. The downward pointing spur is short, being only ¼ the length of the ovary.

Flowers: an early-flowering species; February to April (on hills).

Habitat: old olive groves and stony places on hillsides; always on calcareous soils.

Distribution: Israel (occurring together with the usual forms there are some strikingly coloured plants whose flowers have reddish-violet lip edges and whose helmet is red-veined); Lebanon; Syria. Rather rare and local in all the countries mentioned. **166**

Orchis militaris L.
MILITARY ORCHID; ORCHIS MILITAIRE (F); HELM-KNABENKRAUT (G); GIGLIO-CRESTATO (I).

This species occurs in both small (25cm) and robust (up to 65cm) forms, depending on the favourability of the location. The taller specimens usually occur in damp soils at shady woodland edges.

There are 3–5 broadly lanceolate leaves near the base, with sheaths higher up the stem. The inflorescence is fairly dense and is conical in shape at first, but becomes cylindrical as the upper flowers open. The flower bracts are much shorter than the ovary, often with a violet tinge. Both sepals and petals converge to form a hood which is whitish or greyish-pink outside, with purple veins inside. The lip is 3-lobed, with the laterals more or less curved. The median lobe is nar-

row until the apex where it spreads into a triangular shape which is deeply divided to give 'legs'. There is a very small protuberance which forms a tail. The ground colour varies from white through to deep pink, with the median lobe lighter in shade near the base, where small tufts of reddish hair make up the 'speckling'. The spur is narrowly cylindrical and points downwards.

Varieties: Var. *albiflora* Blümml. has white flowers.

Flowers: April to June.

Habitat: undisturbed calcareous grassland, open woodlands, thickets, forest edges.

Distribution: Britain (now very rare and confined to a few protected sites); Germany (some magnificent colonies); France; Sweden (particularly Götland); Benelux; Switzerland; Austria (up to 1800m); northern Italy; Yugoslavia; northern Greece; Poland; Czechoslovakia; Hungary; Bulgaria; Romania; Russia; Crimea; Caucasus; Turkey (?). **161, 162**

Orchis punctulata Steven ex Lindley
PUNCTATE ORCHID; PUNKTIERTES KNABENKRAUT (G).

The best forms of this orchid can be robust spikes up to 60cm tall, with 4–7 large, oblong leaves forming the lower rosette and upper leaves sheathing the stem. The flower bracts are much shorter than the ovary, and the inflorescence is cylindrical and fairly dense, bearing numerous flowers. The flowers open in the usual bottom-top sequence (which distinguishes it from the closely related *O. galilea*, where the sequence is reversed). The sepals and petals converge to form a helmet, which is yellowish- or whitish-green outside (rarely, there is a pink tinge in evidence). Inside, the helmet is streaked and blotched along the veins with reddish- or purplish-brown. In shape the sepals are oblong-ovate, about 8–11mm in length, whilst the petals are shorter and nearly oblong. The lip is 3-lobed, with the middle lobe deeply divided, giving the same 'arms and legs' appearance as with *O. militaris*, and a small appendage forming a 'tail'. The lateral lobes are rather narrow and oblong.

Two quite distinct colour forms are found growing together: the first has the lip an overall greenish-yellow, with very faint spotting in red on the median lobe; the second is far more striking, with the edges of the lobes a deep chestnut brown and tufts of reddish-brown hairs forming 'blotches' on a median lobe which is deep yellow in colour. The spur is broadly cylindrical, about ⅓ the length of the ovary, and points downwards. The flowers are vanilla-scented.

Flowers: at low levels it is in full flower in mid-February, extending to May in mountainous regions.

Habitat: garigue, deserted vineyards, forest margins, thickets, conifer woodland.

Distribution: Crimea; Turkey; Caucasus; western Transcaucasia; Iran; Cyprus (very rare). Older records from Lebanon and Israel are doubtful because of confusion with *O. galilea*. It does occur in north Lebanon in a form in which the brown edge to the flowers is a deep chocolate colour and spreads to occupy most of the lip.

One of the rarities amongst European orchids. **167, 168**

Ssp. sepulchralis (Boiss. & Heldr.) Soó. This form has a larger helmet (up to 15mm) and a longer lip (up to 15mm) than the nominate race. The lateral lobes of the lip are broader and the spur is about ½ the length of the ovary. The plants are extremely robust and to all intents and purposes are just large-flowered forms of *O. punctulata*. In *Flora Europaea* it is accorded subspecific status, but Sundermann (*Europäische und Mediterrane Orchideen*) and Renz (*Flora Iranica*) suggest that it does not really deserve elevation to this level. From our own observations on the small population growing in Cyprus we have found extremely robust, large-flowered forms growing in the same location as rather small-flowered, slender plants. The large-flowered forms are as much as 3–4 times the height of the others. **169, 170**

Another plant, *O. schelkownikowii* Woronow, from Transcaucasia is now regarded as being identical with *O. punctulata*.

Orchis purpurea Hudson

LADY ORCHID; ORCHIS CASQUE (F); PURPUR-KNABENKRAUT (G).

O. purpurea is among the tallest of European orchids: plants can be from 30–80cm tall in the case of very robust specimens. There are 3–6 broadly lanceolate or ovoid, shiny green leaves on the lower part of the stem, with sheaths higher up. The flower bracts are about ½ the length of the ovary, and the flower spike is cylindrical and many-flowered. Sepals and petals converge to form a rounded helmet, which is deep reddish-to brownish-purple on the outside. Some forms occur with pink helmet with dense purple spots, and very pale forms with a greenish helmet and white lip have also been recorded. The lip is 3-lobed, with narrow laterals and the median spreading to form a broad triangle. At the apex the lip is slightly divided, with a small indistinct protuberance. The ground colour is white or pink, with dark hairs forming purple spots. The spur is broadly cylindrical and points downwards. The flowers have the appearance of country women in broad skirts with a poke bonnet: hence the name 'Lady Orchid'. There is little possibility of confusion with any other orchid because of the very broad lip.

Varieties: Var. *albiflora* Rossb. is the name given to the form mentioned above with the green helmet and whitish lip.

Flowers: April to June (depending on latitude).

Habitat: scrub, grasslands, woodlands – often in quite dense beech, conifer plantations, usually on calcareous soils up to 700m.

Distribution: UK (rare, but there are still superb specimens to be found in reserves in Kent); Denmark; Spain; France; N. Africa; Germany; Benelux; Switzerland; Austria (not on high ground); Italy; Corsica; Yugoslavia; Greece; Turkey; Poland; Czechoslovakia; Hungary; Bulgaria; Romania; Crimea; Caucasus; unconfirmed reports for Sicily and Sardinia. **171, 172**

Orchis saccata Ten.
ORCHIS À FILTRE (F);
SACKSPORNIGES KNABENKRAUT (G).
This is a thick set species, growing 10–30cm tall, with a basal rosette of 2–4 oblong, ovate leaves and dense sheaths above. Occasionally the leaves carry a few dark spots. The bracts are about ½ the length of the ovary and tinged with purple, with 5–7 veins. The flower spike is a rather narrow cylinder or oblong, often with few flowers (anything from 2–15 blooms). The dorsal sepal is curved forward and forms a hood with the petals. The lateral sepals are erect or even curved backwards. The lip is entire and shaped like a fan, with wavy edges. The flowers come in two colour forms, the first pinkish-red to deep purplish-red, with a basal white area on the lip, the second (and less frequent) form with greenish-pink sepals and a greenish-brown lip. The spur is short, conical and downward pointing.
Varieties: Var. *albiflora* Sommier & Gatto – with white lip and greenish-white sepals and petals.
Flowers: an early-flowering species, coming into flower in February and usually past its best by mid-March. Occasional late specimens can be found in April, whilst in Cyprus it flowers in mid-January, near the south coast of the island.
Habitat: usually in dry, grassy places or garigue, more rarely in open woodland, on calcareous soils.
Distribution: rather rare and local, although it has a wide distribution; N. Africa; southern Spain; Majorca; southern France (extremely rare); Italy (Mt Gargano); Sardinia; Sicily; Greece; Crete; Rhodes; Cyprus; Turkey; Lebanon; Caucasus; to Persia and Turkestan. **173, 174**

Ssp. *chlorotica* Woronow. An extremely rare and little-known plant from Transcaucasia which has the lateral sepals forming the hood, and a greenish-yellow lip.

Ssp. *cyrenaica* Durd. & Barr. Plants from Libya with slightly 3-lobed lip and a conical spur are thought by some authorities to be a distinct subspecies or even species.

Orchis patens Desf.
GREEN SPOTTED ORCHID; ORCHIS ÉTALÉ (F); ATLAS-KNABENKRAUT (G).
A stately orchid, this species grows 20–45cm tall with a basal rosette or cluster of 3–5 oblong-ovate to lanceolate leaves and sheaths higher up on the stem. The flower bracts are as long as the ovary, and the spike is a long, lax cylinder with as many as 30 flowers on it.

Fig. 33

The dorsal sepals and the petals are curved forwards and are pink in colour on their outside surface. The lateral sepals are erect or, less often, horizontal, with a green blotch near their bases and red spotting, both on the inside surface. The lip is 3-lobed, with the median lobe just longer than the lateral lobes and slightly indented at its apex. In colour it is pink to dark red, with reddish spots on the light area near the lip base. The spur

is thick, conical and points downwards.
Flowers: March to May.
Habitat: open woodland, scrubby places, mountain meadows up to 1600m.
Distribution: a local plant, with a mainly western distribution; Algeria; Tunisia; southern Spain (?); Balearics; northern Italy (Liguria). **175**

In a paper published in 1978, L. Hautzinger suggests that there are a number of orchid species closely allied to *O. patens* and suggests the following names:
O. prisca (also named *O. spitzelii* ssp. *nitidiflora*), found in Crete.
O. clandestina, a very restricted distribution in NW peninsular Italy.
O. bungii, Iran.

Orchis canariensis Lindley

This orchid has 5–7 ovate, unspotted leaves, mostly grouped around the base, with one or two sheathing the stem, and it grows between 15 and 35cm tall. The flower bracts are slightly longer than the ovary, and the spike is moderately lax, carrying anything from 5 to 20 flowers. The dorsal sepal and petals are slightly incurved to form a loose hood, while the lateral sepals are usually spread. The lip is 3-lobed, with the median lobe longer than the laterals. The overall flower colour is pinkish-white to pink, with red spots on the lip, whilst the sepals are tinted greenish on their inner surface. The spur is about ½ the length of the ovary and horizontal or upward pointing.
Flowers: February to March.
Habitat: shady ravines, mountain thickets, pine woodlands.
Distribution: endemic to the Canaries, where it is frequent in the upper xerophytic zone on most of the islands. **176**

Orchis spitzelii Sauter ex Koch

SPITZEL'S ORCHID; ORCHIS DE SPITZEL (F); SPITZELS KNABENKRAUT (G).

The plant stands 20–50cm tall, with a basal rosette or cluster of 2–4 oblong-ovate leaves and the remaining leaves sheathing the stem above (the stem can either be erect or slightly zig-zagged – 'flexuous'). The bracts are about the same length as the ovary, and the flowers are carried in an ovoid or cylindrical spike. There are from 5–20 flowers, with dorsal sepal and petals slightly curved to form a loose hood and the laterals incurving or erect.

Fig. 34

The sepals are brownish on their inner surface, without spots and without a pale margin. The lip is 3-lobed, with the median lobe slightly indented and with a wavy margin and the lateral lobes often folded under it. In colour it is pink to dark red (without the light basal area of *O. patens*) and carries red dots. The spur is only just shorter than the ovary, conical and points downwards.

This species can be confused with *O. patens*, a closely related species, but they may be distinguished by: brownish sepals in *O. spitzelii*, greenish in *O. patens* (see *O. spitzelii* ssp. *nitidifolia* below); the spur in *O. spitzelii* is longer than in *O. patens*; the pale basal area near the lip base, which carries the spots in *O. patens*, is absent in *O. spitzelii*; and, most important, in *O.patens* the base of the lip is cut with a v-shaped notch at the mouth of the spur, whereas in *O. spitzelii* the lip base is curved, producing a much wider opening.
Flowers: from April in the south to July

(at higher altitudes in Italy and in the Alps).

Habitat: mountain grasslands, pine- and beechwoods (up to 1800m), always on calcareous soils. On low ground in Sweden (Götland).

Distribution: a rare and local species, although it has a wide distribution; Algeria; Spain; France (Alps); Austria; Italy (southern Alps); Yugoslavia; northern Lebanon; Turkey; Crimea; Caucasus. It occurs in Sweden (Götland), where it was discovered in 1939 and named as a variety of the nominate race – var. *götlandica*. Many botanists consider it identical with the nominate race. **177, 178**

Ssp. *nitidifolia* (Teschner) Soó. This plant is restricted to Crete, where it is the only race of this species. It has shiny green leaves, the sepals are greenish inside and carry red spots (compare *O. patens*), the margins are pale pink.

The spur is slender with a slight thickening towards the base, is curved and points downwards.

Some have considered the plants closer to *O. patens* and have named them *O. patens* ssp. *falcicalcarata*. More recently they have been raised to specific status in certain quarters as *O. prisca* Hautzinger.

Flowers: April.

Distribution: Crete (plants from Turkey and northern Lebanon often resemble this subspecies).

Orchis mascula L.

EARLY PURPLE ORCHID; ORCHIS MÂLE (F); KUCKUCKSKNABENKRAUT (G); GIGLIO-CAPRINO (I).

Unusually for members of the genus *Orchis* this species has a large number of distinct races which merit subspecific status.

The nominate race is probably the commonest European orchid and the one which most people associate with the name *Orchis*. It stands 20–50cm (exceptionally, 60cm) tall, with 3–5 leaves in the lower part and sheaths above. The leaves are broadly lanceolate and coloured a shining green, with dark purplish spots (rarely, they are unspotted). The flower bracts are lanceolate, with 1–3 veins, shorter than the ovary and tinged with purple. From 6–20 flowers are carried in fairly dense cylindrical or ovoid spikes. The dorsal sepal and the petals are incurved to form a helmet, whilst the lateral sepals are spreading or slightly reflexed. They are coloured mauve or reddish-purple. The lip is 3-lobed, with the median lobe notched at its apex and the side lobes either very slightly deflexed or not deflexed at all. The central part of the lip is whitish, with deep crimson or purple spots. The median lobe can be up to 1½ times the length of the lateral lobes. The spur is usually as long as the ovary, slightly thickened at its end and horizontal or upward-pointing. The flowers have an odour of cats' urine.

Flowers: April to June.

Habitat: open woodlands (one of the few orchids to thrive in oakwoods, where it can carpet the ground, alongside bluebells – *Scilla non-scriptus*), moist grasslands, thickets, usually on cledgy soils, up to 2650m.

Distribution: a locally common orchid over much of west and central Europe; N. Africa; Spain; Balearica; Austria; Switzerland; France; UK; Scandinavia; Germany; Benelux; Italy; Corsica; Yugoslavia; Greece; Crete; Rhodes; Turkey; Poland; Czechoslovakia; Hungary; Bulgaria; Rumania; Russia; Caucasus. **179, 180**

Ssp. *signifera* (Vest) Soó. This distinctive race has a dense flower spike carrying a large number of blooms. The flowers themselves have a remarkable 'whiskered' appearance because the sepals and petals end in long fine points. The perianth segments are curved inwards and form a loose hood with a spiked apex. The median lobe of the labellum can be up to twice the length of the lateral lobes (which are not deflexed). The spur is as long as the ovary.

Distribution: central, southern and eastern Europe: the southern Alps of Austria and Switzerland; Yugoslavia; Poland; Hungary; Bulgaria; Rumania; Russia; Crimea; Caucasus. **181**

Ssp. *olbiensis* (Reuter ex Grenier) Ascherson & Graebner. This is a slender orchid with lanceolate leaves that are usually unspotted. The spike is lax and carries comparatively few flowers (5–15). The lateral sepal is erect, and petals and sepals are pale pink or reddish in colour. The lip is pale, carrying fine purple spots at its centre and with lateral lobes which are deflexed. The median lobe is about 1½ times the length of the laterals. The spur is longer than the ovary and points upwards; the cat odour is lacking.
Distribution: western Mediterranean, more or less replacing the nominate race in N. Africa; Spain; Balearics; southern France; Italy (Liguria); Corsica. **182**

Ssp. *wanikowii* (Wulff) Soó. This is the least likely of the subspecies to be encountered because of its very restricted distribution. It has a lax spike with few flowers, sepals and petals are lilac, the sepals also having brownish-purple veins. The median lobe of the lip is about 1½ times the length of the laterals and the lip edges are not deflexed. The spur is shorter than the ovary.
Distribution: Crimea.

Ssp. *hispanica* (A. & C. Nieschalk) Soó. This is not a particularly distinct race. The flower spike is lax and many-flowered. The sepals and petals are blunt-ended and coloured purple. The middle lobe is only slightly longer than the laterals (which are not deflexed). The spur is variable in length, ranging from equal to to shorter than the ovary.
Varieties: Var. *alba* Goir has white flowers.
Distribution: mountains of western Spain, central Pyrenees.

Ssp. *pinetorum* (Boiss. & Kotschy) Camus. This subspecies has leaves which are broad and unspotted. The flower bracts are about ½ the length of the ovary. The flowers have an unspotted lip, with a middle lobe that is almost kidney-shaped. The spur is shorter than the ovary.

Distribution: Turkey; Caucasus; Iran; and possibly in Lebanon and the Crimea.

Ssp. *scopulorum* Summ. Plants from the island of Madeira have darker, larger flowers than the nominate race. The lip is 3-lobed, spotted and the spur is short (about half the length of the ovary).
Distribution: endemic to Madeira, although similar plants occur at a single station in pine woods on La Palma (Canary Islands).

Orchis pallens L.
PALE-FLOWERED ORCHID; ORCHIS PÂLE (F); BLEICHES KNABENKRAUT (G).
One of the few yellow-flowered orchids found in Europe, this species has 3–5 broadly oblong leaves at the base, with sheaths above, and a total height of 15–35cm. The flower bracts are about as long as the ovary, and the spike forms a dense-flowered oblong or ovoid shape.

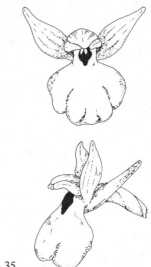

Fig. 35

The dorsal sepal and petals curve to form a loose helmet, with the lateral sepals erect. The lip is distinctly 3-lobed and coloured yellow, like the other perianth segments, but usually with a brighter shade. The spur is slightly shorter than the ovary, cylindrical in shape, and horizontal or upward-pointing (in *Dactylorhiza sambucina* it points downwards). The flowers are strongly scented of elder (*Sambucus niger*), unlike those of the misnamed 'Elderflower Orchid' (*D. sambucina*) which do not have this smell. Possibly the confusion arose over these species because they are both yellow and favour mountain pastures.

Very pale forms are found with a white lip (var. *albiflora*); these, and a form with overall rose-pink colour, are decidedly rare.

Flowers: April to June.

Habitat: alpine and sub-alpine woods and meadows up to 2000m.

Distribution: a rather local orchid, sometimes numerous where it occurs, with a wide distribution in central and southern Europe; Spain; France (especially Maritime Alps and Haute Savoie); Germany; Belgium; Austria; Switzerland; Italy; Yugoslavia; Greece; Turkey; Poland; Czechoslovakia; Hungary; Bulgaria; Rumania; Crimea; Caucasus. **183, 186**

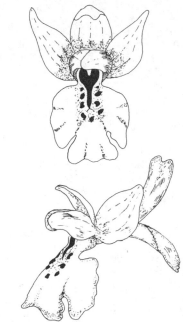

Fig. 36

Orchis provincialis Balbis
PROVENCE ORCHID; ORCHIS DE PROVENCE (F); FRANZÖSISCHES KNABENKRAUT (G).

Like *O. pallens* this is one of the few yellow-flowered *Orchis* species. It is a rather slender plant, 15–35cm tall, with 2–5 broadly lanceolate leaves forming the basal rosette and sheaths higher up the stem. The basal leaves invariably carry dark spots. The flower bracts are narrow, with 1–3 veins, and are at least as long as the ovary. The flower spike is cylindrical and varies from lax to dense, depending on the number of flowers (from 7–20) carried.

The dorsal sepal is erect and the laterals spreading, whilst the petals curve inwards to form a partial helmet. Sepals and petals are pale yellow or creamy white. The lip is 3-lobed and a deep shade of yellow which contrasts well with the sepals and petals. The central part of the lip deepens to orange-yellow in colour and carries a number of purplish-red spots.

Flowers: April to June.

Habitat: grassy slopes, open woodland under pines, thickets and scrub. In its woodland haunts it is often found on slightly acid soils but it also occurs on calcareous soils.

Distribution: N. Africa; Spain; southern France; Switzerland; Austria (southern Alps up to 1300m); Italy; Corsica; Sardinia; Sicily; Yugoslavia; Greece; Crete; Rhodes; Turkey; Bulgaria; Crimea; Caucasus. **184, 187**

Ssp. ***pauciflora*** (Ten.) Camus = *O. pauciflora* Ten. This is very similar to the nominate race but differs in having leaves that are unspotted (or have very few spots) and a lax flower spike – seldom more than 3–7 flowers. The flower bracts are shorter than the ovary. The lip is 3-lobed and the median lobe is indented, while the lateral lobe is bent to give the lip a flattened appearance.

Flowers: April to June (can be in flower in late March in southern Crete).

Habitat: scrubby places on hillsides,

open pinewoods, always on calcareous soils.

Distribution: tends to have an Eastern distribution, being found in the eastern or central Mediterranean, where it seems to be fairly rare and local; Italy (Mt Gargano); Yugoslavia; Corsica (?); Sicily; Greece (frequent on Mt Hymettus near Athens); Crete (not uncommon on low slopes near the sea); Turkey.

185, 188

Orchis quadripunctata Cyr. ex Ten.
FOUR-SPOTTED ORCHID;
VIERPUNKT-KNABENKRAUT (G).

A delicate, slender orchid, usually 10–20cm tall (occasionally up to 25 or 30cm), often with a slightly flexous stem and a basal rosette of 2–5 spotted lanceolate or oblong leaves, with sheaths higher up the stem.

The flower spike is ovoid or an elongated cylinder, with up to 20 flowers, and the flower bracts vary from shorter than to equal to the length of the ovary. The flowers are small, with the lateral sepals more or less spreading, whilst the median is erect and the petals form a loose hood. In length, the sepals are 3–5mm, whilst the petals are 2–5mm. The lip is 3-lobed (rarely entire) and there are two or more often four red spots near its base, which give it its Latin name (*quadripunctata* = 4-spotted). The flowers range from pink to deep violet-pink, with a whitish area near the base of the lip where the spots are carried.

Varieties: Var. *alba* Raulin: has white flowers with red spots and occurs throughout the range of the species.

Var. *brancifortii* (Biv.) Boiss.: known from hillsides in Sicily and Sardinia, this form has very small flowers. The sepals are ovoid and the lip 3-lobed. But in this form the side lobes are very narrow and curved forward, the central lobe is small and parallel for much of its length, coming to a point only at the apex (Fig. 37).

Flowers: April to May (March in Cyprus).

Habitat: scrubby places, stony hillsides, under pines.

Distribution: a rather local and uncom-

mon orchid; Southern Italy (Mt Gargano); Sardinia; Sicily; Yugoslavia; Greece; Crete; Cyprus; Lebanon; southern Turkey.

189, 190

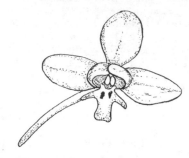

Fig. 37

Orchis anatolica Boiss.
ANATOLIAN ORCHID; ANATOLISCHES
KNABENKRAUT (G).

Rather variable in height, this orchid ranges from 15–40cm, sometimes with a slightly flexous stem. There is a basal rosette of 2–5 lanceolate, spotted leaves, with the rest sheathing the stem for part of its length. The flower bracts are less than ½ the length of the ovary, and the spike is lax, with comparatively few flowers. The lateral sepals are erect, about 8–10mm in length, and the dorsal sepal is incurved with the petals to form a loose hood. The lip is 3-lobed and convex. The lateral lobes are slightly shorter than the median lobe (which has a triangular indentation at the apex). The flowers are variable in colour, from white through pale pink to deep magenta. The base of the lip is spotted with red. The spur is long and gently tapering, either straight and horizontal or upward-pointing, and actually overlapping the main stem.

Varieties: Var. *troodii* Renz: very robust forms (up to 50cm) occur in the upper parts of the Troodos massif in Cyprus, in volcanic soils. At these altitudes it often replaces the small form, but any population of *O. anatolica* on the island will contain large, robust forms. As well as the thicker stem and greater height in the variety the spur is curved upward and is swollen at the tip. The lateral sepals are

spreading and suffused with green near the base. The lip is folded almost in half, and the inflorescence is as much as 20cm in length. The leaves are almost oval.
192

Var. *sitiaca* Renz, from the mountains of Crete, has paler flowers. The sepals and petals are green-veined and the lip strongly folded. The narrow, elongated median lobe is spotted up to its edges. The spur is upward-pointing and thickened at its apex. This form is a similar to var. *troodii*.

Var. *albiflora* has white flowers and occurs throughout the range of the plant.
Flowers: March (late February in the lower parts of the Troodos massif in Cyprus) to late April (at higher altitudes).
Habitat: mountain regions, sparsely grassy places, open scrub and light pine-woods.
Distribution: an eastern Mediterranean, species; Aegean Isles; Crete; Rhodes; Cyprus; western & southern Turkey; Lebanon (frequent in northern mountains); Iran.
191

Orchis laxiflora Lam.
LAX-FLOWERED ORCHID; ORCHIS À FLEURS LÂCHES (F); LOCKERBLÜTIGES KNABENKRAUT (G).

One of the impressive sights of the orchid world is a damp field turned purple with the tall, stately spikes of this orchid. It grows from 30–120cm tall, with 3–8 lanceolate leaves that are both channelled and unspotted . The flower bracts are shorter than the ovary, with a reddish-purple tinge. The flower spike is lax, with 6–20 flowers grouped to give it an ovoid or cylindrical shape. The sepals are 7–10mm long and spread outwards, whilst the petals are slightly incurved, forming a loose helmet. The lip is 7–9mm long and, although it is distinctly 3-lobed, the central lobe is shorter than the laterals, forming a 'tooth' between them. The flower parts come in a range of shades of pink, from light pink, through violet, to a deep red. White

forms are rare. The spur is about ½–⅔ the length of the ovary, thickened at its apex and horizontal or gently upward-pointing.

There is a form, sometimes separated as var. *dielsiana* Camus or even ssp. *dielsiana*, with smaller blooms. The lip has side lobes that are reduced in size, or the lip can be entire.
Flowers: April to June (occasionally late March in Corfu and Samos).
Habitat: always on wet ground; marshes, boggy meadows, dune slacks, where the water tends to be slightly alkaline.
Distribution: although most frequent in the Mediterranean region it reaches as far in the north-west as the Channel Islands (probably the advent of the glacial epochs prevented it making inroads into the UK mainland); N. Africa; Spain; Balearics; France; Channel Islands; Belgium; Austria & Switzerland (lower valleys up to 1150m); Italy; Corsica; Sardinia; Sicily; Yugoslavia; Greece; Crete; Rhodes; Turkey; Lebanon; Cyprus (once common in coastal marshes but now nearly wiped out by their drainage for fruit trees).
193, 194

Ssp. palustris (Jacq.) Bonnier & Layens
ORCHIS DES MARAIS (F); SUMPFKNABENKRAUT (G).

Only in recent years has this orchid been regarded as a sub-species of *O. laxiflora*. Formerly it was treated as a distinct species (*O. palustris*) but the differences are not really sufficient to support any more than subspecific status. The main differences between ssp. *palustris* and the nominate race are: the flower spike is not as 'loose' in appearance because the ovary is shorter in length, thus bringing the flowers closer to the stem; the lip is deeply 3-lobed, up to 10mm in length, with the middle lobe notched and at least as long as the laterals; the spur tapers to the apex, or again can remain parallel for most of its length (only rarely does it become thickened at the end).
Varieties: Var. *albiflora* Guss has white flowers.
Var. *rosea* Cortesi has light pink flowers.

Var. *robusta* (T. Stephenson) Gölz & Reinhard: particularly robust plants with large flowers having 3-lobed lips and straight spurs. Found mainly in the south-west of the plant's distribution.
Flowers: April to June.
Distribution: mainly in the northern and western parts of the range of the nominate race, reaching Götland (Sweden) as the northernmost limit; N. Africa; Spain; France; Sweden (Götland); Germany; Benelux; Austria & Switzerland (Alps, up to 1150m); Italy; Balearics; Yugoslavia; Greece; Turkey; Poland; Czechoslovakia; Hungary; Bulgaria; Rumania; Russia; Crimea; Caucasus.

195, 196

Ssp. *elegans* (Heuffel) Soó. This is a large-flowered form, with a labellum up to 12mm in length and either entire or indistinctly 3-lobed. The median lobe is at least as long as the laterals, and the spur is narrower at its apex, ranging from equal in length to the ovary to shorter.
Distribution: east and east-central Europe.

Aceras

At various stages in the history of botanical classification *Aceras* has been grouped under other headings, *Orchis*, *Serapias*, *Himantoglossum* and even *Ophrys* providing the bedfellows. It seems that botanists have long been aware of the close links between *Aceras* and other genera, although subtle differences in the genus led to confusion in deciding where exactly to place it.

Finally it was put into a genus on its own. The word *aceras* itself means 'without spur', and it is precisely this lack of spur that provides the main reason for not grouping *Aceras* in the genus *Orchis*.

One gains the impression that *Aceras* and *Orchis* are not too far apart, because of the ease with which *Aceras* hybridises with certain species of *Orchis* when they occur in the wild together. Indeed, close examination of the stamens and column of *Aceras* reveals a great similarity between these and the same parts in *Orchis simia*. They differ only in the placing of the viscidia which, in *Aceras*, are very close together and almost adhere to one another. They are covered by a bursicle which stops them drying out prematurely. Not surprisingly, *Orchis simia* is one of the orchids which readily hybridises with *Aceras anthropophorum*; others are the closely related *Orchis purpurea* and *O. militaris*.

In Britain there are parts of Kent where *Orchis purpurea* and *Aceras anthropophorum* occur in the same small area but no hybrids are found. In Britain *O. purpurea* is a woodland orchid whereas *A. anthropophorum* thrives in grasslands, so there is little likelihood of the same insects visiting both species and allowing hybridisation.

A. anthropophorum possesses a slight scent, but it is not to everyone's liking. There is more than a hint of *coumarin* – new-mown hay – about it, which becomes more pronounced as the plant dries out.

Hybrids
These occur most frequently with the genus *Orchis*:
A. anthropophorum x *Orchis coriophora* = un-named Keller

A. anthropophorum x *Orchis italica* = x *Orchiaceras bivonae* Soó
A. anthropophorum x *Orchis militaris* = x *Orchiaceras spuria* Camus
A. anthropophorum x *Orchis purpurea* = x *Orchiaceras duffortii* Keller
A. anthropophorum x *Orchis simia* = x *Orchiaceras bergonii* Camus

A few hybrids with other genera have been noted:
A. anthropophorum x *Barlia robertiana* = x *Barlaceras terraccianoi* Camus
A. anthropophorum x *Dactylorhiza majalis* = x *Dactyloaceras helveticum* Garay & Sweet
A. anthropophorum x *Herminium monorchis* = x *Aceraherminium* (?) (Gremli) Camus.
In some southern French sites where *A. anthropophorum* and *O. simia* grow together there are large numbers of hybrids, more robust in appearance and more numerous than either parent. It seems that conditions are ideal for the survival of the hybrid x *Orchiaceras bergonii* and a swarm has resulted.

Aceras anthropophorum (L.) R. Br.
MAN ORCHID; L'HOMME PENDU (F);
FRATZENORCHIS, PUPPENORCHIS,
OHNHORN (G); BALLERINO (I).

A slender orchid from 10–30cm in height (exceptionally 40cm). The 5–6 leaves are oblong lanceolate in shape, upright when they first unfold, but later spread outwards. The 2 tubers are both ovoid and undivided, and the few roots are short and thick.

The flower spike is long and narrow with many flowers: as many as 90 on a single spike. The flower bracts are membraneous and shorter in length than the ovary.

Both petals and sepals are greenish-yellow; streaked and margined with red. All the perianth segments are incurved to form a helmet.

The dull yellow lip is longer than the ovary and very distinctive in shape. *Anthropophorum* means 'man-like' and most of the local names are direct references to its resemblance to a tiny figure: the English 'Man Orchid', *L'Homme Pendu* (the hanged man) in French, and the delightful Italian *Ballerino*. The median lobe is deeply split forming the legs and the lateral lobes are long and slender forming the arms. In freshly opened flowers there is sometimes a pronounced red tinge to the arms and legs, but this soon fades as the flower spike opens fully.

There is no proper spur – the factor which separates *Aceras* from the genus *Orchis*. Instead there is a shallow depression in which nectar is stored.

Flowers: from late March (in the Mediterranean region) to June. In Britain and other countries in western Europe it flowers through May into June. Late May and early June are the best times to look for it.

Habitat: calcareous soils up to 1500m (in the Alps), hillside pastures, olive groves and woodland edges. In its western European sites it usually frequents the longer grass on calcareous downland where its colour and slender shape make it difficult to see. The Mediterranean plants tend to be more robust and are often found in stony places.

Distribution: north Africa; Spain; Balearic Isles; France; England (Kent and Surrey on chalk, Lincolnshire ar Somerset on Oolitic limestone); Ger many (west and south); Benelux countries; Austria; Switzerland (not on high ground); Italy; Sicily; Corsica; Sardinia; Yugoslavia; Greece (mainland); Corfu; Crete; Rhodes; Cyprus (very rare); Lebanon and south-west Turkey.

197, 198, 199, 200

Himantoglossum

Whether one calls the genus *Himantoglossum* or *Loroglossum* (an alternative found in many books), both words refer to the lip of the flower. The Greek words *himas* and *loros* both mean 'strap' or 'thong', while *glossa* means 'tongue'. The English name, too, is a direct reference to the long tail formed by the lip: hence the name 'lizard orchid'.

Close examination of the members of the genus shows many links with *Aceras*, but the very robust plants and the characteristically shaped flowers justify placement in a genus of their own.

Himantoglossum hircinum and its subspecies are possessors of a strong scent which is sometimes so marked that both Latin and French names are a direct reference to it (*hircinum* refers to goat and so does *Orchis bouc*).

The only widespread member of the genus is *H. hircinum*, but it is by no means a common orchid. It is spread rather thinly through its range, although there are some parts of France where it can be found in large numbers. The subspecies of *H. hircinum* and the remaining species in the genus are all decidedly local and, in most cases, rare.

All members of the genus are robust perennials reaching some 30–90cm. The tubers are large, ellipsoidal and two in number. The flowering spikes are loosely flowered, with large numbers of blooms. The central lobe of the lip is perhaps the most distinctive feature for it is usually greatly elongated, twisted, and divided at its tip. The spur is present but it is short and usually stumpy. As in *Aceras*, the pollinia in *H. hircinum* are fixed to what appears to be a single viscidium so that any visiting insect invariably removes both pollinia at a single visit. Flies, bees and occasionally bluebottles are attracted to *H. hircinum* by its scent and are potential pollinators.

Hybrids
A single hybrid has been recorded between *Himantoglossum hircinum* and a member of the *Orchis* group.
Himantoglossum hircinum x *Orchis simia* = x *Orchimantoglossum lacazei* A. & Gr.

***Himantoglossum hircinum* (L.) Sprengel**
LIZARD ORCHID; ORCHIS BOUC (F);
BOCKS-RIEMENZUNGE (G).
This robust, thick-stemmed orchid can reach a height of 80–90cm although 30–65cm is a more usual range. Leaves number 6–8 and are oval to broadly lanceolate in shape. By the time flowers are produced the lower leaves have already browned and withered: this happens because leaves are produced in the previous autumn and then have to endure the rigours of the winter months.

The inflorescence is moderately dense, with a straggling appearance, due to the long 'lizard tails' formed by the extended middle lobes of the flower lips. As many as 80 blooms have been recorded on a single flowering spike, while less robust specimens can carry as few as 15. The flower bracts are linear and either equal or just exceed the ovary in length.

The sepals and petals are incurved to form a hood, with the sepals green or greyish-green on the outside, striped

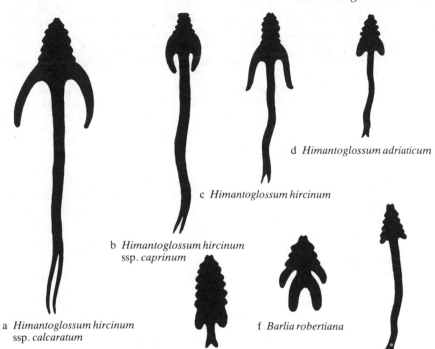

d *Himantoglossum adriaticum*

c *Himantoglossum hircinum*

b *Himantoglossum hircinum*
ssp. *caprinum*

a *Himantoglossum hircinum*
ssp. *calcaratum*

f *Barlia robertiana*

Fig. 38   e *Himantoglossum formosum*   g *Himantoglossum affine*

and spotted inside with red. The petals are narrow, with one vein and some red marks. The lip is 3-lobed with the central lobe much extended and the whole being rolled spirally in the buds. As the flowers open so the lip unfurls. The lateral lobes are crinkled on their outer edges and are narrower and shorter than the central lobe. At the lip base the central portion is white or greenish-white with two long-itudinal rows of red tufts. The extremities of all the lobes are darkened to grey, brownish-purple, olive brown or, in rare cases, pink. The middle lobe is very long, reaching 25–45mm, which makes it two to three times as long as the ovary. The spur is conical in shape and no more than 1.25–2.5mm in length.

Under the ground there are two moderately large ovoid or elliptical tubers.

One can often locate a colony of these plants by smell alone. There is a hint of vanilla in the scent but the general smell is an overpowering one of goat: hence the common names such as the French

Orchis bouc or goat orchid. The smell becomes particularly noticeable towards the evening.

Flowers: May to July. In the southern part of its range the first flowers could appear in late April, while in the UK the plant is at its best in late June to early July.

Habitat: sunny open grassland, scrub or woodland edges, roadside verges (especially in France), open woods and well established sand-dunes (western Europe). On the whole this species prefers an oceanic climate.

Distribution: a rather local and uncommon orchid found throughout much of the southern part of Europe; Spain; Italy; Holland (coastal dunes and South Limburg); Germany (rather rare); France (abundant in some of the southern areas); Switzerland (Jura); Austria (southern Tyrol); Balearics; Corsica; Sardinia; Sicily; Hungary; Yugoslavia; Czechoslovakia and in some parts of north Africa.

In the UK it is decidedly rare but until recently was considered unusual since it was actually spreading while other species were being progressively wiped out. Now this spread seems to have slowed down. It tends to thrive for a number of years in any one colony then inexplicably numbers start to dwindle.   **201**

The two subspecies are so well-defined in terms of appearance and geographical distribution that a number of authors have considered them as worthy of specific status in their own right.

Ssp. **caprinum** (Bieb.) Sundermann. This subspecies seems to replace the nominate race entirely in the eastern part of the range and in parts of the Balkans. In his monograph on the genus E. Nelson considers it as intermediate in characteristics between *H. hircinum* and its other subspecies, ssp. *calcaratum*. This latter he treats as a separate species, namely *Loroglossum calcaratum*.

In appearance it is an altogether more slender plant than the nominate race, with a lax-flowered inflorescence occupying up to 30cm of the stem length. From 9–20 blooms are carried in the spike, and the flower bracts are just about the same length as the ovary.

The helmet is more elongated than in *H. hircinum*, and the petals have 2 veins compared with 1 in the nominate race (according to Schlechter's detailed investigations). The sepals and petals are greenish, with the central part of the labellum base coloured white with red tufts of hair and the lateral lobes greenish-brown.

The middle lobe of the lip is extended as with all forms of *H. hircinum* and is bifurcated, though not nearly as deeply as *H. hircinum* ssp. *calcaratum*. In colour it is pink. The spur is about 4–5mm in length and shaped rather like a skittle.

Flowers: May to early July.

Habitat: rough hillside pastures, edges of woodlands, light woodland and clearings, scrub-covered hillsides always on calcareous soils.

Distribution: northern Turkey (Pontus); Crimea.   **202**

Similar lax-flowered forms of *H. hircinum*, which some botanists have attributed to this race, are found in: Yugoslavia; Bulgaria; Greece (eastern Macedonia on Mt Boz Dag, central Macedonia, Epirus, Euboea, Kephallonia). From Crete there are records of a form of ssp. *caprinum* which occurs in a very limited area of the White Mountains.

Recently some lax-flowered plants have been included with a newly named species, *H. adriaticum* (see description opposite for details). Considerable work needs to be done to determine the exact range of ssp. *caprinum* if *H. adriaticum* is to be recognised as well.

Ssp. **calcaratum** (G. Beck) Soó. This subspecies is sometimes an even more robust plant than the nominate race, ranging from 40–85cm in height. More often if appears as an altogether more delicate plant, with its rosy flowers contributing to an attractive overall appearance. There are 8–10 broadly lanceolate leaves and a pair of tubers which are larger than those of the nominate race.

The inflorescence can contain as many flowers as plants of the nominate race but gives the impression of being more dense because the central lobe of the labellum is much longer even than that of *H. hircinum*. The flower bracts are just slightly longer than the ovary.

Most of the specimens one finds will be fairly lax-flowered, with large showy blooms that are predominately rose-pink in colour.

The lip is drawn out into a long central lobe, some 7.5 to 10cm long which is deeply divided for part of its length – the bifurcation starts at the tip and extends for 15–25mm. Again, the side lobes are extended and have crinkled edges near their basal region. The basal part of the lip separating the side lobes varies from grey-white to pink and carries the same rows of red tufts as the nominate race. The spur in this subspecies is comparatively well-developed, gaining a length of 8–12mm; this contrasts sharply with a spur length of less than 2.5mm for the nominate race. The extremities of all

parts of the lip tend to darken to a deep red-violet.
Flowers: June to July (even into August at high altitudes).
Habitat: pastures, edges of thickets, roadside margins on calcareous soils in mountain regions between 400 and 1000m above sea level.
Distribution: this subspecies has a well-defined and very restricted distribution in southern Yugoslavia and northern Greece: east Bosnia; northern Macedonia; Montenegro; northern Albania; west Bosnia; Dalmatia; Serbia; Romania; Greek Macedonia. **203**

Himantoglossum adriaticum
H. Baumann
This plant was described in 1978 in an OPTIMA leaflet (no. 71). For many years the plants had been overlooked and treated as lax-flowered forms of *H. hircinum*. They have a number of quite distinct characteristics which have led to the award of specific status.

The plants are tall, growing from 45–75cm in height, and have a much more lax inflorescence than *H. hircinum*.

Compared with *H. hircinum*, the helmet formed by the sepals and petals is smaller and more tightly compact. The central lobe of the lip is hardly twisted at all and there is a short furrow at the lip base.
Flowers: May to July.
Habitat: scrub-covered hillsides.
Distribution: around the northern Adriatic region.

Himantoglossum affine (Boiss.)
Schlechter
This is a rather slender species compared with other members of the genus. It has 7–9 broadly lanceolate leaves and reaches 40–60cm in height, with a lax spike that carries 10–30 flowers. The flower bracts are slightly longer than the ovary, and beneath the ground are two very large tubers, both of which are sessile.

The sepals are concave and form much the same helmet as in other members of the genus. On the outside they are greenish-white in colour, tinged with reddish-brown at their edges; inside they are distinctly veined with red.

The lip is relatively short for a plant in this genus, with the median lobe reaching between 2 and 4cm in length, with only a small division at the apex. The lip is held out more or less horizontally form the rest of the plant, it does not have red spots near its base, and the side lobes are short, stumpy and crinkled at their outer edges. Plants have in fact been recorded where the side lobes are absent altogether. The spur is small, being from 3–6mm long.
Flowers: May to June (sometimes into the beginning of July).
Habitat: pinewoods and scrub in mountain areas, juniper woods.
Distribution: western Turkey (near Izmir); southern Turkey (Cadmus, Gheyra Cilicia – near the famous 'gates'); eastern Turkey (Maras); Iraq; Iran; Syria and Lebanon (mountains south-east of Beirut).

This orchid stands out as one of the rarest described in this book. Unfortunately it is everywhere rare and local in its area of distribution. **204**

Fig. 39

Himantoglossum formosum (Steven) C. Koch

This distinctive species would be difficult to confuse with any other member of the genus if one were fortunate enough to find it.

It is a tall plant, 55–65cm in height, with 6–8 broadly lanceolate leaves (3cm wide at their broadest point and up to 16cm in length). By the time flowering starts, the basal leaves have often become browned. The stem is a rather dull green in colour, and both the tubers are large, ovoid and sessile.

The spike is moderately lax, with 15 –30 flowers held in a narrow cylinder about 25cm in length, and the bracts are slightly longer than the ovary.

The lateral sepals are oval, about 11 –13cm in length, and as is usual for members of this genus they form a helmet with the other perianth segments. In colour the helmet is pale green inside and out, becoming rosy purple towards the edges. The inside surfaces of the sepals are veined in purple-red, and the somewhat shorter petals have a single vein. The lip has an extended central lobe but it is shorter than with other members of the genus, seldom exceeding 17mm. This central lobe is greenish-white in colour and very slightly notched at its tip. The laterals are separated from the median lobe over a short length(1– 2mm), and have a distinctly wavy edge, which is olive to purplish-green in colour. The spur is slender and cylindrical, reaching a maximum of 9–10mm.

Flowers: end of May throughout June.

Habitat: mountain woodland and scrub on calcareous soils.

Distribution: restricted to the east Caucasus (Daghestan) and south-east Transcaucasus. It is an exceptionally rare orchid and few specimens have been found. It grows in areas which are not readily accessible to western botanists.

Fig. 40

Barlia

The single specimen in this genus is often a rather massive orchid. It has broad succulent leaves, very long bracts and a thick stem.

It was formerly known as *Himantoglossum longibracteatum* and lumped together with the other species in the genus *Himantoglossum*. However there are quite noticeable differences, particularly in the form of the flowers. In *Himantoglossum* species the central lobe of the lip is very elongated, forming the familiar 'lizard tails', whereas the central lobe of *Barlia* is divided into two thick arms by an indentation at its apex. The side lobes are distinctly sickle-shaped.

The scent is very pleasant, rather like that of lily of the valley.

Hybrids

Only one has been definitely recorded:
B. robertiana x *Aceras anthropophorum* = x *Barlaceras terraccianoi* Camus

Barlia robertiana (Loisel.) W. Greuter
GIANT ORCHID; ORCHIS GÉANT (F);
ORCHIS À LONGUES BRACTÉES (F);
MASTORCHIS (G); GIGLIO BRATTEOSO
(I).

A very robust orchid with thick fleshy stems and a height ranging from 30–80cm. The large broad leaves are coloured a shiny light green and have an almost succulent appearance. The tubers are large and ovoid – two are the usual number but three have been recorded.

The inflorescence is dense and many-flowered. It is oval in shape as it first opens but then becomes cylindrical as the flowers open. The first flowers appear when the flowering stem is still amongst the leaves, the others opening as the stem expands. The flower bracts are very prominent and about twice as long as the ovary.

The lateral sepals are concave and slightly spread, whilst the dorsal sepal and petals are incurved to form the helmet. All the sepals are free. The spur is short, conical and points downwards.

The lip is distinctly 3-lobed, the two lateral lobes crinkled at their outer edges, forming the scythe-shaped arms. The median lobe is divided, providing the 'giant' with legs. The flowers are large – a length of 3.5–4.5cm from helmet to the tip of the median lobe being quite usual – and the overall appearance is of a helmeted warrior.

There seem to be two quite distinct colour forms of this plant, both occurring with equal frequency. The first has a greenish appearance, with grey and green flowers, and the second has flowers of a much deeper purple colour. In the light form the perianth segments forming the helmet are greenish, veined and lightly spotted inside with red. The labellum has dirty greyish-white as a ground colour and spots and streaks of red-purple, the edges forming the 'arms' tend to an olive brown. The dark flowered forms have the segments of the helmet red-purple and are again veined and spotted with a darker shade of the same colour. The ground shade of the labellum is a deep violet pink, and the edges darken to a brownish shade.

The flowers are very fragrant.

Flowers: December to March. This is one of the earliest orchids to flower with plants in north Africa in bloom in December. In Cyprus we have found specimens in full flower in the first week of January. Elsewhere February and March are the best times to see the plant, although by the end of the latter month it is well past its best on lower ground in many places and must be sought on higher ground.

Habitat: found on soils ranging from neutral to definitely alkaline, grassy hillsides, scrubby hillsides under pines, clearings in woodland. Often it occurs on very poor chalky soils where water drains away speedily.

Distribution: widespread around the Mediterranean although it is spread rather thinly in the east of the region; Canary Islands; Spain; Portugal; Balearics (Minorca); Italy (in the south and in Liguria in the north-west); Sicily; Sardinia; Corsica; France (only in the south: Languedoc; Alpes Maritimes); north Africa (Tunisia, Algeria and Morocco); Greece; Crete; Rhodes; Cyprus; Yugoslavia (south Dalmatia); southern Turkey   **205, 206, 207, 208**

Anacamptis

A. pyramidalis, the single species in this genus, is one of the best known orchids of early summer in western Europe. It thrives in open grassland on calcareous soils and can tolerate cultivated or grazed land, provided intensive farming methods are not employed.

The flowers are closely related to *Orchis* but have a much longer, more slender spur than all but a couple of species in that genus. Darwin included a set of illustrations in his classic work on orchid pollination which showed the intriguing mechanism in *Anacamptis*. The flowers are shaped so that moths and butterflies are the only insects that can be successful pollinators. On the lip there are two ridges which make the insect insert its proboscis straight into the mouth of the spur. As it does this the proboscis passes directly below the saddle-shaped viscidium which clasps it, sticking the pollinia firmly in place on the proboscis. At the next flower they come into contact with the two stigmas, since the pollinia are set in a forward-pointing direction.

The insect's reward for its efforts comes from the nectar it finds when its proboscis ruptures the cells on the inside of the spur wall.

The general characteristics of the genus are: two ovoid or globose tubers; stem with numerous leaves; flowers in a dense spike; outer perianth segments spreading; dorsal sepal and petals forming a hood; lip deeply 3-lobed, with two longitudinal ridges at its base; spur long and directed downwards; column short; rostellum small; viscidium solitary, carrying two pollinia; bursicle simple.

Hybrids
A wide range of intergeneric hybrids are known because butterflies and moths visit other orchids for nectar and act as agents for cross-pollination.
A. pyramidalis x *Dactylorhiza maculata* = x *Dactylocamptis weberi* Schulze
A. pyramidalis x *Gymnadenia conopsea* = x *Gymnanacamptis anacamptis* Wilms
A. pyramidalis x *Gymnadenia odoratissima* = x *Gymnanacamptis odoratissima* Wildh.
A. pyramidalis x *Orchis coriophora* ssp. *fragrans* = x *Anacamptorchis simorrensis* Camus et Berg.
A. pyramidalis x *Orchis laxiflora* = x *Anacamptorchis klingei* Fournier
A. pyramidalis x *Orchis morio* = x *Anacamptorchis laniccae* Br.-Blanquet
A. pyramidalis x *Orchis ustulata* = x *Anacamptorchis fallax* Camus
A. pyramidalis x *Platanthera bifolia* = x *Anacamptiplatanthera payotii* Fournier

Anacamptis pyramidalis (L.) L. C. M. Richard
PYRAMIDAL ORCHID; ORCHIS PYRAMIDAL (F); SPITZORCHIS, HUNDSWURZ; PYRAMIDENORCHIS (G).
This slender-stemmed orchid ranges from 20–60cm in height, with 5–8 linear to lanceolate leaves and 2–3 brownish scales sheathing the base of the stem. The flower bracts are about as long as the ovary, and the dense-flowered spike is 2–8cm long, conical when the lower flowers open and becoming cylindrical as the upper flowers open. The dorsal sepal and petals are incurved to form a hood,

and the lateral sepals spread widely. The lip is 3-lobed, with the two ridges (mentioned above) at its base. The flowers are usually pale to dark pink, although other forms are known (see below). The spur is long (12–14mm), very slender and down-curved.
Varieties: Var. *albiflora* Raulin: has white flowers and occasional specimens are found with normal-coloured populations. Unusually, in the open woods on Mt Profitis Elias (Rhodes), it is the dominant form.
Var. *brachystachys* Boiss.: has a rounded spike, with pale pink blossoms, and

frequents stony places in the eastern Mediterranean region. It flowers early (February–April) and often replaces the nominate race (e.g. in Crete). **211, 212**
Var. *sommeriana* Borg: a local Maltese form in which the bracts are shorter than the ovary.
Var. *tanayensis* Chenev.: includes plants from high places in the Alps between 1200 and 1900m; this has a shorter spur and much darker flowers (dark purple) than the nominate race and flowers in May.
Flowers: May to July.

Habitat: an orchid of calcareous grasslands, although it can occur in woodlands where trees have colonised grassland, or at woodland edges.
Distribution: very widespread and often common; N. Africa; Spain; Balearics; France; UK (not in northern Scotland); Scandinavia (southern); Germany; Benelux; Austria & Switzerland (up to 1700m); Italy; Corsica; Sardinia; Sicily; Yugoslavia; Greece; Crete; Rhodes; Turkey; Lebanon; Cyprus; Czechoslovakia; Romania; Hungary; Bulgaria; Russia; Crimea; Caucasus. **209, 210**

Serapias

Egyptian mythology has provided a name for this genus of tuberous-rooted orchids. The word *Serapias* is derived from *Osirapis*, a Greek name for Apis, the sacred bull of Memphis, an animal that was a supposed incarnation of the god Osiris.

The range of the genus extends from the Azores and Mediterranean Portugal, in the west, to Turkey, the Caucasus and the Levant in the east. *Serapias* are found in north Africa and as far north in Europe as the southern Tyrol in Austria and a few low-lying valleys in Switzerland. The genus is essentially a Mediterranean one, for this is the area that has the greatest number of species, forms and varieties.

There is still disagreement amongst botanists about the number of distinct species of *Serapias*, and their classification, like that of *Ophrys*, is fraught with confusion.

Flora Europaea recognises six species: *Serapias lingua*, *S. vomeracea*, *S. cordigera*, *S. neglecta*, *S. parviflora* and *S. olbia*. A seventh, *S. azorica*, has a dubious specific status.

In previous works *Serapias vomeracea* has been separated into: *S. orientalis*, *S. vomeracea* and *S. parviflora* ssp. *laxiflora* (or *S. columnae*). At the eastern end of the Mediterranean, where all three occur together, they merge one into the next, and in the field it is virtually impossible to separate plants conclusively into any of the three categories. These cannot be regarded as distinct species nor are they really good subspecies, for they do not fulfil the criterion of geographical separation that the definition of a subspecies leads one to expect.

In our opinion Sundermann's concept of a prespecies (p. 39) suits them perfectly.

Interspecific hybrids occur with this genus, and some writers claim that it happens with such readiness that the abundance of intermediate forms can be explained. It certainly seems that a lot more work is required to elucidate the tangle and in our opinion the best approach so far comes from Sundermann. He feels that there are two 'good' species: *S. lingua*, with a single dark hump at the base of its hypochile, and *S. vomeracea*, with two furrowed humps in the same place. From *S. vomeracea* have evolved *S. cordigera*, *S. neglecta*, and *S. parviflora* at the western end of the range, with *S. vomeracea* ssp. *laxiflora* and ssp. *orientalis* at the eastern end. In the west the distinctions between *S. vomeracea*, *S. cordigera*, *S. neglecta* and *S. parviflora* have become so marked that they can be considered as separate species. In the eastern part of the Mediterranean, however, *S. vomeracea* and its two subspecies have so far not evolved as distinct species. To us they appear to be a cline (see p. 39).

Ultimately it is a question of labelling, and this is a problem for the taxonomist. Here we have used the analysis detailed in *Flora Europaea*, with the reservations outlined above.

Fig. 41 Dissection of the Serapias flower

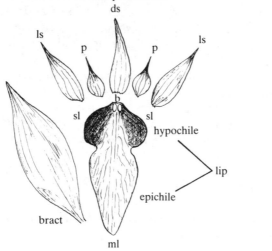

ds dorsal sepal
ls lateral sepal
p petal
b basal region
sl side lobe
ml middle lobe

Key

1 Epichile of the lip usually heart-shaped, at least as wide
   as the hypochile   *2*
   Epichile of the lip narrowed towards the base, narrower
   than the hypochile   *4*

2 Lip with 2 divergent ridges at the base; lateral lobes of
   the hypochile about ⅓ as wide as the epichile; flower
   bracts shorter than the flowers   **S. cordigera**
   Lip with 2 parallel ridges at the base; lateral lobes of the
   hypochile about ½ as wide as the epichile; flower bract
   equal to or longer than the flowers   *3*

3 Epichile directed more or less downwards   **S. vomeracea**
                                                         (ssp. orientalis)

   Epichile directed more or less upwards or forwards   **S. neglecta**

4 Flower bracts much longer then the flowers; lateral lobes
of the lip reddish, becoming black towards the edges   *S. vomeracea*
Flower bracts equal to or slightly longer than the flowers;
lateral lobes of the lip dark purple to black in colour   **5**

5 Lip with a single black ridge at the base, colour of flowers
violet or reddish. Tubers 2–5, 1 sessile the others
on stolons   *S. lingua*
Lip with 2 ridges at base, brownish-red in colour and
2–3 sessile tubers   *S. parviflora*

NB. From this key *S. vomeracea* ssp. *laxiflora* will appear with the nominate
S. vomeracea and *S. olbia* with *S. parviflora*. Positive identification can be
made by referring to the species descriptions.

Hybrids
The whole range of interspecific hybrids (i.e. all combinations of pairs of parents) has
been recorded, but in the field it is extremely difficult to say with conviction exactly
what the origins of the suspected hybrid is. The case is quite different with
intergeneric hybrids. These are often outstandingly attractive plants – especially the
'*Orchiserapias*' which are hybrids between *Orchis* and *Serapias* species. Unfortunately they are far from common.

Interspecific Hybrids
S. cordigera x *S. lingua* = *S.* x *ambigua* Rouy or *S.* x *laramberguei* Camus
S. cordigera x *S. parviflora* = *S.* x *rainei* Camus
S. cordigera x *S. vomeracea* = *S.* x *kelleri* Camus
S. cordigera x *S. vomeracea* ssp. *laxiflora* = *S.* x *halacsayana* Soó
S. neglecta x *S. lingua* = *S.* x *meridionalis* Camus
S. neglecta x *S. vomeracea* = *S.* x *albertii* Camus
S. lingua x *S. parviflora* = *S.* x *semilingua* Camus
S. lingua x *S. vomeracea* = *S.* x *digenea* Camus or *S.* x *philippi* Rouy
S. lingua x *S. vomeracea* ssp. *laxiflora* = *S.* x *demadesii* Renz
S. lingua x *S. vomeracea* ssp. *orientalis* = *S.* x *sitiae* Renz

Intergeneric Hybrids
S. cordigera x *Orchis laxiflora* = *Orchiserapias nouleti* Camus
S. cordigera x *Orchis papilionacea* = x *Orchiserapias debeauxii* Camus
S. lingua x *Anacamptis pyramidalis* = x *Seracamptis forbesii* Godfery
S. lingua x *Ophrys sphegodes* ssp. *mammosa* (?) = (unnamed) Nelson
S. lingua x *Orchis laxiflora* = x *Orchiserapias complicata* Camus
S. lingua x *Orchis morio* = x *Orchiserapias capitata* Camus
S. lingua x *Orchis papilionacea* = x *Orchiserapias barlae* Camus
S. lingua x *Orchis purpurea* = x *Orchiserapias dufforti* Camus
S. neglecta x *Orchis laxiflora* = x *Orchiserapias pisanensis* Godfery
S. neglecta x *Orchis morio* = x *Orchiserapias bevilacque* Penzig
S. neglecta x *Orchis palustris* = x *Orchiserapias mutata* Bergen & Camus
S. neglecta x *Orchis papilionacea* = x *Orchiserapias triloba* Godfery
S. vomeracea x *Orchis coriophora* = x *Orchiserapias tommasinii* Kern
S. vomeracea x *Orchis laxiflora* = x *Orchiserapias purpurea* Camus
S. vomeracea x *Orchis morio* = x *Orchiserapias fontanae* Camus
S. vomeracea x *Orchis papilionacea* = x *Orchiserapias ligustica* Camus

Serapias cordigera L.
HEART-FLOWERED SERAPIAS;
SERAPIAS EN COEUR (F);
HERZFORMIGE STENDELWURZ (G);
SATIRIOBARBONE (I).

Plants of this species range from 15 –45cm in height and have 5–8 channelled, lanceolate leaves. The basal sheaths are usually spotted with deep purplered, a characteristic often quoted as a diagnostic feature for this species. The worth of this observation is open to question because it is not really unusual to find plants that resemble *S. cordigera* in every respect except for this colouring at the stem bases.

4–10 flowers are carried in a rather dense spike, grouped at the end of the flowering stem. The flower bracts are shorter on average than the helmet but are similarly coloured in violet-pink, veined longitudinally with deep maroon red. The lip is heart-shaped, hairy and coloured a deep maroon with fine blackish streaks. The two humps at the labellum base are black and diverge slightly towards the labellum. The lateral lobes are partly hidden by the helmet, and there is little if any darkening in shade compared with the median lobe, although at the edges of the lateral lobes the colouring is almost purple-black.

Varieties: Var. *mauretanica* Camus: a less robust, pale red form restricted to north Africa (Morocco).

Flowers: late March through April to early May.

Habitat: wet and dry grasslands, sanddune slacks, olive groves and marshy places in light woodland.

Distribution: mainly west and central Mediterranean countries; north Africa; Spain; Italy; Greece and the islands; Portugal; Balearics; France; Corsica; Sardinia; Sicily; Yugoslavia and southern Turkey.

This species varies somewhat according to locality. The examples illustrated are as follows: **213**, southern Spain; **214**, Corfu; **215, 216**, northern Spain.

Serapias azorica Schlechter
There is still some argument as to whether or not this deserves the status of a species. It is obviously closely related to *S. cordigera* and should probably be grouped with it.

It is separated from *S. cordigera* on the basis of its smaller flowers in a shorter spike and an epichile which is distinctly wider than the hypochile.

Distribution: Azores (San Miguel) where plants from lower levels tend to have larger flowers than those from higher elevations.

Serapias neglecta De Not.
SCARCE SERAPIAS; SERAPIAS NÉGLIGÉ (F); ÜBERSEHENER ZUNGENSTENDEL (G).

The plants of this species stand 10 –30cm tall, and there are 4–10 leaves that vary in shape from broad to narrowly lanceolate, are channelled and slightly recurved. There are two ovoid tubers, one sessile, the other with a short stalk, and the basal sheaths are green and unspotted.

The small stature of the plants and the large flowers make this one of the most striking species of *Serapias*. There are from 3–8 flowers (exceptionally more), carried in a rather dense inflorescence where they start to open before the spike has cleared the leaves. As the spike elongates so the flowers open. The flower bracts are shorter than the helmet, usually green in colour but sometimes suffused with purple. The helmet varies in colour from a light yellowish-green to a more frequent red-violet, and it partly conceals the lateral lobes of the labellum. At the base of the labellum there are two black-purple ridges, and the middle lobe is an elongated oval. The lip colours span a wider range than any other species of *Serapias*: the central lobe ranges from pale cream to rich yellow at its centre but darkens to reddishbrown at the edges; more infrequently the lip can be red, salmon pink or even orange. The entire lip can then be veined in darker shades of these colours and its surface is hairy.

It is not easy to confuse *S. neglecta* with other members of the genus.

a *S. vomeracea*

b *S. vomeracea* ssp. *orientalis*

c *S. vomeracea* ssp. *orientalis* var. *cordigeroides*

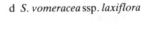

d *S. vomeracea* ssp. *laxiflora*

e *S. vomeracea* ssp. *orientalis* var. *apulica*

Fig. 42 *Serapias vomeracea* flowers

Although some forms of *S. cordigera* have a similarly shaped lip, their stems are invariably spotted whilst those of *S. neglecta* are not.

Flowers: late March, through April, to early May.

Habitat: damp meadows on sandy soils (e.g. dune slacks), light woodland, garigue and spaces in maquis, either on slightly acidic or basic soils.

Distribution: although it occurs in large colonies it is a decidedly uncommon orchid, with a restricted distribution; southern France; northern Italy; Corsica; Sardinia (and possibly Sicily); southwestern Yugoslavia; usually near the coast in all the countries mentioned.
217, 218

Ssp. *ionica* E. Nelson. This is a rather small race with a slender appearance and fewer flowers than the nominate race. The labellum is invariably a deep crimson, and the helmet is red.

Distribution: as the name suggests it occurs on the islands in the Ionian Sea (Corfu, Zante and Kephallinia), where it is found in damp pastures on sandy soils.

Serapias vomeracea (Burm.) Briq.
LONG-LIPPED SERAPIAS; SÉRAPIAS À LONG LABELLE (F); LANGLIPPIGER STENDELWURZ (G).

Plants grow from 20–50cm in height, with exceptional specimens reaching about 60cm. The glaucous green leaves are linear, channelled and reflexed outwards. The basal sheaths are green and unspotted. Two tubers are formed and both are ovoid and sessile.

4–10 flowers are carried in a fairly robust lax-flowered spike. The flower bracts are much longer than the flowers (a useful distinguishing feature from other *Serapias*), varying from pale red through brick red to a deep mahogany brown. They are upward-pointing and strongly elongated. The helmet usually has a pale red ground colour, streaked with distinct longitudinal veins of deep red or purple-brown. The base of the internal flower segments is a deep, almost purple, black. The helmet, like the bracts, is often upward pointing.

The lip has two parallel ridges at its base. The lateral lobes of the hypochile are completely hidden by the hood and their edges are very dark-coloured. The median lobe is elongated and forms the epichile which is 9–11mm long and lighter in colour than the lateral lobes, being pale red, brick red or even a brownish colour. There is sometimes a yellowish centre zone to the epichile but whatever its colour it is always distinctly hairy. The lip narrows towards its base, and its overall appearance is that of an ancient ploughshare.

Two other species, *S. lingua* and *S. parviflora*, have this narrowing at the base of the lip, but *S. vomeracea* is easily distinguished by the length of the bracts.

Flowers: late March to early May in the Mediterranean region. In the sites in Switzerland it flowers in early June.

Habitat: maquis, fields, scrub, grasslands and seepages on hillsides, light Mediterranean pinewood.

Distribution: circum-Mediterranean to Turkey and Lebanon in the east; the Caucasus; north to the lower alpine regions of Switzerland (Tessin and Grisons), the only member of the genus to do so.
219, 220

Ssp. *laxiflora* (Soó) Gölz & Rheinhard. This plant has a somewhat chequered history since it has been linked previously with *Serapias parviflora* as its ssp. *laxiflora*, and also considered as a species within its own right – *S. columnae* (A. & Gr.) Fleischm. or *S. hellenica* Renz. The present tendency is to link it with *S. vomeracea* and it differs from the nominate race in the following respects: the plants are much smaller in stature, seldom reaching more than 30cm; petals and sepals are, as a rule, much shorter than those of the nominate race, the hypochile is narrower, and the epichile usually reflexed against the ovary; the leaves are narrow, elongated and pale green in colour.

It is restricted to the eastern end of the Mediterranean, where it occurs in places with the nominate race and ssp. *orienta-*

lis. In these populations distinctions between subspecies become blurred, and positive identification is often not possible.
Flowers: March through April to early May.
Habitat: as for nominate race.
Distribution: Aegean isles; Crete; Rhodes; Cyprus; Greece; Yugoslavia; southern Turkey; North Africa and southern Italy (Apulia and Calabria).
221

Ssp. *orientalis* W. Greuter. This plant possesses characteristics which link it strongly with other members of the genus: the labellum shape resembles *S. neglecta* and *S. cordigera*, and the general stature is that of a robust *S. vomeracea*. The plants are from 15–30cm tall, with 5–7 moderately long and broad leaves. The basal sheaths are sometimes spotted with red on their external surfaces and so are the lower stems. However, whereas this is a constant characteristic with *S. cordigera* it is not with ssp. *orientalis*.

The flower spike is moderately dense, with 3–6 flowers. The flower bracts equal or slightly exceed the helmet in length and are more or less horizontal, with a slightly upturned end (in the nominate race the helmet and bracts point almost vertically upwards).

The lip is broad, with a barely discernible narrowing towards the base where the two parallel bosses are to be found. The middle lobe forms an epichile which ranges from 11–20mm (in exceptional plants) at its widest; occasionally it is heart-shaped. The epichile has a ground colour varying from yellowish- to reddish-buff with a network of veins in red to light reddish-brown. The lateral lobes are dark red to deep purple-maroon and are not completely covered by the helmet, whereas in the nominate race they are.
Varieties: Var. *cordigeroides* E. Nelson, a dark-flowered form of ssp. *orientalis*, resembles *S. neglecta* but the region of distribution is quite different, since var. *cordigeroides* is restricted to Greece and

Crete. Again, the lip of *S. neglecta* narrows at the base whilst that of var. *cordigeroides* does not. **225**
Var. *apulica* (Nelson) has been considered in some works as a subspecies of *S. neglecta*. It is restricted to Apulia in southern Italy (particularly on the Gargano peninsula) and has flowers which are larger than those of the normal ssp. *orientalis* and are darker in colour. It can be confused with *S. cordigera* but the lower stems and leaf bases are not spotted, the lip although wide is not heart-shaped, and the central portion of the lip tends to a reddish-buff (*S. cordigera* has a distinctive deep red or maroon lip).
Flowers: late March throughout April.
Habitat: as for the nominate race.
Distribution: mainland Greece (Peloponnese); Crete; Karpathos; Rhodes (?); Cyprus; southern Turkey; southern Italy (Apulia). **222, 223, 224**

Serapias lingua L.
TONGUE ORCHID; SÉRAPIAS À LANGUE (F); EINSCHWIELIGER ZUNGENSTENDEL (G); SATIRIO INCAPPUCIATO (I).
The plant stands 10–30cm high with 4–5 linear to lanceolate leaves. The basal sheaths are green and unspotted. The tubers run from 2–5 in number (most commonly 2), one of which is sessile and the others formed on short stolons.

The flower spike carries from 2–8 well-spaced flowers which stand out nearly horizontally from the main stem, with the labellum pointing more or less vertically downwards. The flower bracts are shorter than or equal to the length of the helmet and are reddish-violet or, more rarely, greenish in colour. The petals and sepals forming the helmet are light pink or purple, with distinct parallel veining in dark red or purple. The labellum has a single dark-coloured hump or boss at its base, which has a single longitudinal furrow or groove on it. This boss serves to distinguish *S. lingua* from all other *Serapias* except its own hybrids. In colour the labellum varies from yellowish, through light violet-pink, to dark magenta. Partial albino forms with a yellow lip are known, and there are even plants of a pure white; sometimes these are considered as varieties, e.g. var. *flavum*.

A constant colour feature of this species is the deep purple shade of the lateral lobes of the lip, although they are often obscured by the helmet. The central lobe of the lip forms the epichile. It extends to about 18mm as a maximum and is much narrower than the hypochile.

With a low-powered magnifying glass it is possible to see small warts at the base of the labellum. These are carried by other species of *Serapias* as well and look so much like taste buds on a mammalian tongue that the common name of 'Tongue Orchids' really is appropriate.

Flowers: April to May. In the south, early plants come into flower in the last weeks of March, while in cooler parts of south central France flowers persist until early June.

Habitat: damp meadows, fields, marshlands, sand-dune slacks; less frequently drier parts of garigue and maquis.

Distribution: west and central Mediterranean; north Africa; Italy; Sardinia; Corsica; Sicily; Yugoslavia; Spain; Balearics; mainland Greece; Crete and southern France. **226, 227**

The following subspecies are not included in *Flora Europaea* but are listed by E. Nelson in his monograph on *Serapias, Aceras, Barlia and Himantoglossum*:

Ssp. *duriuei* (Reichenb. fil.) Soó: differs from the type in having larger blooms with a narrower, more elongated helmet. The labellum is concave in front of the basal hump, whilst the hypochile is rather squat in form. The epichile is noticeably narrow and sparsely hairy up to the tip.

Distribution: Algeria and Tunisia.

Ssp. *excavata* (Schlechter) Soó: similar in form to *S. vomeracea* ssp. *laxiflora* but the basal hump is pinched, making it almost violin-shaped. It differs from the

type in having smaller blooms, a strongly curved labellum and an epichile which carries very short hairs along the whole of its length.

Distribution: Corsica and Sardinia.

Ssp. *oxyglottis* (Willd.) Soó: differentiated from the type on the basis of a shorter inflorescence with substantially larger blooms. The sepals are more pointed and the labellum is concave. The epichile is generally larger, narrower and more pointed than with *S. lingua* and has short hairs at its base.

Distribution: southern Italy; Sicily; southern France; Balearics; Algeria and Morocco.

Ssp. *stenopetala* Maire & Stephen: both blooms and bracts are yellowish-green, and the hump at the lip base is obviously furrowed. The labellum is yellowish-green also.

Distribution: Algeria.

Serapias parviflora Parl.
SMALL TONGUE ORCHID; SERAPIAS À PETITES FLEURS (F); KLEINBLÜTIGER ZUNGENSTENDEL (G).

This slender orchid seldom exceeds 25cm in height and possesses from 5–7 linear-lanceolate leaves which are channelled, curved inwards and coloured a glaucous green. The basal sheaths are sometimes red-spotted, and there are 2 tubers, both sessile.

The flower bracts are shorter than or equal to the helmet, and the flower spike is elongated but lax, carrying 3–10 small flowers.

The floral segments form a helmet, with the outer ones coloured reddish like the bracts and the inner ones often a greenish-red. The lateral lobes of the lip are concealed by the helmet and are almost black in colour. The median lobe has two parallel purplish humps near its base and is coloured rusty or brick red. In shape it is small and narrow and invariably folded back to lie along the ovary.

Although the flowers are usually heavily veined, like other *Serapias*, it is not exceptional to find forms which are unveined.

Albino forms with green perianth segments and a yellow lip are not rare, and a white-flowered variant is recorded from southern Greece (Peloponnese).

Flowers: end of March through April (some flowers persist until May).

Habitat: sand-dune slacks, olive groves, both wet and dry grassland, garigue.

Distribution: tends to be more frequently encountered in the western and central Mediterranean countries but it does occur in the eastern area as well although many of the records for the latter region are almost certainly for *S. vomeracea* ssp. *laxiflora* since the plants are often very similar in appearance.

Plants have been recorded from: the Canary Islands; north Africa; Spain; Balearics; southern France; Italy; Corsica; Sicily; Yugoslavia; Greece.   **228**

Serapias olbia **Verguin**
HYBRID SERAPIAS; CÔTE-
D'AZUR ZUNGENSTENDEL (G).

This slender orchid grows 10–25cm tall and has 5–7 narrow lanceolate leaves. The sheathing bracts at the base of the stem are usually unspotted (or very lightly spotted red) and below ground there are 3 rather than 2 tubers.

The flower bracts are shorter than the helmet formed by the petals and sepals, and the spike is lax-flowered, seldom with more than 2 or 3 blooms.

The perianth segments forming the helmet are coloured similarly to the flower bracts; the ground colour is pale to reddish-violet and the veining is in a deeper shade.

As with all *Serapias* the labellum is 3-lobed, with the lateral lobe in this case dark purplish-brown and the middle lobe a very dark red-purple. The median lobe is rather narrow, it is reflexed and overhangs the sepals by 5–6mm: two dark bosses are to be found at its base.

Varieties: Var. *gregaria* (Godfery) Nelson. This pale red form of *S. olbia* has been given the status of a variety rather than a subspecies. The labellum is much lighter than in the nominate race and it overhangs the sepals by 6–9mm. It, too, carries few flowers with 3, 4 or, rarely, 5 blooms. *S. olbia* is considered to have arisen from hybrid populations: *S. cordigera* x *S. lingua* and *S. parviflora* x *S. vomeracea* have been suggested as possible parents but *Flora Europaea* prefers the combination of *S. lingua* x *S. parviflora*.

Flowers: mid-April to mid-May.

Habitat: restricted to slightly acid soils in coastal dune slacks and beside lakes.

Distribution: the plant is restricted to a small area in south-eastern France; Var (particularly Tamaris, Cavalière, Creux St Georges, the Giens peninsula, Hyères).

Drainage of the sites where this orchid once grew has been carried out to satisfy the lust for land for tourist facilities, and its existence in its remaining localities can only be described as precarious. **229**

Ophrys

The members of the genus *Ophrys* have a distinctive appearance that clearly separates them from other orchids. Their dominant feature is a rather fleshy spurless lip. This can be entire or 3-lobed, is usually hairy (the name *Ophrys* means 'eyebrow'), and often carries a shiny area (speculum) or other markings. Together with the spreading sepals the overall appearance is often insect-like, as one can see from illustrations of *O. insectifera* and *O. speculum*.

Before flowering, the leaf rosettes of all species are quite similar, making identification difficult until the flowers appear on the glabrous stem. The 3 sepals are petal-like and longer than the petals, and the column is drawn out into a projection that looks like a duck's head in profile. Underground there are 2 tubers, one being used to produce the leaves and flowering stem, the other in the process of formation for next year's growth.

Although *Ophrys* flowers are spectacular in close-up, they are remarkably easy to overlook until the first is spotted. Others then seem to appear, as if by magic, as the eye becomes able to pick them out.

The greatest number of species and varieties occur in and around the warm Mediterranean lands where the enforced summer dormancy is an essential part of their growth cycle. Only a few species stray as far north as the UK: *O. apifera*, *O. sphegodes* ssp. *sphegodes*, *O. fuciflora* ssp. *fuciflora* and *O. insectifera*. The last-named orchid has the widest distribution, reaching Scandinavia and Finland in the north, but getting no nearer the Mediterranean than northern Spain, central Italy and parts of the Balkans.

Considerable problems occur with the classification of *Ophrys* because of the wide geographical variation, the numbers of subspecies and the differences in individuals in populations of the same species. One has only to read through volumes on European orchids to discover that plants change status with remarkable frequency. Today's variety is tomorrow's subspecies, or perhaps it is ignored completely.

Consider *O. sphegodes* as an example. This is the name used for a number of distinct races which, in line with *Flora Europaea*, we have called subspecies. If one wants to be strictly accurate, these races do not satisfy the criteria for subspecific status because they overlap geographically, and as for being species, they interbreed with impunity. One solution, which we support, is the idea of 'prespecies'. This concept has been successfully used by Prof. Sundermann and is explained in the section on classification (see p. 39).

According to another view *O. sphegodes* is an aggregate species, i.e. a group which consists of a number of closely related species. They are then named as if they were completely separate species.

Thus we have the choice: do we use *O. sphegodes* ssp. *mammosa*, *O. mammosa*, or *O. sphegodes* psp. *mammosa*? The problem is one of attaching a label, and perhaps the amateur enthusiast should be grateful that at least the word *mammosa* is common to all these schemes. That is now accepted as a fact; it is merely the question of its relationship to *O. sphegodes* in the context of accepted definitions of species, subspecies, prespecies and varieties that is debated.

The appearance of volume V of *Flora Europaea* has for the moment put the issue into abeyance because it uses 'subspecies', a term we are quite happy to adopt.

Ophrys is the genus where any field worker, however inexperienced, soon forms his or her own opinions about the rights and wrongs of the classification schemes, and much work still remains to be done. Many believe that the genus is still actively evolving and a number of the species are not yet stable.

One of the greatest contributions to *Ophrys* classification has been made by Dr Erich Nelson, and we recommend that anyone with an interest in the genus should look at the exquisitely painted *Ophrys* faces in his monograph (see Bibliography). The range of forms within a species complex such as *O. sphegodes* is scarcely credible. The work of Dr Jany Renz has also done much to sort out taxonomic problems and a lot of the excellent work being done by the OPTIMA project deals with *Ophrys*. Anyone intending to photograph plants would do well to look at the superb portraits of *Ophrys* in books by Othmar and Edeltraud Danesch.

Numerous groupings have been made for *Ophrys* species according to shared characteristics, and here we have adapted the arrangement used in *Flora Europaea*.

The striking resemblance of some *Ophrys* to insects (and the often fanciful resemblance of others) has intrigued botanists over the years. Darwin was clearly puzzled by the insect-mimicry aspect. Later Pouyanne suggested that male insects were deceived by the appearance of the flowers into believing that they were females and, when attempting to copulate, dislodged the pollinia, carrying them away to the next flower. Pouyanne, who called this pseudocopulation, observed *O. speculum* over the many years he held legal office in Algiers.

Colonel M. J. Godfery was able to confirm his observations by examining other species in southern France. It seems that *O. speculum* is only regularly visited by a single insect, a species of wasp called *Campsocolia ciliata*. The males appear about a month before the females and fly over dry, sunny banks whilst the females spend time underground, hunting for the worms on which their larvae will feed. The males have no probosces and thus need neither nectar nor other food, yet they seek out the flowers of *O. speculum*. Thus it seems that a scent is the major attractant and, with the rather crude resemblance of the flower to the female wasp both visually and tactually with hairs and bumps, serves to convince the male to carry out pseudocopulation. Pouyanne claimed that as many as 40% of flowers of *O. speculum* then form fertile capsules.

Fascinating accounts of the insect visitors to other species of *Ophrys* are detailed in Kullenberg's *Studies in Ophrys Pollination*, and one of the many facts that emerges is the apparent fidelity of one species of insect to a single *Ophrys* species. This tends to account for the relatively small number of interspecific hybrids formed in the wild.

The scents produced by the *Ophrys* flowers have been analysed and have been found to resemble the sexual attractants (pheromones) secreted by corresponding bees and wasps. There is no doubt that the plant scents are powerful, for in controlled experiments male insects actually went for flowers of *O. lutea* in preference to females of their species. Kullenberg writes of Pouyanne's experiment where *O. speculum* flowers were hidden away from the insects' vision in layers of newspaper, but they were still found by persistent males following the scent.

The scent alone is not enough, however, and some sort of tactile contact with the hairs, humps and bumps on the lip is essential to act as a stimulus.

It is quite difficult to witness pseudocopulation but we have been fortunate to see it with plants of *O. sphegodes* ssp. *mammosa* and also with *O. fuciflora* ssp. *bornmuelleri*. It is certainly true that the insect male is attracted easily and then stimulated by contact. After a short time it realises something is wrong, and starts changing position, whirring its wings and even biting the surface of the lip. Kullenberg terms this behaviour 'displacement activity', but it seems to us to be a case of intense sexual frustration.

One is forced to wonder just how such an unlikely chemical deception evolved. In their book on pollination, Proctor and Yeo suggest that a fairly specific attractive scent was first evolved with a flower pattern close enough to that of the female to provoke a reaction from the male – an accident in fact. The plant was pollinated and the way opened for its progress to adapt closer and closer to the insect pattern. Again, females emerge after males and are in short supply, thus ensuring a competitive spirit which favours pseudocopulation with *Ophrys*.

Unlike other species of *Ophrys*, *O. apifera* is usually self-pollinated. One often finds the pollinia bent down on their elastic caudicles towards the front of the stigma, and this can happen almost as soon as the flowers open. The viscid disc at the base of the caudicle actually remans inside the bursicle. A breeze or even a visiting insect will bring the pollinia in contact with the stigma. This self-pollination, although effective in most cases, does not prevent occasional cross-pollination.

Normally all the flowers are fertilized, even if there are many in one inflorescence.

Fig. 43 Pseudo-copulation on an *Ophrys*. A drawing made from a photograph taken in the field.

Hybrids

The list of interspecific hybrids for this genus increases from year to year and now that techniques for cross-pollinating *Ophrys* are becoming more successful perhaps those hybrids not found in the wild can be obtained artificially.

Some species of *Ophrys* show such a considerable range of patterns that even experienced field workers can be deceived into thinking that hybrids have been encountered. Earlier, the fidelity of insect pollinators to particular *Ophrys* species was mentioned, and for this reason hybrids tend to be uncommon.

The book *Ophrys Hybriden* by O. & E. Danesch contains a wealth of photographs of hybrids. Some of the putative parents seem fanciful but the pictures do show the vast range of offspring possible.

The list is by no means exhaustive but the authors have tried to include the more likely combinations to be encountered.

A single intergeneric hybrid is known between *O. sphegodes* ssp. *mammosa* and a *Serapias*, possibly *S. lingua*. A painting appears in E. Nelson's monograph including the genus *Serapias*.

O. bertolonii x *O. apifera* = (unnamed) Harbeck

O. bertolonii x *O. scolopax* = *O.* x *neo-ruppertii* Camus ap Ruppert

O. bertolonii x *O. tenthredinifera* = *O.* x *kallista* Keller

O. bombyliflora x *O. arachnitiformis* = *O.* x *semi bombyliflora* Bergon et Camus

O. bombyliflora x *O. bertolonii* = *O.* x *cataldi* Gölz

O. bombyliflora x *O. scolopax* = *O.* x *olbiensis* Camus

O. bombyliflora x *O. speculum* = *O.* x *fernandi* Rolfe

O. bombyliflora x *O. tenthredinifera* = *O.* x *sommieri* Camus ap Cortesi

O. carmeli x *O. reinholdii* = *O.* x *rhodi* Frey et Keller

O. ferrum-equinum x *O. cretica* = *O.* x *kalopissi* Hermjakob

O. ferrum-equinum x *O. scolopax* ssp. *cornuta* = *O.* x *petri* Hermjakob

O. ferrum-equinum x *O. tenthredinifera* = *O.* x *zeidleri* Hermjakob

O. fuciflora x *O. apifera* = *O.* x *albertiana* Camus

O. fusca x *O. bertolonii* = *O.* x *spuria* Keller et Reinhard

O. fusca x *O. lutea* = *O.* x *subfusca* Reichenb. fil.

O. fusca x *O. scolopax* = *O.* x *enigmatodes* Keller

O. fusca x *O. sphegodes* = *O.* x *pseudofusca* Albert et Camus

O. fusca ssp. *iricolor* x *O. tenthredinifera* = *O.* x *lievreae* Maire

O. insectifera x *O. apifera* = *O.* x *pietschii* Kümpel

O. insectifera x *O. fuciflora* = *O.* x *devenensis* Reichenb. fil.

O. insectifera x *O. sphegodes* = *O.* x *hybrida* Pokorny ap. Reichenb. fil.

O. lutea x *O. bertolonii* = *O.* x *opaca* Keller

O. lutea x *O. ferrum-equinum* ssp. *gottfriediana* = (unnamed) Renz

O. lutea x *O. sphegodes* = *O.* x *quadriloba* Camus

O. lutea x *O. tenthredinifera* = *O.* x *personei* Cortesi

O. scolopax ssp. *cornuta* x *O. argolica* = *O.* x *delphinensis* Danesch

O. scolopa ssp. *cornuta* x *O. cretica* = *O.* x *regis-minois* Halx

O. scolopax ssp. *apiformis* x *O. tenthredinifera* = *O.* x *peltieri* Maire

O. speculum x *O. apifera* = (unnamed) Bouchard

O. speculum x *O. argolica* = *O.* x *rasbachii* Eberle

O. speculum x *O. bertolonii* = *O.* x *emmae* Keller et Wettstein

O. speculum x *O. ferrum-equinum* = (unnamed) Waldmann

O. speculum x *O. fusca* = *O.* x *eliasii* Sennen ap. Camus

O. speculum x *O. lutea* = *O.* x *chobautii* Keller

O. speculum x *O. scolopax* = *O.* x *kelleriella* Denis ap. Keller

O. speculum x *O. sphegodes* = *O.* x *macchiatii* Camus

O. speculum x *O. tenthredinifera* = *O.* x *heraultii* Keller
O. sphegodes x *O. apifera* = *O.* x *flahaultii* D'Abzac
O. sphegodes ssp. *aesculapii* x *O. argolica* = *O.* x *epidavrensis* Eberle
O. sphegodes x *O. bertolonii* = *O.* x *saratoi* Camus
O. sphegodes x *O. cretica* = (unnamed) Baumann
O. sphegodes ssp. *mammosa* x *O. ferrum-equinum* = *O.* x *rechingeri* Soó
O. sphegodes x *O. fuciflora* = *O.* x *aschersonii* Nanteuil
O. sphegodes x *O. tenthredinifera* = *O.* x *grampini* Cortesi
O. tenthredinifera x *O. argolica* = (unnamed) Waldmann

Key
Aggregates such as *Ophrys scolopax*, *O. fuciflora* and *O. sphegodes* are only partly reduced by the key. To separate into subspecies refer to the species descriptions.

1 Connective tissue between the anthers with a blunt end **2**
  Connective tissue between the anthers with a pointed end **8**

2 Inner perianth segments (petals) white, yellowish or green **3**
  Inner perianth segments purplish or blackish-violet at
    least at their base **5**

3 Lip with a flat margin and a marginal zone which is yellow
    and either glabrous or hairy **O. lutea**
  Lip with a more or less deflexed margin and velvety
    marginal zone (perhaps with a fine yellow edge); inner
    perianth segments green **4**

4 Inner perianth segments white to greenish-white, lip
    7–9mm, lower portion of the lip directed backwards **O. pallida**
  Inner perianth segments green, lip 13–23mm, side lobe
    shorter than the central lobe **O. fusca**

5 Lip deeply 3-lobed with velvety lateral lobes deflexed
    so that the lip appears globular and inflated **O. bombyliflora**
  Lip entire to 3-lobed; lateral lobes neither velvety
    nor deflexed **6**

6 Outer perianth segments pink or purplish; lip entire
    (rarely with slight side lobes) **O. tenthredinifera**
  Outer perianth segments green or yellowish; lip distinctly
    3-lobed **7**

7 Inner perianth segments very narrow, velvety, blackish;
    middle lobe of lip entire or slightly indented at the
    apex; speculum small pale violet blue **O. insectifera**
  Inner perianth segments ovate to lanceolate, hairy;
    middle lobe of lip entire; speculum large bright
    iridescent blue sometimes with a yellow margin **O. speculum**

8 Lateral lobes of lip with basal protuberances; speculum
    often with white or yellowish margin **9**
  Lateral lobes without basal protuberances; speculum with
    or without a pale margin **21**

9 Outer perianth segments green; lip with or without an
    appendage **10**
  Outer perianth segments pink or purplish; lip usually with
    an appendage **16**

10 Lip entire   *11*
   Lip 3-lobed   *12*

11 Speculum without a coloured margin, usually H-shaped;
   inner perianth segments at least half as long as the outer   *O. sphegodes*
                                                                 (aggr.)

   Speculum with white yellowish or greenish margin, variable
   in shape from 'H' to shield shape. Inner perianth segments ¹/₅ to ¹/₃ as long as the outer   *O. fuciflora*
                                                                 (aggr.)

12 Lateral lobes of lip glabrous, speculum usually H-shaped   *13*
   Lateral lobes of the lip hairy; speculum variable H- or
   shield-shaped, or of small spots and rings   *14*

13 Speculum without pale margin; lip 5–16mm   *O. sphegodes*
                                                                 (aggr.)
   Speculum often with a white margin; lip 10–14mm   *O. spruneri*

14 Lip blackish-purple; speculum H-shaped, shield-like or
   degencrating into lines, white or bluish with a white
   margin   *15*
   Lip brown; speculum more or less shield-shaped, blue or
   dark violet with a yellow margin   *O. carmeli*

15 Lip with lateral lobes spreading   *O. cretica*
   Lip with lateral lobes strongly reflexed   *O. kotschyi*

16 Inner perianth segments about ⅔ as long as the outer;
   speculum crescent-shaped without a coloured margin   *O. lunulata*
   Inner perianth segments up to ½ as long as outer segments;
   speculum variable but not crescent-shaped, with a white
   or yellowish margin   *17*

17 Lip entire or sub-entire   *18*
   Lip 3-lobed   *19*

18 Basal protuberances of lip up to 3mm, appendage of lip
   large   *O. fuciflora*
                                                                 (aggr.)
   Basal protuberances of lip short and almost incon-
   spicuous; lip appendage small   *O. arachnitiformis*
                                                                 [complex]

19 Outer perianth segments normally 10–15mm; lip append-
   age long or absent altogether, margin of speculum yellow   *O. apifera*
   Outer perianth segments normally 8–10mm lip appendage
   short, margin of speculum yellow or white   *20*

20 Inner perianth segments ½ as long as outer segments, lip
   with small basal protuberances, margin of speculum
   white   *O. cretica*
   Inner perianth segments ¹/₅ to ½ the length of the outer
   segments; lip with large or long horn-like basal protuberances; margin of speculum whitish or yellow   *O. scolopax*

21 Lip entire   *22*
   Lip 3-lobed   *27*

22 Outer perianth segments green   *23*
    Outer perianth segments pinkish or purplish   *25*

23 Speculum with whitish, greenish or yellow margin   *26*
    Speculum without a coloured margin   *24*

24 Lip 5–15mm without an appendage; speculum basically   *O. sphegodes*
    H-shaped   (aggr.)
    Lip 10–12mm, with appendage; speculum usually shaped like
    a horseshoe, sometimes reduced to two vertical lines   *O. ferrum-equinum*

25 Speculum usually horseshoe-shaped; lip velvety, not curved
    up forwards   *O. ferrum-equinum*
    Speculum usually shield-shaped, lip velvety, curved forwards
    at the apex   *O. bertolonii*

26 Inner perianth segments at least ½ as long as the outer; lip
    roundish to ovate in outline   *O. argolica*
    Inner perianth segments ⅕ to ⅓ the length of the outer, lip
    broadly obovate to almost square   *O. fuciflora*

27 Inner perianth segments at least ⅔ length of outer, speculum   (aggr.)
    crescent-shaped; outer segments of perianth pinkish-violet   *O. lunulata*
    Inner perianth segments about ½ as long as the outer or even
    shorter   *28*

28 Inner perianth segments about ½ the length of the outer,
    speculum variable but not crescent-shaped; outer
    segments green, pink or purplish   *29*
    Inner perianth segments much shorter than outer, 2mm or
    less   *34*

29 Speculum usually horseshoe-shaped, inner perianth
    segments glabrous   *O. ferrum-equinum*
    Speculum variable but if shaped like a horseshoe then the
    inner perianth segments are velvety   *30*

30 Speculum of two thick comma-shaped lines or "eyes",
    sometimes much reduced with the white marginal area
    extended over much of the lip surface   *O. reinholdii*
    Speculum not as above   *31*

31 Speculum H-shaped with lower uprights considerably
    lengthened, white lateral sepals large and
    downward pointing   *O. kurdica*
    Speculum H-shaped or shield-shaped, or of one or two
    lines or spots; lateral sepals not very large   *32*

32 Outer perianth segments pinkish violet or purple, inner
    segments velvety, speculum with a white margin   *O. argolica*
    Outer perianth segments green or greenish-purple; inner
    perianth segments glabrous or hairy; speculum with or
    without a white margin   *33*

33 Lip 5–15mm, usually entire; speculum without a white
    margin   *O. sphegodes*
    Lip 10–13mm 3-lobed; speculum with a white margin   *O. spruneri*

34 Side lobes of lip small

Side lobes of lip very large in comparison to the rest
of the lip and directed upwards

O. fuciflora
(ssp. *bornmuelleri*)

O. schulzei

Ophrys insectifera L.
FLY ORCHID; OPHRYS MOUCHE (F);
FLIEGEN RAGWURZ (G); PECCHIE (I).
Plants of this species are slender and
can grow up to 60cm tall, although 20
–50cm is more usual. There are 7–9
broadly lanceolate leaves which grow up
the stem, unlike those of other *Ophrys*
species where leaves form a basal rosette.
  The lax inflorescence can carry 2–14
flowers, and the flower bracts are longer
than the ovary.
  The sepals are small (6–8mm), green
and more or less concave. The petals are
very narrow and 4–6mm in length. They
are blackish-violet in colour and form a
pair of antennae to the insect body of the
lip.
  The lip is 3-lobed, with the central
lobe elongated and indented at the base.
In colour it is a velvety dark brown or
chestnut, with a dark rectangular blue or
violet speculum at its base. Exceptional
forms occur with a narrow, yellowish
margin to the central lobe.
Varieties: Var. *ochroleuca* Camus has a
yellow or greenish lip with a whitish
basal pattern.
Flowers: from May through to July depending on latitude and altitude.
Habitat: grasslands, pine- and beechwoods (up to 1850m), thickets and
woodland edges.
Distribution: it occurs over much of
Europe but is absent from the south-east
and rare in the extreme south and much
of the north. It extends further north
than any other *Ophrys* species, reaching
central Sweden and parts of Norway.
  Middle and southern Sweden; Norway; southern Finland; east Spain;
France; England; Ireland; Germany; the
Benelux countries; Switzerland and Austria; northern Italy; northern Yugoslavia; Czechoslovakia; Hungary; Rumania and Russia.   **230**

Ophrys speculum Link = *O. vernixia*
Brot.
MIRROR ORCHID; OPHRYS MIROIR (F);
SPIEGEL-RAGWURZ (G).
  A rather small plant reaching 10–
30cm in height with 5–7 oblong leaves.
From 2–10 flowers are carried in a lax
spike, and the flower bracts are longer
than the ovary.
  The sepals are 6–8mm long, coloured
green with fine reddish-brown stripes
and the dorsal sepal curved forwards.
The petals are ¼ to ⅓ the length of the
sepals and are coloured dark purple-
brown or in rare cases green.
  The lip is 3-lobed with its margins
covered in dense purple-brown hairs and
maximum dimensions of 13 × 15mm.
The central area of the lip is occupied by
a large, shiny blue speculum which is
sometimes framed by a yellow margin.
This last feature is especially noticeable
in some of the plants from Spain.
Varieties: Var. *regis-ferdinandii* (Acht.
& Kellerer) Soó, from Rhodes and western Turkey, has the side lobes much
reduced and the lip edges so recurved
that the lip appears very narrow and
almost completely blue, giving it a remarkably insect-like appearance.   **233**
Var. *klosii* Hermjakob, a form from
Greece where the mirror is coloured
blue and white.
Flowers: March to April, although in
southern Greece it is past its best by the
beginning of the latter month.
Habitat: undisturbed grassy areas, garigue, woodland (under light pine cover).
Distribution: north Africa; Spain; Balearics; Italy; Corsica; Sardinia; Sicily;
Greece; Rhodes; Turkey and Lebanon.
                            231

Ssp. *lusitanica* O. & E. Danesch. This is
a much more robust plant than the
nominate race, with stems up to 50cm
tall and an inflorescence that can carry as
many as 15 blooms.

The central lobe of the labellum is oblong, and the side lobes are considerably extended downwards. The marginal hairs of the lip are dark yellow or rusty brown.
Distribution: west and central Portugal.
232

Ophrys lutea (Gouan) Cav.
YELLOW BEE ORCHID; OPHRYS JAUNE (F); GELBE RAGWURZ (G); OPHRYS GIALLO (I).
The plant stands 10–30cm tall, with 4–5 broadly lanceolate leaves. There are 2–7 flowers carried in a lax inflorescence, with flower bracts longer than the ovary. The sepals are green and about 10mm in length, with the median curved forwards. The petals are yellowish-green and about ½ the length of the sepals. The lip is 12–18mm long and 3-lobed, with well-developed side lobes and the median lobe indented at the apex. There is a broad yellow margin (2–3mm) and a 2-lobed dark blue speculum (which is narrow in relation to the lip) on a central brown area. The margin is glabrous; the rest of the lip has small hairs on it.
Flowers: March to April.
Habitat: Grassy areas and maquis/garigue, under pine trees.
Distribution: North Africa; Spain; Balearics; southern France; Italy; Corsica; Sardinia; Sicily; Yugoslavia; Greece; Crete; Rhodes; Turkey; Lebanon.
234, 235

Ssp. *melena* Renz. This has a labellum 9–12mm in length, often with the middle lobe smaller than the lateral lobes. The marginal zone is 1–2mm wide, brown with blackish-purple hairs. The speculum is 2-lobed and wide in relation to the lip. The ground colour of the lip is blackish-purple.
Hybrids of *O. fusca* with *O. lutea* produce flowers with the same characteristics as ssp. *melena* and this is possibly the origin of the plants. Ssp. *melena* occurs with *O. lutea* and perhaps deserves no more than varietal status.
Flowers: March to April.
Distribution: southern Greece. Similar

forms also occur in places in Sicily and Sardinia.
236

Ssp. *murbeckii* (Fleischm.) Soó = var. *minor* Guss. This has a smaller lip than the nominate race (9–12mm) and the central lobe is often smaller than the laterals. The yellow marginal zone is 1–2mm wide, and the speculum is 2-lobed and wide in relation to the lip. The lip invariably carries a small brown inverted 'V' at the base of the central lobe.
Flowers: March and April (late February in Cyprus).
Distribution: throughout the range of the nominate race. It is the only form of *O. lutea* found in Cyprus.
237

Ophrys fusca Link
DULL OPHRYS; OPHRYS SOMBRE (F); BRAUNE RAGWURZ (G); MOSCARIA GIALLOGNOLA (I).
The name *Ophrys fusca* includes a number of races which are so distinct that many now think they deserve specific status in their own right.
The nominate race grows from 10–40cm tall, with 4–6 often rather broad leaves. The flower bracts are larger than the ovary, and the lax inflorescence carries 2–8 small flowers.
The sepals are green to yellow, with the dorsal sepal curved forwards. The petals are about ⅔ the length of the sepals and usually green, although they can be yellowish or light brown. The lip is 3-lobed, with side lobes that range from well developed to almost indistinct, and has a length of 10–15mm. The median lobe is indented at the apex, and there is often a thin white or yellow margin. The edges of the lip can be recurved or not. The speculum is in two parts near the base of the lip and varies from dull greyish-blue to bluish-violet, carried on a dark brown lip.
Flowers: February to April.
Habitat: Maquis, garigue, olive groves – often on very poor, bare, stony soils; under pine trees.
Distribution: throughout the Mediterranean region. It is one of the commonest *Ophrys*.
238, 239, 240

In *Flora Europaea* a number of subspecies are listed, but difference in size and colour compared with the nominate flowers seem to us to justify specific status. However, the races are listed here as subspecies.

Ssp. *omegaifera* (Fleischm.) Nelson. This is another large-flowered subspecies, with the size and shape of the lip comparable with ssp. *iricolor* (about 20mm long). The petals are strap-like, green to reddish-brown, with a wavy edge. The lip is 3-lobed, arched and does not have a yellow margin. The speculum is red-brown or brownish-violet, and there is a large yellowish or whitish 'W' (omega) mark.

Recent painstaking work (H. Baurmann and A. Dafni) has shown that what has been assumed to be a rather variable subspecies is in fact three races with a number of quite distinct features and separate distributions. These are:

Ssp. *fleischmannii* Soó. This has a smaller lip than ssp. *omegaifera* (10–14mm), with a violet-black ground colour and speculum area bluish to reddish-grey sometimes broken into patches. The side lobes are slightly spread from the median lobe but only slightly directed backwards.
Distribution: mainly Cyprus, Turkey and Lebanon, with some records from Crete and Greece. **241**

Ssp. *omegaifera*, which has a lip 14–20mm long with a chestnut brown ground colour and speculum from light brown to bluish. The side lobes are definitely backward pointing, while the apex of the lip is hardly, if at all, notched.
Distribution: Crete, Karpathos and Rhodes. **242**

Ssp. *dyris* (Maire) Soó. The lip in this race is 10–14mm long, with reddish-violet ground colour and a speculum area which is a lighter shade of the same colour. The side lobes have well rounded ends and spread sideways from the median lobe.

Distribution: southern Spain and north Africa (Morocco). **243**

Ssp. *iricolor* (Desf.) O. Schwartz. On first sight it is difficult to believe that this plant and the nominate race are related at all. *O. fusca* ssp. *iricolor* is usually a large plant, with much larger flowers than the nominate. The lip is distinctly 3-lobed and up to 25mm long. The sepals are broad and green with petals that are strap-like, yellowish-green or reddish-brown. The speculum is large and iridescent metallic blue, while the lip ground colour is a rich purple-brown, almost black, with a velvety texture. The lip edges are recurved.
Flowers: February (in Cyprus), March and April.
Distribution: Italy (Riviera, Mt Argentario); Corsica; Sardinia; Yugoslavia; Greece; Crete; Rhodes; Corfu; Cyprus; Turkey. **244**

Ssp. *durieui* (Reichenb. fil.) Soó. This race is closely related to ssp. *iricolor*, and was previously known as ssp. *atlantica*, referring to its main habitat in N. Africa. It is 15–25cm tall, with 4–7 broadly lanceolate leaves and 2–3 not very variable flowers in a lax inflorescence. The sepals are long and green, and the petals are green and about ¾ the length of the sepals. The lip is 3-lobed, with the side lobes nearly as long as the median lobe (the length of the side lobes distinguishes it from ssp. *iricolor*). The lip tapers towards the base, giving a marked triangular shape, and the ground colour is purplish-black with a blue speculum.
Flowers: late April to June (after ssp. *iricolor*).
Distribution: Morocco and southern Spain, in mountain regions. **245**

Ophrys pallida Rafin
A rather small, slender species, 10–20cm tall, with 4–7 short, broadly lanceolate leaves. The lax inflorescence carries 2–5 not very variable flowers, and the flower bracts are longer than the ovary.

This species is closely related to *O. fusca* (and is sometimes considered as a

subspecies of it). The sepals are broad and pinkish-white or greenish-white. The petals are about ½ the length of the sepals and whitish to pale greenish. The lip is rectangular and shallowly 3-lobed. The feature which distinguishes it from *O. fusca* is that the lip is deflexed at the base, so that the apex points backwards. The ground colour is maroon brown, and the speculum consists of 2 patches, pinkish-white to blue-grey in colour.
Flowers: March and April.
Habitat: grassy hillsides and maquis.
Distribution: a rare and local species, found in north Africa (Tunisia and Algeria); Sicily; possibly Sardinia; Malta.
                                                    246

Ophrys sphegodes Miller
EARLY SPIDER ORCHID; OPHRYS
ARAIGNÉE, OISEAU-COQUET (F);
SPINNEN-RAGWURZ (G);
CALABRONE (I).

This is an exceptionally variable species, with numerous races cited in the literature on orchids. Some authors spell the name *sphecodes*.

In general the plants are from 10–45cm in height and bear 5–9 broadly lanceolate leaves. The flower bracts are longer than the ovary, and the lax inflorescence carries 2–10 flowers. The perianth segments are glabrous and the outer between 6 and 10mm in length, with the inner at least half as long as the outer and 4–8mm in length. The lip margins are deflexed or flattened, and the surface is velvety in appearance – rarely with a small appendage. The speculum is usually H-shaped or deformed into an X.

In the nominate race the sepals are green and comparatively large. The petals are about ½ the length of the sepals and are green or slightly tinged with a reddish-brown. The lip is ovoid, with average dimensions 10–12mm × 8–12mm – although smaller-flowered forms occur. The side lobes are reduced to 2 humps and a basal protuberance is often present. The overall colour of the velvety lip is a rich maroon brown and the speculum is usually H-shaped, although sometimes the cross line is absent.

Varieties: Var. *planimaculata* has been described as an *apochromic* or pattern-free form where the lip is dominated by a light blue speculum. It is occasionally encountered in small numbers growing with ssp. *atrata*, ssp. *mammosa* and ssp. *sintenisii*.   **249**
Flowers: late March (in the Mediterranean) to June (further north). Late April in the UK.
Habitat: woodland clearings, grasslands, maquis and garigue, always on basic soils.
Distribution: western, central and southern Europe, from southern England (Dorset and Kent in isolated populations); France (common on the southwest edges of the Massif Central); Italy; Corsica; the Balkans to northern Greece; Cyprus and the Crimea. **247, 248**

Ssp. *litigiosa* (Camus) Becherer. This is a very small-flowered race, with 6–10 blooms. The sepals are green, usually with rounded edges. The green petals are broad with a single vein. The labellum has dimensions 5–8mm × 5–8mm, and the basal protuberance is mostly absent. It is very dark brown, edged with greenish-yellow, and the side lobes are barely developed in most specimens. The speculum is small, blue and irregularly H- or saucer-shaped.
Flowers: March to mid-April.
Habitat: grasslands, garigue and open woodland in the Mediterranean region.
Distribution: Spain; France; Corfu; Crete; Greece.   **250**

Ssp. *tommasinii* (Vis.) Soó. There are rarely more than 3–5 flowers on a stem. The petals are 3-veined and the lip is rounded, with dimensions 6–10mm × 6–10mm. In colour the lip is pale brown, and the speculum is U- or saucer-shaped. This race is very closely related to *O. sphegodes* ssp. *litigiosa* and often included with it.
Flowers: April to early May.
Habitat: Mediterranean grasslands, light pinewoods, garigue, on the coast.
Distribution: coastal region of western Yugoslavia; north-west Greece.

Ssp. *provincialis* E. Nelson. This resembles very closely, small-flowered forms of ssp. *garganica*, and there is good reason for treating it as a variant of the nominate race. Its characteristics are: green or pinkish sepals, green or brownish-green petals, and a labellum shape and pattern very close to *O. sphegodes* ssp. *garganica* (p. 164).
Flowers: March.
Distribution: restricted to southern France.   **251**

Ssp. *atrata* (Lindley) E. Mayer. A subspecies with large rounded or pointed petals, usually green, but individuals with reddish-pink perianth segments can be found in some of the larger populations on Mt Gargano in Italy. The petals are broad, with wavy edges, and coloured green (often with reddish edges) or completely reddish. The lip varies in shape from round to pointed-oblong (8 −12 (13)mm × 8−12(13)mm). The basal protuberances are well-developed, usually outspreading and triangular. The lip is coloured blackish-brown or purple, with hairy margin and an H- or U-shaped speculum. The lower arms of the 'H' are much longer than the upper, and it often extends to the protuberances.
Flowers: late March (in southern Italy) to May.
Distribution: Mediterranean, from Portugal and Spain east to Yugoslavia. Very frequent in Gargano.   **252**

Ssp. **mammosa** (Desf.) Soó. This subspecies has long sepals which are either plain green or, in the case of the laterals, coloured reddish on their lower halves. Exceptional examples have sepals reddish-pink overall. The petals are narrow and rather acute, coloured green or reddish and with a wavy edge. The lip is round to oblong (10−17 × 8−17mm) and entire or, more rarely, indistinctly 3-lobed. In colour it is blackish-brown or purple, with two very marked basal protuberances, and it is velvety rather than hairy. The speculum is sometimes H-shaped, but equally often reduced to 2 vertical lines. Occasionally, narrow-lipped forms occur.

In parts of Cyprus, where ssp. *mammosa* and ssp. *sintenisii* grow together, large-flowered forms of *O. sphegodes* occur, with a lip that is shallowly 3-lobed, has an apical protuberance and a wide yellow margin. These form quite distinct populations that seem intermediate between ssp. *mammosa* and ssp. *sintenisii*. As with many members of the *O. sphegodes* aggregate, distinctions between so-called subspecies are frequently so blurred that the wisdom of the accepted classification can often be questioned.
Flowers: February (in Cyprus) to April.
Habitat: Mediterranean grasslands, under open pine trees and in garigue.
Distribution: a distinctly eastern race from Greece; western Turkey; Crete; Cyprus; Israel.   **253, 254**

Ssp. *parnassica* (Vierh.) Soó. The lip is more or less 3-lobed, and the basal protuberances are small or absent. The overall colour is dark brown or purplish, with a white or yellow margin. The speculum has a variable shape. It is probably no more than a local race of *O. sphegodes* ssp. *mammosa*. Despite its name, this is a race from the Peloponnese.
Flowers: late March to April.
Habitat: garigue, grassland.
Distribution: Greece; Crete.

Ssp. *sintenisii* (Fleischm. & Bornm.) E. Nelson. This is often a very robust plant, up to 40cm in height, with rather long, broadly lanceolate leaves in an extended basal rosette, where the upper members usually partly sheath the stem. The leaves are prominently veined, recurved, and a duller, lighter green than the leaves of ssp. *mammosa*. The flowers differ from those of ssp. *mammosa* in the following respects: the column is more attenuated, so that is looks like a long-billed duck in profile; the lip is distinctly 3-lobed, and the speculum invariably H-shaped, with the basal arms of the H reduced; basal protuberances are much reduced or absent altogether.

Flowers: mid-March to April, about 1–2 weeks after *O. sphegodes* ssp. *mammosa* comes into flower, where they occur together, as in Cyprus.

Habitat: stony hillsides, garigue, light hillside pinewoods.

Distribution: Cyprus (in chalk and limestone hills); Turkey; Lebanon; Syria; Israel.   **255**

Some of the Lebanese forms are intermediate between ssp. *sintenisii* and ssp. *amanensis*, with sepals the colour of the former and extended side-lobes and markings like the latter. There seems to be little justification for treating these plants as separate subspecies. *O. sphegodes*, ssp. *transhyrcana* (Czernjah) Soó is generally regarded as identical with ssp. *sintenisii*. *Ophrys caucasica* Woronow is probably another orchid which is identical with ssp. *sintenisii*.

Ssp. **amanensis** E. Nelson. This plant is very similar to ssp. *sintenisii*, and some authorities class them together. The flowers usually have bright pink sepals, although this is by no means always true; some forms have green sepals. The lip is distinctly 3-lobed, with very well developed side lobes.

Attempts have been made to include this ssp. with *Ophrys spruneri*.

Flowers: May.

Habitat: hillside garigue, under light pine cover.

Distribution: southern Turkey (Taurus and Amanus mountains).

Ssp. **aesculapii** (Renz) Soó. This is one of the most attractive of the wide range of *O. sphegodes* subspecies. The petals and sepals are coloured green to pale olive. The lip has a velvet texture and is coloured dark brown, with a wide glabrous yellow margin. The speculum is in the form of an elongated H more or less framed in white.

Flowers: March and early April.

Habitat: stony hillsides or under pines.

Distribution: Greece (Attica and the Peloponnese).   **256**

Ssp. **hebes** (Kalopissis) B. & E. Willing. This recently described form is rather similar to ssp. *aesculapii* in appearance but may be distinguished from it as follows: ssp. *hebes* has a slightly 3-lobed lip with a broad yellowish-green edge, while ssp. *aesculapii* has an entire lip with a bright yellow edge and a well-defined area of dark brown at the centre. In ssp. *hebes* the central lip area is brown but degenerates to a mottling around its perimeter.

Both subspecies have greenish petals but in ssp. *hebes* they are ⅔ to ¾ the length of the sepals compared with just over ½ for ssp. *aesculapii*. Finally, the outer perianth segments of ssp. *hebes* point more or less downwards.

Flowers: early April to late May.

Distribution: central and southern Greece including the Peloponnese.

Ssp. **helenae** (Renz) Soó & D. Moresby-Moore. This subspecies has petals and sepals green to dark-green. The labellum is 11–13 × 16–19mm, with no basal protuberances and dark or reddish velvety brown in appearance. The speculum is absent or very indistinct, which makes the appearance of the subspecies unmistakable. In some books it is mentioned merely as an aberrant form due to the lack of lip markings, or else it is omitted altogether. Until recently this was justified because few good populations were known.

Flowers: March and April.

Distribution: north-west Greece – Epirus, Thessaly and Corfu (rare).   **257**

Ssp. **garganica** E. Nelson. This large-flowered form has green sepals and very broad petals, either green or brown, with wavy edges. The lip is usually rounded and entire, with dimensions up to 12mm × 16mm. Rarely, individuals have very slight development of 3 lobes. The ground colour is a dark purplish velvet brown, and the margins are hairy. The speculum is basically 2 parallel lines, meeting at the base and forming a distorted H-shape. In many flowers the speculum degenerates into a more complicated pattern that can cover the whole of the labellum.

It is sometimes considered merely as a variant of the nominate race, but in parts of southern Italy (e.g. Mt Gargano) it is the dominant form.

Flowers: March and early April.
Distribution: Spain; central and southern Italy. **258, 259**

Ssp. *sipontensis* Gump. This very striking plant has large flowers, with pale or deep-pink sepals and petals that are deep pinkish red. The lip is entire and very dark brown, with a hairy edge, giving it a furry appearance. The speculum is a deep blue, sometimes H-shaped but often more complex and extending ove the whole of the labellum.

This subspecies is omitted in the text of *Flora Europaea*, and the index lists it with *Ophrys arachnitiformis*. It is unlike any form of *O. arachnitiformis* we have seen in the area. It occurs in very local populations with ssp. *atrata* and ssp. *garganica*, and the pink sepals make it strikingly different from any of their usual forms. The lip shape and markings do, however, resemble closely those on forms of ssp. *garganica*.

Flowers: April and early May.
Distribution: restricted to the southwestern parts of Mt Gargano in southern Italy. **260**

Ssp. *sicula* E. Nelson. This robust subspecies can carry up to 18 flowers in an inflorescence of 32cm length. More often the flowers are between 5–15 in number, and the plant has an overall height of up to 40cm.

It is not a very well-defined race, but Nelson justifies its subspecific status on the basis that it occurs mainly in Sicily, where the nominate race is absent.

The blooms tend to be larger than those of the nominate race, and the sepals are generally white to pale pink. Occasionally flowers occur with light green sepals. The petals are relatively long – about ⅔ the length of the sepals – and white with a yellow or greenish edge, or just gently pink. Rarely, they

are green. The lip is very definitely recurved at the edges, giving it a rounded appearance, and it is distinctly 3-lobed. The speculum consists of 2 short strips which are sharply divergent and are linked together only at their base.

Flowers: March and early April.
Habitat: stony hillsides, maquis, under shrubs.
Distribution: mainly Sicily but also recorded in southern Italy. **261**

Ophrys spruneri Nyman
This species is so closely related to *O. sphegodes* and its subspecies that some authorities label it as *O. sphegodes* ssp. *spruneri*.

The plant stands 10–30cm tall, with 3–6 oblong lanceolate leaves and a lax flower spike that carries 2–4 blooms.

The sepals are some 8–10mm in length and rounded, with the lateral sepals drooping slightly. They can range in colour from deep pink, with a central green vein, to green or purplish-green. The petals are at least ½ as long as the sepals, lanceolate or oblong in shape and coloured pink or pinkish-orange.

The lip is ovoid and usually 3-lobed, with the lateral lobes forming two drooping arms. The edges are deflexed and there is a small appendage. The ground colour varies from deep reddish-brown to dark purplish-brown, and the speculum is bluish-violet with a white margin. The pattern formed is generally H-shaped, often with the cross bar missing.

Although the presence of lateral lobes is often a distinguishing feature of *O. spruneri*, in some populations the lips are almost entire and one is hard pressed to find the 3-lobed forms.

Flowers: March and April.
Habitat: grassy areas and garigue.
Distribution: southern Greece (especially the Peloponnese); Crete; southern Turkey. **262, 263**

O. sphegodes ssp. *amanensis* is probably best considered as a form of *O. spruneri*.

Ssp. *panormitana* (Tod.) Soó. This has sepals ranging from whitish-green through pink to deep carmine red, and petals that are orange-pink or pink. Both sets of perianth segments can have green veining.

There is no appendage to the lip, which is 3-lobed with the lateral lobes scarcely deflexed. The lip markings are usualy more X- than H-shaped.

Flowers: March and early April.

Habitat: grassy areas and roadside banks.

Distribution: Sicily only, where it is rather local.   **264**

Ophrys ferrum-equinum Desf.

HORSESHOE ORCHID; OPHRYS FER À CHEVAL (F); HUFEISEN-RAGWURZ (G).

This handsome orchid stands 15–30cm tall, with 5–6 broadly lanceolate leaves. The flower bracts are longer than the ovary, and there are 2–5 blooms carried in a lax spike.

The sepals are 8–10mm in length and usually coloured pink or purple – although green sepalled forms occur. The petals are at least ½ the length of the sepals, glabrous with a wavy edge, and coloured reddish or pinkish-brown.

The lip is entire (rarely indistinctly 3-lobed) and dark velvety purple in appearance. The speculum is dark bluish-purple, with or without a narrow pale margin, and it is shaped like an inverted horseshoe or, less frequently, is reduced to two parallel lines or narrow wedges.

Flowers: March to May (depending on altitude).

Habitat: grassy places, garigue or under loose pine cover on calcareous soils.

Distribution: southern Greece (Attica and the Peloponnese); Aegina; Corfu; Rhodes; Crete; west and southern Turkey.   **265, 266**

Ssp. **gottfriediana** (Renz) E. Nelson. The sepals in this subspecies are far more variable in colour than for the nominate race, ranging from green to greenish-purple, through whitish, to pale pink. The lateral sepals are sometimes tinged reddish on their lower halves.

The lip is distinctly 3-lobed (only in exceptional cases are the lobes indistinctly separated), with a tapering appearance.

This subspecies is often considered to be a transitional form between the nominate race and *O. spruneri*.

Varieties: Var. *flavescens* Renz has a yellow lip with a white pattern.

Distribution: Greek Islands – Kephallinia; Zante; Kythera; Paros; Syros; Karpathos.   **267**

Ophrys bertolonii Noretti

BERTOLONI'S BEE ORCHID; OPHRYS DE BERTOLONI (F); BERTOLONIS RAGWURZ (G); OPHRYS BERTOLONI (I).

Plants of this species grow from 15–35cm tall, with 5–7 lanceolate to broadly lanceolate, acute leaves. The flower bracts are longer than the ovary, and the spike carries 3–8 not very variable flowers.

The sepals are 8–10mm long and coloured pink or lilac, whilst the petals are similarly coloured but shorter – about ½ the length of the sepals. There is an unusual form from Mt Gargano in southern Italy which has greenish sepals and pink petals.

The lip is large and usually entire, although occasionally it can be just differentiated into 3 lobes. Its centre is depressed so that the whole of the lower part of the lip points forwards. It is velvety blackish-purple in appearance, with a blue-violet patch towards the apex which sometimes is enclosed by a narrow pale margin. At the lip apex there is a conspicuous yellow appendage, and the whole lip is surrounded by a narrow glabrous zone.

Flowers: late March and April.

Habitat: dry grassland, roadside banks, thickets and forest margins.

Distribution: Balearics; southern France; southern Italy; Corsica; Corfu (first found by one of us in 1979); Sicily and Yugoslavia. There are very old records from Spain (only in Catalonia) but we have been unable to substantiate these and it is feasible that such records refer to *O. catalaunica* mentioned later in connection with forms of *O. bertolonii*. **268, 269**

There are a number of orchids closely linked with *O. bertolonii* which are thought to have hybrid origins or even to be mutant forms, exactly which is not certain. Over the years they have developed in isolated populations to an extent where some think they should be considered as species in their own right. These are described below.

Ophrys bertoloniiformis O. & E. Danesch
This differs from *O. bertolonii* in the following respects: the plants are generally smaller; height varying from 15–25cm; both the sepals and the petals are often greenish in colour; and the lip is smaller, scarcely curved forwards, and the appendage is small or absent altogether. In some plants the flowers have marked protuberances near the base but such flowers are unusual.

The suggestion is that this species arose from hybrids of *Ophrys bertolonii* and *O. sphegodes* ssp. *atrata*. *Flora Europaea* suggests that it is possibly more widespread than the true *O. bertolonii* (with which it has often been confused) and that this latter species is confined to the eastern part of the range.

Populations of plants from the southern Tyrol have been variously called *Ophrys benacensis* or *O. bertoloniiformis* ssp. *benacensis* Reisgl. They do not merit separate specific status and here they are included with *O. bertoloniiformis*.

Flowers: mid-April to early June.
Distribution: exact range uncertain for the reasons explained above. Populations exist in the southern Tyrol, northern Italy and southern Italy (Mt Gargano). **270**

Ophrys catalaunica O. & E. Danesch
Erich Nelson (*Monographie und Iconographie der Gattung Ophrys*) cites *Ophrys bertolonii* as probably occurring in Spain, in Catalonia. Records of this plant from that area are in all probability for *Ophrys catalaunica*, which was 'discovered' in 1967, growing in the Rio Segré valley near Berga. Since that time searches in successive seasons have revealed it in other localities within the same general area.

In appearance it is quite distinct from *O. bertolonii*. It is usually 20–25cm tall, with pink sepals that carry a green median vein. The petals are a brighter shade of pink and vary in length from ½ to ¾ the length of the sepals.

The lip is narrow and entire, with a small yellow appendage that points forwards. In colour it is dark brown and has a velvety surface, with reddish-brown hairs near the margin. The speculum is variable in shape and colour but is basically circular or even roughly hexagonal, with a deep indentation at its lower end. This indentation bisects the pattern in some specimens, and again forms occur where there is a narrow pale margin to the speculum. O. & E. Danesch (*Ophrys Hybriden*) suggest that this orchid arose from *O. bertolonii* and *O. arachnitiformis*. Over the years this has presumably become distinct from *O. x neocamusii*, a hybrid between the two which Godfery recorded from the south of France.

It has already been mentioned that *Ophrys bertolonii* has been doubtfully recorded from Catalonia. The same is true of *O. arachnitiformis* which has not been found in the area in spite of diligent searching. Perhaps early workers confused *O. catalaunica*, which is rather variable, with both these orchids and so for years it was overlooked. The origins of this plant are obviously puzzling, and more work is needed to determine whether it does have hybrid origins or is, in fact, a mutant species.
Flowers: May.
Distribution: Spain (Rio Segré and Ripoll in the Berga region of Catalonia). **271**

Ophrys promontorii O. & E. Danesch
Small populations of plants with characteristics intermediate between *O. bertolonii* and *O. sphegodes* ssp. *garganica* occur on the Gargano peninsula in

south-eastern Italy. It is probable that these plants arose from hybrids between the two orchids mentioned and over the centuries have stabilised to form what to all intents and purposes is a new species. The plants are up to 20cm tall, with 3–5 flowers. The lateral sepals are wider at their bases and at the apex become rounded, whilst the dorsal sepal is narrow. The petals are unusually large, with a broad oval shape – in some cases they can be nearly as large as the dorsal sepal. Their edges are wavy, and they range from green to brownish in colour, whereas the sepals are invariably green.

The lip is entire, with the margins deflexed and hairy. Its upper surface is convex, and it is more or less oblong in shape. The speculum is a shiny steel-blue in colour and varies in form from two blotches to a shield or horseshoe shape.
Flowers: second half of April.
Distribution: high parts of the Gargano peninsula in south-eastern Italy.

Ophrys lunulata Parl.
CRESCENT OPHRYS; MOND-RAGWURZ (G).

A rather tall, slender plant, usually from 30–40cm in height, with up to 7 oblong-lanceolate leaves. The lax flower spike carries 4–7 blooms, and the flower bracts are longer than the ovary. The sepals are broad and pink, with a green vein; only rarely are they whitish in colour. The petals are long (about ⅔ the length of the sepals), slender and coloured pink. The lip is 3-lobed, with the sides of the median lobe strongly deflexed to give it a long (10–12mm) slender appearance. The overall colour is a deep maroon-red, with a central crescent-shaped marking, ranging from white or lilac to shiny brown. The lower margins of the lip are greenish-yellow.

In colour and size the flowers are among the least variable of all species of *Ophrys*.
Varieties. Two forms are recognised: Var. *flavescens* Schulze has a yellowish-green lip and a white crescent; var. *planimaculata*, in which the lip may be

bluish, brown or olive, with a more extensive pale area.
Flowers: March to April.
Habitat: stony slopes in shrub or grassy areas, always on calcareous soils.
Distribution: almost entirely restricted to Sicily. It was recorded from Sardinia (Mt Fiocca) by Macchiati in 1880 but its presence there now is doubted by many who have searched for it. In Sicily it is certainly not a common orchid, occurring in small plantations widespread over the island. It has been recorded from Malta and is listed in *A Flora of the Maltese Islands* by Haslam, Sell and Wolseley.   **272, 273**

Ophrys argolica Fleischm.
EYED BEE ORCHID; ARGOLISCHE RAGWURZ (G).

The plant stands 15–35cm tall, with 4–6 broadly lanceolate leaves and a lax inflorescence with 2–8 flowers.

The sepals are 8–12mm long and almost invariably rosy pink or lilac. Forms with white or greenish sepals are rare. The dorsal sepal stands upright or is recurved, and the petals are about ½ as long as the sepals, lanceolate or triangular, and coloured pink or lilac.

The lip is rounded, broad (10–12mm) and usually entire, although some plants occur where the lip is indistinctly 3-lobed. The lip surface is slightly convex or flat, coloured red-brown to deep maroon, with a small pattern consisting of a violet area surrounded by white. This usually takes the form of two 'eyes', but can be horseshoe-shaped, semi-circular, or even H-shaped. The lip margin is very hairy and near the base becomes lighter in colour, often forming a pair of whitish or yellowish 'shoulders'. Nelson illustrates some unusual small-flowered forms found near Delphi in Greece.
Flowers: late March and April.
Habitat: scrub-covered hillsides and rough grassland, roadside banks on calcareous ground.
Distribution: Greece (Delphi; Peloponnese). Also recorded from Crete; Karpathos; Kasos.   **274, 275**

Ssp. *elegans* Renz. This subspecies has a distinctly 3-lobed lip with very hairy recurved lateral lobes. The dorsal sepal is recurved, and the laterals are broadly triangular. In colour they range from whitish-pink to deep rose, with a green vein. The petals are deep pink and about ½ the length of the sepals. The median lobe of the lip has a smooth velvety appearance and is coloured a rich chestnut brown. Its edges are curved under, giving it a triangular appearance. The lip pattern does not vary much and consists of two roughly triangular specula surrounded by a narrow pale border.

Varieties: Var. *flavescens Renz* has white sepals and a yellowish lip.

Flowers: early March (in Cyprus late February) to April.

Habitat: scrubby hillsides; in Cyprus it is most frequently encountered under low pine trees near the coast or on low hills.

Distribution: Cyprus and possibly southern Turkey.   **276**

Ophrys delphinensis O. & E. Danesch (pro Hybrid)

O. & E. Danesch were the first to describe a hybrid of *Ophrys argolica* and *Ophrys scolopax* ssp. *cornuta*, calling it *Ophrys x delphinensis*.

Further investigations have revealed a large number of sites for similar orchids in the N. Peloponnese east of Patras. For reasons unknown, it seems that the area has proved ideal for the formation of hybrid swarms which are far more numerous than either of the parents. Indeed in this part of Greece both *Ophrys argolica* and *Ophrys scolopax* ssp. *cornuta* are rather rare.

Many *Ophrys* now enjoying specific status are considered to have evolved from similar fertile hybrid swarms.

There are always problems in classifying these orchids because they are far more frequent than the parents and form stable populations. They are variable in appearance but clearly still intermediate between the parent forms.

The flowers of these plants are characterised by a dark brown lip with prominent 'shoulders' and a much reduced lip

pattern. In shape the lip is closer to *O. scolopax* ssp. *cornuta* than to the rather broad, entire *O. argolica*.

Ophrys reinholdii Spruner ex Fleischm.
RHEINHOLD'S BEE ORCHID;
REINHOLDS-RAGWURZ (G).

This species has 4–5 broadly lanceolate leaves and varies between 20 and 40cm in height. The flower bracts are longer than the ovary, and the lax inflorescence carries 2–8 flowers.

Possible sepal colours range from lilac, through pink, to whitish-green or even greenish-purple, and the petals are olive brown, pink or greenish and about ½ as long as the sepals.

The lip is distinctly 3-lobed, with the lateral lobes strongly deflexed. The ground colour is dark maroon-brown to blackish-purple, and the pattern consists of two thick comma-shaped lines or of two separate or connected spots, white or pale lilac in colour.

In the Greek Peloponnese it occurs with *O. argolica*, and some confusion can arise in identification when both plants are present in forms where the pattern consists of two eyes. Usually the 3-lobed lip of *O. reinholdii* is enough to separate them, since 3-lobed forms of *O. argolica* are extremely uncommon. Again, the lip colour of *O. reinholdii* is far darker.

Flowers: late March to May (depending on altitude).

Habitat: on hillsides amongst scrub, or in coniferous woodland; often on the banks of roads or tracks where the overhead cover starts to break up.

Distribution: Rhodes (one of the few *Ophrys* still in flower in late April); Greece (Peloponnese); Corfu; Crete (a small-flowered form has recently been noted here as well as more typical forms); south-west Turkey.   **277, 278**

Ssp. *straussii* Fleischm. & Bornm. This differs from the nominate race in that the flowers are larger; the side lobes are not as obviously recurved; the speculum area of the lip pattern is reduced but the pale area spreads out over more of the lip.

Dramatically coloured forms are found in south-east Turkey, where the speculum is absent altogether and the lip pattern is white on a very dark brown background.
Flowers: mid-April to mid-May.
Distribution: replaces the nominate race from southern Turkey (east of Mersin) to Syria, Iraq and Iran.   **279**

Ophrys cretica (Vierh.) E. Nelson.
CRETAN BEE ORCHID; KRETISCHE
RAGWURZ (G).

Growing from 20–30cm tall, this species has 3–6 broadly lanceolate leaves and a lax inflorescence, carrying 3–8 flowers. The flower bracts are longer than the ovary. The sepals are green, pinkish-green or, exceptionally, bright reddish-pink. The petals are reddish-green or purplish-brown and about ½ the length of the sepals. The lip is blackish-maroon, with a white-bordered H-marking and well-developed side lobes that are not reflexed (an important distinguishing feature from *O. kotschyi*). As a rule the lip markings are not very variable, but some Cretan populations exist where the markings are reduced to white vertical streaks or crescents, perhaps interconnected by white bars – scarcely two individuals having the same markings.
Flowers: mid-March to April.
Habitat: on hillsides amongst low scrub.
Distribution: Greek islands of Crete (well scattered over the island with some of the best populations in the south), Naxos and Karpathos. There are also records claimed for Attica and the Peloponnese.   **280, 281, 282**

Two rather ill-defined races have been given subspecific status by Nelson, mainly on the basis of slight differences in lip markings. These are:
Ssp. **karpathensis** E. Nelson, from the island of Karpathos.
Ssp. **naxia** E. Nelson, from the island of Naxos.

Ophrys kotschyi Fleischm. & Soó.
CYPRUS BEE ORCHID;
ZYPERN-RAGWURZ (G).

The plant stands 15–35cm tall, with 3–6 broadly lanceolate leaves. The inflorescence is lax, with 2–6 blooms and flower bracts that just equal or exceed the ovaries in length.

The sepals are usually green, although pink-sepalled forms (with green veining) can occur, but they are exceptionally rare. The dorsal sepal is curved forward, and the petals are ½–⅔ the length of the sepals, usually coloured olive green but sometimes brown or even red.

The flowers are among the largest and most impressive of any species in the genus *Ophrys* – due mainly to the dramatic colouring of the large (up to 15mm in length) lip. The ground colouring is almost black, with white-edged, elongated 'H' markings. There is remarkable little variation in lip markings from one population to another. The side lobes are distinctly reflexed.

It is closely related to *O. cretica* but differs in having a larger lip, reflexed side lobes and a forward curving dorsal sepal. Sometimes green sepals are cited as an invariable characteristic of *O. kotschyi* but this is not true.

We would agree with Sundermann's linking of *O. kotschyi* and *O. cretica* as prespecies of a single plant – *O. kotschyi*. The small differences in structure have certainly evolved because of the geographical isolation of the races.
Flowers: early March to early April. In Cyprus it is one of the later *Ophrys* to flower, coming into bloom in the second week of March in most years.
Habitat: dry, stony hillsides in garigue, or under pine trees in open woodland, always on calcareous soils.
Distribution: endemic to Cyprus, where it is an uncommon orchid. Most of the sites listed by E. Nelson around the capital, Nicosia, have been destroyed by urban expansion. The strongest accessible colonies are scattered and occur near the southern coast of the island.

Claims that *O. kotschyi* is frequent in Cyprus are probably based on mistakes in identification. *O. carmeli* occurs abundantly in Cyprus where it grows in a remarkable variety of shapes and patterns. The larger forms with the forward-curving dorsal sepal called by some *O. flavomarginata* might be confused with *O. kotschyi*; that is, until one is lucky enough to see the real thing.   **283, 284**

Ophrys kurdica Ruckbrodt
KURDISH BEE ORCHID; KURDISCHE RAGWURZ (G).

This species has 3–5 broadly lanceolate leaves and grows between 15 –30cm. It has a lax inflorescence, with 3–7 flowers and leaf bracts that are much longer than the ovary.

The sepals are large and broad, coloured greenish or pink to pinkish-brown. The lateral sepals are remarkable in that they curve to point downwards. The petals are green, brown or reddish, and about ½ the length of the sepals.

The lip is distinctly 3-lobed, with the edges of the median lobe curved under to give it a long cylindrical appearance. The side-lobes are small, hairy and recurved. The lip markings form a white elongated H-shape.
Flowers: May.
Habitat: damp grassland and hillside seepages.
Distribution: this is an extremely rare orchid that was discovered as recently as the early 1970s (Ruckbrodt detailed it in a paper dated 1975). It is known from a few small populations in south-east Anatolia, and according to some authorities is identical to *O. cilicica*, although earlier authors have treated this latter plant as synonymous with *O. schulzei*.   **285**

This is another species closely related to *O. kotschyi* and *O. cretica*. They all possibly arose from common ancestors, and geographical isolation has ensured their separate evolution. At the eastern end of the range of the genus *Ophrys*, J. Renz has recently described two distinct new species which are obviously closely related to the species related above:

Ophrys kurdistanica Renz.
This is closely related to *O. reinholdii* ssp. *straussi* and is a rather robust species

with a lax, well-spaced inflorescence containing 4–9 fairly large flowers. The sepals are green to brownish-olive in colour and up to 15mm long. The petals are dark velvety brownish-purple, with a length of up to 6mm.

The lip is rather narrow, 11–14mm in length, with 3 lobes starting near the base. The side lobes are small with a brownish or dark purple surface to the lip which has white markings consisting of two thick white lines or spots.
Flowers: April to May.
Habitat: meadows and open grassy places in oak woods.
Distribution: West Kurdistan.

O. kurdica has much smaller flowers with a narrower lip and compact inflorescence.

Ophrys turcomanica Renz.
This is a slender species growing up to 30cm tall and it looks something like a small-flowered *O. kotschyi* but has a much smaller lip, shallower lobes and lacks the well-developed apical appendage of that species.
Flowers: May
Habitat: hillsides up to 1300m altitude.
Distribution: Kophet Dag and Turcomania in north-eastern Iran.

Each of the orchids described above obviously has close links with the other species but they all have well-defined geographical limits: *O. kotschyi* – Cyprus; *O. cretica* – Crete and the south Aegean islands; *O. kurdica* – eastern Turkey; *O. reinholdii* – east Mediterranean with its ssp. *straussii* in south-east Turkey and western Iran; *O. kurdistanica* – western Iran; *O. turcomanica* – north-west Iran.

Ophrys schulzei Bornm. & Fleischm.
LURISTAN OPHRYS; LURISTANISCHE RAGWURZ (G).

A very slender plant, from 25–65cm tall, with 4–7 broadly lanceolate leaves. The flower bracts are as long as the ovary, and 4–12 flowers are carried in a lax spike. The sepals are large, recurved, and coloured pink to pinkish-violet. The petals are tiny, being some 1–1.5mm long, and coloured pink. The lip is 3-lobed and remarkable for the relative size of the side lobes. These are large, hollowed, and directed upwards. The lip is deep maroon-brown, with white markings covering a large part of its surface.

This species has a distinctive appearance but there are obvious links with the *scolopax* group. Its outposts are in areas remote from most other orchids, and it was 'discovered' in 1973 and given the name *O. luristanica* Renz. Further research showed that the specimens were identical with plants named as *O. schulzei* as early as 1911 and *O. cilicica* Schlechter in 1923; though there is some confusion in the literature about this latter plant (c.f. p. 171).

Flowers: May and June.
Habitat: mountain grassland and scrub, oak scrub on limestone on high ground (800m and above).
Distribution: eastern Turkey (Antioch); western Iran; Syria (close to the borders with Turkey – Amanus Pass); Iraq; north Lebanon (very rare). This orchid is an extreme rarity within the area covered by this book but according to Renz (*Flora Iranica*) it enjoys a wider distribution in the mountains of Iran and Iraq.
                                         286
Ophrys scolopax Cav.
WOODCOCK ORCHID; OPHRYS BÉCASSE; OPHRYS OISEAU (F); GEHÖRNTE RAGWURZ (G).

This rather variable orchid has four recognised subspecies other than the nominate race. The various races are so distinct that some botanists think they should be awarded specific status. The lip is the linking factor. The nominate race plants are from 15–45cm tall, with 5–6 lanceolate or broadly lanceolate, pointed leaves. The sepals are pink or purplish-violet, about 8–12mm in length, oblong to ovate, and the median is *not* incurved (unlike *O. carmeli* and *O. scolopax* ssp. *orientalis*). The petals range from ⅕ to ½ the length of the sepals and are pink or red. The labellum is distinctly 3-lobed, 8–12mm in length, with small, wide, basal protuberances.

The median lobe is ovate, with the edges sharply recurved, giving it a rounded appearance . The margin is very narrow and glabrous. The lip pattern is complex and variable. The speculum can be saucer-, ring- or H-shaped, and even X-shaped on some small-flowered forms. It is comparatively large and is violet or blue, with a yellow or whitish margin.
Flowers: March and April.
Habitat: scrub-covered hillsides, woodlands and sparsely grassy areas, roadside verges, always on calcareous soils.
Distribution: southern Spain; southern France; Italy; Corsica; Sardinia; central Greece; Cyprus.   **287**

Ssp. *apiformis* (Desf.) Maire & Weiller. This is a rather slender plant, some 15 –40cm in height, with 3–12 flowers in a lax inflorescence. The sepals are pink or whitish (rarely green), and the petals are about ½ the length of the sepals and of a similar colour. The lip is 3-lobed, with the side lobes prolonged but not to the same extent as in ssp. *cornuta*. The median lobe is very recurved, giving the lip the appearance of a small, fat insect body (hence the name *apiformis* – bee like). The appendage is large, pointing upwards or forwards.
Flowers: early March to April.
Distribution: southern Spain; the only *scolopax* form to stray into north Africa – Morocco; Algeria; Tunisia.   **288**

Ssp. *cornuta* (Steven) Camus. HORNED OPHRYS. This has pink sepals and petals. The lateral lobes of the lip are developed into long horns, up to 1cm in length.
Flowers: late March and April.
Distribution: widespread but local throughout southern Europe to Turkey; southern Italy (Mt Gargano) – at its western limit; Yugoslavia; Greece; Crete; Rhodes; Aegean isles; north-west & southern Turkey; Hungary; Bulgaria; Romania; Crimea; Caucasus.   **289**

Ssp. *heldreichii* (Schlechter) E. Nelson. This subspecies replaces the nominate *O. scolopax* in parts of the range. It differs in that the flowers are larger, with

a labellum 13–15mm long and lateral lobes with basal protuberances up to 5mm. The middle lobe is as long or longer than its width and has a wide, glabrous margin.
Flowers: late March to April.
Distribution: south-western Turkey; Rhodes; Karpathos; Crete; Kos. Plants from Turkey once called *Ophrys phrygia* are now regarded as identical to ssp. *heldreichii*.   **290, 291**

Ssp. **oestrifera** (Bieb.) Soó. This is similar to *O. scolopax* ssp. *cornuta*. Its labellum is 8–12mm, but the lateral lobes have fairly small protuberances. The middle lobe is oblong, being wider than long. There seems to be little justification for treating it as a separate subspecies since the variability of ssp. *cornuta* produces similar forms. Authorities like Nelson and Renz treat it as identical with ssp. *cornuta*.
Flowers: April to early May.
Distribution: Crimea; Caucasus.

Ssp. **orientalis** (Renz) E. Nelson. This plant is close to the nominate *O. scolopax*, but the sepals tend to be paler in colour (pinkish-white or greenish yellow). The sepals are broad and the median is curved forward so much that it nearly conceals the column. The petals are triangular. The brown lip is 3-lobed and yellow-edged, with a well-developed appendage that points downwards and upwards. To all intents and purposes this species is a light pink-sepalled *O. carmeli*. In Cyprus both ssp. *orientalis* and the nominate race occur together, but differences between them are often very slight – in fact mainly geographical, with ssp. *orientalis* on the coast and the nominate race in the chalk hills.
Flowers: March to early April.
Distribution: Cyprus, southern and western Turkey; Lebanon; Israel. **292**

Ophrys carmeli Fleischm. & Bornm.
MT CARMEL OPHRYS; ATTISCHE RAGWURZ (G).
   The plant is usually 15–35cm in height, with 4–6 linear, lanceolate leaves. The flower spike is often rather dense, with 3–8 blooms. The sepals are 6–10mm in length, ovate in shape and coloured green; rarely whitish. The median sepal is usually incurved. The petals are ⅓ to ½ the length of the sepals, lanceolate or triangular, and green, although they can be whitish or purplish.
   The labellum is small (6–10mm), ovate or oblong, widening towards the apex, with the edges deflexed for most or all of their length. It is 3-lobed, usually with a forward-pointing appendage. The surface carries fine hairs and is coloured brown or dark brown, with a glabrous margin. The lateral lobes are pointed and hairy. The lip pattern is very variable and is similar to that of *O. scolopax*. In fact, the only criterion for separating *O. carmeli* as a distinct species seems to be the green sepals and petals. The speculum is blue or dark brownish-violet, roughly saucer-shaped, with the pale area forming an H or series of connected rings.
   Because of the obviously close affinity with other members of the *scolopax* complex the old name of *O. scolopax* ssp. *attica* seems more appropriate than *O. carmeli*. Indeed, so close is this affinity that *O. scolopax* ssp. *orientalis* differs from *O. carmeli* in only two respects: it has pink sepals and, where they occur together, as in southern Cyprus, *O. scolopax* ssp. *orientalis* comes into flower some 2–3 weeks after the first flowers appear on *O. carmeli*. Some workers believe that small-flowered races from Greece and the eastern Mediterranean form a distinct subspecies and should be called *O. carmeli* ssp. *attica*.
Flowers: from mid-February (in Cyprus) but from March to mid-April elsewhere.
Habitat: sparse grassland, olive groves, maquis, pine plantations, on calcareous soils.
Distribution: southern Greece (frequent in Attica); Rhodes; Cyprus; western Turkey, Lebanon; Syria; Israel.
                          293, 294, 295

**Ophrys fuciflora (F. W. Schmidt)
Moench** = *O. holoserica* (Burm. fil.)
Greuter
LATE SPIDER ORCHID; OPHRYS
FRELON, O. BOURDON (F);
HUMMELRAGWURZ (G); VESPARIA
CRESTATA (I).

Like *Ophrys sphegodes*, *O. fuciflora*
has a large number of subspecies.
Although the number of *O. fuciflora*
subspecies is considerably less than
those recognised for *O. sphegodes*, there
is far more variation of individuals within a particular subspecies. *O. fuciflora* is
notorious for the wide range of patterns
carried on the labellum. In recent literature there has been a move to replace the
name *fuciflora* with *holoserica*. In strict
technical terms *O. holoserica* is correct
but we have retained *O. fuciflora* since it
is far better known.

The nominate race carries 4–7 broadly
lanceolate leaves on a stem which varies
from 15–50cm in height. The flower
bracts are longer than the the ovary, and
the inflorescence is lax. 2–6 flowers are
usual, although 10–14 flowers have
been found on exceptional plants.

The sepals are broad and often rounded. In colour they range from bright
pink, through pale pink, to whitish with
a green median line. The petals are
about ½ the length of the sepals, pink,
and usually triangular in shape.

The lip is variable in size but tends to
be squarish and entire (rarely 3-lobed),
coloured a velvety dark brown to yellowish-brown. Sometimes there is a yellowish marginal zone. There are often well-
developed basal protuberances and a
large, forward-pointing apical appendage. The lip markings are very variable,
but formed from white and blue lines
and patches.
Flowers: March (in south of range) to
May or early June (in UK).
Habitat: dry grassy areas, scrub and garigue, open places in maquis.
Distribution: UK (very rare, in Kent);
eastern Spain; France; Germany (mostly
in the south); Benelux; Austria &
Switzerland (lower slopes up to 1300m);
Italy; Corsica; Sardinia; Yugoslavia;

Greece (only in southern Peloponnese);
Crete; Rhodes; south and west Turkey;
Lebanon; Israel; southern Czechoslo-
vakia; western Hungary.   **296, 297**

A number of distinct forms of the nominate race have been recorded:

Ssp. **apulica** O. & E. Danesch. This is a
large-flowered form (25–35mm) with
petals ½ to ¾ the length of the sepals and
well-developed basal protuberances resembling horns. The lip edges are often
curved forwards. Like *O. fuciflora* ssp.
gracilis (Büel) O. & E. Danesch from
the Salerno region, it is not a well-
defined race and its status as a subspecies
is questionable.
Flowers: mid-April to May.
Distribution: southern Italy (Gargano
and Puglia).

This subspecies has been linked to
Ophrys scolopax ssp. *heldreichii* (which
is found in Greece) by E. Nelson. They
are certainly very similar, and the main
objection raised to the link is that *O.
scolopax* ssp. *heldreichii* has a 3-lobed lip
(like all members of the scolopax
group), and this is rare with *O. fuciflora*
ssp. *apulica*.   **298**

Ssp. **maxima** Fleischm. This is a very
large-flowered form from the islands of
Rhodes and Crete.   **299**

Ssp. **celiensis** and ssp. **parvimaculata** O.
& E. Danesch. These are not generally
accorded subspecific status. They are,
however, very distinct green-sepalled
forms that were recorded by O. & E.
Danesch from Puglia in southern Italy.

Ssp. **candica** E. Nelson ex Soó. This
differs from the nominate race in having
short petals (about 1/5 the length of the
sepals), and there are well-developed
basal protuberances. The lip pattern is
distinctive and consists of a small speculum area – blue or purple brown – surrounded by a yellowish or whitish margin, giving a more or less square shape
near the base of the lip.
Distribution: There are two separate

areas of distribution: southern Greece (Peloponnese) and Crete; south-east Italy (Puglia). It is also reported amongst the very wide range of forms in Rhodes and in south-western Turkey. **300**

Ssp. *chestermanii* J. J. Wood. A large-flowered race from a very restricted area of Sardinia has recently been listed as a new subspecies of *O. fuciflora* (*O. holoserica*).

The lip is large and coloured a uniform deep purple-brown. The pattern is reduced to a small dark blue speculum near the lip base without the white or yellowish border evident with most other subspecies.

Flowers: April.
Distribution: Sardinia (known only from Cagliari province, north-east of Iglesias).

Ssp. *oxyrrhynchos* (Tod.) Soó. This has green sepals and tiny green petals (⅛ to ⅓ the length of the sepals). The basal protuberances on the lip are indistinct. There are two main colour forms. The most frequently found has a more or less H-shaped speculum, bluish or purple-brown in colour, with a whitish margin. The lip margin is light brown or yellowish.

The much rarer var. *lacaitae* (Lojacono) Camus has a triangular yellow labellum with a reduced speculum area. Var. *lacaitae* is known from Sicily and southern Italy. **303**
Flowers: mid-April to May.
Distribution: Sicily and Sardinia. The usual form is by no means a common plant. In Sicily it has a number of well-scattered local populations, mainly in the north-east and south-east of the island. **301, 302**

Ssp. *bornmuelleri* (Schulze) B. & E. Willing. This is another member of the *O. fuciflora* complex that has sometimes been given specific status. The plant stands 10–30cm tall, with 4–6 broadly lanceolate leaves. The flower bracts are only slightly longer than the ovary, and the lax inflorescence carries 2–5 blooms.

The sepals are broad, white to pale pink with green veining or, rarely, plain green. The pink petals are very short – no more than 1–2mm. The lip is a rich red-brown, with a restricted white edge speculum at the base. The flowers tend to vary far less in lip markings than any other subspecies of *O. fuciflora*.

Large-flowered forms, with pinkish-white or rosy sepals occur in Cyprus. These have well-developed basal protuberances which in some flowers resemble horns and are named var. *grandiflora* Fleischm. & Soó. **305, 306**
Flowers: late February to April.
Habitat: scrubby places, usually on low ground near the sea.
Distribution: Cyprus; Lebanon; Israel; south-east Turkey. **304**

Ssp. **exaltata** (Ten.) E. Nelson. This very distinct race has been given specific status by some botanists. The plant is robust (up to 45cm), with broadly lanceolate leaves and a lax inflorescence carrying 3–8 flowers. The sepals are normally pink, with green veining, but can also be deep pink or green tinged with pink The petals are ⅓ to ½ the length of the sepals and coloured deep pink or pinkish-brown (olive). The lip is distinctive, being 3-lobed with small side lobes and indistinct basal protuberances. The markings on the lip are much reduced in comparison with other subspecies, and the ground colour is a dark purplish-brown. The apical protuberance is often forward-pointing. **307, 308**
Flowers: late March to April.
Distribution: Corsica; Capri; central and southern Italy.

Some workers have divided ssp. *exaltata* into 2 subspecies:
Ssp. *exaltata* usually has green perianth segments, and the median lobe of the lip has a swollen, smooth, rounded appearance. The appendage is well developed and forward pointing. This is the form found in the west of Italy (Capri, Mt Argentario) and Corsica.

Ssp. *sundermannii* Soó (also called ssp. *pollinensis* E. Nelson). This has pink or white sepals and red petals. The lip is dark purplish-brown, and the appendage is very small. This form occurs on Mt Gargano in eastern Italy and on Mt Pollino in east-central Italy. The forms are so variable in the populations on Mt Gargano and Mt Argentario that plants fitting both descriptions are found together. We would tend to place both forms under ssp. *exaltata*. The name *O. biscutella* has been given to plants from Mt Gargano where the lip pattern consists of the 2 blue "eye" patches on a wide dark purplish-brown lip.

Ophrys arachnitiformis Gren. & Phillippe

FALSE SPIDER ORCHID; OPHRYS EN FORME D'ARAIGNÉE (F). SPINNENFORMIGE RAGWURZ (G).

The name *O. arachnitiformis* has been applied to a remarkable range of orchid forms from southern France, Corsica, mainland Italy and the islands of Sicily and Sardinia.

For many years botanists have believed that *O. arachnitiformis* arose from hybrids between *O. fuciflora* and *O. sphegodes*. The fact that the putative parents exist in a wide range of forms suggests there is enormous potential for variation in the offspring.

Not all hybrid forms will inherit the best set of characteristics for survival in a particular region but those that do could, with the passage of time and much backcrossing, evolve into populations that are fertile and reasonably stable in pattern and colouring. In another locality conditions might favour the survival of quite different hybrids and ultimately the forms could be changed to the extent that they might be labelled separate species.

In the field it is apparent that forms of *O. arachnitiformis* from any one region are closely linked, but when compared with plants from another region there are obvious differences. It seems that what is now called *O. arachnitiformis* is really in a process of evolution which will eventually result in a number of distinct species.

P. Gölz and H. Reinhard have suggested that plants from southern France which are closely linked to *O. sphegodes* should be called *O. splendida*, while plants from southern Italy with closer affinities to *O. fuciflora* be named *O. tyrrhena*.

Plants included in the past with *O. arachnitiformis* share the following characteristics:

They are usually robust, with thick stems and a height ranging from 15–45cm (occasional plants exceed 50cm). There are 3–7 large, broadly lanceolate leaves, and the flower bracts are twice the length of the ovary.

The flower spike is lax and carries 2–9 flowers which show considerable variation in colour and patterning.

The sepals are spreading and usually coloured with various shades of pink, ranging from a delicate light hue to deep carmine with a green central vein. Other forms with purplish-violet, whitish or pale greenish flowers are found but are fairly rare. The lateral sepals are oblong-ovate in shape, while the median sepal is oblong-elliptical. The petals are 6–7mm in length, making them ½ to ⅔ as long as the sepals with a more intense colouring.

The lip is variable in shape, from oblong to square, with a length of 8–10mm and side lobes so reduced that lip appears entire. In colour it is a rich reddish or dark brown, and there is a small apical protuberance sometimes accompanied by short, but conspicuous, basal protuberances.

Lip patterns can vary considerably even within the same population. For example: the speculum can be square, annular, H- or X- shaped; in colour it can be blue, dark purple or purple-brown, often with a whitish or yellow margin. In some specimens the pattern breaks down into a series of blotches and mottlings.

Flowers: mid-March through to the end of April and early May (in parts of southern France).

Habitat: grassy areas, maquis, undisturbed areas in pastures and old vineyards.

Distribution: south-east Spain; southern France; Corsica; Italy (Riviera, Mt Gargano, Mt Argentario); Sardinia; Sicily; Yugoslavia and possibly Algeria. **310** (France), **311** (N. Italy), **312** (Sicily)

Recent research work indicates that the plants originally described as *Ophrys arachnitiformis* are no more than aberrant forms of *Ophrys sphegodes*. Later some plants from Sardinia were given a specific status as *Ophrys morisii* (Martelli) Ciff. et Giac. **309**

In strict technical terms the name *arachnitiformis* should be abandoned but we have retained it here as a well-known name for a group of poorly understood orchid forms. There is little doubt that within a few years the nomenclature will be properly sorted out.

Ophrys apifera Hudson
BEE ORCHID; OPHRYS ABEILLE (F);
BIENEN-RAGWURZ (G); VESPARIA (I)

Plants of this species range in height from 15cm in open dry places to as much as 50cm at the edges of thickets. The basal leaves are lanceolate to ovate in shape, and the flower bracts exceed the ovary in length. 2–7 (exceptionally more) flowers are carried on a lax spike.

The sepals are large and broad (10 –15mm long) with the median sepal either erect or deflexed. Their usual colour is pale or bright pink although whitish or greenish-white sepals can occur. In parts of southern Spain there are forms with deep carmine sepals growing with the more usual forms.

The petals are variable in length but are usually less than ½ the length of the sepals. In colour they are either greenish or pinkish.

The lip is 3-lobed with prominent side lobes which are hairy, triangular in shape and deflexed. It has a rounded, oval appearance because the edges are considerably deflexed. The median lobe is a rich chestnut brown to blackish-purple, and carries a violet or reddish-brown speculum surrounded by a variable white or yellowish pattern, with clear yellow spots near the apex. It is unique among European *Ophrys* in

being the only species to rely almost entirely on self-pollination.

In the UK *Ophrys apifera* has the reputation of being monocarpic. This tendency to use up all its reserves in a single flowering is often exhibited in western Europe simply because it is at the edges of its range and optimum conditions for its growth are not always found. In the Mediterranean region, where the climate suits it better, it certainly goes on producing flowering stems in successive years, whereas in north-western Europe this is an infrequent occurrence. Recent work has shown that even in Britain plants can flower in several successive seasons.

Varieties: Several distinctive varieties occur throughout the range of the species: var. *bicolor* (Naegeli) E. Nelson has a lip coloured greenish where the speculum area and white pattern should be, with the rest of the lip a dark brown. **316**

Var. *chlorantha* (Hegetschw.) Richter (also called var. *flavescens* Rost.) has whitish sepals and an all greenish-yellow lip. **315**

Var. *trollii* Hegetschw. was at one time given specific status as *Ophrys trollii* Hegetschw. This 'Wasp Orchid' has a pointed lip without the normal clear-cut markings, having instead a mottled or barred pattern of brown and yellow.

There is often a tendency to confuse recently opened specimens of *O. apifera* with var. *trollii* because the apical appendage has not yet become deflexed and the lip appears pointed. In the UK the true var. *trollii* has a very restricted distribution, being found in the Cotswold hills and other parts of southern England (Dorset, Wiltshire).

Flowers: mid-April (in Cyprus) to July in the north of its range. In most areas of the south it is at its best throughout the month of May where it flowers some weeks after most other species of *Ophrys*, when the ground is becoming dry.

Habitat: a variety of surroundings provide a home for this species; chalk grasslands, woodland margins (the authors even found it in deep woodland where once there had been chalk grassland the year after the hot summer of 1976), scrub, edges of sand-dune slacks, maquis.

Distribution: north Africa; Spain; Balearics; France; UK (rare in Scotland); Germany; Benelux; Switzerland; Austria; Italy; Corsica; Sardinia; Sicily; Yugoslavia; Greece; Crete; Rhodes; Cyprus; Turkey; Lebanon; Israel; Hungary; Rumania; Crimea; Caucasus.

Where conditions suit it large numbers of plants can be found, especially in places where the ground has been disturbed some years before, e.g. chalkpits and disused vineyards.   **313**

Ssp. *jurana* Ruppert has also been called *Ophrys apifera* var. *botteronii* Chodat and *O. apifera* var. *friburgensis* Freh. This subspecies has petals almost as long as the sepals. The lip colouring is brown, with a small speculum, and the surrounding yellow area extended to two vertical stripes.

Distribution: found locally over much of west and central Europe, also infrequently in the south.   **314**

Ophrys tenthredinifera Willd.
SAWFLY ORCHID; OPHRYS GUÊPE (F); WESPEN-RAGWURZ (G); VESPARIA BARBATA (I).

A rather robust species standing 10 −45cm tall, with 6–9 broadly lanceolate leaves. The flower bracts exceed the ovary in length, and the lax inflorescence carries 3–8 flowers.

The flowers themselves are large and well coloured, making this one of the most impressive of the Mediterranean *Ophrys* species. There is comparatively little variation in flower size and colouring: the sepals are large (11–14mm long), broad oval in shape, and pink, often with green veining; the petals are about ⅓ the length of the sepals, pink and broadly triangular in shape, with a rounded apex. Specimens occurs infrequently with the sepals purplish-violet, whitish or pale greenish.

The lip is large and rectangular, with the edges flared near the apex. Although it is usually entire it is possible to find flowers that are indistinctly 3-lobed, with the side lobes reduced to rounded humps. The lip margin is very hairy and pale, ranging in colour from yellow, through greenish, to pale brown, and is notched deeply near the forward-pointing apex. A more or less rectangular brown area with a dark purple or blue speculum at its base covers much of the lip surface. The speculum itself is surrounded by a fine whitish or yellow margin, and there is a tuft of rather coarse hairs just above the apical protuberances which often extends to provide a small hairy "border" to the brown area of the lip.

Where it occurs in abundance there is a possibility of finding some very striking hybrids, notably with *O. bertolonii* or *O. bombyliflora*.

Varieties: Var. *viridiflora* Cort. has white sepals and a greenish-yellow lip.

Flowers: March, through April, to early May.

Habitat: grassy, stony areas or hillside scrub and garigue.

Distribution: widespread around the Mediterranean from central and southern Portugal to Spain; Balearics (some of the largest forms occur in Majorca); mid- and southern Italy; Corsica; Sardinia; Sicily (forms with large round sepals and a lot of yellow on the lip); Greece; Crete and western Turkey. It is also known from the Levant (not Cyprus) where it was once listed as *O. rosea* (Desf.) Grande.

317 (Greece), **318** (Spain), **319** (Sicily)

Ophrys bombyliflora Link
BUMBLE BEE ORCHID; OPHRYS BOURDON, OPHRYS BOMBYX (F); BREMSEN-RAGWURZ (G).

This is one of the smallest *Ophrys* species, with plants as small as 7cm tall and rarely more than 25cm, often occurring in clumps of severed rosettes. There are 4–6 broadly lanceolate leaves, with the lower ones spread out horizontally. It differs from other *Ophrys* in that the tubers are produced at the end of a 'stalk' from 2 to about 10cm in length. As many as 6 tubers of varying sizes can be formed in a year, producing a tangled mass of roots and tubers below ground. The lax inflorescence carries from 1–5 small flowers, and the flower bracts are shorter than the ovary.

O. bombyliflora is one of the least variable species of *Ophrys*. The sepals are broad and green (9–12mm) and the petals are about ⅓ their length, triangular in shape, and greenish-purple in colour near their bases.

The lip is deeply divided into three lobes, with the side lobes so deflexed that it has a globose appearance. The ground colour is usually brown to dark purple-brown, and there is no apical appendage.The side lobes are formed into two large hairy humps. The specu-lum area is dark purple or blue, and if pale markings are present they have a very restricted area.

Hybrids of this species with *O. tenthredinifera*, *O. speculum* and *O. bertolonii* produce curious flowers with small globose lips, variously patterned, and coloured sepals.

Flowers: mid-March to April.

Habitat: short grassland and garigue.

Distribution: widespread in the Mediterranean region but its small stature has made it easy to overlook, so it is often cited as a rather local and uncommon orchid; Canary Islands; north Africa; Spain; Balearics; southern France; Italy; Corsica; Sardinia; Sicily (common in some parts); Yugoslavia; Greece; Crete; Rhodes; southern Turkey and Lebanon. **320**

Corallorhiza

The name of this genus literally means 'coral root' and refers directly to the rhizome which forms a much-branched coralloid structure.

Like *Epipogium aphyllum* and *Neottia nidus-avis*, it depends on mycorrhizal activity for most of its food, but it differs from them in having a considerable amount of chlorophyll in its stems – enough at least to give the plant a green colour. Thus it is capable of manufacturing some of its food by photosynthesis. In common with all European saprophytic orchids, there are no green leaves and, like *E. aphyllum* it has no proper roots, having instead small tufts of hair on the rhizome where mycorrhizal fungus threads are able to live.

It is the only European member of the genus and it also occurs in north America, where it is one of about a dozen species of *Corallorhiza*.

The characteristics of the genus are: coral-like rhizomes with no roots; stems with a few sheathing scales and no green leaves; flowers pendent in a spike-like raceme; perianth segments more or less patent and free for all their length; lip entire or 3-lobed (with minute lateral lobes); spur absent or very short; a long column with small rostellum and two distinct viscidia without bursicles.

Although there is a rostellum it usually proves ineffective, for the flowers are fertilized by pollinia falling from the stamen on to the stigmatic surface below. The ovary and sepals remain green after flowering, to produce food for the developing seeds.

Vegetative propagation is not as highly developed in this species as it is with *N. nidus-avis* and *E. aphyllum*, consisting only of the separation of branches of the rhizome as the rear parts die away.

Corallorhiza trifida Chatel

CORAL-ROOT ORCHID; RACINE DE CORAIL (F); KORALLENWURZ (G).

This is a slender orchid with stems from 7–30cm tall, although it is more usual to find plants between 10–13cm in height in groups of 3–10 stems produced from the same rhizome. The stem surface is glabrous and coloured yellowish-green with a few scales sheathing it.

The spike is lax, with 2–12 small flowers and short bracts. The flowers hang downwards and have sepals that are about 5mm long and coloured greenish. The dorsal sepal is oblong in shape, while the laterals are narrow and spreading. The petals are narrow, coloured green or yellowish with reddish margins or spots, and curve inwards with the dorsal sepal.

The lip is usually entire but can also have tiny lateral lobes near its base. It is about the same length as the other perianth segments and is oblong in shape with red lines or blotches on a whitish surface. Near its base there are two wide longitudinal ridges.

The column is comparatively long and there is a small rostellum and two distinct viscidia.

Flowers: May to August.

Habitat: grows in damp forests, tundra and more rarely in dune slacks or alpine marshy areas.

Distribution: a rather local orchid widely distributed in western, northern and central Europe; France; Iceland; north England (though occasional records for the south exist); Scandinavia; Germany (not the north); Benelux countries; Switzerland and Austria; northern Italy; Yugoslavia; northern Greece; Poland; Czechoslovakia; Hungary; Bulgaria; Rumania; Russia; Crimea; Caucasus; throughout north and middle Asia; north America and Greenland. **321, 322**

Calypso

There is still some uncertainty about the number of species in this genus. Sometimes it is claimed that there is a single species and the north American plant is a geographical variant. Alternatively, the north American plant is considered as distinct from the Eurasian *Calypso bulbosa*.

Appropriately for this exquisite orchid the name is taken from the beautiful Greek nymph Kalypso whose charms, both magical and otherwise, kept Ulysses on her island for seven years.

The flowers have a vanilla scent and contain no nectar, yet this does not deter insects from visiting them. Pollination is effected by female bumble bees which crawl deep inside the flowers. On leaving they contact the pollinia, which become fixed to their backs and are there correctly positioned to contact the stigma in the next flower. The pollinia are protected by a hood, and the rostellum prevents self-fertilization by separating the anthers from the stigma.

The genus is characterised by: a single pseudobulb bearing a solitary leaf; a single flower; perianth segments joined at the base; flowers patent with a large inflated slipper shaped lip; a petaloid column; a small 3-toothed rostellum; two distinct viscidia but no bursicles; no spur, but the rear part of the lip is indented and extended to make a double spur-like projection.

Calypso bulbosa (L.) Oakes

It is impossible to confuse this species with any other orchid in Europe because the flowers are so distinct in appearance. The plants are small, growing from 10 –20cm tall, with a solitary pseudobulb from which rises a single stalked leaf. There is a distinct veining on the surface of the leaf, and it has an elliptical to oblong shape. Only one flower is formed, and it grows out of the axil of a sheath-like bract which surrounds the lower part of the stem.

The perianth segments spread widely and are held vertically or even reflexed; all are approximately the same length and coloured bright pink.

The lip forms an inflated slipper which is pale pink or whitish in colour, with pink or yellow markings. Its frontal surface is flattened, while the rear part is extended and indented to make a double 'spur'. The column is developed into a large, pink, petal-like structure, and the rear of the lip is streaked with brown.

Flowers: end of April through to May (after the snows melt).

Habitat: damp mossy places in coniferous woods.

Distribution: northern Scandinavia; northern Russia through northern Asia to north America.

Occasional rumours circulate that *C. bulbosa* has been found growing in Scotland. This is by no means impossible because the climate and habitats are suitable. No-one of the authors' acquaintance can substantiate these claims; but like many other orchid lovers we would like the rumours to be true.   **323**

Microstylis

Some authorities consider a single genus *Malaxis* and include in it the two European plants, *Microstylis monophyllos* and *Hammarbya paludosa*.

Apart from the obvious difference in size – *H. paludosa* is a tiny orchid – the flowers of both species are very similar.

Like *Liparis* both species have a pair of pseudobulbs, but here they are borne one above the other, with the younger of the two uppermost.

As the specific name *monophyllos* suggests, there is usually a solitary leaf (*monophyllos* = single-leafed); the flowers are twisted through 360°, with the labellum upwards and the column short.

This species is reputed to be mostly self-pollinating, but it is possible that small insects act as pollinators too, although this has not been fully investigated.

Microstylis monophyllos (L.) Lindley

SINGLE-LEAVED BOG ORCHID; MALAXIS D'UNE FEUILLE (F); EINBLATTORCHIS (G).

This slender, graceful species is now rare, and it is all the more difficult to see because it blends well with its surroundings.

Plant height ranges from 10–30cm and there is a basal pseudobulb, surrounded by old leaf sheaths. The single broad leaf is a special feature but, very rarely, plants with two leaves can be found. The inflorescence is lax, with numerous green flowers in a spike-like raceme stretching over 3–15cm of the stem length.

The perianth segments are 2–2.5mm

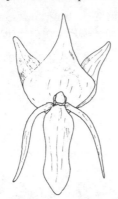

Fig. 44

long, with the sepals ovate or ovate-lanceolate. In this species, just like the closely related *Hammarbya paludosa*, the flowers are rotated through 360°, so

that the lip points upwards with the lateral sepals, and the median sepal points downwards. The petals are slender, linear and widespread and the lip is entire.

Flowers: usually in July.

Habitat: fens, calcareous swamps and wet ground in woods and scrubland – especially where alder grows.

Distribution: drainage and clearing of trees in marshy forests have led to the rapid decrease in numbers of this species and it is now a rare orchid; Scandinavia; Germany (in the north and the Alps); Austria; Switzerland; northern Italy (Alps); Yugoslavia (Croatia); Poland; Czechoslovakia; Hungary; Rumania; Russia and then circumpolar.   **324**

Liparis

Liparis loeselii is the single member of the genus found in Europe, although others occur in China, Japan and north America. Outside the temperate countries its relatives are showy epiphytes of the treetops in humid tropical jungles.

The name is derived from *Liparos* which means 'fatty' or 'greasy' and refers to the appearance of the bright green leaves.

It is one of the few European orchids possessing a pseudobulb, although this is a common feature in tropical epiphytes, where the base of the stem forms a fleshy swelling which has the outward appearance of a bulb.

Another of its unusual characteristics is the stamen which forms a cap at the top of the column. This drops off easily, allowing the pollinia to slide out and attach themselves to the stigma. This form of self-fertilization is efficient, and one often finds all the flowers on a single stem giving rise to large seed pods.

Vegetative propagation is made possible by the production of root tubers at the base of the plant. In the early years of its growth the plant is infected with mycorrhizal fungus but this dependence stops as absorptive roots develop.

The characteristics shared by the orchids in this genus are: an ovoid pseudobulb enclosed in dead leaf sheaths, with the new pseudobulb beside it at the base of the stem; 2 oval basal leaves; a flowering stem with a triangular cross section; perianth segments spreading, with an upward-pointing lip; a slender column and minute rostellum, but no spur.

Liparis loeselii (L.) L. C. M. Richard
FEN ORCHID; LIPARIS DE LOISEL (F);
GLANZKRAUT (G); OFRIDE
DELLEBORDE (I).

This orchid is difficult to find because of its green colouring and small stature. It grows from 6–20cm tall, with a flowering stem that has a more or less triangular cross-section. At the base of the stem there are 2–3 basal scales which enclose the 'developing pseudobulb, and above these a pair of oblong-elliptical or ovate leaves arranged on opposite sides of the stem. The surface of the leaves has a greasy appearance and is bright green in colour.

The inflorescence is lax, with 3–8 flowers (more have been recorded on exceptionally strong plants) which are yellowish-green in colour.

All perianth segments spread, and the sepals are linear-lanceolate in shape while the petals are shorter and narrow-er. The lip is as long as the sepals but is broader and has wavy or crinkled edges. It points upwards, since the flower is not twisted at all – unlike *Hammarbya* where the rotation is 360°. There is no spur.

After fertilization flowers can persist for some time, provided they are in a sheltered place in reeds. If they are growing in dune slacks the flowers can wither in the sun before fertilization has a chance to take place. The seed pods are large, and it is often easier to find the plant at this stage when it tends to be more conspicuous.

Varieties: The form growing in the dune slacks of south Wales is sometimes called var. *ovata* because of its oval leaves.

Flowers: from the end of June through-out July.

Habitat: fens or even bogs provided that the drainage water is alkaline or neutral. It also flowers in dune slacks, accompanied by *Salix repens* and *Anagallis tenella*. In such places it is particularly vulnerable, for a dry summer can cause its disappearance for a few years until young plants, which survived the drought, reach flowering strength.

Distribution: this is now a rare and local species which is fast disappearing as its fenland sites are drained; France; UK (in the fens of Cambridge and Norfolk, dune slacks in south Wales and Devon); Scandinavia (absent from the north); Germany; Austria and Switzerland (up to 800m); northern Italy; Yugoslavia (Bosnia); Poland; Czechoslovakia; Hungary; absent from the Mediterranean area. **325, 326**

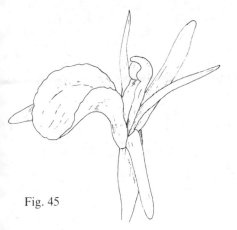

Fig. 45

Hammarbya

The single plant in this genus differs from *Microstylis monophyllos* in its smaller size and 2–5 leaves. The column is very short and the anther persistent (in *M. monophyllos* it is not).

Roots are reduced to root hairs, which are heavily infected with mycorrhiza. The two pseudobulbs, placed one above the other, are formed by swellings of the stem base. The older one is underneath and carries the remains of the previous season's leaves; the younger one is hidden at the bases of the new leaves.

Tiny flies living in the boggy haunts of this species are the main pollinators and a lot of seed is set. The fact that the seed can float on water is probably what enables the plant to spread.

The vegetative propagation of this plant is more interesting, however, because it is the only European species to rely on small buds called 'bulbils', which develop at the tips of the leaves. These drop into the cushions of sphagnum surrounding the plants and are quickly infected by fungus. Since they are not forced into manufacturing their own food, these bulbils develop comparatively quickly (a few years) into adult flowering plants.

The conditions in a sphagnum bog, where there is little oxygen, and the tiny leaves of *H. paludosa* make it dependent on mycorrhizal activity throughout its life.

Hammarbya paludosa (L.) O. Kuntze
BOG ORCHID; MALAXIS DES MARAIS (F); WEICHWURZ (G).
This species consistently produces some of the smallest flowering stems of all European orchids, with plants ranging from 3–12cm. The stems have a cross-section which is 3- or 5-sided and carry 2–3 small (0.5–1mm) leaves, whose bases sheath the stem and enclose the daughter pseudobulb. The tiny bulbils on which the plant relies for vegetative propagation are formed at the free ends of the leaves.

The spike carries numerous tiny green flowers and is dense when the flowers first open but elongates as the upper flowers upen.

The sepals are ovate-lanceolate, with a length of 2.5–3mm; the laterals are erect and the median sepal points downwards, due to the flower being rotated through a full 360°, making the lip point upwards. The petals are deflexed at the apex and are around 1.5mm in length.

The lip is shaped similarly to the sepals but has a bowl-shaped hollow on its surface.

Flowers: July to early September.
Habitat: acidic marshes and bogs, growing in sphagnum moss, where its tiny flowers, small stature and green colour make it difficult to see.
Distribution: a local and uncommon orchid; France; British Isles (a few scattered sites in southern England, much of Ireland and Scotland); Germany; Scandinavia; Benelux countries; Switzerland; Austria; Poland; Czechoslovakia; Russia, then circumpolar to north-east Asia and north America.   **327, 328**

Fig. 46

5 – In search of orchids

Great Britain

About fifty species of wild orchids are reliably recorded for the British Isles, but, sadly, the days when any of them could be regarded as common are long past. As in the case of other western European countries, the need to feed the population has led to much land being used for farming. Modern intensive methods and artificial fertilisers are anathema to terrestrial orchids, and in the battle for survival with man they are inevitably the losers. Urban expansion in the crowded islands making up the British Isles has taken its toll too. Vast tracts of calcareous grassland, where orchids were once abundant, have disappeared beneath the developer's bulldozer or the farmer's plough.

Old books cite, as one of the joys of spring, swathes of *Orchis morio* spikes growing with cowslips. Unhappily this is no longer the case. Again, there are references to large numbers of *Orchis militaris* in Buckinghamshire woodlands: Victorian collectors and a horde of so-called 'botanists' ensured their demise.

Some of the orchids described in this book reach the westernmost limits of their range in Britain. Slight changes in climate or ecological conditions can place them in jeopardy: *Orchis simia*, *O. militaris* and *Cephalanthera rubra* are examples. These plants are some of the real rarities amongst British orchids and efforts have been made to protect them, with varying degrees of success.

For those interested in finding orchids in Britain we would heartily recommend the reserves run by local Naturalist Trusts. Access to rarities in these reserves is controlled because experience with unscrupulous and careless people makes wardens understandably wary about revealing their sites. Too many people troop each year to see *Cypripedium calceolus*, for example; they trample the ground in its one site and, by making it unlikely that the plant will spread, jeopardise its survival.

Indeed, if one wants to see plants which are rarities in Britain (*Orchis militaris* and *Cypripedium calceolus* are good examples) it is best to think 'European' and go to countries where they grow in abundance and are easily photographed. With this in mind, our account of British orchids is based around reserves, although careful searching in surrounding areas could prove rewarding. Most reserves are run by County Naturalist Trusts, and addresses can be obtained from the Nature Conservancy Council.

Chalk & limestone in southern England: the South Downs

By far the greatest range of orchid species occurs in the grasslands and beechwoods of the counties of southern England. Kent is the home of many of the rarer orchids, such as *Himantoglossum hircinum*, *Ophrys fuciflora*, *Orchis simia* and *O. purpurea*. Careful reserve management has paid dividends, and good populations of some of the orchids have been encouraged to develop. The special orchid of Kent is *Orchis purpurea* which, although far from common, can still be found in woodlands. *Ophrys sphegodes* occurs near the coast around Folkestone and Dover, as does the far rarer *O. fuciflora*.

There are numerous reserves in Kent, detailed in a handbook available to those who join the County Naturalist Trust. Among them is the now famous reserve at Wye and Crundale downs where access is controlled and many orchids are to be seen. *Ophrys apifera*, *Aceras anthropophorum*, *Gymnadenia conopsea*, *Anacamptis pyramidalis*, *Orchis mascula* and *Dactylorhiza fuchsii* are frequent in the grassland in the chalk downs, whilst the beechwoods, characteristic of the same areas, hold *Cephalanthera damasonium*, *Epipactis helleborine* (plus the occasional *E. phyllanthes*), *Neottia nidus-avis* and *Ophrys insectifera*.

Further west, the same plants occur on the Sussex downs and in Hampshire. In the latter county the beechwoods hold some good populations of *Cephalanthera longifolia* which in Britain is far less common than the closely related *C. damasonium*. In the New Forest the tiny *Hammarbya paludosa* flourishes in a few sphagnum bogs, but *Spiranthes aestivalis*, which once grew there, now appears to be extinct. Many dream of rediscovering this orchid which seems to be decreasing throughout Europe as its sites are drained.

Dorset adjoins Hampshire and possesses both chalk and limestone regions. *Ophrys sphegodes* thrives in a number of places near the coast in Dorset, on limestone soils.

In all these counties there is a basic orchid flora of the undisturbed calcareous grasslands and beechwoods, comprising the orchids already mentioned. Remarkably good populations of orchids can often be found in disused chalk pits, too. Indeed, surprise finds of *Orchis simia*, *Himantoglossum hircinum* and *Orchis militaris* have been made in just such places. The thin turf that covers the chalk in these sites provides an ideal home for wild orchids and other now seldom-seen plants of the chalk.

The Chilterns

Buckinghamshire has long been famous for the beechwoods which line the escarpments of the Chilterns. Here, in days gone by, *Orchis militaris* was a not infrequent woodland orchid: nowadays it merely hangs on in one or two places. *Epipactis leptochila* occurs in some of the Chiltern beechwoods, growing with the later-flowering *E. helleborine*. Other members of the family are also to be found: *E. purpurea*, and an occasional *E. phyllanthes*. *Cephalanthera damasonium* is common, and *C. rubra* persists in a vegetative state in one place, where the overhead cover prevents enough light reaching it.

Unfortunately, proximity to London brings much of the Chilterns into commuter-belt country. The resulting urban expansion, plus the fact that the ground on the low hills makes first-rate farmland, means that much of the chalk grassland has ceased to exist.

Several very good reserves exist, controlled by the Bucks, Berks & Oxon Naturalist Trust, and these are detailed in the Trust's handbook. *Ophrys apifera, Anacamptis pyramidalis, Gymnadenia conopsea, Platanthera chlorantha, Listera ovata, Dactylorhiza fuchsii* and, very occasionally, *Orchis ustulata* exist in this area.

Many of the rarest orchids in Britain are to be found in the three counties which make up the Bucks, Berks & Oxon Naturalist Trust. *Orchis simia* hangs on in Oxfordshire in a population which is rather sad in comparison with the Kent one, and *Epipogium aphyllum* exists in its only known site in Britain, near Marlow in Buckinghamshire. Unfortunately, the 'secret' of its whereabouts is known to far too many people, and the future of this plant is in danger from orchid enthusiasts and unscrupulous collectors alike.

Bix Bottom, near Henley, is the location of a superb reserve, set up in memory of E. F. Warburg (of Clapham, Tutin & Warburg fame – authors of *Flora of the British Isles*). Here there are numerous orchids growing in grassland and woodland settings. Well over a dozen orchids can be seen here and include *Platanthera chlorantha, Ophrys apifera, O. insectifera, Gymnadenia conopsea, Anacamptis pyramidalis, Neottia nidus-avis*, as well as several helleborines: *Cephalanthera damasonium, Epipactis helleborine, E. purpurea* and *E. leptochila*.

West of Oxfordshire lie the Cotswolds where the only good colony of *Cephalanthera rubra* still flourishes and the true *Ophrys apifera* var. *trollii* occurs.

Wetlands of the south: the Broads

The Norfolk Broads are widely known to holiday-makers and thus their unique value to naturalists is jeopardized by their use for leisure purposes. Drainage and pollution are affecting the area, and plants and animals suffer accordingly.

Liparis loeselii is a special plant of fens in Cambridge, Norfolk and Suffolk, growing where the water is alkaline or neutral. It flourishes only at certain stages of poolside colonisation, with reeds, sedges and moss. It is a rare plant and sometimes occurs with *Dactylorhiza incarnata* var. *ochroleuca*, an attractive yellow marsh orchid.

The South Wales dunes

Lying along the south Welsh coast there are extensive dune systems. For many years these proved attractive to builders of chemical factories and giant steelworks, and their plant and animal life decreased alarmingly. Large areas still remain, however, and have now been designated as nature reserves.

Dune slacks are wet areas between stabilized dunes where the soil is calcareous, due to the presence of shell fragments from long-dead molluscs. Here one can see orchids growing in abundance – something rather unusual in Britain and well worth preserving. Marsh orchids such as *Dactylorhiza incarnata* and *D. majalis* ssp. *praetermissa* comprise the main part of the display, with a bewildering range of colour forms. *Epipactis palustris* flourishes, with a variety devoid of red colouring, var. *ochroleuca*. In drier places one finds *Orchis morio* in May and, in September, the tiny *Spiranthes spiralis*. At the edges of the slacks *Ophrys apifera* occurs in good colonies, followed by large numbers of *Epipactis helleborine*, showing flower colours ranging from green, through pink, to deep purple-violet. Undoubtedly, the treasured find is the tiny *Liparis loeselii* var. *ovata* – a difficult plant to spot, for not only is it inconspicuous but it occurs in very scattered populations, growing with *Salix repens*. Forms of *Epipactis phyllanthes* have been recorded but they are extremely difficult to find.

North Wales and Lancashire dunes
In North Wales large dune systems are found in Anglesey, where *Dactylorhiza majalis* ssp. *praetermissa* is replaced by ssp. *purpurella*. Another marsh orchid, *Dactylorhiza traunsteineri*, is known here, and *D. majalis* ssp. *occidentalis* (better known as an Irish plant) was recently discovered. Stabilized dune land in Anglesey provides a home for the rather rare *Epipactis dunensis*. These plants occur in especially good forms on some of the coastal dune systems in Lancashire. An unusual plant of the Norfolk dunes is *Goodyera repens*. It thrives under pine trees and, at one time, it was assumed that it was 'imported' with young trees from Scotland. It now seems that some of the plants are indigenous.

Northern limestone

Limestone areas, such as the Great Orme in North Wales and the pavements of Yorkshire, are places to look for *Epipactis atrorubens*. Easily one of the most attractive members of the genus, it is at its best growing in cracks in cliffs and limestone pavement.

In the north and west ridings of Yorkshire, where there is carboniferous limestone, and on magnesian limestone in Durham the magnificent *Cypripedium calceolus* once flourished. It is such an easily spotted plant, however, that its numbers were decimated by picking and collecting. It hangs on in one locality but is visited by far too many people. One can only hope that efforts to secure fertile seed from the stock will one day produce the sort of populations that are offered in the Italian Dolomites, the Austrian Tyrol and the Swiss Alps.

Pseudorchis albida occurs in a few scattered localities in Derbyshire, Yorkshire and Teesdale but is more in evidence further north, in Scotland. The limestone of the Midlands and north of England hold populations of *Orchis ustulata*, a plant which is difficult to find and which appears small and unattractive until viewed in close-up (see plate 152).

Scotland

Although there are extensive pine plantations throughout Britain, only in Scotland has a natural pinewood flora and fauna developed. A small group of orchids occurs in such places where the pines are not densely packed and the ground is moss-covered. *Goodyera repens* threads its stolons through the moss cushions, *Corallorhiza trifida* grows in damp leaf mould, and *Listera cordata* flourishes near the woodland edges, growing under heather and bilberry.

In Argyll, Inverness and one or two places in the Hebrides, *Spiranthes romanzoffiana* is a rare find. It is better known from its Irish sites in west Cork and south Kerry and around Lough Neagh.

In the Scottish Islands and on parts of the mainland *Dactylorhiza fuchsii* is replaced by its subspecies, ssp. *hebridensis*.

Rumours have circulated over the years concerning the finding of *Calypso bulbosa* in Scotland. This is by no means impossible since it occurs in north Norway, Russia and Sweden.

Ireland

The limestone region of the Burren in north-west Ireland has long proved a magnet for botanists from all over Europe. The flora is exceptionally rich in species rare elsewhere in the British Isles. It is the youngest landscape in Europe, with its carboniferous limestone rocks cut and twisted by weathering and intense glaciation, suffered as recently as 15,000 years ago. All the typical limestone land forms are there, ranging from swallow holes, caves and grykes to underground rivers.

Before the last glaciation there was a warm climate which allowed a southern (Lusitanian) flora to exist. Ice sheets slowly invaded from the north-east and left debris when they melted. It is thought that there were seeds of northern plants in amongst the debris, thus accounting for the present existence of northern (Hibernian) and southern plants side by side. Before man's intervention the Burren was covered with pine, hazel and yew – this has been deduced from examination of pollen buried in the limestone cracks.

Nowadays orchids thrive in the area. There are familiar ones, such as *Ophrys apifera*, *O. insectifera*, *Gymnadenia conopsea*, *Anacamptis pyramidalis*, *Platanthera bifolia* and *Orchis mascula*. One attraction, however, is the presence of some unusual orchids: *Epipactis atrorubens* thrives in cracks in the limestone, the marshy places hold *Dactylorhiza majalis* ssp. *occidentalis* and *D. incarnata* ssp. *cruenta*, while *D. fuchsii* ssp. *okellyii* flourishes on grassy heaths and beside the roads. Without doubt *Neotinea maculata* is the special orchid of the region. It is not an attractive orchid, being small with a dense spike of barely opened flowers, but the Burren is the only place it occurs in any number outside the Mediterranean region. Recently, it has been discovered in the Isle of Man.

The most famous of the Irish orchids is *Spiranthes romanzoffiana*, which is a member of the north American orchid flora. Its presence in western Ireland has puzzled botanists for many years. It was thought to be a relic of the last Ice Age, 10,000 years ago. Recent discoveries of the plant in some of the Scottish islands and on the Scottish mainland have caused further confusion. In Ireland it occurs in west Cork, south Kerry and on the shores of Lough Neagh.

Additions to the orchid flora

Although the orchid species flowering regularly in Britain are well-known, there are occasional reports of what might be termed 'continental visitors'. *Ophrys bertolonii* flowered in Dorset in 1976, during the long, hot summer of that year; *Chamorchis alpina* has been reported from the New Forest in Hampshire, and *Gymnadenia odoratissima* is known from a single specimen found in the last century in Durham. Two *Epipactis* species, *E. muelleri* and *E. confusa*, have also been reported, and it seems that these might occur with a regularity which puts them above mere 'erratics'. Finally, there are the persistent rumours of *Calypso bulbosa*, already mentioned in this section.

Germany

Germany and the British Isles have similar land areas, with large populations and heavy industrialisation which over the years have led to the disappearance of many orchid sites. However, in Germany orchids have fared somewhat better than in Britain, which may be connected with the fact that much of the literature on European orchids has been published in that country. There is even a strong working group in the shape of the AHO (*Arbeitskreis 'Heimische Orchideen'*), set up under the auspices of the Institute for Environmental Research and Nature Conservation, which deals entirely with the problems of looking after the country's wild orchids.

It was mainly through the energies of German botanists that the OPTIMA organisation (see p. xi) was founded. Every year extensive field work is carried out, and already much useful information has been gathered concerning the distribution and classification of Mediterranean flora, including wild orchids, which feature prominently in the publications.

With such a botanical tradition it is not surprising that Germany has been well botanised, and there are now numerous reserves throughout the country where orchids can be found.

Although Britain and Germany enjoy many species in common, several orchids which are known only as great rarities in the United Kingdom exist in much better colonies in Germany; for example *Orchis militaris*, *Ophrys fuciflora*, *Cypripedium calceolus*, *Cephalanthera rubra* and *Epipogium aphyllum*.

Of the German orchids which are not shared with Britain, an important group are the species most often associated with alpine regions. Thus in the Bavarian Alps one finds *Orchis pallens*, *Dactylorhiza sambucina*, *Traunsteinera globosa* and *Chamorchis alpina*, although they are often very local. Also, in Germany there are still sites for two rare orchids, *Spiranthes aestivalis* and *Microstylis monophyllos*, which are decreasing everywhere throughout Europe as their wetland habitats disappear, and for the less rare but still endangered *Orchis coriophora*.

The region of Baden-Württemberg is one of the richest in Germany for wild orchids, and it is here that both the AHO and OPTIMA have their headquarters.

A comprehensive booklet of orchid distribution maps was published in 1973 by the *Landestelle für Naturschutz und Landschaftspflege Baden-Württemberg*. Orchids can be found on numerous reserves and elsewhere in the forests, hills and meadows of this large area. Some sixty-two orchid species have been recorded, although one, *Orchis spitzelii*, has disappeared from the area.

Of particular interest are a number of sites for *Epipactis muelleri*, a plant closely related to the British *E. dunensis*, and for the diminutive *E. microphylla* with its small leaves and vanilla-scented flowers.

The rosy-flowered *Cephalanthera damasonium* is widespread in the woods with its less common relatives *C. rubra* and *C. longifolia*. The elusive *Epipogium aphyllum* occurs in a few good colonies in Baden-Württemberg and further west into the Black Forest, where it can be counted in hundreds rather than the usual ones and twos.

In the south of the region around the Bodensee, there are still colonies of the greatly endangered *Spiranthes aestivalis* and the rare *Liparis loeselii* growing in wetland areas. Another orchid of wet places, *Microstylis monophyllos*, has a few sites in Baden-Württemberg but it is always one of the hardest orchids to find: not only is it a rare plant, but its slender shape and green colouring make it difficult to discern against the surrounding vegetation.

Orchis pallens, by no means a common orchid, occurs in a large number of sites in the mountainous parts. Finally the extensive woods and glades of this rich area are the home of numerous populations of orchids such as *Epipactis helleborine*, *Neottia nidus-avis* and *Listera cordata*.

South of Munich, in the forests and hills of Bavaria, lies a reserve called the Pupplinger Au, where the Isar and Loisach rivers meet before their combined waters flow towards the great city. This region is well known to botanists for its collection of alpine plants growing amongst the stones brought down by the river. Here they survive on the flood plain at a much lower altitude than is usual. For the orchid hunter the reserve is remarkable for enormous scented spikes of *Gymnadenia conopsea* and a colony of *Cypripedium calceolus* with literally thousands of flourishing plants.

Proceeding south to where both rivers rise, the mountains become higher and merge into the Austrian Tyrol. Much of this mountain area is limestone and contains a rich collection of orchids. Apart from *Gymnadenia conopsea*, *Platanthera bifolia* and *P. chlorantha* there are small numbers of the high-mountain orchids, *Pseudorchis albida*, *Traunsteinera globosa*, *Nigritella nigra* and *Chamorchis alpina*. The latter orchid occurs at lower altitudes than one normally expects.

The Kaiserstuhl mountains lie in the upper reaches of the Rhine in south-west Germany and for many years have attracted orchid lovers. Of some 54 species of orchid growing in Germany about 35 have been recorded from this limited area.

Unfortunately in recent years the climate and soil have proved ideal for viticulture to the detriment of the orchid population. In spite of this the area is still worth visiting.

Although this account concentrates on the southern part of the country, orchids can certainly be found in many parts of the Rheinland and Hessen, wherever there are calcareous soils.

Scandinavia

The countries of Scandinavia – Norway, Sweden, Denmark, Finland and Iceland – occupy a vast part of the area of north Europe and they are, for several reasons, of considerable interest to anyone interested in wild orchids.

First, a number of orchid species found in Germany and the UK occur in Denmark and southern Sweden, wherever there are calcareous soils: further north they disappear, as their northern limits are passed. Then, there is a collection of orchids that frequent high mountains in the rest of Europe but flower down to sea level in Scandinavia. These are *Dactylorhiza sambucina*, in both the yellow and red forms, *Nigritella nigra* and the tiny *Chamorchis alpina*. Finally, there are the Scandinavian specialities: marsh orchids, *Dactylorhiza pseudocordigera* from Norway and Sweden, and *D. traunsteineri* ssp. *lapponica* from northern Scandinavia (Lapland); the exquisite *Calypso bulbosa* from the forests of northern Scandinavia, and – a great rarity – *Platanthera obtusata* ssp. *oligantha*, known from very few sites. The Swedish island of Götland, lying in the Baltic sea, has a rich flora growing on its calcareous rocks, laid down in the Cambro-silurian period. *Cephalanthera damasonium* is found in its northernmost outpost here; *Dactylorhiza sambucina* occurs in both colour forms, but the red one tends to be confined to places near the coast (it is quite a common orchid in parts of Sweden, notably on islands near Stockholm). The Swedish name of 'Adam and Eve' is more probably due to the likeness of the tubers to human bodies pressed together than a reference to the two colour forms. Another marsh orchid, *Dactylorhiza majalis* ssp. *purpurella*, occurs in dune slacks in the northern part of the island. There are magnificent colonies of *Orchis militaris* on Götland (and elsewhere in Sweden), but it is for another member of the genus that the island is famous. In 1939 European botanists were startled when *O. spitzelii* was found growing in Götland. It had obviously been overlooked because of the rather similar *O. mascula*, which is common on the island. It is a rare orchid, occurring in sites spread widely through Europe into Turkey, where it has survived the various ice ages.

In northern Sweden (northern Lapland) lies the national park of Abisko, at the western end of the big lake Torne Trask. Here, in two separate sites, grows the exceptionally rare *Platanthera obtusata* ssp. *oligantha*. It only flowers sporadically, near the lake and on the northern slopes of nearby Mt Nuolja, where its small stature (6–20cm) makes it easy to overlook. It is also known from a few sites in the far north of Norway (Finmark and Troms-fylke).

To the south-west of the park and across the peninsula near the coast lies Boden and its fortress. In nearby woods grows *Calypso bulbosa*, one of the most delightful of all orchids, and also *Cypripedium calceolus* (which occurs in small numbers in a few places in northern Sweden).

In parts of Lapland, where there are calcareous deposits, the tiny and often overlooked *Chamorchis alpina* is found growing amongst *Dryas octopetala* on exposed heathland.

Iceland is a country of impressive scenery but few orchids. There are two local specialities and both are quite frequently encountered in low parts of the island. The first, *Platanthera hyperborea*, is locally frequent, growing in a number of open places such as heath and moorland. The second is a marsh orchid, *Dactylorhiza maculata* ssp. *islandica*.

Holland

Wild flowers have suffered the same fate in Holland as in other western European countries where the demands of agriculture have been met. Ironically, it is to provide for the needs of cultivated forms that large areas of land have been denuded of wild flowers. Areas which were formerly sandhills and marshes, complete with wild orchids, are often a riot of colour in springtime, when Holland's justifiably famous bulbfields are in bloom.

The Dutch Nature Conservation Act of 1973 designated 31 species of plant and four groups of plants as protected species, and there is one small area, a region called South Limburg, where many of these plants occur together. Here the landscape is formed of Cretaceous chalks and limestone, loosely referred to as marl. It is an area of outstanding natural beauty, with gentle hills and valleys eroded by streams into plateaux and terraces. The area also has a unique orchid flora which is particularly abundant in the chalk and limestone grasslands of the numerous Nature Reserves set up in this area (Wolfskop, Bemelerberg, Kundeberg, Wrakelberg, Wahlwiller and Geremdal), all with carefully marked paths and signposts warning of the legal perils of straying from them.

From May onwards the parade of orchids includes *Orchis morio*, *O. simia*, *O. militaris*, *O. mascula*, *Aceras anthropophorum*, *Ophrys apifera*, *O. fuciflora*, *Himantoglossum hircinum*, *Anacamptis pyramidalis* and *Gymnadenia conopsea*.

The woodlands are no less impressive and have their orchid flora too, with such specimens as *Orchis purpurea*, *O. mascula*, *Cephalanthera damasonium* and *Ophrys insectifera*. Unfortunately there are few marshes and bogs in South Limburg that can be found in their original state. Those remaining occur in the Geul and Gulp valleys and along the valley of the Roste Beek stream, near Schinveld. The hillside bog along the last-named stream provides a home for a number of orchids – *Dactylorhiza incarnata*, *D. maculata* ssp. *ericetorum* and *Platanthera bifolia*.

France

It is perhaps fitting that France, the largest country in the EEC, should also possess the richest European orchid flora. Orchids seem to be everywhere, in numbers that make photography a joy. There is no need here for lengthy pilgrimages to well-protected sites to photograph a bedraggled *Orchis simia* or a battered *Cypripedium calceolus*.

The varied terrain of France, with vast areas of calcareous rocks and soils, provides homes for a range of orchids with very different requirements. As well as a climate which permits the growth of nearly all the orchid species found in Germany and Britain, France has an alpine region with its attendant orchid flora. Again, the Mediterranean climate of the South permits the growth of a large variety of *Ophrys* and *Orchis*.

So much of the French landscape is either limestone rock or the *terra rossa* soils derived from it that there is a problem in deciding where to start a search for orchids. The areas given below are only a guide; thankfully there are many more places, ripe for discovery.

Central France
Massif Central. This largely unspoilt area of France offers some of the wildest and most beautiful scenery in Europe, especially when the spring flowers are at their best in May and June. In the north-west lie the volcanic mountains of the Auvergne, in the north-east rise the granite mountains of Forez. The south-west holds the strange Causse country of limestone plateaux, deeply divided by gorges, while the south-east is occupied by the Cevennes.

The flora, too, has four distinct elements: *Central European*, characterized by silver fir trees and beechwoods; *Mediterranean*, in the south of the region; *Atlantic*, characterized by heathers and broom; and *Boreal*, comprising arctic and alpine species.

Causse Country: South to Cevennes. Particularly good orchid finds can be made near the edges of the Causse country. Roquefort, famous for its cheese and for the flocks of sheep that provide the milk for its manufacture, is a good base. In the surrounding country *Himantoglossum hircinum* is frequent beside roads, *Orchis militaris* and *O. purpurea* occur in such numbers that hybrids between them are not rare, while *Orchis ustulata*, *Anacamptis pyramidalis* and *Plantanthera bifolia* are often encountered.

Rodez is a large town on a hill, dominated by a cathedral. It provides a base for exploratory journeys along the numerous small roads that thread the surrounding countryside. In May and June stone-strewn fields between Brive and Decazeville hold populations of *Himantoglossum hircinum*, *Orchis militaris*, *O. purpurea*, *O. ustulata*, *Ophrys sphegodes* and *O. apifera*. The roadsides are equally rich, before the scythe is used to 'neaten' them.

Espalion lies surrounded by *terre rouge* and an amazing collection of orchids. First one finds, as elsewhere, *Himantoglossum hircinum*; then there are the various 'bee orchids' *Ophrys apifera*, *O. scolopax* and *O. sphegodes*. Under pines there are small colonies of *Limodorum abortivum*, at woodland edges *Cephalanthera longifolia* and *Orchis militaris*, in open places *Orchis purpurea* and *O. ustulata*. The undoubted prize here, as in many other parts of the region, is the rose-coloured *Cephalanthera rubra*.

Estaing lies in a deep valley on the river Lot where the soil is acidic and no orchids grow. However, to the south the *terre rouge* begins again, and orchids abound beside the roads and in deserted vineyards. As well as the species mentioned, *Dactylorhiza elata* occurs in marshy places such as roadside ditches, and the occasional *Serapias lingua* is found in wet fields. Further south one can take many roads and tracks towards St Affrique and the Cevennes region – all worth searching, for in this area grows the curious and confusing *Ophrys arachnitiformis*.

Orchids seem to thrive in soil that was disturbed about twenty years earlier: thus, old disused vineyards on stony, well-drained slopes are ideal habitats for orchids. Now that artificial fertilizers are used this is less frequently the case, for orchids are particularly susceptible to the chemicals employed. In our modern world the French farmer is often criticized for his lack of efficiency and because subsidies have to be awarded to make his products competitive in the European marketplace. For the conservationist the longer the farmer adheres to his old-fashioned methods the better, for then we might still enjoy the sight of myriads of insect-mimicking orchids in old vineyards, where they often rival the blades of grass in number.

The South of France
To the north of the eastern Pyrenees lies a group of predominantly limestone mountains, les Corbières. In places they rise to a little over 1000m, and the flowers are at their best in the latter part of April and early May. As well as dwarf narcissi, muscari, irises and tulips there is a good selection of *Ophrys* and *Orchis* amongst the low scrub in open areas. *Ophrys sphegodes*, *O. fuciflora*, *O. arachnitiformis*, *Orchis simia*, *O. tridentata*, *O. provincialis* are all fairly frequent on slopes with a northerly aspect.

When H. Thompson wrote his *Flowering Plants of the Riviera* many years ago and spoke with great enthusiasm of the orchids of the region, he could not have anticipated the army of tourists that descends each year on the coastal resorts. To fulfil the demands of these visitors camp sites have sprung up, often in pinewoods where orchids once grew. The better-off have built their villas around the chic resorts of St Tropez, Juan-les-Pins and Nice. This development puts the orchid flora under great pressure, and many sites have long disappeared. Fortunately orchids are not above ground in the summer months when the tourist influx is greatest and pickers would eradicate whole species. There are still many orchids to be found, although one would be unlikely to rediscover all the species that Thompson lists for the province of Var alone.

Away from the coast road which leads from Toulon to Nice there are seepages which are long dry by the time the sun-seekers arrive. Here one finds *Serapias*, sometimes in abundance. Undoubtedly the most impressive is *S. neglecta*, with large flowers in a range of colours from yellow through orange to a brick red. It is a plant of restricted distribution, being confined to the South of France, northern Italy and Corsica, with a few sightings in Sardinia. *Serapias cordigera*, with its dark lip and spotted stems, is also to be found over the whole area, whereas *S. olbia* is confined to the peninsula near Hyères. This curious plant is supposed to be of hybrid origin, and there has been some conjecture as to its parentage. *S. lingua* and *S. parviflora* are the most likely contenders, although *S. vomeracea* and *S. parviflora* have also been cited. In recent years drainage of wet lands in the dune region where it grows in slightly acid soils has led to its disappearance in a number of places. Its future looks decidedly grim.

Other than *Serapias* there are *Ophrys* such as *O. sphegodes*, *O. fuciflora*, *O. bertolonii*, the occasional confusing *O. arachnitiformis* and, very rarely,

O. speculum (possibly extinct in most of the French sites). *Orchis* are to be found too, particularly in the high parts of the Var. Among them are *O. simia*, *O. purpurea*, *O. mascula*, *O. provincialis* and *O. tridentata*.

Lying to the north of the Côte d'Azur are the incomparable warm hills of Provence. Here rivers thread their way through woods and gorges in what is essentially a limestone plateau lying at over 1000m above sea level.

The spring air is fragrant with lavender in April, and the cistus scrub holds large numbers of orchids. The flora is Mediterranean, and thus *Orchis* and *Ophrys* predominate. *Ophrys bertolonii* is particularly handsome here, growing with *O. sphegodes* ssp. *litigiosa* and ssp. *provincialis* and robust plants of *O. arachnitiformis* and *O. fuciflora*. *Orchis provincialis* is common, as one would expect from its specific name, and *Orchis simia*, *O. purpurea*, *O. tridentata* are frequently found on the east-west ridges which cross the region.

The High Mountains
Haut Dauphiné (the Cottian Alps). The busy road from Grenoble to Turin via Briançon takes one through some of the most magnificent mountain scenery in France. From Freney d'Oisans the road skirts the Lac de Chambon until the far end of the lake where the Romanche enters it. The road now closely follows the river to La Grave, a small, pleasant town remarkable mainly for the views of La Meije, one of the Dauphiné giants with huge snow fields and the highest of its peaks stretching to 3657m.

The path from La Grave to the river leads to a national park, Le Parc des Ecrins, which includes La Meije. If one is not feeling energetic enough to climb to the heights, a walk in the Bois des Fréaux which runs along the Romanche will bring a mixed bag of orchids to light.

First, the grassy places hold huge spikes of *Gymnadenia conopsea*, mixed with *Orchis militaris* and an occasional *Dactylorhiza fuchsii*. On the wooded slopes, in the rich humus under the trees, the curious *Corallorhiza trifida* grows in small colonies. The saprophytic orchid is not an imposing plant, for its stature is small, its colour dingy and its flowers tiny, yet a hand lens or extreme close-up photograph reveals a quiet beauty.

The roadside banks are covered with thick cushions of moss, punctured by the creeping green stems of *Goodyera repens*, another orchid whose beauty eludes the casual observer not equipped with a hand lens (see plate 52). Further along the river bank there are helleborines to be found: *Epipactis atrorubens* and *E. helleborine*.

To the north of La Grave the road winds steeply to a series of mountain villages, perched on the hillside and looking out across the valley to the snow-capped heights of La Meije. The villages all have alpine meadows around them where *Orchis militaris*, *O. ustulata*, *Gymnadenia conopsea* and

G. odoratissima flourish, with a backdrop of rugged snow-capped peaks to set them off to full advantage.

Higher up on the hills various mountain seepages play host to an amazing variety of Marsh Orchids. Here *Dactylorhiza majalis* and its subspecies grow with *D. traunsteineri* and *D. incarnata* ssp. *cruenta* as reasonably distinguishable forms, but it is the hybrids and multitude of variants that baffle all but the handful of specialists when identification is required.

From Les Hyères there is a very pleasant walk up to the Lac du Goléon at 2435m. Here *Nigritella nigra* and *Traunsteinera globosa* are to be found, as well as a wealth of narcissus and, higher up, an abundance of alpines.

Beyond La Grave the road winds up to the famous Col du Lautaret, whose virtues as a place for alpine plants have long been extolled by writers on the subject. Here, within easy walk of the hotel and on a high hilltop with a great ring of peaks around, *Nigritella nigra*, *Traunsteinera globosa*, the unimpressive *Pseudorchis albida* and various forms of *Dactylorhiza majalis* are all readily found. The descent from the Col takes one past the Prés des Brunets, an area full of small trees where *Dactylorhiza sambucina* grows in its magenta form and, rather more frequently, in its yellow form where the ground is moist.

The road descends towards Briançon, reputedly the highest town in France, where the surrounding woods and hills contain *Orchis militaris* and *O. purpurea*.

The Jura. One way of crossing Europe leads through the Mont Blanc tunnel from France into Italy. From here one can make an easy detour into the Jura, a region of moderately high mountains raised by disturbances in the Jurassic era. Here beech trees flourish in the extensive woodlands, giving way to pines at higher altitudes, and there are areas of limestone rock and basic soils. From a base such as Morez it is possible to spend some time profitably exploring for orchids.

One trip involves a circular tour of the Forêt du Massacre where, under the beech trees, large numbers of the saprophytic orchid *Neottia nidus-avis* may be found growing in the beech litter hidden from the sunlight. *Epipactis leptochila* occurs in very fine form in more than one place, and in areas where the woods give way to sunny slopes strewn with lumps of limestone one can find its relative, *Epipactis atrorubens*, often in large numbers. Rumour has it, too, that the very rare *Epipogium aphyllum* is as frequent here as anywhere. As the forest gives way to mountain pastures *Gymnadenia conopsea* is much in evidence, while *Coeloglossum viride* is common on roadside banks.

The route takes one near La Dôle, a mountain reaching 1677m and which offers a taste of the mountain flora, although it is but a dwarf compared with giants like Mont Blanc. A walk of half an hour or so takes one past groups of pines where *Epipactis atrorubens* is to be found. Higher up there are a few plants of *Pseudorchis albida* and the very dark red *Nigritella nigra*.

The Jura has the great advantage that it remains flower-filled even until late August when most other montane regions have given of their best.

Annecy, a lakeside resort, is a good place to stay for a few days before continuing a journey to Chamonix and Mont Blanc. In the height of summer its lake attracts hordes of holidaymakers and it is a place to avoid. However, at 'orchid' times, in late May and June, things are better.

To the east of the lake, near Talloires and Menton, there is some good limestone country where orchids thrive. A short journey by car takes one to the Col des Aravis where, apart from breathtaking views of Mont Blanc, there are masses of *Orchis purpurea* in the woods, as well as *Platanthera bifolia* and an unusual white form of *Orchis mascula*, growing happily with the normal purple form. In later months orchids such as *Traunsteinera globosa* and various *Dactylorhiza* species grow freely.

Just outside Annecy itself, towards the west, there are quite extensive beechwoods where orchids may be found. *Neottia nidus-avis* is a regular constituent of the beechwood flora in France, and these woods are no exception, but one plant of interest here in July is a very narrow-lipped *Epipactis* showing distinct characteristics of both *E. helleborine* and *E. leptochila*.

The Pyrenees. Running for over 400km from the Mediterranean to the Atlantic, the Pyrenees form a natural frontier between Spain and France. As a mountain range they do not compete in height with the Alps, but they nevertheless offer some memorable scenery and an abundance of wild flowers, many of which qualify as endemics. We have not found the mountain orchids in such large numbers as in the Alps but there is the added advantage of a very good Mediterranean springtime orchid flora in places like les Corbières, to the north of the eastern Pyrenees.

Climatically there is quite a difference between the western and eastern ends of the range and the centre. The coastal ends tend to have hotter summers and wetter winters than the centre, and this produces differences in the flora.

It is difficult to recommend a 'best' time for a visit to the Pyrenees, for in some years the Route des Pyrénées can be blocked by snow until July. Again, if it is the Mediterranean flora of the lower eastern slopes that provides the reason for a visit then late April or early May is a good time. Usually the greatest number of orchids can be found in June.

We first visited Gabas in the western Pyrenees as a result of reading a comment in Polunin and Smythies' *Flowers of South Western Europe* to the effect that the woods around Gabas were full of orchids. We were not too disappointed since we found *Orchis ustulata*, *Platanthera bifolia* and *Gymnadenia conopsea*.

Above the village on the Pic de Sagette *Nigritella nigra* grows, but the special prize in this area is *Spiranthes aestivalis*, a plant uncommon in France in damp hillside meadows but now probably extinct in its British sites.

Roughly south-east of Gabas lies Gavarnie and its famous Cirque, a marvellous example of nature's architecture and an exceptional place for wild flowers. Unfortunately Gavarnie can be spoiled by the daily influx of pilgrims from Lourdes, so it is best to visit the Cirque either in the early morning or in the evening when the crowds have gone.

There are many walks to be taken. One can find without difficulty the following orchids, which are fairly well-spread over the area: *Pseudorchis albida*, *Orchis ustulata* and *Dactylorhiza sambucina* in both its colour forms (in one place abundant enough to qualify as a drift). *Gymnadenia conopsea* in the robust form called var. *densiflora*, *Epipactis atrorubens* and *Nigritella nigra* make up the rest of the collection in high places, while on lower ground *Ophrys apifera* is present together with its uncommon var. *chlorantha*.

Switzerland

Apart from the low-lying plateau in the north, bounded by the Jura, the greater part of the country consists of high peaks and deeply incised valleys.

In the meadows and woodlands orchids flourish, for the Swiss are conscious of the beauty of the wild flowers in their country and have taken trouble to protect by law both orchids and other plants.

In the valleys, however, cultivation is intense and few orchids survive in the hayfields. The woods and their edges present a different story, with *Corallorhiza trifida*, *Listera cordata*, *Platanthera chlorantha*, *Cephalanthera damasonium*, *C. rubra*, *Orchis militaris*, *O. purpurea*, *Gymnadenia conopsea*, *Anacamptis pyramidalis*, *Orchis mascula* and *Cypripedium calceolus* all in evidence.

In the sub-alpine pastures and woods the orchids are those discussed on page 31.

Two particularly good areas for orchids are the Bernese Oberland and the Valais. Of course, orchids occur in abundance elsewhere in Switzerland, but the accounts of these two regions should convince the reader of the worth of the country as a venue for orchid hunting.

The Bernese Oberland
Of all the alpine regions in Europe which are visited for the flowers the Bernese Oberland is perhaps the best known and the best loved. Here one can find an extremely rich flora, with plants of low meadows, woodlands and high alps all to be seen in a single day's excursion.

The orchids are particularly splendid, and there are a number of very good sites for that Queen of European orchids, *Cypripedium calceolus*. This plant, with its inflated yellow 'clog' lip and its contrasting deep purple-brown sepals, is very strictly protected by the Swiss. As if its beauty alone was insufficient, the sites where *C. calceolus* flourishes often have the added benefit of a backdrop of giant mountains and cool pinewoods to heighten their appeal.

Kandersteg, long known as a centre for plants, lies at the head of a valley whence the Lötschberg tunnel carries the railway under the mountains to the Rhône valley. There are many walks to be taken in the area, and orchids can readily be found. The rose-coloured helleborine *Cephalanthera rubra* is at its best here with *Platanthera bifolia* and numerous plants of both *Gymnadenia conopsea* and the intensely scented *G. odoratissima*. The valley between Kandersteg and Selden holds *Cypripedium calceolus* in a superb woodland setting, with *Corallorhiza trifida* to be found in places where the litter of the floor has become moss-covered.

Anyone who intends to visit one of the high holiday centres like Wengen and who is travelling by train comes first to Lauterbrunnen. Here a change is made onto a little rack-and-pinion railway which then climbs at an impossible gradient to its destination.

The Lauterbrunnen valley deserves exploration in its own right, for *Cypripedium calceolus* is found in small numbers in one or two sites and, at the far end of the valley, the meadows contain most of the orchids characteristic of this type of habitat.

To reach the higher ground one either walks or takes the aforementioned train which carries on up to the dizzy heights of Kleinerscheidegger and Jungfraujoch stations. For the traveller on a budget these trains are by no means cheap, especially if one uses them to connect with cable cars to reach the really high places where the high alpine plants flourish.

From Wengernalp one can walk up or down with reasonable ease, but for those who find even this amount of walking tiring there are orchids right outside the station where seepages hold *Dactylorhiza majalis* and its broad-leaved ssp. *alpestris*, as well as a few *Pseudorchis albida*.

To return to Wengen one can go via Biglenalp and find *Listera cordata* and *Corallorhiza trifida* in the woods or one can retrace one's steps along the main path and find exactly the same things.

In this area, in a site known to far too many people, grows *Cypripedium calceolus*, not in a wood this time but in an open valley beside a stream with pine trees beyond and, in the distance, the towering snow-capped peaks of the Jungfrau, the Eiger and the immense Finsteraarhorn (4274m).

Valais
The resorts of Zermatt and St Luc are two of the famous resorts in the area. St Luc is a little more accessible by car because travellers to Zermatt can only travel as far up the valley as St Niklaus. It also has the advantage that a

circular drive around the flanks of the Val d'Anniviers is possible from here, taking in all types of montane vegetation.

Parts at least of the spruce forests and meadows lie on limestone. On the north-west of the valley limestone predominates up to 2700m, and here orchids grow in abundance. Rarities such as *Cypripedium calceolus, Cephalanthera rubra* and the more common *Orchis militaris, O. purpurea, Platanthera chlorantha* and a host of others are strictly protected by law from the depredations of pickers and collectors.

The whole valley has long been famous for its almost unrivalled range of alpine plants – a richness due to the varied geology of the region with its rocks of gneiss, limestone and calceschists.

Austria

Austria, like Switzerland, is a land of breathtaking mountain scenery – the stuff of which picture postcards and calendars are made. There are extensive areas of limestone, both in the high Alps and in the hilly areas of the south-east and southern Tyrol, and here orchids abound in the woods and meadows.

The Tyrol is perhaps the best-known region of Austria, visited for its scenery in the summer and for skiing in the winter. It is a superb area for the plant lover, with a wide range of species to be found, most notably orchids. The reasons for this are threefold: there is a variety of soils of both basic and acidic natures; the climate is quite different in the south of the region compared with the north, for the southern Alps are influenced by the Mediterranean region while the northern Alps have a temperate climate; and there is a wide range of habitats, from forests of beech, pine, oak and spruce through to wetlands and grasslands.

Using Innsbruck as a centre there are four main areas:

To the north-west, between the chalk chain of the Lechtaler Alps and the Allgau range the climate is cool and damp and orchids are abundant.

South-east of Innsbruck lie the Zillertaler Alps, with one of the best-known and most easily accessible of the Tyrolean Alpine valleys. Here one can find wet meadows, woods and pasture land on calcareous soil.

Halltal, which stretches from the Karwendel range to Hall and is well-known to lovers of mountain flowers.

The South Tyrol Dolomites are almost certainly the most interesting for the orchid lover because this is where the rarities grow. The climate is mild and heavily influenced by the Mediterranean. It is in this region that Mediterranean orchids, such as *Serapias vomeracea* and *Ophrys bertoloniiformis* (*O. benacensis*) can be encountered.

In all of these regions there are orchids, and it pays the visitor to look for particular habitats where there will be a good chance of finding the orchid one is seeking (c.f. Chapter 2).

In the pine forests one regularly finds *Goodyera repens*, *Ophrys insectifera*, *Cephalanthera rubra*, *Epipactis atrorubens*, *Platanthera bifolia*, *Listera cordata* and *Corallorhiza trifida*. In spruce and mixed forests *Cypripedium calceolus* is widespread and well-protected. The beech forests provide a home for *Cephalanthera longifolia* and *C. damasonium* and, if one is lucky, *Epipogium aphyllum* might be found.

The orchid population of the grasslands varies according to altitude. In the high mountains there is the easily overlooked *Chamorchis alpina* and a fine display of *Nigritella nigra* in a wide range of colour forms. Lower down but still in alpine meadows there is *Traunsteinera globosa*, *Coeloglossum viride*, *Herminium monorchis* and *Pseudorchis albida*. Both colour forms of *Dactylorhiza sambucina* are widespread, but the yellow *Orchis pallens* tends to be rare. In damp flower meadows of the sub-alpine zone one can occasionally find *Microstylis monophyllos*, with a wide range of *Dactylorhiza* species and hybrids sharing the habitat. *Gymnadenia conopsea*, *G. odoratissima*, *Orchis militaris* and *O. mascula* are all to be found in large numbers.

Spain

The Iberian peninsula occupies a vast area, divided between Spain, Portugal and the small state of Andorra. The four main islands of the Balearics (Majorca, Minorca, Ibiza and Formentera) form a province of Spain and the Canaries form another. About 85 per cent of the peninsula is bordered by the sea, the remainder being separated from France by the high wall of the Pyrenees.

With an Atlantic coast, a Mediterranean coast, an area only 13.7km from Africa at its nearest, and with countryside that is generally mountainous, Spain naturally has a very rich flora. In fact the Spanish flora numbers 6,000 species, with numerous endemics. A large number of orchid species occur, but few of them are rare. What makes the region special is that the orchids seem to occur in especially magnificent forms. For example, the mahogany spikes of *Serapias cordigera* on the Picos de Europa, *Orchis papilionacea* and *Ophrys tenthredinifera* in southern Andalucia, all grow in magnificent, robust spikes with large flowers which compare with the best from anywhere in Europe.

Southern Spain (Andalucia)
Costa del Sol. This is an area that is often missed by the flower seeker on holiday, for the simple reason that it is known and avoided as a tourist trap.

In the springtime, though, before the influx of the summer visitors, the area has a rich display of wild flowers, including a notable collection of orchids. Malaga is a useful centre, although the tasteless development of the coastal region has spoiled its attraction.

The area is divided into two distinct parts: one towards Gibraltar and the entrance to the Atlantic, the other to the east. The former has a heavier rainfall than the latter, which includes Cabo de Gata, near Almeria, the driest part of Spain.

From Malaga a road runs roughly north towards Puerto del León. Beyond Colmenar the road forks, the eastern branch heading towards the Sierra Tejeda where grow some of the largest spikes of *Orchis papilionacea* (the form var. *grandiflora*) that the authors have seen. The other fork leads towards Antequera, which lies in an area of grotesquely weathered limestone. The whole area is a plateau which has been eroded, and the orchid list from this region alone is very impressive. In early spring (March) *Ophrys lutea*, *O. bombyliflora*, *O. speculum*, *O. tenthredinifera*, *Orchis italica*, *O. saccata*, *O. papilionacea* and *Barlia robertiana* flower, followed by *Ophrys fusca* ssp. *durieui*, *Ophrys scolopax*, *Ophrys apifera*, *Serapias lingua*, *S. cordigera*, *S. parviflora*, *Neotinea intacta* and the curious *Gennaria diphylla*. The display does not end with the spring, for after the first orchids are past their best *Orchis laxiflora* and its ssp. *palustris* flower in damp places, *O. coriophora* comes into bloom, and from May onwards *Himantoglossum hircinum*, *Cephalanthera longifolia* and, later, *Epipactis helleborine* and *E. atrorubens* flower. The very rare *Spiranthes aestivalis* also occurs in the same district.

This is not the only region near Malaga where orchids flourish, for near the old spa of Carratraca, north-west of Malaga, lies the Sierra de Alcaparain. This is of Jurassic limestone with extensive woods of *Pinus halepensis* where orchids thrive in amazing numbers. Most species of the list mentioned above are to be found, and the striking *Ophrys fusca* ssp. *durieui* is at its best here. It was only discovered there in 1963 by one of us, the first European record, although it has since been found in many other localities. It is better known as *O. fusca* spp. *atlantica*.

Orchis pallens is a rather uncommon yellow orchid that grows with *Orchis mascula* in May in the mountain woods and on slopes near Puerto de Penas Blacas in the Sierra Bermeja, a region of Malaga province.

Serrania de Ronda. About 64km west of Malaga lies the little Moorish town of Ronda. The fact that it lies at the centre of some thousand square kilometres of rugged mountains, much of them Triassic and Jurassic limestone, has made it a magnet for discerning botanists.

To get there one has a choice of approaches, for at least five roads converge on the town from various directions. First, from Malaga there is the small cross-country road via Coin and Burgos, through the area of

Alhaurin de la Torre. There are orchids in fine form along the roadside, especially *Ophrys lutea* and *O. fusca*.

Alternatively, if one can stomach the tasteless coastal development without thinking of what once grew there, take the road to San Pedro Alcántara, west of Marbella, and then head northwards into the hills. The road climbs up through cork oakwoods, growing on red volcanic rocks composed of peridotite. The plants here indicate the acid nature of the soil, but this changes abruptly when the volcanic soils give way to a grey-white dolomite. From here on the journey to Ronda can take a long time because of the temptation to stop and search for orchids along the roadside. *Ophrys fusca* and *O. lutea* are very frequent, with some attractive colour variants of the former in evidence. Scattered throughout the area one can also find, at various times from March to June, *Ophrys speculum*, *O. scolopax*, *O. tenthredinifera*, *Orchis italica*, *O. mascula*, *O. pallens*, *O. morio*, *O. papilionacea*, *O. lactea*, *Barlia robertiana*, *Aceras anthropophorum*, *Neotinea intacta* and *Himantoglossum hircinum*.

Various members of this orchid list grow wherever the limestone is in evidence – the Serrania de Grazalema and its cliffs, Sierra Blanca and many other places. A stay of several days is essential to explore all the small roads and tracks in the environs of Ronda.

Sierra Nevada. East of Malaga lie the highest mountains in south-west Europe. The highest peak, Mulhacén, reaches 3478m. Although we cannot recommend the region for its orchid display, it is a botanical paradise in either late April or early May, when the spring flowers appear after the winter snows, or else in August, when the high alpines are at their best. The isolation of the mountains has ensured a large number of endemics. The flanks of the mountains consist of Triassic limestone and sandstones, and orchids are to be found. Travelling up from Granada, at the Pico Veleta (where the road is the highest in Europe), large forms of *Ophrys lutea* are in evidence and *Orchis mascula* ssp. *olbiensis* flourishes in a range of colours, wherever the soil is *terra rossa*.

Cadiz to Gibraltar. This region, facing the Atlantic, is noticeably cooler than the Mediterranean Costa del Sol.

From Tanta to Cape Trafalgar the rocky coast is wild and unpopulated. For the ornithologist it is an area of great fascination because of the number of migrants that pass on their way north. Access to parts of the coast is restricted in places because of military activities. Although there are no spectacular displays of orchids a number of species can be found. Dunes near the Faro de las Palomas are the place to find *Ophrys speculum* and a few *O. scolopax*. Near Cape Trafalgar there is a tableland of calcareous sandstone, dating from the Miocene era, which carries extensive pinewoods. Here grow

Ophrys speculum, O. scolopax, O. fusca, O. lutea, O. bombyliflora and *Gennaria diphylla.*

To the west of Cadiz lies the famed Coto de Donăna, with its unbelievable range of species of wild birds and animals, protected as a reserve and to which access is strictly controlled.

Central Spain

Southern Iberian Mountains: the Montes Universales. Some 80km north of Cuenca lies a limestone range with a profusion of deep, narrow gorges and imposing cliffs. From Cuenca one takes the road to Tragacete, across part of the Montes Universales chain. This portion is called the Serrania da Cuenca and is remarkable for the Ciudad Encantada, a collection of rocks produced by erosion of a soft, tufa-like limestone. There are arches, bridges and 'mushrooms' up to 20m high. In the woodlands *Ophrys lutea* thrives with the rather local *Orchis spitzelii.*

Towards Tragacete the countryside is well-wooded, mainly with *Pinus nigra* and thickets of *Buxus sempervirens*. There are plenty of forest roads, not shown on maps, and there are orchids to be found. Indeed one of the authors was fortunate enough to share in the find of a dramatically coloured variety of what was then called *Dactylorhiza romana*. The plant was later named *D. insularis* var. *bartonii* Huxley & Hunt. Now that *Flora Europaea* is available it seems that *D. insularis* has become a subspecies of *D. sambucina*. Thus a lovely, yellow orchid with reddish-brown patches on its lip now has the ungainly name *Dacylorhiza sambucina* ssp. *insularis* var.*bartonii.*

The Tragacete area is a fertile valley with steep pine-clad hills on either side. In the damp areas near the streams several orchids grow in abundance: *Epipactis palustris, Gymnadenia conopsea* var. *densiflora* and *Dactylorhiza elata*. In the woods *Epipactis helleborine*, *E. leptochila* and *E. microphylla* all grow well, and where the woods give way to grassy meadows one can find *Orchis morio, O. mascula, O. spitzelii* and one or two *O. pallens*. Slightly earlier in the year *Ophrys scolopax* and *O. sphegodes* flower in the open places, and around the same area grow *Dactylorhiza incarnata, Anacamptis pyramidalis, Coeloglossum viride, Cephalanthera damasonium, C. longifolia, C. rubra* and *Limodorum abortivum.*

The Central Sierras: Gredos.. The Central Sierras run for some 400km in length, in a south-west to north-east direction, across the centre of the Iberian peninsula.

From Madrid one can escape to the Sierra de Gredos, which forms part of the chain. There is an overwhelming sense of relief at escaping the heat and bustle of the city and reaching these high (2592m) mountains.

On one of the mountains, the Arenas de San Pedro, there are extensive pinewoods where, in late May, *Orchis laxiflora* is common in open spaces and beside roads where the ground is damp. Very good specimens of *Orchis coriophora* can be found often where the soil reaction is slightly acid. The subspecies *fragrans* seems to take over where there are limestone outcrops in parts of the Gredos. *Dactylorhiza elata* thrives in northern parts of the massif in marshy places on granitic soils. Some of the spikes are very robust and splendid white forms are not rare.

Catalonia. In Europe there is such a long tradition of interest in plants that it seems unlikely that an orchid should have eluded discovery. In fact, this is just what seems to have happened in the case of *Ophrys catalaunica*. First discovered in 1967, it has been located since in several places in a wide radius of Berga. Its exact status is not yet certain but it is certainly an attractive plant (c.f. description on p. 167). In the same area magnificent spikes of *Dactylorhiza* occur in wet places and *Ophrys sphegodes* is found infrequently.

At Monserrat there is a monastery, high up amongst the masses of rock. Since the Holy Grail was reputed to have been kept there it tends to be a popular place – as the cable cars and funiculars testify. Fortunately the forests on the lower and middle slopes of the mountain are untouched. *Orchis mascula* flowers in abundance, and where there are rocky gulleys *Ophrys fusca*, *Dactylorhiza fuchsii*, *Aceras anthropophorum and Limodorum abortivum* flower in May.

Northern Spain

Picos de Europa. For 240km the Cantabrian mountains rim the north coast of Spain. Near the centre of the chain the highest mountains rise, forming the Picos de Europa. They are impressive, wild mountains, reaching 2648m in the Torre Corredo, and they are not too easy of access. There is a road which more or less rings them, and from this a number of rough branch roads partially penetrate the massif. The central parts can only be reached on foot.

From Santillana, at the north-east end of the Picos, one can travel to Altamira for the prehistoric cave drawings. Far more of an attraction for the orchid lover lies along the coast road via Comillas. *Serapias cordigera* abounds in fields at the roadside, to the extent that there is a dark purple tint to the ground in places. *Ophrys apifera* rivals it in numbers, with both varieties, *chlorantha* and *bicolor*, in some abundance.

From Panes one can travel to Potes, through some 24km of dramatic limestone gorge carved out by the rushing Rio Deva. The gorge is called the Desfiladero de la Hermida, and *Aceras anthropophorum, Barlia robertiana, Ophrys fusca, O. apifera, O. scolopax* and *Serapias cordigera* all grow here.

From La Hermida a small road goes to Reinosa via Puentenansa, and orchids are found here too. Again there is *Serapias cordigera*, which seems to find its favourite conditions in this part of the world, and its relative *S. lingua*. *Ophrys tenthedinifera* occurs, too, in almost as fine a form as in Andalucia. Others exploring the same region have found *Orchis provincialis* and *O. papilionacea*, both in unusually robust spikes.

Beyond Potes, on the road up to the Puerto de Piedrasluengas, the roadsides are full of spikes of *Himantoglossum hircinum*, growing even more freely than in Central France.

A very interesting collection of orchids occurs near the Parador Fuente Dé. It is a delightful place in peaceful pastures, overshadowed by huge cliffs – part of the Peña Vieja. For the mountain flower enthusiast a cable car takes one up to the top of the cliffs and one can walk to the Refugio de Aliva. From mid-June orchids appear near the Parador itself and they form an interesting mixture. First there are *Aceras anthropophorum*, *Gymnadenia conopsea*, *Ophrys insectifera*, *O. sphegodes* and *Orchis ustulata*, then a month or so later *Coeloglossum viride* and *Nigritella nigra* appear while *Epipactis atrorubens* is in flower on limestone screes.

Portugal

Algarve. The southern part of Portugal is a mixture of intense cultivation and wild land. The small towns are clean and one is left with an impression of neatness.

The Barrocal is the limestone zone of the Algarve, stretching in a thin curve from near Cape St Vincent in the west and disappearing north of Tavira in the east. Orchids are found in good numbers in this region. For example, between Benafim and Louie there are the familiar Mediterranean species: *Ophrys lutea*, *O. speculum*, *O. fusca*, *Orchis italica* and *O. papilionacea*. There is also that speciality of limestone in southern Portugal, *Ophrys speculum* ssp. *lusitanicum*. This is much more robust than the nominate race, with large, extended side-lobes to the flowers. It occurs with *Ophrys speculum*, and the difference between them is pronounced.

Serra da Arrabida. Another limestone region, lies in the west of the area. It is an isolated outcrop, running parallel to the coast and rising to 500m at its highest point. Orchids grow here, too, the same species as mentioned for the Barrocal.

Estoril. Near Lisbon lie the Cintra mountains in an isolated outcrop some 13km long. To the south of these mountains there are Cretaceous limestone where development has not occurred and where orchids might still be found. This is a region which the authors have not checked, but it seems that orchids did once abound there. A small booklet, *List of Plants Collected around Estoril*, published in 1910 by Lady Markham and her Friends, lists numerous species of flowering plants as well as the following orchids: *Ophrys sphegodes* ssp. *atrata*, *O. apifera*, *O. bertolonii*, *O. bombyliflora*, *O. lutea*, *O. speculum*, *Limodorum abortivum*, *Serapias lingua*, *Aceras anthropophorum* and *Cephalanthera longifolia*. Let us hope these have not all disappeared: the visitor to Portugal might find it worthwhile to check.

Majorca

The Balearic islands form one of the provinces of Spain. The best known are Majorca, Minorca and Ibiza, and for those in search of orchids Majorca is of the greatest interest because the mountains which dominate the island are Jurassic and Triassic limestone and the soils of the lower levels are calcareous.

In the spring (March to early April) there is a very good display of orchids in the lower-lying parts of the island. In the west the roadsides between Puigpunyent and the turn-off to Galilea are a good place to search. The road twists and turns up the mountain in a series of hairpin bends, and one need not stray far from the roadsides to find orchids. In fact, the scrub which lies beyond the edges of the roads is difficult to penetrate. Here, at about 300m altitude in April, the orchids to be found are those which are over on ground nearer the sea. *Serapias parviflora* is abundant (it tends to be one of the commonest orchids in Majorca) and occurs with *Serapias lingua*. *Ophrys speculum* is widespread and there are occasional specimens of *O. apifera* and *O. tenthredinifera*. *O. fusca* is represented by the nominate race and by ssp. *iricolor*, and the rather inconspicuous *O. bombyliflora* can be sought. The most handsome of the roadside orchids is undoubtedly *Ophrys bertolonii*, while under pines there are the no less impressive spikes of *Limodorum abortivum*. In early March *Barlia robertiana* can be found, but not in large numbers. *Aceras anthropophorum* occurs high up on the mountainside.

Orchids grow on the Alcudia peninsula, too. *Ophrys speculum* abounds on open ground, and the woods contain *Limodorum abortivum*. From Alcudia there is a road to Arta which passes between the coast and the extensive Albufera wetlands. On open dunes and in the pinewoods *Ophrys speculum*, *O. bombyliflora* and *O. apifera* are all to be found. *Serapias parviflora* abounds where the soil is poor, and *Serapias lingua* occurs less frequently. *Orchis coriophora* ssp. *fragrans* occurs on open ground throughout the area. In the wetlands themselves there are good colonies of *Orchis laxiflora* ssp. *palustris* growing near paths.

In woods in the Formentor peninsula the curious, small-leaved *Epipactis microphylla* flowers in May. *Orchis longicornu* occurs on the island, but in much smaller numbers than in Sicily or Sardinia and is, on the whole, rather uncommon. *O. mascula* ssp. *olbiensis* grows in the mountains.

The Canary Islands; Madeira

Politically speaking the Canary Islands belong to Spain and Madeira to Portugal. In terms of distance they are far closer to the African coast, and from a botanical standpoint they are unique. They have been isolated from any landmass for so long that they share a considerable number of endemic species. Fossils of leaves and fruits of plants found in the Mediterranean region and south Russia dating from the Miocene and Pliocene periods (up to 20 million years ago) are identical with species surviving in Madeira and the Canary Islands.

Some authorities have suggested that the islands arose independently from the sea-bed; others that they formed part of Africa. Volcanic rocks and ash dominate the landscape on these islands, and the usual Mediterranean orchids are absent. In fact the orchid flora is limited in numbers of species, but they are of considerable interest. The first, *Habenaria tridactylites*, is endemic to the Canary Islands and differs from all other orchids in this book. Its flowers are green and resemble some species of *Platanthera*, but the lip is deeply divided into three equal straps. It occurs from sea-level up to about 700m, usually on acid soil near forest cliffs and ledges. It is found on a number of the islands: on Tenerife it is locally common (Sierra Anaga, Icod el Alto, Barranco de Masca) and it also occurs on Gran Canaria, Gomera, Las Palmas and Hierro (forests of El Golfo). It comes into flower very early or very late, depending on one's viewpoint, for it flowers from November to January.

Another orchid, *Gennaria diphylla*, is known from Spain and north Africa and occurs with some frequency in laurel forests and on cliffs and banks on many of the islands (Tenerife, Las Palmas, Hierro and Gomera).

Neotinea intacta, a familiar Mediterranean orchid, occurs on the islands mentioned above, always in forest regions.

The second Canaries endemic is the rather delicate *Orchis canariensis*. This species grows in ravines and amongst thickets on undisturbed ground or in pine woodland between 800 and 1400m altitude on Tenerife (where it is frequent), Gran Canaria and Hierro.

Madeira has its own endemic, *Dactylorhiza foliosa*, an attractive pink marsh orchid with large-lipped flowers. Like many other members of the family it frequents marshy places. It is one of the few European orchids cultivated in gardens.

Corsica

The 'mountain in the sea' is the name by which the French island of Corsica has been known for a long time. A more apt title could not have been chosen, for the island is very mountainous, with the granite peak of Mt Cinto rising to a height of 2710m and six other peaks to over 2350m. The valleys are threaded by a spider's web of roads which makes travelling there an adventure, with dramatic views at every turn. Most people arriving in Corsica will land at either Calvi or Ajaccio, both places providing good centres for further exploration.

The island is famous for the thick maquis in which bandits still hide from the authorities. Along the coast from Calvi to Ajaccio this vegetation type is in evidence, with its thick tangle of bushes of *Arbutus unedo*, *Cistus* species, *Erica arborea*, *Pistacia lentiscus*, and the vicious *Calicotome spinosa* with its long spines.

Whenever the maquis gives way to open ground there is a good chance of finding orchids. Besides the common Mediterranean *Ophrys* species, such as *Ophrys fusca*, one can find *Orchis tridentata*, the unusual *Gennaria diphylla*, *Dactylorhiza sambucina* ssp. *insularis* and *Orchis papilionacea*. Corsica is perhaps unrivalled for its display of *Serapias*. These occur with the other orchids, in clearings in the maquis and on grassy hillsides.

If one arrives at Calvi and goes just to the north of the town, along the sweeping bay, *Serapias* are in evidence, on grassy slopes away from the road. The undoubted prize is *Serapias neglecta*. This gem of the orchid world has a low stature but large flowers, with lips in a range of shades from yellow, through orange to flesh pink or deep red. The taller *S. cordigera*, with its deep wine-coloured flowers, is frequent, and *S. lingua* completes the list of representatives of the genus in Corsica (*S. parviflora* is reported but we have not found it so far).

Numerous stops can be made on the route from Calvi to Ajaccio to take in the beauty of villages like Piana, near Porto, where again orchids are to be found. *Orchis pauciflora* is particularly good here. Diversions can be made into the hills where one can search for Corsican endemics.

Using Propriano in the south as a centre one can spend time exploring the country towards Bonifacio. Here the ground is less mountainous and the granite is replaced suddenly by calcareous rocks. Orchids abound on the calcareous peninsula, stretching towards the Bonifacio straits, and as well as those species earlier mentioned there are numerous *Ophrys*. The list is impressive, starting with the tiny *O. bombyliflora* and continuing with *O. speculum*, *O. fusca* and its ssp. *iricolor*, *O. lutea*, *O. sphegodes* (both the nominate race and ssp. *atrata*), *O. bertolonii*, *O. tenthredinifera* and the occasional *O. fuciflora* ssp. *exaltata*.

The hills and mountains must not be ignored, however, for here the orchids are later to flower than on the coast and one can find a number of different species, such as *Orchis mascula* ssp. *olbiensis*, *Orchis morio* ssp. *picta*, *Orchis provincialis* and, later still, *Epipactis microphylla*.

The orchids mentioned above are by no means a complete list, but will serve to give the reader the impression that a visit to Corsica is not to be missed.

Sardinia

Sardinia, one of the largest Mediterranean islands and belonging to Italy, is also one seldom visited by people in search of wild flowers. Although a mainly mountainous island with a wide range of soil types, it has much to offer the botanist. Its proximity to Corsica and Sicily means that it shares many plant species with them, including a wide range of orchids. In the south of the island, Cagliari is a reasonable centre from which to make trips on small roads threading into the surrounding mountains.

Several species of *Orchis* are widespread throughout the island and without doubt *O. longicornu* is at its best here, with forms including a red and white one. *O. papilionacea* is another plant occurring throughout the island on a wide range of soils but the magnificent var. *grandiflora* seems to be restricted to higher places on limestone soils. Wherever marshy meadows are encountered one stands a good chance of finding *O. laxiflora*, and *O. provincialis* is not unusual on dry calcareous soils. Near Laconia there are good populations of *O. lactea* which, although growing in many places in the island, is not as generally frequent as it is in neighbouring Sicily.

The mountain slopes of Monte del Gennargenta are the places to look for *Dactylorhiza sambucina* ssp. *insularis*, which flowers best from early May onwards.

The genus *Ophrys* is well represented here, as it is throughout the lands washed by the Mediterranean. The common component of the orchid flora is made up of *Ophrys lutea*, *O. fusca*, *O. bombyliflora*, *O. speculum* and *O. sphegodes* ssp. *atrata*. On suitable ground one can find *O. tenthredinifera*, and in one site in the south-east there are forms even larger than those in northern Spain.

Ophrys arachnitiformis is perhaps the most puzzling of all European *Ophrys*, not only for the wide variation in lip patterns shown within a single population, but also for the totally different forms embraced by the species. Forms from southern France are quite distinct from those in south-east Italy (Gargano) while those from Sardinia and Corsica are similar to one another but quite obviously different from other populations. Before the behaviour of this orchid is fully understood there will have to be much exhaustive field work.

Here, as in Corsica, there are numerous plants of the genus *Serapias*. Of these *S. parviflora* and *S. lingua* are widespread but *S. cordigera* is more plentiful along the north coast. The most attractive species, *S. neglecta*, also grows here but is not nearly as easily found as it is in Corsica.

Later in the year the mountain woodlands in the south provide a home for an interesting collection of orchids – *Cephalanthera longifolia*, *Epipactis helleborine*, *E. microphylla* and an occasional *Neottia nidus-avis*.

Ophrys lunulata is at the centre of a dilemma at present for, although reported for the island, it has not been rediscovered in spite of diligent searching. For the moment it seems to be mainly Sicilian but this is obviously subject to a change of opinion if the plant turns up in Sardinia as it has in Malta.

Sicily

The orchid flora of Sicily is as rich in numbers as that of Crete or Cyprus but, as in the latter island, goat-grazing has rendered much of the ground unsuitable for orchid growth. However, orchids still abound at roadsides and on more sheltered north-facing slopes, away from habitation.

Much of the island is dominated by limestone mountains, a continuation of the Apennines which form the backbone of Italy and which culminate in Sicily. In the north of the island, to the west of the Straits of Messina, one finds the Nebrodi, which merge with the Madonie around Collesano. The capital, Palermo, is dominated by the huge limestone rock of Monte Pellegrino.

In the early weeks of April a unique collection of orchids can be found in the Palermo region. Away from the bustle of the main roads tracks take one past roadside banks and cuttings where orchids flourish. Near Monreale one finds *Ophrys spruneri* ssp. *panormitana*, *O. sphegodes* ssp. *sicula*, stately spikes of *Orchis longicornu* and the dense-flowered *O. lactea*.

High up on the stone-strewn hillsides of the Piana di Moarda and further to the Piana degli Albanesi, *Orchis longicornu*, *O. lactea* and *O. tridentata* abound. The strange *Ophrys pallida*, obviously closely related to *O. fusca*, occurs in small numbers, its flowers remarkable for the pinched recurved lip. In the same area is another orchid with unusual flowers, *Orchis quadripunctata* var. *brancifortii*.

Near Palermo itself the slopes of Monte Pellegrino at Mondello hold *Ophrys bertolonii*, *O. lutea*, *O. speculum*, *O. arachnitiformis*, *O. bombyliflora* and *Orchis longicornu*. *Ophrys lunulata* has survived urban development, just hanging on in small numbers in one or two places. Fortunately it occurs more frequently around Syracuse, in the south-east of the island.

To the west of Palermo, out beyond the airport, lies Monte Palmeto. To reach the summit of the mountain one travels along a poor road which leads through flower-filled hillsides where *Ophrys speculum*, *O. bertolonii* and *O. tenthredinifera* thrive. The lucky researcher might even find one of the hybrids between them.

Moving from Cefalu and on to Collesano one reaches the Madonie, where orchids again flourish. Because of the increase in altitude they are best seen some two weeks after those at Palermo. The same species grow in both regions, and there is the possible bonus of *Ophrys fuciflora* ssp. *oxyrrhynchos* var. *lacaitae*, a great rarity with a large yellow lip, recorded from 'somewhere around Collesano'.

Ophrys fuciflora ssp. *oxyrrhynchos* proper was reported by Nelson from several localities around Palermo but its sites on Monte Pellegrino seem to have disappeared. It grows more frequently in the Monte Iblei region near Syracuse.

Because of its mountainous nature and poor secondary roads, distances covered in a day in Sicily are short, but one can be assured that wherever one travels in the limestone hills there are orchids to be found.

Maltese Islands

Some 93km south of Sicily lie the Maltese Islands. When the ice of the last glaciation retreated, the level of the Mediterranean rose and effectively isolated the islands from north Africa and Sicily.

Malta is the largest of the three islands, being some 27km long and 14.5km wide, with an area of 246sq km. Gozo is next, with an area of 67sq km, and tiny Comino has an area of barely one square mile.

The greater part of the surface of all the islands is limestone of various forms; either the rather soft yellow Globerigina type or the harder Corallian. In some places there is also an overlay of blue clay.

With a Mediterranean climate and limestone soils one might expect a good orchid flora, but a high population density and extensive cultivation for centuries have had a considerable effect.

Nonetheless, in early spring there seem to be flowers everywhere, and on the upper Corallian plateaux in the north and west of Malta there are many orchids to be found. The plateaux are rugged and exposed, with very little soil left except in fissures and the ancient 'cart-ruts', so tend to be largely uncultivated, but as elsewhere in the Mediterranean goats pose a threat to the survival of orchids.

A particularly good area is the Marfa Ridge in the north of Malta, a flattish promontory near the ferry embarkation facility at Marfa Point, where there is much interesting flora besides the orchids in exposed fields beside the road going along the promontory roughly eastwards. Another rewarding area is the flat, undeveloped ground above the western cliffs near Dingli, especially around a stone quarry a little to the south on a bluff called Gebel Cantar.

Gozo is more fertile than Malta and as a consequence much more of the island is cultivated and there are fewer wild plants. However, there is plenty of exposed limestone to explore around the coasts where orchids appear.

A comprehensive flora of the islands has been recently published (Haslam, Sell & Wolseley) and it lists some 25 species of orchid. Of these 12 are *Ophrys*, six *Orchis* and four *Serapias*.

Some of the special orchids are shared with Sicily; for example the small *Ophrys pallida*, closely related to *O. fusca*, has been recorded in a number of sites but it nowhere frequent. *O. lunulata* is reported here too from arid rocky places, a habitat it shares with *O. bertolonii*, *O. bombyliflora*, *O. fuciflora* and various forms of *O. sphegodes*.

Orchis tridentata and *O. saccata* are fairly frequent in rocky places but both *O. italica* and *O. longicornu* are rare here although often found in Sicily.

Anacamptis pyramidalis is found in two forms: the normal race, where bracts exceed the ovary in length, and a local form, var. *sommeriana* Borg., which has bracts shorter than the ovary.

Italy

In terms of its appeal to botanists, mainland Italy is often a third choice after the Balkan and Iberian peninsulas.

Though most often visited for the exceptional alpine flora of the Dolomites or the Aosta valley, springtime in the south can yield orchids in numbers and varieties to rival Greece or Spain.

Throughout the country there are large areas of calcareous soils on gentle hills to high mountains. In the far south one encounters a lot of calcareous sandstone and *terra rossa* but the orchids away from roadside banks and waste places are few and far between. Farmers are usually struggling to make a living in this region where there is a high degree of poverty and grazing is not controlled.

The varied terrain in Italy provides a wide range of habitats ranging from mediterranean to alpine, and if one follows spring from south to north the diversity of orchid species is remarkable.

Calabria

As one motors from Sicily through Italy's deep south the autostrada threads its way through Calabria, which forms the 'toe' of the boot-shaped Italian peninsula. It is a very hilly region, with a good deal of limestone and *terra rossa* soil. This combination is invariably a good one for orchid hunters, and Calabria is no disappointment. Roadside stops away from the autostrada quickly reveal *Orchis purpurea*, *O. italica*, *Ophrys lutea*, ssp. *lutea* and *O. sphegodes* ssp. *garganica*.

In the north of the region Monte Pollino rises to 2271m, and here one can find *Ophrys fuciflora* ssp. *exaltata* (plants here have been called *O. fuciflora* ssp. *pollinensis*), *Orchis tridentata*, *Orchis italica* and *Ophrys lutea*. The spring orchids are at their best on this mountain in late April.

Salerno

The province of Salerno is dominated by limestone hills which, at the coast, tumble into the sea and form a peninsula. Beyond lies the island resort of Capri.

The region is good for orchids, with *Ophrys fuciflora* ssp. *oxyrrhynchos* to be found in the hills near Salerno, and *O. fuciflora* ssp. *exaltata* near Positano and Castellamare di Stabia. To the south lies Paestum with its famed ruins and its no less impressive orchids: *Ophrys sphegodes* ssp. *sicula* is particularly good here.

Puglia

To the south-east of the Gargano peninsula and forming the 'heel' of Italy lies Puglia. Near the coast and at its southern end it is a flat, monotonous country with roads full of traffic heading towards the ports of Bari and Brindisi. In spite of this there are some particularly good sites for orchids on the rather sandy, calcareous soils of the area.

Around Lecce, Ostuni and Ceglie Messapico agriculture has destroyed much of the natural vegetation. But in old vineyards and on a few low hills orchids still flourish. *Orchis coriophora*, *O. italica*, *Ophrys lutea* and *Barlia robertiana* are worth looking for, but the specialities of the area are a range of forms of *Ophrys fuciflora*. They flower from the end of April into early May, when most of the other orchids have fruited and dried up. *O. fuciflora* ssp. *candica* is especially attractive, with large flowers and a square, whitish pattern on the lip. There are also green-sepalled forms of *O. fuciflora*, some of which are given subspecific status by Danesch in his book *Orchideen Sudeuropas* (e.g. *O. fuciflora* ssp. *celiensis*). Finally *Serapias vomeracea* ssp. *orientalis* occurs in its var. *apulica* form.

Gargano

The mountainous Gargano peninsula rises from the plains of northern Apulia and forms the spur to Italy's boot. Tourists are now becoming aware of its wooded white hills plunging down to a clear blue sea, but for the botanist it has always been an area of exceptional beauty. Orchids abound, and the stony fields and limestone pavements are full of dwarf yellow, white and blue irises.

In mid-April the hotels are empty, so one can stay on the coast and make forays into the mountains. Along the north of the peninsula, on the road to Peschici *Ophrys sphegodes* ssp. *garganica* is found in large numbers and in two forms. In the one form the petals are brown, in the other olive green. *O. arachnitiformis* is at its most confusing, with a bewildering range of flowers on robust stems.

Around Peschici many orchids are to be found, including *Ophrys bombyliflora*, *O. fuciflora* ssp. *apulica*, *O. tenthredinifera*, *Orchis italica*, *O. tridentata*, *O. papilionacea* and *Barlia robertiana*. From here one can cross the peninsula, via the Foresta di Umbra – a cool woodland haven where *Dactylorhiza sulphurea* ssp. *pseudosambucina* grows in both pink and yellow forms.

Where the woods end the stone-strewn hillsides are little grazed and the orchid flora is remarkable. In a small area *Aceras anthropophorum*, *Orchis morio*, *O. italica*, *Dactylorhiza sulphurea* ssp. *pseudosambucina*, *Ophrys tenthredinifera* and *O. bombyliflora* are all to be found. *O. fuciflora* ssp. *exaltata* is the special orchid here, its well-rounded labellum sporting a very pointed basal protuberance. The plant on Mt Gargano has been called *O. fuciflora* ssp. *sundermannii*, to distinguish it from the closely related form on Mt Argentario in the west of Italy. *O. fuciflora* ssp. *exaltata* is very variable and we think, from experience of it in the field, that there is little justification for splitting it even further. *Orchis purpurea* is particularly impressive in Gargano and occurs on the hills which rise from the roadside edges.

High up on the peninsula one finds Monte san Angelo. Stone-filled pastures near the picturesque town are full of the orchids already mentioned. From here to San Giovanni Rotondo the picture is the same, with orchids to be seen everywhere one stops. Towards the end of April one can find *Ophrys promontorii*, a plant which probably originated from hybrids between *Ophrys sphegodes* ssp. *garganica* and *O. bertolonii*. At this altitude orchid growth is at least some two weeks behind that near the coast.

Near the town of Manfredonia two more interesting orchids occur. The first is a rather robust form of *Serapias vomeracea* ssp. *orientalis*, its large, broad-lipped flowers distinguishing it as var. *apulica*. The second is perhaps the most striking form of *Ophrys sphegodes* one could wish to see. With pink sepals and large brown lip *Ophrys sphegodes* ssp. *sipontensis* is not easy to confuse with anything else. *Flora Europaea* cites it in the index as a form of *Ophrys arachnitiformis*, but we would not be so sure. It is an extremely local plant, growing in a few places with *Ophrys sphegodes* ssp. *garganica* and *O. sphegodes* ssp. *atrata*.

Mount Argentario

About 100km north-west of Rome lies a limestone pensinsula, much smaller in area than Mt Gargano but a haven for orchids, nonetheless. *Ophrys fuciflora* ssp. *exaltata* is the special orchid here, and it grows in large numbers. *Orchis provincialis*, *O. purpurea* and *O. morio* occur, too, with some of the more common *Ophrys*.

Liguria

The Ligurian Alps are the home of a rather rare orchid, *Orchis patens*. It is recorded from Crete and southern Spain, but it is only found in appreciable numbers in Algeria. Cretan forms are now *O. spitzelii* ssp. *nitidiflora*.

The coast between La Spezia and Sestri Levante is well developed for tourism – a fact which usually has disastrous effect on wild orchids. Thankfully orchids do persist and some most impressive *Serapias neglecta* flourish here, particularly near Sestri Levante. The colour forms range from yellow through orange to flesh pink or brick red. Other members of the same genus grow here too: *S. cordigera*, *S. lingua* and *S. parviflora*.

The Apennines
To the north and east of Rome lie calcareous hills. Further east these hills become the Abruzzi mountains, part of the Apennine range.

On low hills, where cultivation permits, a Mediterranean flora still persists. The orchids to be seen are: *Ophrys fuciflora* ssp. *fuciflora*, *O. bertolonii*, *Orchis purpurea*, *O. tridentata* and *O. italica*. On higher ground the orchid flora changes. Whether one is in the Tuscan Apennines, near Florence, in the Apuan Alps with their famous Carrara marble or in the Abruzzi, the orchid species occurring are the same: *Orchis morio*, *O. provincialis*, *O. purpurea*, *O. militaris*, *Dactylorhiza sambucina* (in both colour forms) and *Dactylorhiza sulphurea*.

In the Abruzzi, near Campo Imperatore, the rather rare *Orchis pallens* occurs.

The Northern Mountains
The mountains of northern Italy form the frontiers with its European neighbours. The more or less continuous chain is broken only by the area around the lakes which Italy and Switzerland share.

In the west the road from Turin takes one to Briançon in France and beyond to the Col du Lautaret (see p. 198). In the north-west lies Gran Paradiso, the highest mountain in Italy, much of it lying in a national park which adjoins the French park of Vanoise. The whole area is geologically varied, with calcareous schists, dolomite and gneiss present. In the lower parts of the valleys of this region the familiar 'alpine' orchids are fairly frequent: *Pseudorchis albida*, *Traunsteinera globosa*, *Nigritella nigra* and various forms of *Dactylorhiza maculata*.

Again in the north there are the Pennine Alps which separate Italy from the Valais in Switzerland. The flora is the same on both sides, and orchids occur here too.

Further to the east lies the Ortles and, near Bormio, good orchid country. Here there is a limestone region which includes the Val di Fraele and its two reservoirs. Among the orchids to be found are *Platanthera chlorantha*, *Gymnadenia conopsea* and the occasional *Cephalanthera rubra*.

Dolomites
In our opinion all these mountain areas pale in comparison with ‚the Dolomites in north-east Italy. Although they are lower than other mountains in northern Italy (reaching 3300m) the great pinnacles and castellations of rock seem to change colour with the sun, making a photographer's paradise. The region takes its name from the type of crystalline magnesian limestone which predominates, and the abundance of marine fossils indicates that the mountains were pushed up out of the sea bed some 200 million years ago.

More than a few European botanists maintain that the Dolomites are not to be surpassed by any other region of Europe for its wealth of wild flowers, and the alpine meadows certainly seem more flower-filled than anything on offer in either France or Switzerland.

Of course the limy nature of the soil means that orchids can thrive, and woods and meadows have a rich display. Indeed, *Cypripedium calceolus* was, at one time, more abundant here than anywhere else, but the picking of blooms to adorn the dining-tables of hotels and for sale in markets changed that. Fortunately good colonies of the plant still survive, away from the well-trodden paths.

If one has a car, the drive to the Rolle pass is worthwhile because one can travel through the Val Travignolo, near Predazzo. The roadside meadows are rich in flowers, with magnificent displays of both yellow and pink forms of *Dactylorhiza sambucina* in late June or early July. Earlier, *Orchis militaris* flourishes with *Gymnadenia conopsea* and *G. odoratissima* and numerous forms of *Dactylorhiza maculata*.

It is difficult to single out any one part of the region, for wherever one travels orchids can be found. Even when journeying along the main Dolomite road sorties along the branch roads into the surrounding countryside can often prove rewarding.

Lake Garda
The lake stretches from the Lombardy plain into the southern end of the Dolomites. At its southern end the hills are low, but at the northern end lie the Monte Baldo and Monte Tombe ranges. The wide range of altitudes and climate around the lake permit the growth of a wide range of plants, particularly orchids. *Orchis militaris* and *O. simia* frequently occur together. *O. coriophora* is found, and there are a number of *Ophrys*, such as *O. apifera*, *O. fuciflora* and *O. bertolonii*.

Yugoslavia

Yugoslavia is an amalgam of six republics, and shares its borders with Italy, Austria, Hungary, Romania, Bulgaria, Greece and Albania. Much of the country is mountainous, with limestone predominating.

The West Coast
Our first trips to Yugoslavia were made as students, more in search of the sun than flowers. As the train wound its way down from Ljubliana to Rijeka, one of the northern ports, we became aware of limestone country with promising-looking grassland and woods. Later visits, in spring rather than summer, proved that our early suspicions were well-founded: this was, indeed, orchid territory.

To the east of Trieste and just north of Rijeka lies a region of limestone hills. Here, on the grassy hillsides and at woodland edges, orchids abound. *Ophrys scolopax* ssp. *cornuta*, with its prominent horns, is particularly impressive here (and in many places along the Dalmation coast) and *Orchis morio* is abundant.

South of Rijeka the road winds along precipitous cliffs towards the walled resort of Dubrovnik. One cannot help being impressed by these cliffs of gleaming marble and then, realising that marble is a form of calcium carbonate (limestone), one naturally looks for orchids. Away from the cliffs there are extensive areas of hillside grassland, maquis and open pinewoods. Here one can find *Ophrys bombyliflora*, *O. fusca*, *O. fusca* ssp. *iricolor* and *O. lutea*. *Ophrys sphegodes* occurs in a number of places, as the nominate race and also the subspecies *litigiosa*, *atrata* and, more rarely, *tommasinii*. This latter race is restricted to the western coast of Yugoslavia and only just ventures into north-west Greece.

On nearing Dubrovnik one enters the province of Montenegro. Botanically it is a rich area, with the centre of interest for orchid lovers lying in the range of limestone hills (Mt Orjen) roughly east of Dubrovnik. In the hills *Ophrys scolopax* ssp. *cornuta* abounds, and also *Orchis morio*. Higher up *Orchis pallens* is frequent and there are occasional spikes of *Traunsteinera globosa*.

Our usual passage through Yugoslavia has been en route to Greece, a journey fraught with problems because of the driving habits of the road users. Skeletons of 'dead' vehicles are a familiar site along the main roads, and for those who botanise from the car it is advisable to get onto side roads. But be warned – the standard of roads in the hills can at best be described as 'poor'.

Macedonia

Macedonia is the name of the ancient territory partitioned by Yugoslavia, Greece and Bulgaria. Between Mavrovo and Ohrid there are orchids to be found. Near Mavrovo is a reservoir and roads, leading through woods to the hills, where *Orchis purpurea* flourishes. Near Lake Ohrid one can find *O. scolopax* ssp. *cornuta* and, a couple of months or so later, *Limodorum abortivum* flowers under pines near the roadside. The special orchid in this area is *Himantoglossum hircinum* ssp. *calcaratum*, which flowers in late May and early June. At its best this plant can be even taller and more robust than the nominate race, but most of the specimens we have seen look even more delicate – probably because the flowers are pink or reddish-violet, with their lizard tails deeply divided and spread out from the plant. *H. hircinum* ssp. *calcaratum* occurs along the roadsides south of lake Ohrid and in a number of other places in the region. Its distribution is nearly restricted to southern Yugoslavia and northern Greece.

The Julian Alps

North-west of Ljubliana lie the Julian Alps, forming part of Yugoslavia's border with Austria. This limestone range is best known for Mt Triglav (2863m), the highest peak in Yugoslavia.

From Bled and its lake one can make inroads into the wooded mountains and valleys. The area can be recommended for its *Cephalanthera rubra*. Spikes of this exquisite orchid occur frequently in its woods, especially near the lake. *Epipactis atrorubens* grows on open stony ground and at woodland edges, and *Cephalanthera longifolia* tends to be rather uncommon here, in comparison with *C. rubra*.

Greece & its islands

For the person whose holidays are restricted to two weeks of the year a springtime visit to the Greek mainland or to one of the numerous islands affords an unrivalled introduction to the orchid flora of the Mediterranean region.

On a first visit to mainland Greece most people are struck by the ruggedness of the scenery. Whether they arrive by road in the north or fly into Athens airport, hills and mountains are everywhere. The many hidden valleys in the country have provided a sort of isolation that has made the development of a rich endemic flora inevitable. In fact, over 800 endemics are claimed for Greece, with a total flora count of some 6,000 species, not including subspecies and varieties.

Dr Constantine Goulimis, one of the great authorities on the flora of Greece as well as the discoverer of many endemics in the last thirty years, has suggested that Greece, in proportion to her size, has more than fourteen times as many species as the USA. Indeed, with an area of 132,000 square kilometres and 6,000 species, Greece compares more than favourably with America which has 25,000 species of flowering plant in an area some sixty times larger.

The geographical position of Greece, coupled with her climatic conditions, has made it a recipient of flora contributed from all directions. There are not only many Mediterranean species but also a considerable number of Central European species and several from the European Alps too. This is well demonstrated in the orchid flora of Greece, with a list that includes many *Ophrys* species and forms as well as central European representatives, like *Orchis purpurea*, and 'alpines' like *Dactylorhiza sambucina* and *Nigritella nigra*.

Dr Turrill, in his classic *The Plant Life of the Balkan Peninsula*, attributes the richness of the Mediterrranean flora in Greece partly to the extensive deforestation which has been going on there since classical times, pointing out that the dry, stony ground which remained was eminently suitable for the growth and spread of xerophytic species.

Likewise many species have reached Greece from the Caucasus, Asia and Africa without spreading into western Europe, while a large contingent of species is found in northern Greece which appear in the northern Balkan countries but do not spread beyond.

Some of the endemic plants of Greece are relics of pre-glacial flora, probably from the Tertiary period, which perished in Europe in the Ice Age but were able to survive in Greece. These relicts represent a small proportion of the endemic flowers, with the majority having evolved 'where they stood'.

Much of the Greek landscape comprises limestone rocks or the soils such as *terra rossa* derived from them, so orchids thrive. More than one author has described Greece as a 'huge rock garden', a statement which few who have walked on the scrubby, boulder-strewn hillsides amidst orchids, anemones and the numerous bulbous plants, would dispute. Alas, some of the the classical sites have misguidedly been treated with weedkiller in recent years, much reducing their previous botanical interest.

When is the best time to come? For orchids the season starts in February in the south, the Peloponnese and many of the islands. Most of the orchids can be found in March and early April, and without too much effort it is possible to find and photograph 25 to 30 different kinds in a two-week stay.

In the mountains orchids flower later, and June to early July would be the time to arrange a holiday. As with most Mediterranean countries a mild or prolonged winter can advance or retard spring by several weeks, and although one might miss a particular orchid at its best because of the vagaries of the climate there will usually be a few stragglers which can be searched out on higher ground or in places away from the sun's direct glare.

Many people reckon that the richest finds of orchids are made on north-facing slopes away from the direct heat of the sun. This comes as no surprise to those who have stood on a Greek hillside under a July sun and seen the desiccated landscape: the comparison with the spring appearance is beyond belief. Most orchids need a summer 'baking' but there is a limit to what they can take before dehydration occurs and the tubers shrivel and die. This does not mean that orchids are not found on south-facing slopes, but we have always found the richest populations away from the full glare of the sun.

With so many hills and valleys to explore it is difficult to imagine any complete account of orchid-rich localities in Greece. Thus the places given are those which the authors and their friends have found particularly rewarding.

Athens
Athens itself is a dry, dusty city, full of tourists and taxi drivers: hardly the place to look for orchids – or so one might wrongly think.

Just a twenty minute bus ride from the centre of the city, on the lower slopes of Mt Hymettus, lies the cemetery and the chapel of Kaisariani. Here the noise and the heat of Athens are just a memory. The hillsides have been planted with cypresses and other trees by a dedicated group of people who refused to see the complete destruction of the wooded haven after its wartime deforestation. Thanks to them it is a place of peace unequalled in Athens. Under the trees, away from the road, orchids quickly begin to appear and one can find *Ophrys carmeli*, *O. sphegodes* ssp. *aesculapii* with its attractive yellow-bordered lip, *O. sphegodes* itself and *O. sphegodes* ssp. *mammosa*. *Ophrys ferrum-equinum* is magnificent here. A few plants of *O. speculum* are to be found but they are past their best when *O. ferrum-equinum* comes into its own. As one ascends Hymettus one passes through a natural rock garden, with the occasional wild tortoise for company. In this area there are *Ophrys scolopax* ssp. *heldreichii*, *Serapias vomeracea* and its ssp. *laxiflora*, while higher still *Orchis italica*, *O. pauciflora*, *O. quadripunctata*, *Ophrys fusca* ssp. *iricolor*, with its velvet lip and shining blue mirror, and *Barlia robertiana* are all to be found in the course of a few hours' walk.

Even if one has just a few hours between planes, the lower slopes of Hymettus are infinitely preferable to a stay in Athens airport.

Sounion

Just over 60km south of Athens, at the tip of the Attic peninsula, lies the famous temple of Poseidon, high on a promontory above the sea. It is a spot favoured by visitors from Athens and, judging by the queues of luxury coaches lining the approach road as the sun descends, a view of the sunset there seems to be *de rigueur* for tourists.

On the site itself around the temple there is little but well-trodden ground as the area has been thoroughly sprayed. However, just a short distance away there are ruins of a much smaller temple, dedicated to Athena. Here, in the surrounding scrub, there are a number of orchids growing, oblivious to the streams of visitors to the main site. *Ophrys carmeli*, *O. lutea* ssp. *murbeckii*, the tiny but curiously interesting *Ophrys bombyliflora*, *O. ferrum-equinum* and *O. fusca* all occur in the space of a few square metres.

Outside the site and away to the east *Ophrys lutea* var. *melena* is frequent in a large form, and there are small populations of two of the real beauties of the orchid world, *Ophrys tenthredinifera* and the wide-lipped form of *Orchis papilionacea*.

Delphi

Formerly known throughout the classical world for its oracle, Delphi is one of the most imposing of all the Greek sites. The sheer cliffs of Mt Parnassus tower above Delphi, and the vast chasm of the Pleistos gorge lies below, while beyond, towards the Gulf of Corinth, seemingly limitless olive groves stretch silvery grey in the bright sunlight.

Besides the paths leading to the stadium and in the stadium itself there is an abundance of wild orchids. *Barlia robertiana, Ophrys sphegodes* forms, the handsome *O. tenthredinifera* and the intriguing *O. speculum* all occur in appreciable numbers. Erich Nelson, in his superb monograph on the genus *Ophrys*, has painted the 'faces' of some very unusual forms of *O. argolica* from the Delphi region, thus adding to the list of species found here.

The Peloponnese

The toll road to the south-west of Athens takes one to the Gulf of Corinth and beyond to the plains and mountains of the Peloponnese. However the old road to Corinth, although longer, is a more attractive route for the enthusiast since it affords the chance of roadside stops for orchids such as *Orchis papilionacea, Ophrys tenthredinifera, O. lutea* and *O. ferrum-equinum*. Many of the famous place-names of the ancient world (Epidavros, Olympia, Mycenae and Sparta) still exist as towns or as the site of the ruins of their former glories.

It takes a week at least to sample the variety of places where orchids are found, and the countryside surrouding the ancient sites provides many good places to begin.

Olympia lies on a low site which becomes very wet in winter, and there is a host of flowers to be found. The low, heathy hills around are full of orchids such as *Ophrys fusca, O. lutea* and superb specimens of *Orchis simia*.

In the hills behind the citadel at Mycenae there are orchids a-plenty, provided you get there before the goats do! There is a particularly good form of *Ophrys lutea* noted here by a number of people.

On the road leading up to the site of the enormous amphitheatre at Epidavros there are patches of scrub where the olives do not reach. Many orchids grow in these places, but a special prize is *Ophrys argolica*. Although a form ssp. *elegans* exists in Turkey and Cyprus, *O. argolica*, as its name suggests, has its main distribution in Argolis. It is an attractive plant with a variety of lip markings ranging from white-bordered blue eyes to two stripes on a chestnut background. When it occurs with *O. ferrum-equinum* the population ranges through strange intermediate forms between the types.

At Mistras, it was our good fortune to arrive in the driving rain of an early spring storm. The whole area was shrouded in grey mist and we had no idea of the lie of the land until, from the window of our hotel room, we saw the mists rise to reveal the towers of the Byzantine ruins on the steep, lush hillside. From a distance it is difficult to tell where the modern village ends and the ancient begins, so complete are some of the buildings and so imposing the setting.

The site itself is a haven for orchids, with the *Ophrys* stealing the show in the weeks before they are swamped by lush grass, filled with poppies and a bewildering array of other flowers. There are abundant forms of *Ophrys sphegodes*, with ssp. *mammosa* in fine form and the closely related but now separately classified *O. spruneri* also in evidence. *O. argolica* is there too, but the finest forms are along the roads, away from the ruins, where they occasionally provide some identification problems when found with one or two unexpected plants of *O. reinholdii*. *O. argolica* can be remarkably similar to a particular form of *O. reinholdii* that has an eye pattern on the lip, although in most cases the distinctly three-lobed lip of *O. reinholdii*, with the strongly reflexed side-lobes, distinguishes it from the entire-lipped *O. argolica*. Just to complicate matters further, large populations of *O. argolica* show the very occasional plant whose flowers are three-lobed!

Above the village of Mistras lies a deep gorge, dominated by the snow-capped bulk of the main ridge of the Taygetus mountains. The Parori gorge, as it is called, is a delightful place for an evening walk for anyone staying at Mistras. The path takes one above a torrent to one of the most flower-filled places we have seen. Scarlet anemones, cyclamen and a host of other flowers fill the picture, and inevitably there are orchids too. *Orchis simia* occurs along the path, while on the disused terraces further on *Ophrys spruneri* grows as the dominant orchid.

Unfortunately the annual beauty of this gorge and the valley beyond is transient, for goatherds from a village high up in the valley bring their flocks this way.

South of Sparta lies Gythion, at the head of the middle finger of the Peloponnese, called the Mani. The countryside en route to Gythion is good for orchids being, for the most part, scrub on calcareous soils. Here, just beyond Gythion itself, one can find *Ophrys carmeli*, *O. speculum*, *Orchis italica* and many others.

The Mani beyond Gythion is wild country with a number of endemics to its credit and, moreover, it is orchid country. Most of the usual orchids of the Greek spring are here, together with a few 'specials', such as *Ophrys reinholdii* and a number of forms of *O. fuciflora* including the rather rare ssp. *candica*.

The modern fishing-port of Pylos is near the site of the famous Nestor's palace, and here *Ophrys speculum* and *Orchis coriophora* ssp. *fragrans* occur. Away from the site, in the surrounding countryside, there are some magnificent populations of *Ophrys ferrum-equinum* and *O. argolica*, with a whole spectrum of intermediate forms where they occur in close proximity.

The Mountains of the Greek Mainland
The lower slopes of the Greek mountains possess the invariable rich orchid flora of the Mediterranean spring, wherever the soils are calcareous. The lowland flowers include many of the orchid species mentioned in connection with Mt Hymettus near Athens, but higher up, in May and June, the picture changes to include a number of species often found in Central and Western Europe. *Orchis purpurea*, *Neottia nidus-avis*, *Cephalanthera rubra* – all find a place to suit their needs on the mountains. Even *Nigritella nigra* and

Dactylorhiza sambucina (more familiar to wanderers in the Alps) are found in a handful of places.

Mount Olympus. Of the many mountains so named in Greece and the Islands, none is as magnificent as the best-known Thessalian Olympus whose many peaks were reputedly the home and playground of the ancient gods, and from whose lofty heights vengeful Zeus hurled his thunderbolts on those foolhardy persons who incurred his wrath.

The middle slopes of Olympus are well-wooded, with large areas of beech trees where, on the north-east slopes of the mountain, in the Prionia area, *Epipactis helleborine* and the saprophytic *Limodorum abortivum* flower together in the early days of June.

A little later, the beechwoods shelter the pink spikes of *Cephalanthera rubra* and the honey-brown *Neottia nidus-avis*.

Mount Boz-Dag (Mt Phalakron), lying in eastern Macedonia, must not be confused with another of the same name, also in Macedonia. With its highest peak rising to 2229m and enclosing a snow-filled crater or snowpit in which the snow is said never to melt since it lies in perpetual shade, Boz-Dag has been a magnet for botanists in recent years, all of whom are attracted by its rich and varied flora.

Unfortunately the mountains are often mist-covered and the mountain flowers are thus hidden, but when the sun does shine through the mist *Nigritella nigra* and *Gymnadenia conopsea* can both be found.

A subspecies of *Himantoglossum hircinum*, ssp. *caprinum*, is a rare plant , found in small numbers on Boz-Dag in the area around Moni Prodhromou.

In early May, on the road north of Granitis, *Orchis pauciflora* can be found in very good colonies, but the special orchid here is *O. purpurea* which produces very large spikes.

The Pindus Range. In mid-May in the Katara pass, at about 1700m and where there are thick bushes of box growing, one can find a number of orchids. *Orchis ustulata* can often be a rather insignificant plant because of its diminutive size, but here the plant seems to do rather better. *Dactylorhiza sambucina*, the so-called Elderflower Orchid, is found in both purple and yellow forms.

In the same area, north of Metsovo, there are valleys covered with forests of beech and mountain pine where, in recent years, *Epipogium aphyllum* has been rediscovered in the litter under the beech trees. This orchid is widespread, but everywhere rare. It flowers irregularly wherever it occurs and seems to do better after a wet spring. It is easily overlooked because in the half-light of its chosen habitat it blends well with the beech litter.

On the northern ridges of some of the Pindus ravines *Cephalanthera rubra* grows with one of the more attractive *Epipactis*, *E. atrorubens*.

The yellow *Orchis provincialis* can be found in drifts in grassy areas in southern Pindus near Katerini.

Peloponnese. Mount Taygetus has already been mentioned in connection with Mistras, which lies on the lower slopes. The orchid flora mainly occur in spring on the lower ground, but it is possible to find a number of the same orchids growing later in the year higher up.

On the northern slopes of Mt Chelmos in the western Peloponnese lies a valley which is wild and desolate and strangely attractive. The ancient Greeks were strongly affected by this place, for the river Styx and its waterfall had sufficient impact on their superstitious beliefs to have become the barrier which the dead had to cross in order to enter the Elysian Fields, on their way to the underworld. There are a number of orchids to be found, but the most noteworthy is a large-flowered Dactylorchid, known as *Dactylorhiza cordigera*. The flowers are deep rose-red to magenta in colour and have a very wide heart-shaped lip.

Rhodes
The flora of Rhodes bears a close resemblance to that of south-west Turkey which is hardly surprising since Rhodes, the easternmost of the Greek islands, is only 20 km off the Turkish coast. It is some 80km long by 30km wide, and although it does not have any really high mountains it is certainly hilly, with Mt Ataviros rising to 1215m and the well-wooded Mt Profitis Elias to 798m.

Because of its proximity to the Turkish coast, Rhodes enjoys a warmer spring and winter climate than Crete, which means that the orchid flora of the lower regions can be well past their best as early as the middle of April.

As well as *Ophrys lutea* ssp. *murbeckii*, *O. carmeli* and *O. fusca* ssp. *iricolor*, all of which are a common element of the orchid flora of the island, Rhodes possesses a number of species and forms belonging principally to the eastern Mediterranean region. These are *Ophrys fuciflora* ssp. *maxima*, *O. speculum* var. *regis-ferdinandii*, *O. reinholdii* and *Orchis sancta*.

For the visitor, one of the most worthwhile trips to take is from the medieval walled town of Rhodes, along the northern coast, and then into the hills leading to Mt Profitis Elias. As soon as one turns away from the coast and the sandy soil there orchids become apparent in the grass and scrub away from the raodside.

The most obviously striking flowers are those of *Ophrys fuciflora* in the form sometimes called ssp. *maxima* because of the size of the large, rounded lip (up to 2cm in length) and the spreading pink tepals. A similar form is found on Crete and on the mainland of western Turkey but it is especially on Rhodes that the greatest variety of labellum markings is seen. *Ophrys fuciflora* ssp. *candica* is also reputed to occur in Rhodes but none of the authors has seen it growing there. *O. fuciflora* ssp. *bornmuelleri* is also found on the same mountain and, in drier places, the curious *O. speculum* var. *regis-ferdinandi*, its pinched labellum and exaggerated side-lobes giving it a realistic 'bluebottle' appearance. This orchid is not rare on Rhodes but it flowers early and is small enough to be inconspicuous.

Higher up Profitis Elias, in the woods, large forms of *Limodorum abortivum* are common, while white forms of *Anacamptis pyramidalis* and good spikes of *Ophrys reinholdii* are not difficult to find. Recently *Comperia comperiana* has been found in small numbers under pines on the mountain.

In later weeks both *Orchis sancta* and *Serapias vomeracea* ssp. *laxiflora* are evident everywhere in the rapidly drying grassy places.

South of Rhodes lies the famous citadel of Lindos which is an excellent site for orchids, with good forms of *Ophrys fusca* ssp. *iricolor*, *O. sphegodes* ssp. *mammosa* and *O. ferrum-equinum* to be found. Lindos is unfortunately overrun with trippers at holiday times so, in order to see orchids in flower before trampling and sun-scorching have taken their toll, late March is a reasonable time for a visit.

The area south of Lindos is little frequented by tourists, so searches here could result in good finds, assuming one arrived early enough in the year.

Samos

Two mountains, Kerketus (1436m) and Ambelos (1140m), visible from afar, are the first sights to greet the traveller. As one approaches the island the greenness and lush vegetation comes as a shock to anyone accustomed to the drier islands of the south, such as Rhodes or Crete.

Samos has a number of spring-fed streams which tumble down steep hillsides through cool woods of sweet chestnut, oriental plane and white poplar. On lower ground, near the coast, there are marshy areas, particularly near the temple of Hera – once one of the wonders of the ancient world but now sadly reduced to a single standing column, with the remains of the rest strewn around. In the adjacent marshes *Orchis laxiflora* ssp. *palustris* grows in impressive pink spikes, of a size seldom found elsewhere (the so-called *Orchis robusta*). Orchids abound in the spring in Samos, with *Ophrys speculum*, *O. lutea* ssp. *murbeckii* and various forms of *O. scolopax* seemingly everywhere.

Early May is the best time to see the flowers of the mountains, especially on Mt Ambelos (also called Mt Karvouni) where there are mainly beautiful treasures, apart from the rich orchid flora. Here one can find *Orchis anatolica*, *O. simia* and *Dactylorhiza sulphurea* ssp. *pseudosambucina* together with a number of *Ophrys*, including *Ophrys reinholdii* in quantity.

Lesbos

Lesbos, a green and peaceful island, has not suffered from tourists in the same way as Rhodes and Crete. It remains an island for the connoisseur, a place of flowers, woodlands, hills, countless olive trees and sea.

The springtime orchid flora is rich in much the same way as that of Samos, with a wide variety of *Ophrys* and *Orchis* and the marshy places holding large spikes of *Orchis laxiflora* ssp. *palustris*.

In June Mt Olympus holds a special attraction in *Comperia comperiana*. This extremely rare orchid is better known from Turkey, parts of Syria and Iran, and represents an Asian infiltration into the flora of Europe. It is an intriguing plant, unlike any other orchid found in Europe, with distinctive long four-whiskered lip and attractive colouring of magenta and brown/green.

Crete
Any visitor to the museum in Heraklion, the largest town in Crete, soon realizes that flowers were of great importance to the Minoan people. Their mosaics are frequently decorated with flowers and these were surely inspired by the floral wealth around them.

The floral richness of Crete is no less impressive today, for the island possesses elements of western and eastern Mediterranean floras as well as over 20 endemics and a total of some 2,000 species of flowering plants. This gives Crete roughly the same number of plants as the British Isles, despite the fact that the latter's territory is about 35 times larger than Crete.

The orchid flora of Crete is rich, with an exceptionally fine display of *Ophrys* on the low ground in early spring. Late March is probably the best time to visit the lowlands, while May and June will see the mountains at their best.

The exact timing of a visit is not too critical, for one can always take to the hills when the lowlands are past their floral peak and still find orchids in flower. However, a short, wet winter can make a big difference to the flowering times of the spring orchids: one can arrive in Crete at the beginning of April and find that the early *Ophrys* and the lovely long-lipped form of *Orchis papilionacea* which, during a previous visit, were so much in evidence at this time, are now past their best, having given way to a display of later *Ophrys* and *Serapias*.

If one follows botanical protocol, the start of a visit should be in the east of the island, for that is where spring comes first. One can then move 'with the spring', first westwards and later into the mountains.

Most visitors to Crete arrive in Heraklion and here the voyage of discovery can begin in earnest. Just outside Heraklion lies Knossos and the famous restorations for which Sir Arthur Evans is either responsible or guilty, depending on taste. Beyond Knossos the road goes to Archanes and thence to Mt Jouktas. Here, in the garigue on the hillside, there are many orchids. Early to flower is *Ophrys fusca* ssp. *omegaifera*, followed by *O. fusca* ssp. *iricolor*, two forms of *Ophrys lutea* and the occasional *Ophrys cretica*.

To the east the main road takes the traveller past a number of archaeological sites, all of which are worth exploring for their orchids. The first, at Gournia, is a small town set on a low hill overlooking the sea. Here, outside the town wall, there are *Ophrys* to be found, as well as the distinctive large fleshy flowering stems of *Barlia robertiana*. Further along the road lies Mallia (again worth a visit) and, near to Aghios Nikolaos, the strikingly situated site of Lato. This must be one of the most flower-filled of the Cretan sites and although there are, of course, orchids to be seen – notably *Orchis quadripunctata* – it is the wealth of other wild flowers that will remain in the memory.

Further east lies Zakros, a comparatively recent addition to the dis- covered sites in Crete and well worth a visit, since the scrub-filled hills around the site are ideal orchid country.

On the way back to Heraklion lies the road to the Lassithi plateau. Strictly speaking this should be visited later in April because of its elevation but it is 'on the way back' and convenient to include in a general discussion of the area. The Lassithi plain, with its claimed ten thousand windmills, is virtually an alluvial plain where the run-off from the northern slopes has deposited a thick fertile soil. As a result it is heavily cultivated and well populated by Cretan standards. Around the edges of the plain, where the plough does not reach, there are orchids in the shape of *Ophrys fusca*, *O. fusca* ssp. *omegaifera*, *Ophrys lutea* and the striking *Ophrys tenthredinifera*, held by many to be the loveliest of the *Ophrys* tribe (although its specific name, taken from an unimpressive earth wasp, is less than flattering): *Orchis* are represented here by *O. coriophora* ssp. *fragrans*, *O. papilionacea* and the delicate yellow *O. pauciflora*.

At the southern edge of the plain lies the Dhikti cave, the legendary birthplace of Zeus, which is most conveniently reached from the village of Psykhro. On the path up to the cave all the orchids previously mentioned in connection with the plain are again to be found.

Once back in Heraklion the next route should be south, over the moun- tains, to Timbaki, taking in Aghia Varvara, Mires, the incomparable ancient site of Phaestos and its close neighbour, Aghia Triada.

Aghia Varvara, situated some 28km from Heraklion, has some attractive scrub-filled hills nearby. Here, on the north-facing slopes, there is an abundance of orchids. At the end of the village there is a road leading to Kamares which is a convenient point from which to start the ascent of Mt Idha or from which one can reach the Kamares cave. In this region, the endemic helleborine *Cephalanthera cucullata* has its headquarters. It is not an imposing plant: indeed, its rather dingy flowers pale into insignificance if compared with cousins such as *C. rubra* and *C. kurdica*, and it is perhaps best described as 'quietly' rather than 'obviously' attractive. There is a pink form which is even more uncommon than the cream.

Continuing south from Aghia Varvara one comes out of the hills to see the fertile Mesaoria plain stretching out below. On the plain the road goes through Aghia Dheka to Mires. On the hills near Mires a very interesting form of *Ophrys fuciflora*, called *O. fuciflora* ssp. *candica*, is to be found. It is certainly not present in large numbers but is well worth searching for.

Phaestos, a few kilometres beyond Mires and the site of a famous Minoan palace, holds a special place in our affections because it was here, armed with a copy of Polunin & Huxley's *Flowers of the Mediterranean*, that we (P. & J.D.) were first overwhelmed with the abundance of Mediterranean orchid flora. It is the ideal place for any novice to start, not only because of the wealth of orchids but also because one can see where they grow: for instance, which orchids prefer the drainage at the top of a slope, which the bottom, which relish the dry, scrubby areas and which flourish in lush, grassy places. One will quickly notice how localized populations of orchids can be: for example *Ophrys cretica* will be abundant over a small area but outside that the next population might be some considerable distance away, with no stragglers in between.

In the hillside scrub, on a north-facing slope between the palaces of Phaestos and Aghia Triada, the following can be found: *Orchis italica*, with particularly massive spikes, *O. simia*, *O. papilionacea*, *O. saccata*, *Ophrys fusca*, *O. fusca* ssp. *iricolor*, *O. fusca* ssp. *omegaifera*, *O. tenthredinifera*, *O. scolopax* ssp. *cornuta*, *O. bombyliflora*, *O. spruneri*, *O. sphegodes* ssp. *mammosa* and *O. cretica*. The last-named orchid is a very striking plant which, on our early visits to Crete, always seemed to possess stable labellum patternings but which on later visits appeared to have 'gone mad', with many specimens having their patterns reduced to black and white, and no trace of any other colour. *O. cretica* is not an endemic, as its name suggests, but occurs also on Naxos and Karpathos to the east of Crete. Erich Nelson has identified two separate races (ssp. *naxia* and ssp. *karpathensis*), and it has been suggested that it previously occurred in Attica on Mts Penteli, Hymettus and Lycabettos in Athens itself.

Slightly later than the main flood of *Ophrys* come the *Serapias*, with *Serapias vomeracea* and its two subspecies *laxiflora* and *orientalis* all present in large numbers. The last-named is also present in a form called var. *cordigeroides*. The curious dense-flowered *Neotinea intacta* is found locally in the scrub and, early in the year, *Barlia robertiana* also occurs.

After Phaestos there is a danger that anywhere else will be an anticlimax – anywhere, that is, except the Samaria Gorge, deep in the White Mountains to the west. To get there one can travel from Phaestos to Rethymnon via Spili and en route find spikes of *Orchis laxiflora* ssp. *palustris* in the damper places. Eventually one comes to Chania, a good centre for exploration of this part of the island. From Chania the road climbs through the interior to the high Omalos plateau, famous for its access to Faranghi Samaria – the Samaria Gorge. One can make the descent into the gorge and walk to the south coast where a boat will take one back to Chora Sfakion. From the tourist pavilion at the top of the Xyloskalon (wooden ladder) one has a choice of either searching for alpines in the mountains above (May and June are best for this) or descending into the gorge. In April the wind can howl over Omalos but, safe in the depths of the gorge, the orchids are in flower. As well as the usual Cretan display of common orchids there are many *Orchis pauciflora* under the pines at the bottom of the gorge, while down beyond the deserted chapel of Samaria there are *Ophrys tenthredinifera* and various forms of *O. fuciflora*.

Back at Chania itself there are good places to visit: a short walk to the east of the town, past the tanneries, brings one to an area of coastal scrub where *Ophrys fusca* ssp. *iricolor*, *O. tenthredinifera*, *Serapias lingua* and *S. vomeracea* are among a good selection available to the diligent explorer. The Akrotiri peninsula itself, further to the east, is good for orchids but some of it is used for military purposes and is therefore inaccessible.

Later in the year, in June, there are orchids to be found high in the mountains. Perhaps in some of the hidden gorges there are new species to be found. This is not a wild dream, for just a few years ago a variety of *Himantoglossum hircinum* was found at Kloumoussi which may have been ssp. *caprinum* – the form usually found in southern mainland Greece.

Corfu

The position of Corfu at the very north-west corner of Greece, opposite its frontier with Albania and at one point only 3km away from that country, makes it the wettest and hence one of the lushest places in Greece, with an annual rainfall of 114cm. Despite many new roads and hotels and a big annual influx of tourists, there are large unspoilt tracts where wild flowers abound, including orchids which reach a total of 44 species. The peak month is April.

An unexpected place to start orchid-hunting is the old British cemetery in Corfu town itself. This is south-west of Theotaki Square on the road running in that direction to the airport and the south of the island. About 200m from the square the small, rough Kolokotroni Street forks left, and 50m up it, on the left, is the entrance to the cemetery. The War Graves Commission ensures that the garden-like setting of some fascinating nineteenth-century monuments, among pines and cypresses is preserved, and at the time of writing the local guardian is passionately interested in the orchids which grow in both grass and pathways. These include five species of *Ophrys*, *Orchis italica* and some rather sickly *O. simia*, *Serapias lingua* and *S. vomeracea* ssp. *laxiflora*, *Anacamptis pyramidalis* and the Giant Orchid, *Barlia robertiana*.

North of Corfu town Ipsos is a very popular beach resort in summer, but few tourists penetrate behind the narrow strip of buildings. Here woodland and small meadows contain many orchids. *Ophrys* abound: there are *O. bombyliflora*, *O. ferrum-equinum*, *O. scolopax* and its long-horned subspecies *cornuta*. and it was here, within a hundred yards of the beach, that one of us found *O. bertolonii* in 1979, a new record for Greece. *Orchis italica,* *Cephalanthera longifolia* and *Epipactis helleborine* grow on dryer slopes and tall spikes of *Orchis laxiflora* in damper places, with here and there *Serapias lingua.*

North of Ipsos rises Corfu's highest mountain, Mt Pantokrator, reaching 906m. After a long series of hairpin bends the road becomes less twisty beyond the village of Spartilas, and a stop on its flatter reaches around here is worthwhile for *Orchis morio* ssp. *picta, O. quadripunctata* and massive *Barlia robertiana* among others. The actual summit is reached from the village of Strinilas along a narrow track which is passable by car; it is well worth walking this since many orchids grow along it. On the summit spur itself, from which the daunting looking mountains of Albania can be seen, there are a few clumps of *Ophrys reinholdii;* nearer Strinilas many *O. tenthredinifera.* All along the trackway a fine form of Man Orchid, *Aceras anthropophorum,* with rich brown helmet can be seen along with *O. italica, O. saccata* and *O. quadripunctata,* with here and there on the rocks yellow spikes of *O. provincialis,* which can indeed be found all over the northern mountainous region.

A smaller, less-frequented peak is that of Ayii Deka (576m) south of Corfu town, near the village of that name. A path leads to a small deserted monastery with old vineyards on the summit, and a display of orchids similar to that on Pantokrator can be found, together with *Orchis lactea.*

At the very northernmost tip of the island, around the salt-water lagoon called Lake Antionioti near the hamlet of Ayios Spiridon, there is the most amazing quantity of *Serapias.* A form of *S. cordigera* with markedly heart-shaped lip is notable, together with *S. neglecta* ssp. *ionica, S. vomeracea* and its ssp. *laxiflora, S. lingua* and a variety of apparently intermediate forms guaranteed to make your head swim after attempting to identify them. Here too one sees *Ophrys fusca, Orchis laxiflora,* and the distinctly ugly Corfiot form of *Orchis papilionacea* with markedly narrow lip (plate 135).

The north coast, which has long sandy stretches, will reveal other concentrations of *Serapias,* for instance west of the curious Canal d'Amour at Sidari, but none so mind-boggling as those at Antinioti.

A roadside stop or ramble along paths almost anywhere in Corfu will reveal orchids; one particularly pleasant stroll is between Kavos and the quaint deserted monastery of Pantatika at the southern tip of the island. Among orchids not mentioned before are *Limodorum abortivum,* to be seen for instance on the coast near Agios Matteos and along with *Orchis papilionacea, Serapias cordigera* and others around Kouloura Bay, where Lawrence Durrell's villa may be visited; *Dactylorhiza sulphurea* ssp. *pseudosambucina* is among finds on the path from Kouloura to Agios Stefanos, and *Orchis coriophora* ssp. *fragrans* in the rather unpromising terrain near the Alikes saltpans.

Turkey

Western Anatolia

The part of the Turkish coast near the Greek islands of Chios and Lesbos is a good place to start looking for wild flowers. *Cephalanthera epipactoides* grows in pinewoods around Izmir, on the nearby peninsula, out towards the seaside resort of Cesme, and also inland. *Comperia comperiana* is nowhere a common plant, but it grows in small numbers under pines in this region, in greater quantities near ancient Troy and also under the extraordinary calcite terraces of Pamukkale. The small form of *Ophrys speculum*, var. *regisferdinandii*, grows to the south of Izmir, and so does *O. reinholdii*, one of the most attractive of the *Ophrys*. Further south in Anatolia, from Mersin eastwards, *O. reinholdii* ssp. *straussii* replaces the type plant.

In the countryside around Maras one can find the lax-flowered *Himantoglossum affine*. In appearance it is rather like the recently named *H. adriaticum* and must rank as one of the rarer orchids described in the book. It grows on calcareous soils in open pinewoods and in oak scrub.

Not all the orchids found in the area make such exciting finds as those mentioned above. *Ophrys carmeli*, *O. scolopax* ssp. *orientalis* and *O. fuciflora* ssp. *bornmuelleri* are orchids with a wider distribution, found throughout southern and western Turkey wherever there are calcareous soils and grazing is not severe.

Southern Anatolia

Behind Mersin the snow-capped Taurus mountains rise steeply to well over 3000m. On clear days they are even visible from parts of Cyprus, some 70 miles distant.

In the lower hills there are extensive forests and valleys where one can find *Comperia comperiana* growing on slopes under pine trees, often in the company of *Limodorum abortivum*.

Around Mersin *Ophrys sphegodes* ssp. *amanensis* occurs: it has a bright pink perianth, but *Flora Europaea* groups it with *O. sphegodes* ssp. *sintenisii*, a plant with greenish-brown tepals.

In the province of Diyarbakir in south-east Anatolia grows one of the rarest of all the orchids mentioned in the text. It was discovered by Ruckbrodt, and a paper was written on it in 1975. Its name is *Ophrys kurdica* and it seems to be related to *O. kotschyi* and *O. cretica*. It has been found in only a few sites, growing in damp grassland or hillside seepages.

In eastern Anatolia, east of lake Van, flat marshy areas are full of purple spikes of *Dactylorhiza cilicica*, accompanied by a yellow *Pedicularis*.

Turkey is also the home of the very rare *Ophrys schulzei*. This is the earlier, and therefore accepted name of *O. luristanica*. It has been recorded on both sides of the border with Syria, near Antioch and Alexandretta, flowering in May and June on high ground above 800m.

In the same area, near the pass over the Amanus mountain from Antioch to Iskenderun, the imposing pink spikes of *Cephalanthera kurdica* are found in sizeable clumps in coniferous woodlands. Refugee camps now occupy one of the spots where both *O. schulzei* and *C. kurdica* used to grow, and the future of both plants is far from secure.

The last of the rarities to be mentioned, *Steveniella satyrioides*, grows in the Pontus region and is rather insignificant looking with green flowers.

Although some of the rarest of our orchids grow in Turkey, travellers are often disappointed that the display of plants does not rival that of the Greek islands or the Peloponnese. In addition, goat-grazing and peasant agriculture have so decimated orchid populations that one often has to travel great distances in order to find viable orchid sites.

Cyprus

Cyprus, the third largest of the Mediterranean islands, is at a botanical crossroads. Its proximity to its nearest neighbours, Turkey, Syria, Lebanon, Israel and Egypt, gives its flora a distinctly Eastern flavour, although it has been long enough separated from the mainland masses to have established a strong endemic flora. Also present are a great many plants more familiar in places in the western Mediterranean region.

For a small island Cyprus has a very varied topography and a correspondingly rich flora (about 1500 species, of which 75 or so are endemics, in an area comparable to that of Wales). Spring arrives early here, the first orchids appearing in the first week of January and some species continuing to flower in the mountains until July.

The island is dominated by two mountain ranges. In the Turkish-held north lie the limestone hills of the Kyrenia range, their north-facing slopes and mountain pathways rich in orchids; in the south-west there is the Troodos massif, volcanic in origin and reaching 1940m at Chionistra on Mt Olympus.

To the south and west of the Troodos massif lie large areas of chalky hills where orchids abound. A descent from Troodos to the coast by any of a number of roads takes one over hills and through valleys where, away from cultivation, fleshy spikes of *Barlia robertiana* are found in early March and *Ophrys fusca*, ssp. *iricolor* and ssp. *omegaifera* flower, together with a range of intermediate forms. *O. sphegodes* ssp. *mammosa* is common, and in a few places the rarer *O. sphegodes* ssp. *sintenisii* can be found. *O. scolopax* and its ssp. *orientalis* occur here, as well as the closely related *O. carmeli*.

In the south, near the coast, chalk hills between Larnaca and Limassol are the home of the endemic *O. kotschyi*, although this is nowhere common for its sites are few in number.

Outside Larnaca, near the salt lake, wattle scrub and the secondary grassland nearby are rich in orchids: *Ophrys lutea* ssp. *murbeckii, O. carmeli, Orchis saccata* and *Barlia robertiana* are the first to appear. These are followed by *Ophrys scolopax* ssp. *orientalis, O. fusca* and its subspecies, *O. argolica* ssp. *elegans*, and *Orchis italica*; and, as the grass dries, *O. coriophora* ssp. *fragrans* comes into bloom.

In Cyprus, as elsewhere in the Mediterranean region, widespread goat-grazing is having a ruinous effect on the flora. It is thus interesting to contrast the floral displays of the Sovereign Base area of Akrotiri (where goats are controlled) with the land immediately around. Under pines at Akrotiri the ground is carpeted with *Anemone coronaria* and the yellow form of *Ranunculus asiaticus*, as well as numerous orchids. There are large numbers of *Ophrys argolica* ssp. *elegans, Orchis quadripunctata* and the occasional *Ophrys kotschyi*.

The unexplored Cyprus lies to the west or north-west of the Troodos massif, beyond Paphos. Here on sandy, calcareous soils the floral display is magnificent. Amongst the orchids to be found in March are thick mahogany spikes of *Serapias vomeracea* ssp. *orientalis*, the smaller *S. vomeracea* ssp. *laxiflora* in a range of colours, and intermediate forms that make a mockery of any attempt to classify them. *Ophrys fuciflora* ssp. *bornmuelleri* occurs here too, both in a form with a small lip and as the large-lipped var. *grandiflora*. All the other orchids mentioned earlier are found here, with the exception of *Ophrys kotschyi*.

In the north-west of the island lies an area of limestone which forms the Akamas peninsula. It is a wild area of deep gorges and spectacular displays of wild flowers. Unfortunately it is grazed by feral goats, and its promise in early spring is often curtailed by flowering time.

Somewhere in this region grows the rare and impressive *Orchis punctulata*, surrounded by a host of other orchids including *Barlia robertiana, Ophrys fusca* ssp. *iricolor*, both the pink and white forms of *Neotinea maculata* and *Ophrys fuciflora* ssp. *bornmuelleri*. When the ground is rapidly becoming baked *Orchis coriophora* ssp. *fragrans* and the closely related *Orchis sancta* come into flower.

By mid-April the land and hills below 600m are becoming desiccated but now, on higher ground in the Troodos massif, *Orchis anatolica* flowers in abundance (high up in the massif there is a robust form, var. *troodii*, which flowers later in the year). *Dactylorhiza sulphurea* ssp. *pseudosambucina* also appears, but only in its yellow form.

In May the woods of mixed *Quercus alnifolia, Pinus brutia* and *Arbutus andrachne* hold the white-flowered form of *Neotinea maculata* and a curious form of *Platanthera chlorantha*, sometimes called *P. chlorantha* ssp. *holm-*

boei. It is completely green and quite different in appearance from the usual white form of *P. chlorantha*.

By early June huge spikes of *Limodorum abortivum* have appeared under the *Pinus brutia* and again, higher up in the *Pinus nigra* ssp. *pallasiana* zone, where they are accompanied by *Epipactis troodii*. Amongst bracken on the heights of Chionistra there are small colonies of *Cephalanthera rubra* and the very occasional spike of the rare *Epipactis condensata*.

Besides one or two permanent streams in the mountains the impressive *Epipactis veratrifolia* flourishes in clumps of up to 40 stems, each as much as 1m in length.

The last of the orchids to flower, the familiar *Spiranthes spiralis*, does so in late September, bringing a touch of the ordinary to an otherwise exotic list.

Syria & Lebanon

These two countries have figured much in the news of recent years because of their internal troubles. As a result many may be discouraged from going there and, indeed, some of the areas most attractive to botanists are difficult if not impossible to reach because of military restrictions.

Syria
Much of Syria is too dry for orchids to grow. However, near the coast where there is a more normal Mediterranean climate with some rain in winter orchids can be found.

To the north and east of Latakia the arid hills become mountains, clothed in extensive mixed forests, where rainfall and shade have produced a good moss cover and rich leaf-mould. *Cephalanthera kurdica* is not unknown in these woods, and the green *Platanthera chlorantha* ssp. *holmboei*, once thought to be a Cyprus endemic, has been recorded there too. Further north, near the Turkish border, *Ophrys schulzei* has been reported from Alexandretta.

Lebanon
The spring display of flowers in the hills and mountains near Beirut is without equal anywhere in the Mediterranean. In a small publication entitled *Petite Flore des Environs de Beyrouth* (published in 1935) over 1200 species of wild flowers were recorded as growing within a 10km radius of Beirut itself.

The area has a typically Mediterranean climate in winter and spring, but with rather higher summer temperatures. This is also true of the coastal areas and the western slopes of the hills below about 1400m.

In hills around Beirut one can find *Ophrys fusca* and its ssp. *iricolor, O. lutea* ssp. *murbeckii, O. fuciflora* and its ssp. *bornmuelleri, O. carmeli* and the closely related *O. scolopax* ssp. *orientalis.* Both *Ophrys apifera and O. sphegodes* ssp. *sintenisii* are also found, but less frequently than the others mentioned.

As well as *Ophrys,* the genus *Orchis* is well represented around Beirut, with *Orchid papilionacea, O. morio* ssp. *picta* var. *libani, O. sancta, O. italica* and *O. anatolica* all present.

Orchis galilea is a rather special orchid of Lebanon and Israel. In appearance it is not unlike forms of *Orchis punctulata,* and there is some confusion over records of *O. punctulata* in Lebanon for this reason. Although widespread, it is rather local and grows early in the year (flowering from February) on limestone hills and in old vineyards in grassy areas amongst rocks, such as one finds around Ghazir.

Lebanon has been famous through the centuries for its cedars. For the botanist interested in orchids there is the possibility of finding *Comperia comperiana* in these cedar woods. It occurs fairly widely in the Foret d'Ehden which lies near Bcharre, a town high up on the edge of Makmel, the N. Lebanon massif. From Bcharre one can travel to Baalbek over the Col des Cèdres: *C. comperiana* grows here too. Unfortunately, populations of this intriguing orchid have been decimated by collectors – too often in vain, because the plant flowers in cultivation for a year or so and then dies for reasons not yet understood.

Finally, also in the same region, the very rare *Himantoglossum affine* hangs on in numbers again reduced by collectors.

Israel

South of Lebanon, along the same Mediterranean coast, lies Israel, and since both countries share an appreciable number of interesting orchid species, the latter provides a safer alternative for the visitor.

The near-miracle wrought by the Israelis in turning a once inhospitable land into an efficient fruit and vegetable growing region has inevitably meant that the natural flora has suffered. In spite of the intense cultivation, one can find numerous wild flowers by moving into the hills that separate the coastal strip from the sunken valley that connects the Sea of Galilee with the Dead Sea.

Spring arrives early in these hills, with orchids to be found on stony, scrubby slopes out of the direct glare of the sun or at the edges of vineyards.

Ophrys carmeli is perhaps the commonest orchid, occurring in many places in the hills with forms of *O. fusca* and the later flowering *O. scolopax* ssp. *orientalis.*

Rather less frequent but still widespread is the form of *O. sphegodes* called ssp. *sintenisii* by some and *O. transhyrcana* by others.

Mt Carmel reaches virtually to the coast and has long been known by botanists for its profusion of early spring flowers. *Orchis papilionacea* is particularly fine on the slops of Mt Carmel where it flowers with *O. morio* ssp. *picta* var. *libani* and a number of *Ophrys* such as *O. scolopax* ssp. *orientalis*, and ssp. *cornuta*, *O. fusca* and the inevitable *O. carmeli*.

The prize of this region is the rare *Orchis galilea*. Like the closely related *O. punctulata*, it flowers early in March and April, although lower down near Jerusalem it can be in seed by the beginning of March.

The appeal of Israel for many travellers is the profusion of places whose names are known from childhood days, when Bible stories were read. Many of these places are in hills where wild flowers grow in the brief spring before the summer heat and dryness. Thus it is possible to combine a trip to the biblical sites such as Nazareth, Mt Carmel, the hills of Judea, Bethlehem and Jerusalem with worthwhile finds of orchids and numerous bulbous plants. It is necessary to come early, for spring in this part of the Mediterranean is well underway by the beginning of March.

6 – Photographing wild orchids

There can be few occasions when collecting rare plants can be justified and then only for national herbaria. Far too many wild orchids have ended up on dusty herbarium sheets often inadequately pressed and labelled so that they are worthless to future generations of botanists. A clear colour photograph is a far better record of one's orchid finds than a series of brown, desiccated specimens which bear little relation to the colour and form of the original plant. It is almost impossible to preserve the colour of orchids when pressed, and they almost always end up dark brown with no trace of patterns or markings. Few are fortunate to be able to depict orchids in a sketch or painting, but most people can take good photographs once they have mastered their equipment and learnt to take pains to secure a worthwhile result.

Every photographer who goes out to find orchids, or indeed any form of animal or plant life, should first and foremost have regard for the welfare of the subject. Many conservationists have a low opinion of plant photographers in general. This is, regrettably, justified because groups of people often unwittingly trample plants, especially seedlings, and remove the surrounding greenery in order to get a better shot. Such wholesale 'gardening' is to be deplored, for not only is the plant made more obvious to other people, the habit usually produces very unrealistic photographs. A useful list of suggestions has been published as the 'Nature Photographers Code of Practice' and it is important that every plant photographer follows it.

The choice of camera is very much a question of personal preference, although with so many of similar specification to choose from a decision is not easily made. Modern cameras and lenses are so well made that their potential often far exceeds the ability of the photographer using them. For plant photography a single-lens reflex (SLR) camera is essential, since this permits the user to see exactly what he is aiming at whatever lens, ring or bellows is being used.

Almost all amateurs will choose the 35mm format, and since this is the case, and since the majority of the pictures in this book were taken by two of the authors (P. & J.D.) using 35mm, most of the technical detail which follows, in the hope that it will be of interest to would-be orchid photographers, refers to this format.

The cameras involved are Canons, which have never given trouble and have produced flawless definition and colour rendering. With these cameras were used a range of so-called macro lenses for close-up work, some of which do not have a built-in focussing mount and are designed for use on a bellows. The average photographer will find a 50mm or 100mm macro lens adequate for most purposes. With an extension ring, such lenses will give life-size reproduction, and without it focussing from infinity to half life size is possible. The 100mm lens has the advantage of increased distance between subject and camera, an important factor given the difficulty of using most tripods for close-up work. The 50mm is light and easily hand-held up to half life-size magnification, whereas the 100mm is a bit cumbersome. The disadvantage of the 50mm is the closeness to the subject in use: in some the front lens element is so deeply recessed that the lens barrel almost touches the subject, making lighting a great problem.

A 135mm lens is useful for habitat shots on occasions when one cannot get close to the plant. We have a preference for a moderate wide-angle lens for habitat shots. When stopped right down, the subject can occupy a large part of the foreground, with the background also in focus. There is sometimes a distortion in perspective but this can be exploited very successfully.

All the 35mm photographs were taken on Kodachrome 64 and 25 transparency films, which are the only easily obtained 35mm materials which had the desired definition and contrast. Colour prints, although handy to look at, do not have the same sparkle and colour rendition. On occasions when prints are required these can easily be made from transparencies.

Over the years we have found that a tripod is indispensable for most of our work, especially since many of our pictures necessitate the use of a bellows. It is possible to hand-hold a camera at half life-size magnification and 1/30th of a second shutter speed; the results look good when projected but used for printing the transparencies will not have the same sharpness as when a tripod is used. The smallest amount of camera shake causes softening of the edges of the subject.

When camera shake has been eliminated the next problem is movement of the subject. A natural light shot of one or more orchids showing habitat is easily made even on a windy day by waiting for periods of calm – but great patience is often needed, for a breeze usually starts up just as the sun comes out from behind the clouds and the picture looks perfect in the viewfinder! Even on a calm day flowers viewed in close-up always seem to be moving slightly, and the higher the magnification the more exaggerated this becomes. What are the remedies? First, some people carry portable windbreaks made from transparent plastics; but for the photographer who walks long distances to find subjects they are an extra encumbrance.

Another possibility is the use of faster films which allow a higher shutter speed when an aperture has been selected to give the required depth of field. Their only disadvantage lies in the higher film speed being obtained at the expense of fine grain in the film. Often one has to compromise and accept less sharp transparencies unless flash lighting is used.

Carefully used, flash can be the answer for sharp close-ups, but all too often the shadows and dark backgrounds one gets tell the viewer that artificial light has been used. It is possible, however, to obtain excellent results by using one or two flashguns and a few pieces of white card to reflect light into potential shadow areas. For the photographs in this book a powerful gun was used since it can be held quite far from the subject and then there is not such a great fall-off in light intensity between subject and background.

Successful use of flash requires some experimentation, and there is a lot of useful information to be gleaned from the books listed in the bibliography. Our present set-up involves two flash guns and one or two reflectors. Recently a modified flash meter has been calibrated to read through the eye-piece of one of our cameras and is taking much of the guess-work out of the tricky business of lighting extreme close-ups.

Articles in the photographic press often debate advantages or disadvantages of 35mm and 6 × 6cm photography. The question of what to use does demand some thought, and one of the authors (A.H.) is a confirmed user of the larger format while the others changed from that format to 35mm some years ago and would never reverse their decision.

The 6 × 6cm camera is bulkier and heavier than any 35mm, and much less flexible in lens possibilities. There is no equivalent of the 35mm macro lenses fixed directly onto the standard lens fitting. The close-ups in this book which have been reproduced from 6 × 6cm transparencies were taken on Zeiss Pentacon cameras with the standard lens fitted on a bellows or extension tubes, with a moderately powered flash gun placed fairly near the front of the lens. For orchid portraits needing less magnification, screw-on close-up lenses were used with the standard lens.

There is no doubt that the larger transparencies look impressive on a screen and can often be examined without a viewer. At one time art editors would use nothing smaller than 6 × 6cm transparencies for reproduction in books. Those days have changed, mainly because the exceptionally fine grain of photographic emulsions available nowadays allows 35mm film to be used for all but giant enlargements, without the image breaking down as grain becomes apparent. There is no question that film for the small format is cheaper and that there is a far wider choice of relatively light equipment available at moderate prices.

Besides the fact that Kodachrome films are not made in 6 × 6cm format and this is the stock we feel best for our work there is a technical reason for the choice of 35mm. For the close-up photographer there is an advantage in using 6 × 6cm only if the subject occupies a large part of the film area. To do this in the larger format means a higher magnification for the same subject when compared with 35mm. Whenever there is an increase in magnification the depth of field decreases, and one of the biggest headaches in this type of photography is the difficulty in sharply focussing small subjects. One is forced to use apertures of f16 or smaller to get the required depth of field with 35mm, so that the 6 × 6cm user with a higher magnification of subject has to suffer because his lenses cannot be stopped down enough to give the required depth. Even if it were mechanically possible, lenses are not usually made to stop down beyond f32 because the tiny aperture brings problems in getting enough light without using too slow a shutter speed, and the image starts to deteriorate due to the phenomenon of diffraction.

To improve as a plant photographer takes time and patience but the rewards come when one views the results. One way of improving is by looking at the work of expert photographers in the subject and considering exactly what it is about their work which makes it stand out. These people often seem to disobey the so-called rules of composition and use lighting and choice of viewpoint in an innovative way.

We have gained a great deal by looking at the work of such gifted plant photographers as Othmar Danesch and Paula Kohlhaupt. Work such as theirs provides an inspiration, not to copy but to go out and try to capture the personality of a plant on film. We often sit for some time admiring a plant before remembering to photograph it and this is always worthwhile, for certain flowers on a spike are often just begging to be photographed.

Bibliography

Roses and lilies may be the only flowers that have received similar coverage to orchids in botanical literature. And many talented artists over the past 300 years have chosen to depict the innumerable flower forms of this, the most intriguing of plant genera.

There is a wide range of literature dealing specifically with European orchids, from monographs preoccupied with a single genus to more general works. Orchids feature, too, in the Floras of individual countries or districts; these can be useful in deciding where to search for particular species.

Some outstanding works have appeared in print in the last 50 years: of these the drawings and paintings of Dr Erich Nelson must rank supreme. His three monographs on *Ophrys*, on *Dactylorhiza* and on *Serapias*, *Aceras*, *Loroglossum* and *Barlia* are works of art as well as of botanical scholarship, and we would recommend that any lover of orchids should try at least to see the volume of plates dealing with *Ophrys*. The paintings of myriads of *Ophrys* faces, each precisely depicted, brings home to the reader the diversity of form even within a single species. The three monographs can be found in specialised libraries, such as the one at Kew or the Natural History Museum at South Kensington.

A quiet revolution has occurred in plant photography over the past 20 years, and now photographic illustrations rival accurate paintings and drawings in their ability to show fine detail. In the field of orchid photography, the work of Othmar and Edeltraud Danesch set new standards when their three-volume set, *Orchideen Europas*, appeared in print. The illustrations of Paula Kohlhaupt in *Bunte Welt der Orchideen*, of Dr Jany Renz in *Flora Iranica*, and of Dr Gerd Hermjakob in *Orchids of Greece and Cyprus* are also examples of orchid photography at its best.

Of the wide range of handbooks available, Professor Hans Sundermann's *Europäische und Mediterrane Orchideen* has long been our favourite, and a tattered, much-thumbed copy accompanies us on all our travels. (This is now in its third edition.)

The traveller in search of wild orchids will find much of interest in the bulletins of the Alpine Garden Society. Here there are articles on growing, plant-hunting and other topics, with orchids receiving a very fair share of coverage.

The final mention must go to V. S. Summerhayes' now almost classic work, *Wild Orchids of Britain*. This appeared in 1951, as one of the Collins New Naturalist series, and is written clearly and with obvious enthusiasm. Many lovers of wild orchids, the authors included, can trace the origins of their interest to their first reading of this book.

Included in the list below are those books and more general papers that the authors have found useful for reference. For more detailed research, extensive bibliographies of early papers and books can be found in Godfery and Nelson. An excellent and exhaustive study of European orchid literature has been made by Dr E. Willing and B. Willing. Published in 1977 by OPTIMA (Organisation for the Phyto-Taxonomic Investigation of the Mediterranean Area), it forms the first part of an ambitious programme for the mapping of orchids in the Mediterranean area.

Baumann, H., & Kunkele, S., *Die wildwachsenden Orchideen Europas* (Kosmos, Stuttgart, 1982)

Bacon, L., *Mountain Flower Holidays in Europe* (Alpine Garden Society, 1979)

Brooke, J., *The Wild Orchids of Britain* (Bodley Head, London, 1950)

Binz, A., & Thommen, E., *Flore de la Suisse* (Lausanne, 1941, 1953)

Bonnier, G., *Flore complète de France, Suisse et Belgique*, Book XI (Paris, 1929–31)

Camus, E. G., & Camus, A., *Iconographie des Orchidées d'Europe et du Bassin Méditerranéen* (P. Lechevalier, Paris, 1928)

Clapham, A. R., Tutin, T. G., & Warburg, E. F., *Flora of the British Isles* (Cambridge University Press, 1962)

Correvon, H., *Album des Orchidées d'Europe* (Geneva, 1923)

Darwin, Ch., *The various contrivances by which Orchids are fertilized by insects*, ed. II, (J. Murray, London, 1877)

Danesch, O. & E., *Orchideen Europas* (I – *Sudeuropa*; II – *Mitteleuropa*; III – *Ophrys Hybriden*) (Hallwag, Berne & Stuttgart, 1962–73)

– *Orchideen* (Hallwag Taschenbuch 114, 1975)

– *Tiroler Orchideen* (Athesia, Bozen, 1977)

Ettlinger, D. M. T., *British and Irish Orchids* (Macmillan, London, 1977)

Godfery, M. J., *Monograph and Iconograph of Native British Orchidaceae* (Cambridge University Press, 1933)

Gölz, P., & Reinhard, H. R., *Die Orchideenflora der ostagaischen Inseln Kos, Samos, Chios und Lesbos (Griechenland)* (OPTIMA–Projekt 'Kartierung der mediterranen Orchideen', Karlsrue, 1981)

Haslam, S. M., Sell, P. D., & Wolseley, P. A., *A Flora of the Maltese Islands* (Malta University Press, 1977)

Hegi, G., *Illustrierte Flore von Mitteleuropa*, Vol II (Munich, 1939)

Hermjakob, G., *Orchids of Greece and Cyprus* (Goulandris Museum, Kifissia, 1974)

Huxley, A. J., & Hunt, P. F., 'A New Orchid from Spain', *R.H.S. Journal* (Vol XCII, part 7)

Huxley, A. J., & Taylor, W., *Flowers of Greece and the Aegean* (Chatto and Windus, London, 1977)

Kohlhaupt, P., *Bunte Welt der Orchideen* (Stuttgart, 1978)

Kullengerg, B., *Studies in Ophrys Pollination* (Uppsala, 1961)

Kunkele, S., & Paysan, K., *Die Orchideenflora von Euböa (Griechenland)* (OPTIMA–Projekt 'Kartierung der mediterranen Orchideen', Karlsruhe, 1981)

Landwehr, J., *Wild Orchideeën van Europa* (Amsterdam, 1977)

Lang, D., *Orchids of Britain* (Oxford University Press, 1980)

Lazaro, E., & Ibiza, B., *Compendio de la Flore Española* (Madrid, 1921)

Marret, L., *Fleurs de la Côte d'Azur* (Lechevalier, Paris, 1926)

Meikle, R. D., *Flora of Cyprus*, Vol II (Orchids detailed by J. Wood) (Bentham and Moxon Trust, to be published)

Mouterde, P., *Nouvelle Flore du Liban et de la Syrie* (Beyrouth, 1966)

Nelson, E., & Fischer, H., *Die Orchideen Deutschlands und der angrenzenden Gebiete* (Munich, 1931)

Nelson, E., *Monographie und Iconographie der Orchidaceen* (*Ophrys*, 1962; *Serapias, Aceras, Loroglossum und Barlia*, 1968; *Dactylorhiza*, 1976) (Verlag Speich ag Zurich)

Polunin, O., *Flowers of Greece and the Balkans* (Oxford University Press, 1980)

Polunin, O., & Huxley, A. J., *Flowers of the Mediterranean* (Chatto and Windus, London, 1972)

Polunin, O., & Smythies, B. E., *Flowers of South West Europe* (Oxford University Press, 1973)

Procter, M., & Yeo, P., *The Pollination of Flowers* (Collins, London, 1973)

Rechinger, K. H., *Flora Aegaea* (Orchid section by J. Renz) (Denkschr. Akad. der. Wiss., Vienna, 1943)

Renz, J., *Flora Iranica, Flora des Iranischen Hochlandes und der umrahmenden Gebirge, Persien, Afganistan, Teile von West Pakistan, Nord Iraq, Azerbaidjan, Turkmenistan* (ed. K. H. Rechinger, Graz, 1963–79)

Roger-Smith, H., *Plant Hunting in Europe* (Alpine Garden Society)

Ross-Craig, S., *Drawings of British Plants*, part XXVIII (G. Bell & Sons, London, 1971)

Ruckbrodt, D. & U., 'Eine neue Ophrys aus der südöstlichen Türkei', *Die Orchidee* (1975)

Schlechter, R., & Keller, G., *Monographie und Iconographie der Orchideen Europas und des Mittelmeergebietes* (Berlin, 1928)

Summerhayes, V. S., *Wild Orchids of Britain* (Collins London, 1951, 1968)

Sundermann, H., *Europäische und Mediterrane Orchideen – Eine Bestimmungsflora* (Brucke-Verlag Kurt Schmersow, Hildesheim, 1970, 1975, 1980)

Synge, P. M., *In Search of Wild Flowers* (Michael Joseph, London, 1973)

Tauhourdin, C. B., *Native Orchids of Britain* (H. R. Grubb, 1925)

Tutin, T. G., & others, *Flora Europaea*, Vol V – Monocotyledons (Cambridge University Press, 1980)

Willing, E., & B., *Index der Verbreitungskarten für Orchideen Europas und der Mittelmeerländer* (OPTIMA–Projekt 'Kartierung der mediterranen Orchideen', Karlsruhe, 1979)

Journals

Alpine Garden Society Bulletin (Quarterly, from 1929–   ): various articles on plant-hunting and aspects of terrestrial orchid culture, classification etc.

Die Orchidee: written in German, this journal contains papers, usually illustrated, on orchid biology and classification.

Orchid Review (from 1893): occasional articles on Britain and Europe.

Orchid Society of Great Britain Journal: a few articles on native British species.

Scottish Rock Garden Club Journal: similar in coverage and content to the *Alpine Garden Society Bulletin*.

Watsonia (Journal of the Botanical Society of the British Isles): twice-yearly articles on classification, ecology and discovery of orchids in new localities.

Plant photography

Angel, H., *Nature Photography – its art and techniques* (Fountain Press, London, 1972)

Croy, O., *Camera Close-up* (Focal Press, London, 1961)
Ettlinger, D. M. T., *Natural History Photography* (Academic Press, 1974)
Freeman, M., *Wildlife and Nature Photography* (Croom Helm, London, 1981)
Holmåsen, I., *Nature Photography* (Cassell, London, 1976)
Izzi, G., & Mezzatesta, F., *The Complete Manual of Nature Photography* (Gollancz, London, 1981)
Kinne, R., *The Complete Book of Nature Photography* (Barnes, New York, 1962)
Kodak, *Close-up Photography* (Kodak Technical Publication, Rochester, 1969)
Kodak, *Photomacrography* (Kodak Technical Publication, Rochester, 1969)
Nuridsany, C., & Perennou, M., *Photographing Nature* (Kaye and Ward, London, 1976)
Ray, S., *Focal Guide to Close-ups* (Focal Press, London, 1978)
Ray, S., *Focal Guide to Photographing Wild Flowers* (Focal Press, London, 1980)
Time-Life, *Photographing Nature* (Time-Life Books, New York, 1973)

Index to species descriptions and plates

Entries in small capitals are to genera and the remainder to species, except those in italics which are English names. The bold italic numerals refer to the colour plates (numbers *1–328*); other numbers refer to the text pages. A page number followed by d refers to a drawing on the page indicated. Synonyms, indicated by =, include all important synonyms likely to be encountered, even if not referred to in the text.